CRIMINAL PRACTICE

The
University of
Law
1 Royal Standard Place
Nottingham
NG1 6FZ

CRIMINAL PRACTICE
THIRD EDITION

Sean Hutton

Third edition published 2023 by
The University of Law
2 Bunhill Row
London EC1Y 8HQ

First edition published 2021

Second edition published 2022

British Library Cataloguing in Publication Data

A catalogue record for this book is available from the British Library.

ISBN 978 1 805020 09 7

Preface

This book is part of a series of Study Manuals that have been specially designed to support the reader to achieve the SQE1 Assessment Specification in relation to Functioning Legal Knowledge. Each Study Manual aims to provide the reader with a solid knowledge and understanding of fundamental legal principles and rules, including how those principles and rules might be applied in practice.

This Study Manual covers the Solicitors Regulation Authority's syllabus for the SQE1 assessment for Criminal Practice in a concise and tightly focused manner. The Manual provides a clear statement of relevant legal rules and a well-defined road map through examinable law and practice, including the relevant parts of the Police, Crime, Sentencing and Courts Act 2022 on the expanded use of police bail, and the updated grounds for a remand into youth detention accommodation along with the changes to the length of a detention and training order for youths introduced by s 236 of the Sentencing Act 2020. The important case of *R v Arie Ali* [2023] EWCA Crim 232 is also included in relation to sentencing and the impact of the current, very high prison population, along with the reversion to the magistrates' court's sentencing powers for a single either-way offence from 12 months back to six months. The Manual aims to bring the law and practice to life through the use of example scenarios based on realistic client-based problems and allows the reader to test their knowledge and understanding through single best answer questions that have been modelled on the SRA's sample assessment questions.

For those readers who are students at the University of Law, the Study Manual is used alongside other learning resources and the University's assessment bank to best prepare students not only for the SQE1 assessments, but also for a future life in professional legal practice.

We hope that you find the Study Manual supportive of your preparation for SQE1 and we wish you every success.

The legal principles and rules contained within this Manual are stated as at 1 April 2023.

Author acknowledgments
I should like to thank Deborah Sharpley, Cheryl Weir and Gary Atkinson for their help in the preparation of this book and my fellow SQE1 Criminal Practice course designers, Sue Evans and Matthew Nash, for their comments and support. Thanks must also go to David Stott for his editorial support and guidance.

For Alfie, Eva and Esme

Contents

Table of Cases

Table of Statutes

PART 1
ADVISING CLIENTS ABOUT THE PROCEDURE AND PROCESSES AT THE POLICE STATION

PART 1

Advising clients about the procedure and processes at the police station

---

SQE1 syllabus

The first four chapters will enable you to achieve the SQE1 Assessment Specification in relation to Functioning Legal Knowledge concerned with the following procedures and processes:

Rights of a suspect being detained by the police for questioning:

- right to legal advice;
- right to have someone informed of arrest;
- reviews and detention time limits under PACE 1984, Code C.

Advising a client, including vulnerable clients, whether to answer police questions:

- right to silence;
- adverse inferences.

Procedure for interviewing a suspect under PACE 1984:

- role and appropriate conduct by defence legal representative/solicitor including representation of vulnerable client;
- role of appropriate adult and who can be an appropriate adult.

Identification procedures:

- when an identification procedure must be held;
- different types of identification procedure under PACE 1984, Code D;
- procedure for carrying out an identification procedure.

Note that, for SQE1, candidates are not usually required to recall specific case names or cite statutory or regulatory authorities. These are provided for illustrative purposes only unless otherwise stated.

1 Detaining a Suspect at the Police Station and Police Interviews

Learning outcomes

By the end of this chapter you will be able to apply relevant core legal principles and rules appropriately and effectively, at the level of a competent newly qualified solicitor in practice, to realistic client-based and ethical problems and situations in the following areas:

- How the decision to detain a suspect is made and the maximum periods a suspect may be detained for before charge.
- The rights of a suspect who has been arrested and detained (or who attends as a volunteer).
- How to advise a client whether or not to answer police questions.
- The procedure for interviewing a suspect under PACE 1984.
- The role of a legal adviser before and during interview.
- A range of conduct issues which may arise at the police station.

1.1 Introduction

This chapter examines the powers the police may exercise when a suspect has been arrested and detained at the police station and what rights a suspect has whilst so detained and what advice a solicitor (or accredited police station representative) would be expected to give such a client. What occurs at the police station is likely to represent a critical stage of the investigation and influence the decision whether or not to charge the suspect with any offences. This may also be of great significance when a case gets to trial, particularly if the defendant's solicitor attempts to argue that prosecution evidence obtained whilst their client was detained at the police station is inadmissible because the police behaved improperly or unlawfully.

References to section numbers in Part 1 (**Chapters 1** to **4**) are, unless otherwise stated, to the Police and Criminal Evidence (PACE) Act 1984. References to Code C are to the Code of Practice to PACE for the Detention, Treatment and Questioning of Persons by Police Officers. References to Code D are to the Code of Practice for the Identification of Persons by Police Officers. References to Code E are to the Code of Practice on Audio Recording Interviews with Suspects, and references to Code F are to the Code of Practice on Visual Recording with Sound of Interviews with Suspects.

This chapter looks at:

- the procedure on arrival at the police station;
- the rights of a suspect being detained by the police for questioning;
- advising a client whether to answer police questions;
- the procedure for interviewing a suspect under PACE 1984 and the role of the legal adviser before and during the interview; and
- how to deal with a range of conduct issues which may arise at the police station.

1.2 Procedure on arrival at the police station

A suspect who has been arrested other than at a police station must usually be taken to the police station 'as soon as is practicable after the arrest' (s 30(1A)) unless the arresting officer decides to grant 'street bail'. Paragraph 1.1 of Code C provides that 'all persons in custody must be dealt with expeditiously, and be released from the police station as soon as the need for detention no longer applies'.

1.2.1 The custody officer

A suspect who has been arrested must be brought before a custody officer in the custody suite on their arrival at the police station (or after their arrest if they were arrested at the police station). The custody officer is responsible for authorising the detention of the suspect and supervising their welfare whilst in police custody. The custody officer will normally be a police officer holding at least the rank of sergeant, who should not be involved in the investigation of the offence for which the suspect has been arrested.

Paragraph 2.1A of Code C confirms that a suspect who has been arrested (or who is attending the police station to answer bail) should be brought before the custody officer as 'soon as practicable'.

1.2.1.1 What initial steps must the custody officer take?

The custody officer is responsible for opening and then maintaining a custody record for each suspect who has been arrested and brought to the police station. This is an electronic document which records certain key information:

(a) the suspect's name, address, telephone number, date of birth and occupation;

(b) the offence for which the suspect has been arrested and why the arresting officer considered it necessary to arrest the suspect (Code G, para 4.3);

(c) the time of the suspect's arrest and the time of their arrival at the police station;

(d) the reason why the suspect's ongoing detention at the police station has been authorised by the custody officer;

(e) the time such detention was authorised;

(f) confirmation that the suspect has been given details of the rights they may exercise whilst detained at the police station (see below), and whether they have requested legal advice from a solicitor; and

(g) details of the items of property the suspect has on their person, and details of any medical condition they suffer from.

The custody record will also have attached to it a detention log. This is a record of all the significant events that occur whilst the suspect is in police custody. The custody officer must also inform the suspect about their ongoing rights (see **1.3** below).

1.2.1.2 Search of the detained person

The custody officer must also find out what items of property a suspect has on their person and will make a record of these items (ss 54(1) and (2)). The custody officer will therefore authorise a search of the suspect, to the extent the officer considers necessary to ascertain what items the suspect has on their person (Code C, para 4.1).

Section 54(3) allows the custody officer to seize and retain any items the suspect has on their person. Items of clothing and personal effects may be seized only if the custody officer has reasonable grounds for believing that they may be evidence (for example, a blood-soaked shirt), or if the custody officer believes that the suspect may use them:

(a) to cause physical injury to themself or others;

(b) to cause damage to property;

(c) to interfere with evidence; or

(d) to assist them to escape (Code C, para 4.2).

Obvious examples of such items are a penknife, a key, a sharpened comb or a razor blade, but this will also include items such as shoelaces, ties and belts.

1.2.2   The decision to detain a suspect

After opening the custody record and informing the suspect of their rights (see **1.3** below), the custody officer must determine whether there is already 'sufficient evidence' to charge the suspect with the offence for which they have been arrested (s 37(1)). To do this, the custody officer will ask the investigating officer – usually in the presence of the suspect – for details of the evidence that already exists against the suspect. If not, what steps the officer proposes to take if the further detention, before charge, of the suspect is authorised (this will normally be some form of investigative procedure such as an audibly recorded interview with the suspect or the holding of an identification procedure – see **1.5** and **Chapter 2** below). The custody officer should note in the custody record any comments made by the suspect in relation to the account given by the arresting officer of the reasons for the arrest (Code C, para 3.4). The custody officer should not put any questions to the arrested person about their suspected involvement in any offence (Code C, para 3.4).

It is unusual for there to be sufficient evidence at this early stage of the investigation. If there is such evidence, the suspect should be charged straight away, and either released on bail to appear before the magistrates' court on a later date or remanded in police custody until they can be brought before the magistrates' court.

1.2.2.1 Grounds for detention

If there is not sufficient evidence to charge a suspect immediately, the suspect should be released either on bail or without bail, unless:

(a) the custody officer has reasonable grounds for believing that detaining the suspect without charge is necessary to secure or preserve evidence relating to an offence for which they are under arrest; or

(b) it is necessary to obtain such evidence by questioning (s 37(2)).

Despite the wording of s 37, in practice the usual decision will be for the custody officer to authorise the suspect's detention before charge because one or both of these grounds are likely to be satisfied.

The first ground above may be useful in situations where the police want to carry out a search of the suspect's premises (under s 18), or where they are still looking for evidence of the offence. In such cases the police may want to detain the suspect in the police station so that the suspect has no opportunity to hide or destroy the evidence before it can be found. This ground can also be used where the police want to obtain some form of identification evidence and can do so only whilst the suspect is in the police station.

In practice, the second ground tends to be the most common ground to authorise detention but note these grounds may both apply, and they are not mutually exclusive.

If the custody officer becomes aware at any time that the grounds on which a suspect's detention was authorised have ceased to apply (and that no other grounds to justify their continued detention exist), the suspect must be released immediately (s 39).

1.2.2.2 Conditions of detention

The cell in which a suspect is held must be adequately heated, cleaned and ventilated, and also adequately lit (Code C, para 8.2). Any bedding supplied to a suspect must be of a reasonable standard and in a clean and sanitary condition (Code C, para 8.3). A suspect must be provided with access to toilet and washing facilities (Code C, para 8.4). A suspect must be offered at least two light meals and one main meal in any 24-hour period, and drinks should be provided at mealtimes and upon reasonable request between meals (Code C, para 8.6 and Note for Guidance 8B). A suspect should be offered brief outdoor exercise daily if this is practicable (Code C, para 8.7). Suspects should be visited in their cells at least every hour (Code C, para 9.3).

If the custody officer considers that a suspect is injured, appears to be suffering from physical illness or mental disorder or appears to need clinical attention, the custody officer must make arrangements to ensure that the suspect receives appropriate clinical attention as soon as reasonably practicable (Code C, paras 9.5, 9.5A and Annexes G and H). Normally in such cases the custody officer will arrange for the suspect to be seen by the nearest healthcare professional, or an ambulance must be called immediately.

1.3 Rights of a suspect being detained by the police for questioning

Before the custody officer decides whether or not the suspect will be detained before charge, the suspect must first be informed about their ongoing rights which may be exercised at any time whilst the suspect is in custody:

(a) the right to have someone informed of the suspect's arrest (s 56);

(b) the right for the suspect to consult privately with a solicitor (the suspect must be told that free, independent legal advice is available; s 58); and

(c) the right to consult the Codes of Practice.

The suspect must also be advised of their right to be informed about the offence and (as the case may be) any further offences for which they are arrested whilst in custody, and why they have been arrested and detained.

1.3.1   Right to legal advice

A suspect who has been arrested and detained at the police station has the right to receive free and independent legal advice.

Section 58(1) states:

> A person arrested and held in custody in a police station or other premises shall be entitled, if he so requests, to consult a solicitor privately at any time.

If a suspect makes such a request, they must be allowed to consult a solicitor 'as soon as practicable' (s 58(4)).

Paragraph 6.1 of Code C reinforces this by providing that:

> all detainees must be informed that they may at any time consult and communicate privately with a solicitor, whether in person, in writing or by telephone, and that free independent legal advice is available.

In all cases where legal advice is sought, unless a suspect asks for legal advice to be paid for privately, the police must contact the Defence Solicitor Call Centre (DSCC) – even if the suspect has asked for a named solicitor or firm. The DSCC will then determine whether the case is such that telephone advice is sufficient or whether a solicitor should attend.

Telephone advice, where appropriate, is provided for free through Criminal Defence Direct (CDD). A solicitor/accredited police station representative will provide the necessary advice over the telephone. Should the suspect want to speak to their own solicitor, they will be told that they may have to pay for the call.

Should attendance be required, the suspect's own solicitor, or the duty solicitor (if the suspect has not specified a particular solicitor), will be notified. If a solicitor attends the police station to see a particular suspect, that suspect must be informed of the solicitor's arrival at the police station (whether or not they are being interviewed at the time of the solicitor's arrival). The suspect must then be asked if they would like to see the solicitor, even if they have previously declined legal advice (Code C, para 6.15). The solicitor's attendance and the suspect's decision must be noted in the custody record.

Code C also states that at no time should a police officer do or say anything with the intention of dissuading a person from obtaining legal advice (Code C, para 6.4). In addition, para 6ZA of the Notes for Guidance to Code C states that:

> No police officer or police staff shall indicate to any suspect, except to answer a direct question, that the period for which he is liable to be detained, or, if not detained, the time taken to complete the interview, might be reduced:

- if they do not ask for legal advice or do not want a solicitor present when they are; or

- if they have asked for legal advice or ... asked for a solicitor to be present when they are interviewed but change their mind and agree to be interviewed without waiting for a solicitor.

1.3.1.1 Can the right to legal advice be delayed?

Unlike delaying the right under s 56 (see **1.3.2** below), the police have a very limited right to delay the exercise of the right to legal advice. Any delay must be authorised by an officer of at least the rank of superintendent and can be authorised only when a suspect has been arrested for an indictable offence (s 58(6)). The length of any delay can be for a maximum of 36 hours from the relevant time (s 58(5)). Authorisation for delaying a suspect's access to legal advice can be given orally but, if it is, it must be confirmed in writing as soon as is practicable (s 58(7)).

Delay to the suspect receiving access to legal advice may only be authorised if the officer has reasonable grounds for believing that the exercise of this right, at the time when the suspect wishes to exercise it, will:

(a) lead to interference with or harm to evidence connected with an indictable offence, or interference with or physical injury to other persons; or

(b) lead to the alerting of other persons suspected of having committed such an offence but not yet arrested for it; or

(c) hinder the recovery of any property obtained as a result of such an offence (s 58(8)).

Guidelines which the police must follow when determining whether to delay a suspect's access to legal advice are contained in Annex B to Code C.

In R v Samuel [1988] 1 WLR 920, the accused was arrested for armed robbery and taken to a police station where he signed the custody record to the effect that he did not want a solicitor at that time. Later in the evening of the same day he changed his mind and requested a solicitor, but this was refused. During the following morning, his mother arranged for a solicitor to attend the police station to represent him. Access to legal advice was again refused. Later that evening he was again interviewed and finally confessed to the robbery. It was submitted that evidence of the final interview should not be admitted because refusal of access to a solicitor was unjustified throughout. HELD: The appeal was allowed, and the conviction quashed. In doing so the CA set down some guidelines on the power to delay this right. Hodgson J said that the superintendent authorising delay must have a subjective belief that consultation with a legal adviser will result in one of the above three conditions happening and that this 'will very probably happen'. In other words, that the legal adviser will either deliberately do this or do so inadvertently. It follows that this will therefore be very rare and that further, the belief must be towards a particular legal adviser. The CA went on to confirm that the right to legal advice in s 58 of the Act was fundamental. The fear that a solicitor might advise his client not to answer questions would never be an adequate ground to delay such access.

1.3.2 Right to have someone informed of arrest

Section 56(1) states:

> Where a person has been arrested and is being held in custody in a police station or other premises, he shall be entitled, if he so requests, to have one friend or relative or other person who is known to him or who is likely to take an interest in his welfare told, as soon as practicable ... that he has been arrested and is being detained there.

In certain situations, the police may delay the exercise of this right. Any delay must be authorised by an officer of at least the rank of inspector and can only be authorised when the suspect has been detained for an indictable offence (ie either-way and indictable-only offences, see ss 56(2)(a) and (b)). The length of any delay can be for a maximum of 36 hours from the 'relevant time' (s 56(3)). Authorisation may be given orally but, if it is, must be confirmed in writing as soon as is practicable (s 56(4)).

The police officer who authorises the delay may do so only if they have reasonable grounds for believing that telling the named person of the arrest will:

(a) lead to interference with or harm to evidence connected with an indictable offence, or interference with or physical injury to other persons;

(b) lead to the alerting of other persons suspected of having committed such an offence but not yet arrested for it; or

(c) hinder the recovery of any property obtained as a result of such an offence (s 56(5)).

In making this decision the police officer must follow the guidelines set out in Annex B to Code C.

⭐ *Example*

Ashley is a member of a notorious criminal gang. Ashley is arrested on suspicion of having taken part in an armed robbery at a bank, after an image of his face was captured on the bank's CCTV system. A number of other people took part in the robbery, but they have not yet been identified. Several thousand pounds were stolen in the robbery.

Ashley wants to notify Ben, his brother, that he has been arrested. Ben is known to be a member of the gang. The police believe that, if notified that Ashley has been arrested, Ben will alert the other gang members who participated in the robbery and these people will then take steps to dispose of the money that was stolen. The police will be able to take advantage of the provisions in s 56 to delay Ben being notified of Ashley's arrest for up to 36 hours. Armed robbery is an indictable offence (it is in fact an offence triable only on indictment), and the police appear to have reasonable grounds for believing that notifying Ben of Ashley's arrest will lead to the alerting of other suspects and will hinder the recovery of property obtained as a result of the offence.

1.3.3 Detention time limits and reviews of detention under PACE 1984, Code C

Prior to charge there are time limits on how long a suspect can be detained at the police station. There are two different clocks that will apply to such detention.

1.3.3.1 The initial maximum period of detention before charge (the 'detention clock')

Section 41 provides that a person 'shall not be kept in police detention for more than 24 hours without being charged'. This 24-hour period begins from the 'relevant time'. The relevant time is determined as follows:

(a) in the case of a person attending *voluntarily* at the police station (see 1.3.4 below) who is then arrested at the police station, *the time of their arrest* (s 41(2)(c));

(b) in the case of a person who attends a police station to answer *'street bail'* granted under s 30A, the time *when they arrive at the police station* (s 41(2)(ca));

(c) in the case of a suspect who has been *arrested away from the police station*, the relevant time is generally the time when the suspect *arrives at the first police station* to which they are taken after their arrest (s 41(2)(d)). (Note there are some limited exceptions to this usual rule.)

Figure 1.1   The 'relevant time'

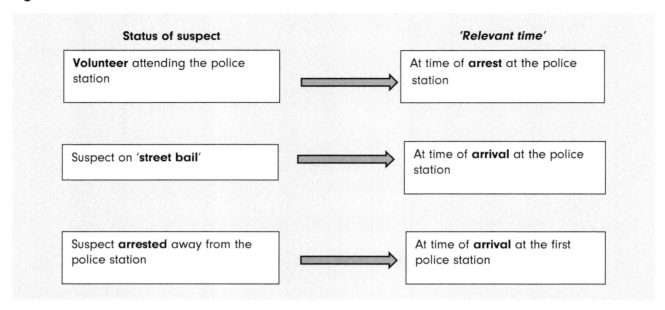

Status of suspect		'Relevant time'
Volunteer attending the police station	→	At time of **arrest** at the police station
Suspect on '**street bail**'	→	At time of **arrival** at the police station
Suspect **arrested** away from the police station	→	At time of **arrival** at the first police station

⭐ *Example 1*

Sam is attending the police station as a volunteer to answer questions about his suspected involvement in an assault. Sam arrives at the police station at 11.00 hrs. His interview begins at 11.15 hrs. During interview, Sam admits to the assault and he is then arrested at 12.10 hrs. The 'detention clock' will start running from 12.10 hrs, the time of Sam's arrest. The police will be able to detain Sam for a maximum period of 24 hours from this time.

⭐ *Example 2*

Jo is arrested by PC Long on suspicion of theft. There are witnesses to the theft from whom PC Long wants to take statements before interviewing Jo. The officer therefore grants Jo street bail, requiring her to attend at the police station at 13.00 hrs the following day. Jo complies with the terms of her street bail and attends the police station at 13.00 hrs the following day. The 'detention clock' will start running from this time. The police will be able to detain Jo for a maximum period of 24 hours from this time.

⭐ *Example 3*

Hamid is arrested at home at 15.30 hrs on suspicion of theft. He is taken to the police station and arrives there at 15.45 hrs. His detention is authorised by the custody officer at 16.00 hrs. The 'detention clock' will start running from 15.45 hrs, the time of Hamid's arrival at the police station. The police will be able to detain Hamid for a maximum period of 24 hours from this time.

Note: In practice the police will not usually need the full 24-hour period and will either release the suspect under investigation (RUI), bail the suspect before charge or charge the suspect well within this 24-hour period. Very occasionally they may need longer.

1.3.3.2   Can the police extend the maximum period of detention?

Under s 42, the police have the power to extend the period of a suspect's detention in the police station up to a period of 36 hours (ie an additional 12 hours on top of the original 24 hours) from the 'relevant time' if certain conditions are met.

Such an authorisation must be given by an officer of the rank of superintendent or above, and may only be given if the superintendent has reasonable grounds for believing that:

(a) the detention of the suspect without charge is necessary to secure or preserve evidence relating to an offence for which the suspect is under arrest, or to obtain such evidence by questioning them;

(b) the offence is an indictable offence (ie an either-way or an indictable-only offence); and

(c) the investigation is being carried out diligently and expeditiously.

✪ Example

Damian is arrested on suspicion of the murder of Esme. He arrives at the police station at 09.00 hrs and is questioned about the offence. Damian refuses to answer any questions, but at 08.00 hrs the following day, during the course of searching Damian's house, the police find a bloodstained knife that they believe Damian used as the murder weapon. The investigating officer wants to question Damian about this new piece of evidence and asks the superintendent to authorise Damian's continued detention to enable him to do this.

The superintendent is likely to authorise the extension of the initial detention period. Murder is an indictable offence (it is indictable-only) and the investigating officer wants to question Damian to find out what Damian has to say about the knife which has only just been found. As long as the superintendent believes that the investigating officer is carrying out the investigation diligently and expeditiously, the officer's request will be granted. If the request is granted, Damian may be detained at the police station until 21.00 hrs that day (a total of 36 hours from the 'relevant time').

1.3.3.3 **Are any further extensions possible?**

The police are able to obtain a warrant of further detention from a magistrates' court if the conditions set out below are satisfied (s 43). If the magistrates are persuaded to grant a warrant of further detention, this can be for such period of time as the magistrates think fit, but up to a maximum period of 36 hours. This is on top of the police superintendent's power to extend the basic detention period up to a maximum of 36 hours from the 'relevant time'. Therefore, if the magistrates grant a warrant of further detention, this may result in the suspect being detained in the police station for a total of 72 hours (ie three days).

The magistrates have the power to grant such a warrant of further detention on very similar grounds to those used by the superintendent under s 42. So only if they consider that there are 'reasonable grounds for believing that the further detention of the person to whom the application relates is justified' (s 43(1)). Such detention may be justified only if:

(a) the suspect's detention without charge is necessary to secure or preserve evidence relating to an offence for which they are under arrest, or to obtain such evidence by questioning them; and

(b) the investigation is being conducted diligently and expeditiously (s 43(4)).

In exceptional cases, the police may make an additional application to a magistrates' court under s 44 for an extension of the warrant of further detention granted under s 43. The magistrates will grant an extension only if the grounds under s 43 above are satisfied and there are reasonable grounds for believing that the further detention is justified (s 44(1)).

An extension granted under s 44 'shall be for any period as the court thinks fit' but cannot:

(a) be longer than 36 hours; or

(b) end later than 96 hours (ie four days) after the 'relevant time'.

This means that the police can detain a suspect in police custody for a maximum period of four days before that suspect must be either released or charged.

1.3.3.4   Detention reviews (the 'review clock')

In addition to the time limits for detention set out above, the police must carry out periodic reviews of the suspect's detention to ensure that the grounds on which the detention was initially authorised by the custody officer are still applicable (s 40). This is a mandatory requirement, and if such reviews are not carried out, any detention after this time will be unlawful and will amount to the tort of false imprisonment (*Roberts v Chief Constable of the Cheshire Constabulary* [1999] 1 WLR 662).

Reviews of detention that take place before a suspect is charged are carried out by an officer of at least the rank of inspector who is not directly involved in the investigation (s 40(2)(b)). This officer is usually referred to as the 'review officer'.

The first review must take place no later than six hours after the custody officer first authorised the detention of the suspect (**note:** not six hours after the suspect first arrived at the police station). The second review must take place no later than nine hours after the first review. Subsequent reviews must take place at intervals of not more than nine hours.

⭐ *Example*

Khaled is arrested at 08.00 hrs. He arrives at the police station at 08.15 hrs (the 'relevant time' for the purpose of the 'detention clock' – see above). The custody officer authorises his detention at 08.30 hrs. The first custody review must be carried out no later than 14.30 hrs (ie within six hours of the 'review clock' starting). If that review takes place at, for example, 14.15 hrs, the next review would need to take place no later than 23.15 hrs that day (ie no more than nine hours after the first review). Further reviews after that would then need to take place at intervals of no more than nine hours.

Table 1.1   Detention and review clocks

s 40 PACE	Within **6 hours** from detention being authorised	A review by an officer not below the rank of inspector to determine whether detention is still necessary
s 40 PACE	Within **9 hours** from the first detention review	A review by an officer not below the rank of inspector to determine whether detention is still necessary
s 41 PACE	Within **24 hours** from arrival	The detainee must be charged or released unless an officer not below the rank of superintendent authorises continued detention (s 42)
s 42 PACE	Within **36 hours** from arrival	The detainee must be charged or released unless a magistrates' court grants a warrant of further detention (s 43)
s 43 PACE	Within **72 hours** from arrival	The detainee must be charged or released unless a magistrates' court grants an extension to the warrant of further detention (s 44)
s 44 PACE	Within **96 hours** from arrival	The detainee must be charged or released

1.3.4 The rights of a volunteer attending the police station

If the police do not have sufficient evidence to arrest a suspect, or where an arrest is not necessary (for example, where a suspect has indicated a willingness to assist the police with their investigation), they may ask that person to attend voluntarily at the police station to answer questions. Section 29 sets out the rights of a volunteer at the police station. There is no obligation to attend as a volunteer, and the volunteer can leave at any time unless formally arrested. Generally, a legal adviser will advise a client to attend voluntarily if the client is given this choice. In addition, the volunteer can request that a friend or a solicitor be present at the interview (see Code C, para 3.21). The police may then arrest a 'volunteer' if, when interviewed, the volunteer makes admissions which then give the police sufficient grounds to arrest them.

1.4 Advising a client whether to answer police questions

A suspect who has been arrested and detained at the police station is entitled to free legal advice and to be represented by a solicitor (s 58 and Code C, para 6).

The role which a solicitor plays at the police station is set out in para 6D of the Notes for Guidance to Code C. This states:

> The solicitor's only role in the police station is to protect and advance the legal rights of their client. On occasions this may require the solicitor to give advice which has the effect of the client avoiding giving evidence which strengthens the prosecution case.

Section 1.4 must be read in conjunction with **Section 9.4**, which deals with the evidential implications of a client exercising their right to remain silent when interviewed at the police station.

1.4.1 Information gathering on arrival at the police station

There are usually three key sources available to a solicitor who attends the police station to represent a suspect. Namely:

- The custody officer (and the custody record)
- The investigating officer
- The client.

1.4.1.1 The custody officer

On arrival at the police station the first person the solicitor is likely to speak to is the custody officer. Although the custody officer is not involved in the investigation of the offence, this officer will be able to supply the solicitor with basic information about the circumstances of the client's detention in police custody. In particular, the custody officer should allow the solicitor to inspect the custody record and detention log (Code C, para 2.4) in which the custody officer will have recorded all the significant events which have occurred since the client arrived at the police station (see above). The solicitor should use the custody record to obtain (or confirm) the client's basic details (name, address, date of birth, etc), unless they already have this information. The solicitor then needs to obtain (or confirm) the following additional details from the custody officer and/or the custody record:

(a) the alleged offence(s) for which the client has been arrested;

(b) the time at which the custody officer authorised the client's detention and the reason such authorisation was given (ie was detention authorised to obtain or preserve evidence and/or to obtain such evidence by questioning);

(c) any significant comments made by the client whilst at the police station (for example, an admission of guilt) (Code C, para 3.4);

(d) any samples, fingerprints or impressions of footwear which may already have been taken from the client;

(e) any identification procedure which may already have taken place (see **1.6** below);

(f) any interview which may already have taken place at the police station (if, for example, the client has decided to obtain legal advice only after already having been interviewed by the police);

(g) whether the client is under any form of physical or mental disability, or requires the attendance of an appropriate adult;

(h) any illness which the client may be suffering from, or any indication that the client is in any way vulnerable or requires medical treatment (or details of any medical treatment which the client has already received whilst at the police station). Similarly, the solicitor should find out if the client is suffering from the effects of drink and/or drugs;

(i) any significant items found as a result of a search either of the client's person, or of any premises owned, used or occupied by the client or premises where the client was arrested (for example, items it is alleged the client has stolen or used in the commission of the offence); and

(j) if the client has already been at the police station for six hours or more, details of any detention reviews which have been carried out and the reason why the client's continued detention has been authorised (see above).

Code C, para 2.4A allows a legal representative or an appropriate adult to request a copy of the custody record when a detainee leaves police detention or is taken before a court. In practice solicitors will usually be provided with a printout of the custody record and detention log when they first arrive at the police station.

1.4.1.2 The investigating officer

Once the solicitor has obtained some basic details about the circumstances of the client's detention, they will then need to speak to the officer who is dealing with the case. The purpose of speaking to the investigating officer is to obtain the following information:

(a) disclosure (the facts of the offence and the evidence supporting those facts);

(b) significant statements and/or silence; and

(c) the next steps the investigation officer proposes to take.

Disclosure

The solicitor first needs to know what the client is alleged to have done which constitutes a criminal offence. Although the police are not obligated to provide the solicitor with any evidence of the case against the client (subject to the requirements under para 11.1A of Code C below), they will normally provide the solicitor with some (if not all) of the details they have. The investigating officer will summarise orally the contents of the witness statements which they have obtained, possibly allow the solicitor to view copies of such statements or supply the solicitor with a typed disclosure statement summarising the evidence which the police have. The last form of disclosure is the more common method now used by the police. The solicitor should push the investigating officer to disclose as much information as possible about the case against their client. The solicitor should try to find out if the police have any other evidence in addition to statements from witnesses. The police may, for example, have obtained forensic evidence such as samples or fingerprints, there may well be CCTV evidence, or there may be an item of documentary or real evidence (such as a weapon it is alleged the suspect used, or drugs found on the suspect's person). If the investigating officer refuses to make any disclosure, or discloses only a very limited amount of information, the solicitor should point out that in those circumstances the solicitor cannot properly advise the client as to the nature of the case against them. This in turn may affect the advice the solicitor gives the client about whether or not to answer questions in interview. An amendment made to para 11.1A of Code C assists the solicitor (and a defendant who is not represented) in respect of obtaining disclosure from the investigating officer. Paragraph 11.1A includes the following:

> Before a person is interviewed, they and, if they are represented, their solicitor must be given sufficient information to enable them to understand the nature of any such offence, and why they are suspected of committing it (see paragraphs 3.4(a) and 10.3), in order to allow for the effective exercise of the rights of the defence. However, whilst the information must always be sufficient for the person to understand the nature of any offence (see Note 11ZA), this does not require the disclosure of details at a time which might prejudice the criminal investigation. The decision about what needs to be disclosed for the purpose of this requirement therefore rests with the investigating officer who has sufficient knowledge of the case to make that decision. The officer who discloses the information shall make a record of the information disclosed and when it was disclosed. This record may be made in the interview record, in the officer's pocket book or other form provided for this purpose.

Significant statements

The solicitor also needs to find out if, prior to their arrival at the police station, the client has made any significant statement (or significant silence) in the presence of a police officer. The client may, for example, have made an admission on arrest which the police will be required to put to the client at the start of the interview and ask the client whether they confirm or deny saying this (see para 11.4 of Code C).

Next steps

The solicitor then needs to find out from the investigating officer what their intentions are. For example, is the client going to be interviewed straight away, will the police require the client to take part in an identification procedure, or to provide fingerprints or samples? It may also be useful to ask the investigating officer their views on bail as this is usually something the client will be concerned about.

1.4.1.3   The client

The solicitor should then speak to the client once they have obtained as much information as they can about the case from the custody officer and the investigating officer. The solicitor needs to discuss the following matters with the client:

(a) *The solicitor's identity and role*

Unless the solicitor has represented the client previously, this is likely to be the first meeting between the solicitor and the client. Although the solicitor may have already spoken to the client on the telephone, this is likely to have been several hours earlier and the client is unlikely to recall much of what the solicitor said. Furthermore, the client may be in a vulnerable, emotional state and may not fully understand who the solicitor is and what their role is at the police station. The solicitor needs to make it clear to the client that they are there to provide the client with free, independent legal advice and that they have no connection with the police. The solicitor should point out to the client that their only role at the police station will be to protect and advance the client's legal rights. The solicitor must also tell the client that anything they are told by the client will remain confidential (even after the solicitor has stopped acting for the client), although the solicitor is bound by certain rules of professional conduct which in certain circumstances may limit what they are able to do or say on the client's behalf.

(b) *Details of the alleged offence*

The solicitor should give the client details of what they have been told by the investigating officer about the offence the client is being investigated for. The level of information the solicitor can give to the client will depend upon the level of disclosure given by the police, but it is important that the client has a clear picture of what the solicitor has been told. As part of telling the client about the police case, the solicitor should also advise the client about the relevant substantive law. In particular, the solicitor should advise the client as to what the police will need to prove in order to obtain a conviction for the offence for which the client has been arrested.

(c) *The client's instructions*

Once the client knows what the police case against him is, the solicitor should then get the client's version of events. Given the pressures of time that exist at the police station, it may not be possible for the solicitor to obtain a full proof of evidence from the client. The solicitor should, however, try to take detailed instructions from the client. Any advice which the solicitor subsequently gives to the client will be based on this information, and it is therefore important that the solicitor takes as full instructions as time permits. In *R v Anderson* (2010) The Times, 23 December, the Lord Chief Justice recommended that counsel and solicitors in criminal cases make a note recording both their client's instructions and the advice that had been given on essential issues.

(d) *The next step in the police investigation*

The client may already have been detained at the police station for several hours and be anxious to know what the police intend to do. The solicitor needs to advise the client as to what the next step in the police investigation is likely to be. In the majority of cases, the next step will be for the police to require the client to take part in an audibly recorded interview.

(e) *Prepare the client for interview*

This involves:

(i) advising the client on whether or not to answer questions put to them in the interview (ie advising the client what is the 'safest option' in the interview);

(ii) preparing a written statement on the client's behalf if the client is to give a 'no comment' interview, but hand the statement to the police so that their defence is put 'on record' (see below);

(iii) advising the client how the interview will be conducted by the police (see below); and

(iv) advising the client what role the solicitor will play in the interview (see below).

1.4.2 The client's options in interview and identifying the safest option

The usual ground upon which the custody officer will authorise the detention of a suspect at the police station is to enable the investigating officer to obtain evidence by questioning the suspect in an audibly recorded interview. One of the main reasons for the police wanting to interview a suspect is their hope that the suspect will make admissions to the offence they have been arrested for. Many suspects who are interviewed by the police end up either making an admission of guilt or contradicting themselves, so that their account of the case is shown to lack credibility when the audibly recorded interview is either played or read out to the court at trial. The most important role the solicitor has at the police station is to advise their client whether or not to answer questions in police interview. A client whom the police wish to interview has four options:

- to answer all the questions put to them;
- to give a 'no comment interview';

- selective silence, where the client answers some questions but not others;
- to give a 'no comment interview', but either during the interview or before being charged, hand a written statement to the police setting out facts the client will rely upon in their defence at trial.

Each of these options will be examined in turn below. Whilst the final decision as to which option to take is that of the client, the client is likely to follow the advice received from their solicitor. It is therefore vital that the solicitor makes an accurate note of the advice given to the client, and the reasons for giving such advice.

1.4.2.1 Answer all questions

Advantages

The advantage of a client answering all questions in interview is that this allows the client to put his version of events on record straight away. This can be particularly important if the client is raising a specific defence which imposes an evidential burden on them, such as self-defence or the defence of alibi (see **Chapter 9**). If the client's defence is particularly strong and the client comes across well when interviewed, answering questions in full may even result in the police deciding not to pursue the case any further if they accept the truth of the client's version of events. Even if the client is subsequently charged by the police, the credibility of their evidence at trial will be boosted if it can be shown that the client placed their defence on record at the earliest opportunity, and have told a consistent 'story' throughout.

Answering all the questions put by the police is also likely to ensure that at trial the court or jury will not be allowed to draw adverse inferences against the client under ss 34, 36 or 37 of the Criminal Justice and Public Order Act (CJPOA) 1994 – see **9.4**.

If the client is admitting guilt, it may also be sensible to answer questions in interview to confirm this, particularly where the police appear to have a strong case. If the client has no previous convictions and has never previously been cautioned, the police may decide to deal with the matter by way of a caution rather than charging the client with the offence if, when interviewed, the client admits their guilt. Even if the police decide to charge the client with having committed the offence, an admission of guilt during the interview at the police station is a matter that may be raised when the client's solicitor is giving a plea in mitigation to the court prior to the client being sentenced (see **Chapter 11**). The solicitor will be able to tell the court that their client co-operated with the police from the first opportunity and that, by making a prompt admission of guilt, the client saved the police spending additional time and resources investigating the offence. Guidelines produced by the Sentencing Council suggest that, when determining the reduction in sentence a defendant will receive for entering an early guilty plea, the court may consider that the defendant should have indicated a willingness to plead guilty when interviewed at the police station.

Disadvantages

The disadvantage in answering questions put by the police in interview is that many suspects will either say something incriminating or make comments which undermine their credibility. Police officers are particularly adept at 'tripping up' suspects in interview, and it is very easy for a suspect to become flustered, confused or angry, particularly if they are in an emotional condition. Suspects in such a state may be led into admitting their involvement in the offence, or into asserting facts which are contradictory or which the police can show to be untrue.

If the suspect is subsequently charged with the offence and pleads not guilty, a transcript of the interview record will be read out at court (or the recording of the interview may be played). A suspect who comes across as being confused or angry, who makes admissions, or who gives a contradictory or implausible account of events is likely to have their credibility severely damaged in the eyes of the jury or magistrates.

Even clients who are able to give their solicitor a clear version of events may be vulnerable to confusion in an interview situation. This is particularly the case with young or immature clients, clients who have not previously been in trouble with the police or clients whom the solicitor believes may be emotionally vulnerable.

The solicitor also needs to consider whether the police have provided sufficient disclosure of the evidence which they have obtained in the course of their investigations in order to enable the client to answer all the questions which the police put. A common tactic employed by the police is to hold back from the suspect's solicitor a particular piece of information which is then put to the suspect in interview, hoping to catch them off-guard. If the solicitor does not consider that the police have made a full disclosure of their case, it is a hazardous step for the solicitor then to advise the client to answer questions in the interview. The client is likely to be caught out when the police raise a matter which was not disclosed to their solicitor.

An additional potential problem with the client answering questions is that the line of questioning pursued by the police may lead the client to make an attack on the character of another person. If the client is subsequently prosecuted for the offence, such an attack may enable the CPS to raise in evidence at trial any previous convictions the client may have (see **9.7**).

1.4.2.2 Remaining silent

Advantages

The advantage of a client exercising their right to remain silent by declining to answer questions in interview (other than to say 'no comment' or 'no reply' to each and every question put) is that there is no danger of the client incriminating themself by making any admissions, or inadvertently giving the police a piece of evidence which they would not otherwise have obtained. If the case against the client is weak and the police are hoping to bolster it by getting the client to say something damaging in interview, giving a 'no comment' interview may mean that the police will not then have sufficient evidence to enable them to charge the client with the offence, and the client is likely to be released without charge.

Disadvantages

The disadvantage of a client giving a 'no comment' interview is that, if the client is subsequently charged and pleads not guilty, the magistrates or jury may in certain circumstances draw an adverse inference under ss 34, 36 or 37 of the CJPOA 1994 from the client's silence in interview. The circumstances in which an adverse inference may be drawn are examined fully in **Chapter 9.4**. In summary, however, if the client fails to answer questions in police interview and then at trial raises a defence, the details of which could reasonably have been given to the police in interview, the court or jury are entitled to conclude that the defence is a sham and was fabricated by the defendant after they had left the police station, when they had the opportunity to 'get their story straight'.

When is a solicitor likely to advise the client to give a 'no comment' interview?

A solicitor may advise a client who admits their guilt to the solicitor to give a 'no comment' interview. This will be important if the solicitor considers that the case against the client is weak and the police do not currently have sufficient evidence to prove the allegation. A client who answers questions in such a situation may make a damaging admission which will give the police sufficient evidence to charge. This course of action would not involve the solicitor being a party to the client lying to or misleading the police, and the police may decide not to pursue the case if they are unable to obtain any admissions from the client in interview.

The other occasions on which a solicitor may advise their client to give a 'no comment' interview are where:

(a) the solicitor considers that the police have not provided adequate disclosure of the evidence they have obtained against the client (so that the solicitor is unable to properly advise the client on the strength of the police case against them). Lack of disclosure from the police creates a real risk that the client may implicate themself if they answer questions in interview. This is a particularly important consideration if a co-accused has also been arrested and interviewed by the police, especially if the police are not prepared to disclose what they consider the role of the co-accused to have been, or if the police are not prepared to disclose what the co-accused has said in interview;

(b) linked to (a), the solicitor considers that the police may attempt to 'ambush' the client during the interview by revealing a piece of evidence which they had not disclosed to the solicitor in advance of the interview (in the hope that, when confronted with this evidence, the client will say something incriminating or be lost for words);

(c) the client denies involvement in the offence and the police do not currently have sufficient evidence to charge the client (since if the client agrees to answer questions in interview they run the risk of giving the police the additional evidence they need to enable them to charge the client);

(d) the client is physically or mentally unfit to be interviewed (if, for example, the client is suffering from the effects of drink or drugs), or the solicitor considers that the client would fail to give a good account of their case in interview because the client is distressed, emotional or fatigued. This is likely to be the case if the interview is to take place late at night, the client has been at the police station for a number of hours before the interview takes place, or the client has been involved in an upsetting incident (often in connection with the alleged offence);

(e) the client is likely to perform badly in interview due to his:

   (i) age

   (ii) lack of maturity

   (iii) psychological vulnerability or

   (iv) previous inexperience of police detention and questioning.

   If the client is particularly young, they may lack the maturity to answer questions properly or may become aggressive during the interview. Elderly clients may become easily confused or 'lost' during interviews at the police station. If the client appears particularly agitated or ill at ease, the solicitor may consider that the client is psychologically vulnerable to the questioning techniques the police may employ during the interview. Similar considerations will apply if this is the first time the client has been arrested and they have no previous experience of custody or questioning by the police. A solicitor may also have suspicions that the client could be suffering from some form of mental impairment if the client is behaving strangely, or if the client is unable to give the solicitor coherent instructions;

(f) the facts of the case are so complex, or relate to matters occurring so long ago, that the client cannot reasonably be expected to provide an immediate response to the allegations made against them, or that any immediate response they are able to give will not be accurate. This may be a particular consideration in a fraud case in which the police want to ask the client about complex financial matters, or in a case involving allegations of physical or sexual abuse carried out many years previously;

(g) although the client says they did not commit the offence, the client does not have a viable case or defence. If the solicitor considers that the client has no case that will, at that time, stand up to police questioning, the safest course of action may be to give a 'no comment' interview, since the client will only come across badly in interview if they attempt to answer questions to which they have no real response; or

(h) where the client has other good personal reasons for remaining silent. A common situation when a client may have such a reason for remaining silent is if the client would suffer extreme embarrassment if they were to tell the police what actually happened.

⭐ *Example*

Peter is arrested on suspicion of burglary in the early hours of the morning. Peter instructs his solicitor that he did not commit the burglary and has an alibi. The alibi is that, at the time the burglary is alleged to have occurred, Peter was at the home of Ida, with whom he is having an affair. Peter is married and doesn't want his wife to find out about the affair. If, when interviewed, Peter tells the police details of his alibi, the police will check it and it is likely that Peter's wife will find out about the affair. Peter may have a personal reason for wanting to remain silent. (In this situation the solicitor would advise Peter that he would need to balance the risk that his wife might find out about the affair against the greater likelihood of his being convicted if he fails to put forward a defence to the allegation made against him.)

If a client decides to give a 'no comment' interview on the basis of the legal advice they have received, the solicitor must explain to the client that this will not necessarily prevent a court from drawing adverse inferences from this silence at any subsequent trial. If the solicitor has advised a client to remain silent, they should ensure that they make a full written note of the reasons for this advice. Such a record may have important evidential value at trial (see **9.4**).

1.4.2.3 Selective silence

A solicitor should not generally advise a client to answer some of the questions put by the police but not others. Doing this comes across very badly at trial when the interview transcript is read out or the recording of the interview is played to the court. By answering some questions but not others, it will appear to the magistrates or the jury that the defendant has something to hide and is refusing to reply to those difficult questions for which they have no satisfactory answer.

1.4.2.4 Making a prepared written statement

(a) *When might a written statement be used?*

Handing in a written statement to the police is a useful strategy to employ if the solicitor considers that the client needs to place their version of events on record to avoid an adverse inference being drawn at trial (if, for example, the client has a positive defence such as self-defence or alibi), but the solicitor is concerned that the client may perform badly if they answer questions in interview. This is likely to be the case if the client is young, emotional or has never previously been arrested and detained at the police station. If the client is to hand in a prepared written statement to the police, the solicitor will advise the client to answer 'no comment' to questions put by the police in interview. The written statement will be read out and then handed to the police either during the interview, or after the interview but prior to the client being charged.

(b) *What should the statement contain?*

A written statement will be drafted by the solicitor and will allow the client to set out their defence in a clear and logical way, but it should be in their own words. As long as the written statement sets out all the facts which the client later relies upon in their defence at trial, handing in a written statement should avoid the risk of any adverse inferences being drawn at trial under s 34 of the CJPOA 1994, even if the client then answers 'no comment' to the questions put by the police in interview. In drafting the statement, the solicitor should also take care to cover those matters about which the police might also ask the client in interview and which may at trial be the subject of an adverse inference under s 36 or s 37 of the CJPOA 1994 (see **9.4**).

The statement should say no more than is necessary to prevent the drawing of adverse inferences at trial, although the statement may need updating if the police make further disclosure of their case.

(c) *When should the statement be handed in to the police?*

The written statement can be handed in to the police either during the interview, or just prior to charge or even kept on the client's file and not disclosed at either of these stages. It is normal practice for the statement to be handed in at the start of the interview and for the suspect to then answer 'no comment' to questions put by the police during the interview. If, however, the defence solicitor feels that the police case is particularly weak, it may be better to hold back the handing-in of the prepared written statement until the police have actually decided to charge the client (but before the client is formally charged). Handing in the statement earlier may give the police some additional information, which might lead them to decide to charge the client when otherwise they might not have done so. For example, in the statement the client may make a partial admission which gives the police sufficient evidence to enable them to charge the suspect with the offence.

✪ *Example*

Fien is arrested on suspicion of burglary of shop premises and is to be interviewed at the police station. Before the interview takes place, Fien's solicitor obtains disclosure of the case from the investigating officer. The solicitor considers that the police case against Fien is weak and that Fien is unlikely to be charged if she gives a 'no comment' interview. In particular, the police do not have any direct evidence placing Fien at the shop premises at the time of the burglary. When the solicitor takes instructions from Fien, she instructs the solicitor that she did not commit the burglary but was outside the shop premises when the burglary took place. Fien's solicitor advises her that if she discloses this fact to the police, this will strengthen the case against her and make it more likely that she will be charged. Fien accepts her solicitor's advice and gives a 'no comment' interview. However, Fien's solicitor also prepares a written statement setting out Fien's defence. The solicitor will not hand this statement in to the police during the interview (but may explain that the client has provided a prepared written statement setting out her defence, which at this stage will be kept on the client file). If the police do decide to charge Fien, however, the solicitor may then hand in the statement before Fien is charged. If the statement contains the facts Fien will later raise in her defence at trial, this may prevent an adverse inference being drawn as to recent fabrication.

Very occasionally a solicitor will take a written statement from their client but, rather than hand the statement to the police whilst the client is at the police station, retain the statement on the client's file. This may occur when the solicitor has doubts as to the accuracy of the instructions they have received from their client and are reluctant to disclose this defence to the police because they believe the facts put forward by the client either will not stand up to scrutiny, or may 'change' later in the case. In such circumstances, the solicitor will retain the statement on file and produce it at a later stage in the case, if necessary, to try and prevent the court drawing an inference that the client's defence was fabricated after they had left the police station. Adopting such a tactic will not, however, prevent other adverse inferences being drawn by the court at trial. This could include an inference that the defendant was not sufficiently confident in their defence to expose it to police scrutiny or investigation, or that they had not thought up all the details of this defence at the time of the interview.

✪ *Example*

Fergus is arrested on suspicion of assault and is to be interviewed at the police station. Fergus tells his solicitor that it is a case of mistaken identity and that he was elsewhere at the time of the assault (although he cannot recall exactly where he was). The identification evidence against Fergus is extremely strong and Fergus's solicitor doubts that Fergus's account will stand up to police scrutiny. The solicitor takes a written statement from Fergus who then gives a 'no comment' interview. The solicitor does not hand a copy of the statement to the police but retains the statement on his file.

Scenario 1 – Fergus is subsequently charged with assault. Fergus's defence at trial is the same as the account he gave to his solicitor at the police station. Fergus's solicitor can produce the statement to the court to prevent the court drawing an inference of recent fabrication (that Fergus thought up his defence only after he had left the police station). The court will, however, be able to draw the adverse inference that Fergus was not sufficiently confident in his defence to expose it to police questioning at the police station.

Scenario 2 – Fergus is subsequently charged with assault. Fergus changes his version of events and now tells his solicitor that he was present at the time of the assault but claims to have been acting only in self-defence. The solicitor will not use Fergus's statement obtained at the police station because the basis of Fergus's defence has changed. The court will be able to draw an inference of recent fabrication. However, by not handing in Fergus's statement when Fergus was originally detained at the police station, Fergus's solicitor has avoided the far more damaging situation of Fergus saying one thing at the police station and then saying something totally different when his case comes to trial. Note: there are also potential ethical issues with continuing to represent a client who has changed their account. Here the solicitor would have to be satisfied that Fergus's new account is the truthful one, otherwise the solicitor would be misleading the court by allowing Fergus to run a positive defence they believed to be untrue.

Conclusion

Giving the correct advice to a client on whether or not to answer questions in an interview at the police station is one of the hardest tasks a defence solicitor will face, because there are a number of considerations that need to be taken into account. Giving the right advice though can have a significant impact on the outcome of a client's case.

1.5   Procedure for interviewing a suspect under PACE 1984

Once the custody officer has authorised the detention of a suspect at the police station, the officer investigating the offence will then take steps to further the investigation. The steps that an investigating officer can take to secure, preserve or obtain evidence whilst the suspect is detained at the police station will involve one or more of the following:

(a) carrying out an audibly recorded interview with the suspect about the suspect's alleged involvement in the offence(s);

(b) arranging for an identification procedure to be conducted by another officer to see if a witness to, or a victim of the offence is able to identify the suspect (see **2.3**);

(c) taking fingerprints from the suspect to see if these match fingerprints found at the scene of the crime, or on any relevant objects or articles which the police have recovered; and

(d) taking samples from the suspect to see if these match any samples obtained during the course of the police investigation.

The first two investigative powers will be considered below, starting with police interviews.

1.5.1   Requirements of Codes C and E

Interviews that take place in the police station must comply with the requirements of Codes C and E. Such interviews are recorded (usually on tape, disc or digitally depending on the police force area) and are referred to in the Codes of Practice as 'audibly recorded' interviews. Code E provides detailed guidance as to the procedure that needs to be followed in such interviews.

The interview will normally be recorded on two or three tapes/discs or as one digital recording. If the recording is on tape/disc, the master tape/disc, is sealed in the presence of the suspect at the end of the interview. This seal will only be broken, and the tape/disc opened at trial, if there is any dispute about what was said. One of the other tapes/discs is called a working copy and will be used by the investigating officer to prepare a written summary or transcript of the interview if the suspect is subsequently charged with an offence. Some police forces will use a third tape/disc, which will be given to the suspect if they are subsequently charged so they will also have a record of what was said in the interview and which they may pass on to their solicitor if they are legally represented.

An interview is defined in para 11.1A of Code C as:

> the questioning of a person regarding their involvement or suspected involvement in a criminal offence or offences which, under paragraph 10.1, must be carried out under caution.

1.5.1.1   Should the suspect be interviewed at all?

Paragraph 11.18(b) of Code C provides that suspects who, at the time of the interview, appear unable to:

(a) appreciate the significance of questions or their answers; or

(b) understand what is happening because of the effects of drink, drugs, or any illness, ailment or condition, should not generally be interviewed (although there are some limited exceptions to this in cases where an interview needs to be held as a matter of urgency).

1.5.1.2   Can a suspect be interviewed before receiving legal advice?

The general position

In general, a suspect who requires legal advice should not be interviewed (or continue to be interviewed) until such advice has been received (Code C, para 6.6). This means that the police should not seek to interview a suspect who has indicated that they require legal advice. Similarly, where a suspect has indicated that they do not require legal advice, is then interviewed and indicates at some point during the interview that they have changed their mind and now require legal advice, the police should stop the interview to allow the suspect to obtain such advice.

Exceptions to the general position

The police may interview a suspect before that person has obtained independent legal advice, but given that access to legal advice is so important (see s 58 and Article 6(3)(c) of the European Convention on Human Rights), the rules permitting this are quite detailed and complex:

(a) Section 58(8) allows the police to delay a suspect receiving legal advice for up to 36 hours. If the police exercise these powers, they may (and usually will) want to interview the suspect prior to allowing them access to legal advice (see **1.3.1.1**).

(b) If the relevant solicitor has agreed to attend the police station but awaiting their arrival would 'cause unreasonable delay to the process of investigation' (Code C, para 6.6(b)(ii)).

(c) If the solicitor the suspect has asked to speak to either cannot be contacted or has declined to attend the police station, and the suspect has then declined the opportunity to consult the duty solicitor (Code C, para 6.6(c)).

(d) If a suspect asks for legal advice and changes their mind about this, the police may interview the suspect, provided:

(i) an officer of the rank of inspector or above speaks to the suspect to enquire about the reasons for their change of mind, and makes, or directs the making of, reasonable efforts to ascertain the solicitor's expected time of arrival and to inform the solicitor that the suspect has stated that they wish to change their mind and the reason for it;

(ii) the suspect's reason for the change of mind and the outcome of the efforts to contact the solicitor are recorded in the custody record;

(iii) the suspect, after being informed of the outcome of the efforts in (i) above, confirms in writing that they want the interview to proceed without speaking or further speaking to a solicitor, or without a solicitor being present, and do not wish to wait for a solicitor, by signing an entry to this effect in the custody record;

(iv) an officer of the rank of inspector or above is satisfied that it is proper for the interview to proceed in these circumstances and gives authority in writing for the interview to proceed; and if the authority is not recorded in the custody record, the officer must ensure that the custody record shows the date and time of the authority and where it is recorded, and takes or directs the taking of reasonable steps to inform the solicitor that the authority has been given and the time when the interview is expected to commence, and records the outcome of this action in the custody record;

(v) when the interview starts and the interviewer reminds the suspect of their right to legal advice, the interviewer shall then ensure that the following is recorded in the interview record:

(1) confirmation that the detainee has changed their mind about wanting legal advice or about wanting a solicitor present, and the reasons for it if given;

(2) the fact that authority for the interview to proceed has been given;

(3) that if the solicitor arrives at the station before the interview is completed, the detainee will be so informed without delay, and a break will be taken to allow them to speak to the solicitor if they wish, unless para 6.6(a) applies, and that at any time during the interview, the detainee may again ask for legal advice, and that if they do, a break will be taken to allow them to speak to the solicitor, unless para 6.6(a), (b) or (c) applies (Code C, para 6.6(d)).

In the situations at (a) and (b) above, the caution given to the suspect at the start of the interview will be as follows:

'You do not have to say anything, but anything you do say may be given in evidence.'

The reason for this wording is that no adverse inferences may be drawn at trial from the suspect's silence in interview if the suspect had not at the time of the interview been allowed access to legal advice (see **9.4**). The suspect is therefore said to have an absolute right to remain silent. This will not apply to the situations at (c) and (d) above, because in these cases the suspect is allowed to speak to the duty solicitor (situation (c)) or a solicitor of their own choice (situation (d)). The caution in these cases will be the normal caution given at the start of the interview (see below).

1.5.2 Start of the interview

1.5.2.1 The caution

At the start of the interview, the police officer conducting the interview will caution the suspect. The wording of the caution is the same as that used at the time of the suspect's arrest and is set out in para 10.2 of Code C:

You do not have to say anything. But it may harm your defence if you do not mention when questioned something which you later rely on in court. Anything you do say may be given in evidence.

The normal caution is worded in this way because, although the suspect has a right to remain silent and cannot be compelled to answer questions in the interview, if the suspect exercises this right but then at trial raises facts as part of their defence which they could have mentioned during the interview, the court may draw an 'adverse inference' from such silence under s 34 of the CJPOA 1994 (see **1.4.2** above and **9.4** below).

1.5.2.2 The continuing right to legal advice

After cautioning the suspect, the officer must also remind the suspect that they are entitled to free and independent legal advice, even if the suspect has a solicitor present at the interview (Code C, para 11.2). The caution and the reminder that the suspect is entitled to free and independent advice must be given at the start of each interview the police have with the suspect.

1.5.2.3 Significant statements and silences

After complying with the above, the interviewing officer must then put to the suspect 'any significant statement or silence which occurred in the presence and hearing of a police officer ... before the start of the interview' (Code C, para 11.4). The interviewing officer must ask the suspect whether they confirm or deny that earlier statement or silence, and if they want to add anything to it. The terms 'significant statement' and 'significant silence' are defined in Code C, para 11.4A. A 'significant statement' is a statement which appears capable of being used in evidence against the suspect at trial, in particular a direct admission of guilt. A 'significant silence' is a failure or refusal to answer a question or to answer satisfactorily when under caution, which might allow the court to draw adverse inferences from that silence at trial (see **9.4**).

✪ *Example 1*

PC Singh is called to a public house where one of the customers has been assaulted. The customer did not recognise his assailant but is able to provide PC Singh with an accurate description of this person. PC Singh leaves the public house and sees Oscar nearby. Oscar closely matches the description of the assailant given by the customer. PC Singh asks Oscar where he has just come from. Oscar replies by saying 'I came from the pub and I was only acting in self-defence'. This would be a significant statement. Oscar has not been told by PC Singh that an assault took place at the pub, and the only explanation for Oscar's reply is that he was at the pub and has some involvement in the incident. This is therefore a partial admission by Oscar and should be put to him at the start of the interview.

✪ *Example 2*

PC Minnikin is called to a jewellery shop in connection with the suspected theft of a gold bracelet by Alice. Following PC Minnikin's arrival at the shop, and in his hearing, the owner of the shop says to Alice: 'I saw you pick the bracelet up and put it in your pocket when you thought I wasn't looking. Why did you try to steal it?' Alice doesn't reply to this. This is a significant silence. Although Alice has not admitted her guilt, had she not done what the owner of the shop accused her of doing, it would have been reasonable to expect her to have denied the shop owner's version of events. The significant silence should therefore be put to Alice at the start of his interview at the police station.

Should the police officer fail to put to a suspect at the start of the interview a significant statement or silence made outside the police station, this may result in the contents of that statement or the nature of that silence being ruled inadmissible at trial under s 78 of PACE 1984 (see **Chapter 9**).

1.5.3 Conduct of the interview

The way in which the interviewing officer may conduct the interview is subject to limitations imposed by Code C. Paragraph 11.5 provides: 'No interviewer may try to obtain answers or elicit a statement by the use of oppression'.

'Oppression' might occur if the interviewing officer:

(a) raises their voice or shouts at the suspect;

(b) makes threatening gestures towards the suspect;

(c) leans towards the suspect so that they are 'in the suspect's face';

(d) stands over or behind the suspect; or

(e) threatens to detain the suspect indefinitely unless they make a confession.

Paragraph 11.5 also states that 'no interviewer shall indicate, except to answer a direct question, what action will be taken by the police if the person being questioned answers questions, makes a statement or refuses to do either'. This means that an interviewing officer should not offer any inducements to a suspect to admit their guilt. This may occur if the interviewing officer indicates to the suspect that they will be released from police detention much more quickly if they admit to having committed the offence under investigation.

1.5.3.1 When must an interview cease?

When the officer in charge of the investigation is satisfied all the questions they consider relevant to obtaining accurate and reliable information about the offence have been put to the suspect; this includes allowing the suspect an opportunity to give an innocent explanation and asking questions to test if the explanation is accurate and reliable, eg to clear up ambiguities or clarify what the suspect said; or the officer in charge of the investigation, or in the case of a detained suspect, the custody officer reasonably believes there is sufficient evidence to provide a realistic prospect of conviction for that offence (Code C, para 11.6).

If interviews with a suspect take place over more than one day, in any period of 24 hours the suspect must be given a continuous period of at least eight hours for rest. This period will usually be at night and must be free from questioning or any other interruption in connection with the offence (Code C, para 12.2).

Similarly, breaks from interviews should take place at recognised mealtimes, and short refreshment breaks should be taken at approximately two-hour intervals (Code C, para 12.8).

If the conduct of an interview breaches any of the above provisions of Code C, at any subsequent trial the court may rule inadmissible any admission or confession made by the defendant in that interview (see **9.6**).

1.5.4 Role and appropriate conduct by defence legal representative/solicitor

1.5.4.1 Preparing the client for interview

The solicitor needs to explain to the client the procedure to be followed in the audibly recorded interview, and to warn the client about the tactics the police are likely to adopt in an attempt to get them to answer questions if they give a 'no comment' interview. The following points need to be explained to the client:

(a) The interview will be audibly recorded and all parties (including the client and the solicitor) will be asked to identify themselves at the start of the interview.

(b) The interview may be stopped at any time if the client requires further legal advice from the solicitor. The client should be told that they can ask for the interview to be stopped for this purpose, or the solicitor may intervene of their own volition to suggest that the interview be stopped so they can give further advice to the client.

(c) The solicitor will be present in the interview to protect the client's interests, and will intervene in the interview when necessary if the solicitor considers that the police questioning is in any way inappropriate, or considers that the client would benefit from further legal advice in private.

(d) If the client is to remain silent in the interview, they should be advised to use the stock phrase of 'no comment' in answer to all the questions which are put to them. It is easier for clients to answer questions in this way rather than to remain totally silent.

(e) A client who is to remain silent should be advised that the police will often employ certain tactics to get them to talk. In particular the police may:

   (i) try to get the client to talk by asking apparently innocuous questions that have nothing to do with the offence under investigation;

   (ii) try to alienate the client from the solicitor by suggesting that the legal advice they have received from their solicitor is incorrect; or

   (iii) warn the client that certain adverse consequences may arise unless they answer questions.

   The client should be advised to ignore such tactics and to maintain their silence.

(f) If the client is advised to answer questions in the interview, the solicitor should remind them not to 'lose their cool' during the interview, and not to become hostile or abusive in their comments towards the interviewing officer. If the recording of the interview is subsequently played out at trial, the client is likely to lose credibility in the eyes of the jury or magistrates if they act in this way. The client should also be warned against making personal attacks on others during the interview. An attack on the character of another person made during the course of an interview may enable the prosecution to adduce evidence of the suspect's previous convictions at his trial (see **9.7**).

1.5.4.2   The interview

Seating arrangements

The solicitor should ensure that they are allowed to sit beside their client during the interview and must never allow the police to prevent them from being able to make eye contact with their client. The police will occasionally try to 'distance' the client from the solicitor by asking the solicitor to sit behind them, so that they are unable to make proper eye contact with their client, thereby isolating the client and making them feel more alone and vulnerable in the interview. The client and the solicitor need to be able to make eye contact, both to give the client the psychological support of being reminded that the solicitor is present in the interview and also to enable the solicitor to detect from the client's facial expressions or gestures if they are becoming fatigued, emotional, confused or frustrated.

The solicitor's role

The solicitor will not play a passive role in the interview. It may be necessary for the solicitor to intervene to object to improper questioning, or to give the client further advice (which may entail the interview being stopped if such advice needs to be given in private).

Paragraph 6D of the Notes for Guidance to Code C provides that the solicitor may intervene in order to seek clarification, challenge an improper question to their client or the manner in which it is put, advise their client not to reply to particular questions or if they wish to give their client further legal advice.

Paragraph 6D also provides that a solicitor may only be excluded from the interview when they are deemed to be engaging in 'unacceptable conduct', such as answering questions on behalf of their client or writing down answers for the client to read out.

Opening statement by the solicitor

It is standard practice at the start of the interview for the solicitor to make an opening statement explaining the role which they will play in the interview. This will put the police officer(s) conducting the interview on notice that the solicitor intends to play an active role in the interview, and may also provide an opportunity for the solicitor to state the advice given to the client and if necessary, the reasons for that advice. A suggested form of wording for the statement is as follows:

> I am [name], a solicitor/accredited or probationary representative with [firm name]. I am now required to explain my role. My role is to advance and protect my client's rights. I shall continue to advise my client throughout the interview and if necessary I shall ask that the interview be stopped in order to allow me to advise my client in private.

I shall intervene in the interview if:

- my client asks for, or needs, legal advice;

- your questioning or behaviour is inappropriate;

- information or evidence is referred to that has not been disclosed to me before this interview;

- clarification of any matter is required; or

- a break is required.

After receiving legal advice my client has decided:

[either]

- to exercise his right to silence [if appropriate, give a reason for this advice] because [reason]. Please respect that decision. [My client is however prepared to hand to you a written statement about this matter.]

[or]

- to answer questions which you may raise which are relevant to my client's arrest/voluntary attendance.

It is important that a solicitor makes an opening statement, both to make it clear to the police that the solicitor knows their role (and if the solicitor does need to intervene, to justify such intervention in advance) and to give the client confidence in the solicitor's ability, which in turn will give the client important psychological support. The Law Society advises that an opening statement should be made at the start of every interview, irrespective of the client's 'experience' at the police station or the seriousness of the charge.

When should a solicitor intervene during the interview?

A solicitor should intervene during the course of the interview if they consider that:

(i) the questioning techniques employed by the police are inappropriate or improper;

(ii) the police are behaving in an inappropriate manner; or

(iii) the client would benefit from further (private) legal advice.

Set out below is a non-exhaustive list of the types of situation which may occur during an interview when it would be appropriate for the solicitor to intervene:

- The solicitor is unhappy about the seating arrangements for the interview.

- The police are acting in an oppressive manner.

- The police are asking inappropriate questions because they are:

  - irrelevant questions

  - making a statement/asserting facts

- ○ misrepresenting the law
- ○ misrepresenting the strength of the case against the client
- ○ 'upgrading' a response from the client/putting words in the client's mouth/making assumptions
- ○ hypothetical/speculative questions.

- The police make threats/give legal advice on the consequences of silence.
- The police offer inducements.
- There is reference to a client's previous convictions.
- New information is introduced that was not disclosed earlier.
- The police ask the client if they would be prepared to take part in further investigative procedures before the solicitor has been able to give the client advice on this.
- The solicitor is concerned about the client's behaviour or conduct.
- The client is making comments that may have adverse consequences later in the case.
- The police provide an inaccurate summary by the interviewing officer.
- There is already sufficient evidence to charge.

1.5.4.3 Can a solicitor be removed from the interview?

Paragraph 6.9 of Code C states that a solicitor may be required to leave the interview only

> if their conduct is such that the interviewer is unable properly to put questions to the suspect.

Paragraph 6D of the Notes for Guidance to Code C provides that para 6.9 will apply only if the solicitor's approach or conduct prevents or unreasonably obstructs proper questions being put to the suspect, or the suspect's response being recorded. Examples of such unacceptable conduct would include answering questions on a suspect's behalf or providing written replies for the suspect to quote. A solicitor should not be removed from the interview simply because they tell their client not to answer questions, or because they intervene when they consider the police are asking questions in an inappropriate manner.

If the officer conducting the interview considers that the conduct of the solicitor is preventing them from properly putting questions to the suspect, the interviewer must stop the interview and consult an officer of at least the rank of superintendent (Code C, para 6.10). This officer must then speak to the solicitor and decide if the interview should continue in the presence of the solicitor or not. If it is decided that the solicitor should be excluded from the interview, the suspect must be given the opportunity to consult another solicitor before the interview continues, and that other solicitor must be given an opportunity to be present at the interview.

1.6 Conduct issues at the police station

There are a number of potential conduct issues which can arise at the police station. They may be with a range of different people the solicitor has contact with, including the client, the police or the appropriate adult where there is a vulnerable client (see **Chapter 4**).

1.6.1 The client who admits guilt

A solicitor may take instructions from a client who confirms that they did in fact commit the offence for which they have been arrested but wants to deny the offence when interviewed by the police. If the client admits guilt to their solicitor, the solicitor must advise the client that they cannot then attend an interview to represent the client if the client intends to deny having committed the offence. The solicitor cannot be a party to the client giving information to the police which the solicitor knows to be false since this would amount to a breach of the solicitor's duty not to mislead the court under para 1.4 of the SRA Code of Conduct. The solicitor could attend such an interview where the client intends to give a 'no comment' response to police questions, since this would not involve the giving of false information.

If the client insists on giving false information in interview, the solicitor should decline to act any further on the client's behalf. As the solicitor owes an ongoing duty of confidentiality to the client (SRA Code of Conduct, para 6.3), the police should not be told why the solicitor is no longer acting on the client's behalf. It is usual in such a case for a solicitor to say that they are withdrawing from the case for 'professional reasons'.

A solicitor representing a client who intends to lie to the police in interview should attempt to dissuade the client from doing so. From the client's perspective, this would be because it will usually be easy for the police to disprove such lies and because it may also result in the client being charged with a more serious offence such as perverting the course of justice. It may also be appropriate for the solicitor to advise the client that, if they admit their guilt in the interview, they will receive credit from the court for cooperating with the police when they are later sentenced.

1.6.2 Conflict of interest

1.6.2.1 When a conflict may arise

A solicitor will often be asked to advise two (or more) suspects at the police station who are jointly alleged to have committed an offence. Although a solicitor is allowed to act for two or more suspects where there is no conflict of interest, the difficulty faced by a solicitor at the police station is spotting when such a conflict may arise. On arrival at the police station the solicitor will know little more than the names of the clients and the offence for which they have been arrested. Until the solicitor knows what the police version of events is (and what version of events their potential clients are giving), the solicitor is not going to know whether there is an actual or potential conflict of interest. It is the responsibility of the solicitor to determine whether a conflict of interest exists. If the custody officer suggests to the solicitor that there is a conflict, the solicitor should ask the officer to clarify why they consider this to be the case, but stress to the officer that ultimately it is the decision of the solicitor alone as to whether a conflict exists and not that of the police (Code C, Notes for Guidance, para 6G).

Steps the solicitor should take:

- Once the solicitor has spoken to the investigating officer, the solicitor should speak to one of the suspects (usually the first suspect to have requested the solicitor's attendance at the police station). If that suspect's account suggests a clear conflict of interest (if, for example, the suspect denies guilt and accuses the other suspect of having committed the offence), the solicitor should decline to act for the second suspect and inform the police that this suspect should receive separate legal advice. To act for both suspects in such circumstances would be a breach of para 6.2 of the SRA Code of Conduct, whereby a solicitor must not act where there is a conflict of interest between two or more clients or a significant risk of a conflict.

- Even if there is no obvious conflict of interest, the solicitor should be alert to a potential conflict of interest arising later in the case. This could occur, for example, if both suspects admit the offence but, when the case comes to court, the mitigation for one of the suspects is going to be that they only played a minor role in the commission of the offence and that the larger role was played by the other suspect, and this is something the other suspect disputes.

- If a conflict of interest emerges only after the solicitor has seen both suspects, the appropriate course of action is for the solicitor to withdraw from the case completely. To continue acting for both suspects would be a clear conflict of interest. It would also be inappropriate to continue to act for only one of them because the solicitor would be in possession of confidential information from the other, which could not be passed on to the one whom the solicitor was continuing to represent. Only if the solicitor is able to act for one client without putting at risk their duty of confidentiality to the other may they continue to represent that first client (SRA Code of Conduct, para 6.3). This is unlikely to be the case, because the confidential information received from the other is likely to assist the case of the client the solicitor is continuing to represent and so confidentiality will be put at risk (and also because the solicitor is under a duty to disclose all relevant information to the remaining client – SRA Code of Conduct, para 6.4).

1.6.3 Should a solicitor disclose to one client information they have been given by another client?

If a solicitor decides that there is no conflict of interest and they are able to represent both suspects, they must still not disclose to one client anything they have been told by the other (in order to comply with their duty of confidentiality to the other client), unless:

(a) the solicitor has obtained the other client's consent (preferably in writing) to disclose this information (ie the client waives their right to confidentiality);

(b) both clients are putting forward consistent instructions; and

(c) the solicitor considers it in their clients' best interests for the information to be disclosed.

Even if the above considerations are satisfied, the solicitor must also have regard to their overriding duty not to mislead the court. Co-accused who are represented by the same solicitor may attempt to use that solicitor to pass information between each other so that they can jointly fabricate a defence and give the police a consistent 'story'. To guard against this, the solicitor should ensure that before telling the second client what they have been told by the first client, they obtain an account of the second client's version of events. If this is consistent with the account given by the first client, the solicitor will then be able to pass on the relevant information (provided the first client has authorised this). If, however, the stories are inconsistent, the solicitor will need to withdraw from the case. As mentioned above, it would be inappropriate for the solicitor to continue to act for just one of the clients because they would be in possession of confidential information about the other and yet also under a duty to disclose it.

1.6.4 Disclosing the client's case to a third party

A solicitor representing a client at the police station may be asked for details of their client's defence by another solicitor representing a co-accused who has been arrested in connection with the same offence. Such a request should be treated with caution. The solicitor owes a duty of confidentiality to their client and should therefore not respond to such a request by releasing any such information. The only exception to this is if the solicitor considers it is in their own client's best interests for such information to be disclosed. This will only very rarely be the case. If the solicitor does consider that it would be in the client's interests to disclose this information, the solicitor should first explain their reasoning to the client and obtain the client's authority (ideally in writing) to disclose this information.

1.6.5 The solicitor's duty of disclosure to a client

This duty is described in para 6.4 of the SRA Code of Conduct. It requires a solicitor to make the client aware of all material information of which the solicitor has knowledge. This is subject to a limited range of exceptions such as where:

- disclosure is prohibited by national security or the prevention of crime;

- the client gives informed consent (in writing) to the information not being disclosed;

- you have reason to believe that serious physical or mental injury will be caused to the client or another if the information is disclosed; and

- the information is contained in a privileged document that has been mistakenly disclosed to you.

✪ Example

You represent Jayne who has been arrested on suspicion of fraud. Whilst obtaining disclosure from the investigating officer, DC Edwards, he says to you: 'Look, I really respect you, so I'm going to disclose some very sensitive information to you about the case, but only if you first promise not to disclose it to anyone'.

In replying to DC Edwards, you should explain that you are required by your professional code of conduct to disclose all relevant information to your client. You should also try to persuade the officer to still disclose this information to you even though you are obliged to let your client know about it (unless you believe that one of the limited exceptions above applies).

1.6.6 Withdrawing from acting

If, for reasons of professional conduct, a solicitor is unable to continue acting for a client (or clients) at the police station, the solicitor needs to do the following:

(a) explain to the client why they are no longer able to represent them;

(b) tell the client that they are entitled to free legal advice from another solicitor of their choice or the duty solicitor;

(c) tell the client that, although they are no longer able to represent them, the solicitor still owes them an ongoing duty of confidentiality and will not therefore tell the police why they are unable to act; and

(d) tell the custody officer that they are no longer able to act (for professional reasons), but not disclose the reason why. If the solicitor told the custody officer why they were no longer able to act, this would be a breach of the ongoing duty of confidentiality owed to the former client under para 6.3 of the SRA Code of Conduct.

Summary

In this chapter you have considered what powers the police have to detain and question a suspect and what rights the suspect has whilst at the police station, including the right to free, independent legal advice and the role a solicitor plays whilst representing a client at the police station, particularly when the client is to be interviewed. Notably:

- *The procedure on arrival at the police station.* The role of the custody officer who decides whether an arrested person should be detained before charge (s 37) and their responsibility for the suspect who is so detained.

- *The rights of a suspect being detained by the police for questioning.* The right to free, independent legal advice (s 58); the right not to be held incommunicado (s 56) and how these two rights can be delayed and also the right to consult the codes of practice.

- *The period of detention and the requirement for regular reviews.* The operation of the 'detention clock' (ss 41, 42, 43 and 44) and the 'review clock' (s 40).

- *Advising a client whether to answer police questions.* The suspect's solicitor will first gather as much relevant information as they can before advising their client of the options open to them in the interview, the advantages and disadvantages of these and which option they believe to be the safest.

- *The procedure to be followed when interviewing a suspect.* Codes C and E provide detailed guidance for the conduct of audibly recorded interviews at the police station. These include: what exactly an interview is; when a suspect should not be interviewed; when an interview can take place without a suspect first receiving legal advice; when the caution and any significant statements or silence shall be given; how the interviewing officer must then conduct the interview; and finally when the interview should stop.

- *The role of the legal adviser.* This is described in para 6D of the Notes for Guidance to Code C. The legal adviser is expected to actively represent and defend their client before and during the interview. This will include preparing the client to cope with the interview; ensuring the seating arrangements are appropriate; explaining their role at the start of the interview by making an opening statement; intervening during the interview whenever the questioning techniques employed by the police are inappropriate, improper or where the police behave in an inappropriate manner; or where the client would benefit from further (private) legal advice.

- *Dealing with a range of conduct issues at the police station.* This included what to do when a client admits guilt; how to deal with a conflict of interest or a significant risk of such a conflict; whether a solicitor can disclose to one client information they have been given by another client; whether a solicitor can disclose the client's case to a third party; and what to do when withdrawing from acting for a client.

Sample questions

Question 1

A man has been arrested on Tuesday at 10.00 hrs on suspicion of common assault (a summary offence) and taken to the local police station by the arresting officer. He arrives at 10.15 hrs and the custody officer authorises his detention to obtain evidence by questioning him at 10.30 hrs.

Which of the following best describes the maximum period of time this man can be detained before charge?

A   He can be detained up until an inspector conducts a review of his detention which must be by 16.30 hrs on Tuesday.

B   He can be detained up until an inspector conducts a review of his detention which must be by 19.30 hrs on Tuesday.

C   He can be detained up until 10.00 hrs on Wednesday.

D   He can be detained up until 10.15 hrs on Wednesday.

E   He can be detained up until 10.30 hrs on Wednesday.

Answer

Option D is the best answer. The 'custody clock' as opposed to the 'review clock' starts from the time the man arrives at the police station, which here is 10.15 hrs on the Tuesday (not the time of his arrest away from the police station, so option C is wrong, nor from the time detention is authorised, so option E is also wrong). According to s 41, the maximum period of detention before charge is 24 hours (note this cannot be extended as common assault is a summary-only offence) so he can only be detained up until 10.15 hrs on the Wednesday. Option A correctly sets out the time by which the man's detention must be initially reviewed by an inspector, but the question asks for the maximum period of detention, not when the first review must be conducted. Option B is wrong because this also refers to a review, and in any event, it gives the wrong time period (9 hours) for the first review to be conducted.

Question 2

A woman has been arrested and taken to the police station. When she is given her rights, she requests legal advice, but she subsequently changes her mind when she learns the police are ready to interview her and there is a delay in her solicitor attending the police station. The custody officer authorises the interview to proceed in the absence of the solicitor and makes an entry to this effect in the custody record. The woman also confirms her change of mind in writing by signing an entry to this effect in the custody record.

Can the interview lawfully proceed on this basis?

A   Yes, because the right to legal advice is an ongoing right, the suspect is entitled to change her mind at any stage during her detention.

B   No, because written authority can only be given by an officer not below the rank of inspector.

C   Yes, because the custody officer has authorised this and made a record of the authorisation in the custody record.

D   No, because written authority can only be given by an officer not below the rank of superintendent.

E   No, because once a suspect has requested legal advice the interview cannot proceed without the solicitor's attendance.

Answer

Option B is the best answer. Whilst a suspect can change her mind about wanting legal advice (so option E is wrong), this must be authorised in writing by an officer not below the rank of inspector (so options C and D are also wrong). Whilst option A is correct in that the right to legal advice is an ongoing right, and the suspect is entitled to change her mind at any stage during her detention, there are some additional safeguards that must be followed for this to be done correctly. These safeguards are actually very detailed (see the key points below), but option B is the best answer because this correctly identifies the role played by an officer not below the rank of inspector, provided:

- this officer speaks to the suspect to enquire about the reasons for their change of mind, and makes reasonable efforts to contact the solicitor;
- the suspect's reason for the change of mind and the outcome of the efforts to contact the solicitor are recorded in the custody record;
- the suspect confirms in writing that they want the interview to proceed without first obtaining legal advice by signing an entry to this effect in the custody record; and
- the officer of the rank of inspector or above is satisfied that it is proper for the interview to proceed in these circumstances and gives authority in writing for the interview to proceed.

Question 3

A solicitor is acting for a client at the police station when it becomes apparent that there is a conflict of interest with an existing client the solicitor is already representing.

Assuming the solicitor will withdraw from acting for the client, what should she now say to the custody officer?

A   That she no longer wants to represent the client.

B   That she can no longer represent the client because there is a conflict of interest with an existing client.

C   That she can no longer represent the client and the custody officer should speak to the client to find out why.

D   That she can no longer represent the client but someone else from her firm will be attending to represent the client.

E   That she is no longer able to represent the client for professional reasons.

Answer

Option E is the best answer because all the solicitor can tell the custody officer is that she can no longer act (for professional reasons) – she must not disclose the reason why. Arguably she could just tell the custody officer that she is no longer able to act, but some practitioners would say it would be discourteous not to explain that it is for professional reasons. Option A is not the best answer because it is misleading for the solicitor to say that she no longer *wants* to represent the client. The reason she can no longer represent the client is because of her professional obligations to this client and her existing client rather than because she no longer wants to do this. If the solicitor told the custody officer why she was no longer able to act (other than for professional reasons) this would be a breach of the ongoing duty of confidentiality owed to the client under para 6.3 of the SRA Code of Conduct, so option B is wrong. It would also be wrong to tell the custody officer to speak to the client about why the solicitor can no longer act, so option C is also wrong. Option D is wrong because if the solicitor has a conflict with this client and an existing client, this will also prohibit anyone else in the firm from representing the client.

2 Identification Procedures

Learning outcomes

By the end of this chapter you will be able to apply relevant core legal principles and rules appropriately and effectively, at the level of a competent newly qualified solicitor in practice, to realistic client-based and ethical problems and situations in the following areas:

- When an identification procedure must be held.
- The different types of procedure available.
- How such procedures should be conducted and who is responsible for conducting these.
- The role of a legal adviser during such procedures and the advice a client should be given about participating in an identification procedure.

2.1 Introduction

In addition to wanting to interview an arrested person about their suspected involvement in a criminal offence, the other main reason for the police to arrest a suspect is to enable them to obtain additional evidence which points to that suspect's guilt. One method which the police use to obtain such evidence is to see if the victim or witnesses to the offence are able to visually identify the suspect, where the suspect is claiming they were not involved.

The procedures which the police need to follow when obtaining identification evidence are contained in Code D. Paragraph 1.2 of Code D provides:

> In this code, identification by an eye-witness arises when a witness who has seen the offender committing the crime and is given an opportunity to identify a person suspected of involvement in the offence in a video identification, identification parade or similar procedure. These eye-witness identification procedures ... are designed to:

- test the witness' ability to identify the suspect as the person they saw on a previous occasion
- provide safeguards against mistaken identification.

If the police do not know the identity of the suspect, they are allowed to take a witness to a particular neighbourhood or place to see if that witness is able to identify the person they saw.

If the identity of the suspect is known to the police and the suspect has been arrested, the police may then use a form of identification procedure to see if the witness can identify the suspect.

> The police must keep a record of the suspect's description as first given to them by a potential witness (Code D, para 3.1). Before any form of identification procedure takes place, a copy of this record should be given to the suspect or their solicitor. This may prove useful at trial if there are discrepancies between this description and the actual appearance of the suspect.

2.2 When an identification procedure must be held

Whenever:

(a) a witness has identified or purported to have identified a suspect; or

(b) a witness thinks they can identify the suspect, or there is a reasonable chance that the witness can identify the suspect, and the suspect disputes being the person the witness claims to have seen, para 3.12 of Code D states that an identification procedure *shall* be held unless it is not practicable or would serve no useful purpose in proving or disproving whether the suspect was involved in committing the offence.

Code D, para 3.12 goes on to give two examples of when it would not be necessary to hold an identification procedure, namely:

(a) when the suspect admits being at the scene of a crime and gives an account which does not contradict what the witness saw; and

(b) when it is not disputed that the suspect is already known to the witness.

In such cases, an identification procedure would serve no purpose because the witness would inevitably pick out the suspect.

In R v Harris [2003] EWCA Crim 174 the victim to a robbery claimed that he knew the accused on the basis that he had gone to the same school. However, they had not been in the same class and it had been two years ago when the accused was only 14 at the time. The accused disputed the identification and also disputed that he was known to the witness. It was held that this was a case where an identification procedure should have been held under Code D, para 3.12.

By contrast, in H v DPP [2003] All ER (D) (Jan) the Court of Appeal held that it would have served no useful purpose for the police to hold an identification procedure given that it was accepted that the victim prior to the assault in question had known his aggressor well for a period of 18 months and the assault had lasted a full seven minutes and so no useful purpose would have been served in then holding a formal identification procedure.

An identification procedure should also be held if a witness to a crime has purported to identify the suspect in the street some time after the crime was committed, since the purpose of an identification procedure is to test the reliability of the eyewitness' identification.

An eyewitness identification procedure may also be held if the officer in charge of the investigation considers it would be useful (Code D, para 3.13).

✪ *Example 1*

Liam is arrested on suspicion of assault. A witness, Baljeet, saw the assault. She does not know Liam but thinks she can identify the person she saw commit the assault. Liam disputes being the person Baljeet claims to have seen. An identification procedure should be held to see if Baljeet can pick out Liam as the person she saw committing the assault.

✪ *Example 2*

Liam is arrested on suspicion of assault. A witness, Baljeet, saw the assault. She recognised Liam as the person who committed the assault because she was at school with him some years previously. Liam disputes being the person Baljeet claims to have seen. He also says that he only vaguely recalls Baljeet from school but did not know her very well. He also comments that it is several years since he left school and Baljeet was two years ahead of him. An identification procedure should be held to see if Baljeet can pick out Liam, since Liam is disputing the fact that he is known to Baljeet (see R v Harris above).

✪ *Example 3*

Liam is arrested on suspicion of assault. A witness, Baljeet, saw the assault. She identifies Liam as the person who committed the assault. Liam disputes being the person Baljeet claims to have seen. Baljeet has known Liam for several years as they are both members of the same gym. Liam does not dispute that he is known to Baljeet. So unlike Example 2, there would be no useful purpose in holding an identification procedure since Liam is known to Baljeet who would clearly pick out Liam were a procedure to be held (see H v DPP above).

✪ *Example 4*

An assault takes place outside a pub and is witnessed by Baljeet. The assailant runs away before he can be apprehended. Baljeet does not know the identity of the person who carried out the assault but thinks she will be able to identify this person if she sees him again. PC Smith later takes Baljeet to the area where the assault occurred. Baljeet sees Liam and recognises him as the person who committed the assault. An identification procedure should be held to test the reliability of Baljeet's street identification of Liam if Liam claims that Baljeet is mistaken.

2.3 Different types of identification procedure under PACE 1984, Code D

There are four different types of identification procedure:

(a) video identification;

(b) an identification parade;

(c) a group identification; and

(d) confrontation by a witness.

2.3.1 Which type of identification procedure should be used?

Paragraph 3.14 of Code D provides that a suspect should initially be offered a video identification unless:

(a) a video identification is not practicable;

(b) an identification parade is both practicable and more suitable than a video identification; or

(c) the officer in charge of the investigation considers that a group identification is more suitable than a video identification or identification parade, and the identification officer considers it practicable to arrange a group identification (Code D, para 3.16).

The decision on which type of procedure is offered to the suspect will be made by the investigating officer in conjunction with the identification officer. A video identification is now the most common form of identification procedure used by the police. Identification parades and group identifications are held only rarely. A video identification is normally preferred to an identification parade, if it can be arranged and completed sooner than an identification parade. Paragraph 3.14 states:

> An identification parade may not be practicable because of factors relating to the witnesses, such as their number, state of health, availability and travelling requirements. A video identification would normally be more suitable if it could be arranged and completed sooner than an identification parade.

Confrontations are very much a last resort.

2.3.2 Can an identification procedure be used if a witness has recognised a suspect from a photograph?

The police will keep photographs of individuals with previous convictions and may show these photographs to a witness when they are trying to identify the person responsible for a crime (see below).

Before a witness is shown any photographs, that witness' first description of the suspect must have been recorded (Code D, Annex E, para 2).

The witness must be shown at least 12 photographs at a time (Code D, Annex E, para 4). As soon as a witness makes a positive identification from photographs, no other witnesses should be shown the photographs. The witness who made the identification and any other witnesses should then be asked to take part in one of the identification procedures outlined above (Code D, Annex E, para 6).

The suspect or his solicitor must be notified if a witness attending an identification procedure has previously been shown photographs, or a computerised or artist's composite (Code D, Annex E, para 9).

If the case subsequently comes to trial, when giving evidence the witness will not be allowed to say that they originally identified the suspect from photographs shown to them by the police (see also *Charles v The Queen* [2007] UKPC 47).

2.4 Procedure to be followed for carrying out an identification procedure

2.4.1 Video identification (Code D, Annex A)

A video identification occurs when the witness is shown moving images of a known suspect, together with similar images of others who resemble the suspect.

The images must include the suspect and 'at least eight other people who, so far as possible, resemble the suspect in age, general appearance and position in life' (Code D, Annex A, para 2). Where two suspects of roughly similar appearance are shown in the same images, they must be shown together with at least 12 other people (Code D, Annex A, para 2). The images that are shown to the witness must show the suspect and the other people in the same positions or carrying out the same sequence of movements (Code D, Annex A, para 3).

The suspect or their solicitor must be given a reasonable opportunity to see the full set of images before they are shown to any witness. If there is a 'reasonable objection' to the images or to any of the other participants (such as one of the other participants not resembling the suspect), the police must take steps, if practicable, to remove the grounds for objection (Code D, Annex A, para 7). Such steps may include not using the image of a participant who does not resemble the suspect, and instead replacing this with an image of someone who does resemble the suspect.

If a suspect has any unusual features (such as a facial scar, a tattoo or distinctive hair style or colour) which do not appear on the images of the other people, the police may take steps to conceal those features on the video or to replicate those features on the images of the other people (Code D, Annex A, para 2A). Such concealment or replication may be done electronically. If a witness, having seen video images where concealment or replication has been used, wants to see an image without the concealment or replication of the unusual feature, the witness may be allowed to do so (Code D, Annex A, para 2C).

A suspect will not be present at the video identification, although the suspect will have attended the police station on an earlier date to be video recorded for the purpose of the video identification. The suspect's solicitor should be given reasonable notice of the time and place of the video identification so that they may attend to ensure that it is carried out properly (Code D, Annex A, para 9).

Only one witness may see the video at a time. The playback of the video may be frozen and there is no limit on the number of times the suspect may see the video (Code D, Annex A, para 11). Before they see the set of images, witnesses must not be able to:

(a) communicate with each other about the case;

(b) see any of the images which are to be shown;

(c) see, or be reminded of, any photograph or description of the suspect, or be given any other indication as to the suspect's identity; or

(d) overhear a witness who has already seen the material (Code D, Annex A, para 10).

The police must not discuss with the witness the composition of the set of images, and a witness must not be told whether a previous witness has made an identification. If a suspect refuses to consent to take part in a video identification, alternative procedures may be followed (see below), including a covert video identification.

2.4.2 Identification parades (Code D, Annex B)

An identification parade occurs when a witness sees the suspect in a line of other persons who resemble the suspect.

The identification parade will consist of at least eight people (in addition to the suspect) who, so far as possible, resemble the suspect in age, height, general appearance and position in life (Code D, Annex B, para 9).

As with a video procedure, if a suspect has any unusual features (such as a facial scar, tattoo or distinctive hair style or colour) which it is not possible to replicate on the other participants in the parade, the police may take steps to conceal those features. For example, a plaster may be used to hide a facial scar, or a hat may be used to hide distinctive hair colour (Code D, Annex B, para 10).

Paragraph 14 of Code D, Annex B provides that the police must make appropriate arrangements to ensure that, before attending the parade, witnesses are not able to:

(a) communicate with each other about the case, or overhear a witness who has already seen the identification parade;

(b) see any member of the identification parade;

(c) see, or be reminded of, any photograph or description of the suspect, or be given any other indication as to the suspect's identity; or

(d) see the suspect before or after the identification parade.

The suspect is allowed to choose their own position in the line (and may change positions between witnesses if more than one witness is to attend the parade), but cannot otherwise alter the order of people forming the line. Paragraph 16 of Code D, Annex B states:

> Witnesses shall be brought in one at a time. Immediately before the witness inspects the identification parade, they shall be told the person they saw on a specified earlier occasion may, or may not, be present and if they cannot make a positive identification, they should say so. The witness must also be told they should not make any decision about whether the person they saw is on the identification parade until they have looked at each member twice.

Sometimes a witness will ask to have a parade member speak, move or adopt a particular posture. If a witness makes such a request, they should first be asked whether they can identify any person on the parade on the basis of appearance only. A witness who asks a parade member to speak must be reminded that the participants in the parade have been chosen on the basis of physical appearance only. Only when the police have done that may a member of the parade then be asked to comply with the request to hear them speak, move or adopt a particular posture. (If a suspect is picked out after they have been asked to speak, whilst this evidence will be admissible at trial, the judge will give a very strong warning to the jury to treat such evidence with the utmost caution.)

A colour photograph or video recording of the identification parade must always be taken (Code D, Annex B, para 23) to help guard against any later dispute that the other members of the parade were not sufficiently similar to the suspect 'in age, height, general appearance and position in life'.

As with a video procedure, the police cannot compel a suspect to take part in an identification parade, but there are practical and evidential implications when this occurs (see **2.5.1** below).

2.4.3 Group identification (Code D, Annex C)

A group identification occurs when the witness sees the suspect in an informal group of people. Group identifications may take place either with the consent and cooperation of the suspect, or covertly if the suspect does not consent (Code D, Annex C, para 2).

The place where a group identification should be held is a place where other people are passing by or waiting around informally (such as on an escalator, or in a shopping centre or bus station). The suspect should be able to join these people and be capable of being seen by the witness at the same time as others in the group (Code D, Annex C, para 4).

In selecting the location for the holding of a group identification, the police must reasonably expect that the witness will see some people whose appearance is broadly similar to that of the suspect (Code D, Annex C, para 6). Beyond that, however, there is no requirement that the other persons whom the witness sees in addition to the suspect have any particular likeness to the suspect.

If a suspect refuses to consent to a group identification and such an identification is held covertly, the police will be required to take the witness to a place where the suspect is likely to be at a given time. If, for example, the suspect is in employment, the group identification could take place outside the suspect's place of work at the time when the suspect is known to start or finish work, since it is likely that the suspect would then be in a group of fellow workers arriving or leaving work at the same time.

2.4.4 Confrontation (Code D, Annex D)

A confrontation occurs when a witness is brought face-to-face with a suspect in the police station. Confrontations are extremely rare and very much a last resort.

Prior to a confrontation taking place, the witness must be told that the person they saw may, or may not, be the person they are to confront and that if they are not that person, the witness should say so (Code D, Annex D, para 1).

Confrontations will usually take place in the presence of the suspect's solicitor and usually occur where the suspect refuses to take part in any of the above alternative procedures.

2.4.5 Who is responsible for the running of an identification procedure?

2.4.5.1 The identification officer

Identification procedures are the responsibility of an officer not below the rank of inspector who is not involved with the investigation. This officer is known as the 'identification officer' (Code D, para 3.11). The identification officer will be in charge of the identification procedure and must ensure that it complies with the requirements of Code D. The identification officer will be present throughout the procedure and must be in uniform. When an identification procedure needs to be held, para 3.11 of Code D provides that 'it must be held as soon as practicable'. If the police decide to hold an identification procedure, the suspect will normally be released on police bail (see **3.3**) with a requirement to re-attend the police station at a later date when the identification procedure will take place. This will then enable the police to arrange for witnesses to attend the police station (in the case of an identification parade) or to obtain the necessary images (in the case of a video identification).

The investigating officer will have no involvement in the conduct of the identification procedure. Paragraph 3.11 of Code D states:

> No officer ... involved with the investigation of the case against the suspect ... may take part in [identification] procedures or act as the identification officer.

This is to ensure there is no risk of the investigating officer seeking to influence in any way the witnesses who are to take part in the identification procedure.

2.4.5.2 Steps to be taken by the identification officer

Before a video identification, identification parade or group identification is arranged, the identification officer must explain the following matters to the suspect:

(a) the purpose of the identification procedure to be used;

(b) the suspect's entitlement to free legal advice;

(c) the procedure to be followed, including the suspect's right to have a solicitor or friend present;

(d) that if the suspect refuses to consent to the identification procedure taking place, such refusal may be given in evidence at trial, or the police may proceed covertly without the suspect's consent (ie by holding a covert video or group identification), or make other arrangements to test whether a witness can identify the suspect (ie by arranging a confrontation);

(e) that if the suspect has significantly altered their appearance between being offered an identification procedure and the time of the procedure, this may be given in evidence at trial and the identification officer may consider other forms of identification;

(f) whether, before the suspect's identity became known, the witness was shown photographs, or a computerised or artist's composite likeness or image by the police; and

(g) that the suspect or their solicitor will be provided with details of the description of the suspect as first given by any witnesses who are to attend the identification procedure before the procedure takes place (Code D, para 3.17).

2.5 Legal adviser's role at an identification procedure and advising a client

2.5.1 Initial advice to the client

An identification procedure will generally take place after the suspect's first interview. It will usually only be at this stage of the investigation that the police will be aware if the suspect disputes they were the person the witness saw at the relevant time (usually committing the offence). If the suspect is then positively identified at such a procedure, they are then likely to be either re-interviewed in light of the positive identification and/or charged with the offence.

As mentioned above, the most likely identification procedure will be a video identification (or possibly an identification parade) and this will usually require the suspect's consent. In such circumstances, there are several matters which the solicitor will need to explain to their client, and various checks which the solicitor will need to carry out prior to the identification procedure taking place. On the assumption that the police will want to hold a video identification or identification parade, the solicitor should advise the client to agree to such a procedure being carried out. If the witness attending the procedure cannot identify the client, the police may release the client without charge.

If the client is not prepared to take part in a video identification or identification parade, the solicitor should warn the client that the police may hold a less satisfactory form of identification procedure, such as group identification or even a confrontation. These procedures are less satisfactory than a video identification or an identification parade because it is more likely that the suspect will be identified by the witness, as the suspect will not be seen in a group of people who resemble them in appearance. The police may also choose to video the suspect covertly for a video identification.

Refusal to take part in an identification procedure is admissible at trial, and the court may therefore draw an adverse inference from the refusal of a suspect to take part in an identification procedure. The adverse inference will be that the suspect refused to take part in the procedure because they thought they would be recognised by the witness(es) who would have attended the procedure.

Occasionally the police will decide not to organise an identification procedure even if the suspect disputes their involvement and is willing to take part in such a procedure and the police have a witness who believes they would be able to identify the person who committed the offence. If the police decide not to hold an identification procedure in such circumstances, this would be a breach of Code D, para 3.12 (see **2.2** above). If the solicitor considers that the police should carry out an identification procedure in order to comply with Code D, they should make representations to this effect to the investigating officer and also ensure their representations are recorded in the custody record as such a failure may allow them to subsequently challenge the admissibility of any later disputed visual identification evidence at trial (see **Chapter 9**).

2.5.2 Video identification

If the police intend to hold a video identification, the solicitor will be entitled to attend this procedure. The solicitor needs to obtain from the police details of the first description of the suspect given by the potential witness (Code D, para 3.1). The solicitor needs to check in advance that the images which are to be used resemble the suspect in age, height, general appearance and position in life. Again, the solicitor will need to object if the images do not comply with this requirement and ensure that the police obtain further images. If the suspect has a distinctive feature (such as a prominent tattoo) the solicitor should ensure that this is covered up both on the image of the client and on the other foils.

The solicitor should attend the video identification to ensure that the witnesses attending the procedure are segregated from each other and that no unauthorised persons (such as the investigating officer) are present. The solicitor should check the number of witnesses who are to attend, where the witnesses will be kept before and after the procedure (making sure that a witness who has attended the procedure has no opportunity to speak to a witness who has not yet taken part), and the route the witnesses will take both to view and then to leave the procedure.

If the solicitor considers that the video identification has been contaminated in any way, they should ask the witness if they have discussed the description of the offender with anyone, either before attending or whilst at the police station. They should also ask that a note of their concerns be made by the identification officer in the written record of the video identification procedure.

2.5.3 Identification parades

Before the parade takes place, the solicitor should ensure that the police provide them with details of the first description of the suspect given by the potential witness (Code D, para 3.1). The solicitor should explain to their client what will happen at the parade (see **2.4.2** above). The solicitor should tell the client that they may choose where to stand on the parade and that whilst the parade is taking place they should not speak or do anything to draw attention to themselves.

The solicitor needs to check that the other participants in the parade resemble their client in age, height, general appearance and position in life. If they do not, the solicitor should make representations to the identification officer and ask either for the parade to be postponed, or for some form of disguise to be used to overcome any disparity in the appearance of the other participants. If, for example, the other participants in the parade are taller than the suspect, the solicitor may ask that all the people taking part in the parade be seated. Alternatively, if the suspect has a distinctive style or colour of hair, the solicitor could ask that all participants in the parade wear hats.

The solicitor should check that the witnesses are properly segregated before the parade and that there is no opportunity for the witnesses to see either the client or the other participants in the parade before the parade takes place. This may involve the solicitor checking the route which the witnesses will take to get to the parade and ensuring that the witnesses who are waiting to take part in the procedure are kept in separate rooms. The solicitor should ensure that there is no opportunity for a witness who has already attended the parade to speak to another witness before that witness has attended the parade. The solicitor should also ensure that the investigating officer is to play no part in the identification parade.

If the solicitor considers that the parade has been contaminated in any way, they should ask the witness if they have discussed the description of the offender with anyone, either before attending or whilst at the police station. They should also ask that a note of their concerns be made by the identification officer in the written record of the parade.

2.5.4 Written records

Whichever form of identification procedure is used, the solicitor needs to keep a detailed record of what happens. The solicitor must ensure that the identification officer complies with the procedural requirements of Code D, Annex A (in the case of a video identification), or Annex B (in the case of an identification parade) when conducting the procedure. The solicitor should also make sure that any objections they make to the conduct of the procedure (if, for example, the solicitor considers that the witnesses have not been properly segregated before an identification parade takes place) are recorded in full by the identification officer. Any comments made during the procedure (whether by the witness, the identification officer or anyone else) should also be recorded.

Summary

In this chapter you have considered when and how the police will be required to conduct an identification procedure and the importance of Code D of the Codes of Practice to PACE 1984 in relation to identification procedures. Notably:

- *When an identification procedure must be held.* This is dealt with by para 3.12 which makes such a procedure mandatory where the police have an identification witness and the suspect disputes being the person the witness claims to have seen, unless it is not practicable or would serve no useful purpose in proving or disproving whether the suspect was involved in committing the offence. Paragraph 3.13 also gives the police a discretion to hold an identification procedure if the officer in charge of the investigation considers it would be useful.

- *The different types of identification procedure.* These are a video identification; an identification parade; a group identification; and a confrontation by a witness. Paragraph 3.14 provides that a suspect should initially be offered a video identification unless this is not practicable.

- *The procedure to be followed when carrying out an identification procedure.* These are set out in considerable detail at Annexes A, B, C and D of Code D and for all four types of procedure an officer not below the rank of inspector and not involved with the investigation is responsible for conducting the identification procedure and preparing a formal record of this.

- *The legal adviser's role at an identification procedure.* The legal adviser will initially advise their client whether or not to consent to taking part in such a procedure and will then be present during the procedure to ensure that it is conducted in accordance with Code D.

Sample questions

Question 1

A man has been arrested on suspicion of burglary. A witness claims to have seen the man climbing out of a window of the burgled premises at the time of the burglary. The witness claims she recognised the man because they were at school together. During interview, the man denies any involvement in the burglary and claims the witness is mistaken. He also claims the witness could not have recognised him on the basis that he is known to her as they were not in the same class or year group at school and he left school six years ago.

Which of the following statements best describes whether the police will now be required to hold an identification procedure?

A   The holding of an identification procedure will be required because the man claims the witness is mistaken and disputes that he is known to the witness.

B   The police may hold an identification procedure if they believe it will help the investigation into this offence.

C   The police may hold an identification procedure if the officer in charge of the investigation considers it would be useful.

D   An identification procedure would not be necessary because the witness would inevitably pick out the man.

E   An identification procedure would serve no useful purpose as it is not disputed that the man is already known to the witness.

Answer

Option A is the best answer. An identification would be mandatory in this case according to Code D, para 3.12. There is a witness who has purported to recognise the man and the man disputes being the person the witness claims to have seen, so an identification procedure *shall* be held unless it is not practicable or would serve no useful purpose in proving or disproving whether the man was involved in committing the offence. The man disputes that he is known to the witness because they were not in the same year group at school and also because of the passage of time since they were at school. This scenario is therefore very similar to *R v Harris* (2003) where the CA stated that an identification procedure was required in such circumstances. Options B and C are not the best answers because although an eyewitness identification procedure may also be held if the officer in charge of the investigation considers it would be useful (Code D, para 3.13), this would not apply where the requirement to hold the procedure is already caught by para 3.12. Option D is wrong because it is not at all inevitable that the witness would pick out the man since the man has proper grounds to dispute that he is known to her. Option E is not the best answer because it is disputed that the man is already known to the witness.

Question 2

Two brothers have been arrested on suspicion of affray. The police have a witness to the incident who believes he would be able to identify the two offenders. Both brothers deny being involved in the incident and both claim they were elsewhere at the time. Because the two brothers are roughly of similar appearance, the police hold a video identification procedure with the images of the two brothers and 10 images of other people who all resemble the suspects in age, height, general appearance and position in life. The investigating officer, who is an officer of inspector rank, conducts the video identification procedure.

Has the video identification procedure been properly conducted?

A   Yes, because the correct number of images have been used and an officer not below the rank of inspector has conducted the procedure.

B   No, because two separate procedures should have been used with one of the suspect's video image and eight other images used for each procedure.

C   Yes, because the other images are of people who all resemble the suspects in age, height, general appearance and position in life.

D   No, because the investigating officer must not be involved in the conduct of the identification procedure.

E   No, because 12 other images should have been used and the investigating officer must not be involved in the identification procedure.

Answer

Option E is the best answer. The video identification procedure has not been conducted lawfully in accordance with Annex A to Code D of PACE 1984 because 12 other images (not 10) should have been used and the investigating officer must not be involved in the conduct of the procedure, so option A is wrong. Where two suspects of roughly similar appearance are shown in the same images, they may be shown together with at least 12 other people (Code D, Annex A, para 2), so although separate procedures would usually be held, option B is not the best answer. Although option C is correct about the other images all resembling the suspects in age, height, general appearance and position in life, it fails to explain why the procedure is still not conducted correctly. Option D is partially correct, because the investigating officer must not be involved in the conduct of the identification procedure, but it is not the best answer, because it fails to mention that the wrong number of images (10 rather than 12) have been used.

Question 3

A street robbery takes place and the victim provides a first description of the robber. The victim does not know who the robber was and so she is shown photographs, in batches of 12, of people who fit this description. The victim makes a positive identification of a man who is then arrested on suspicion of committing the robbery. The man is interviewed and denies any involvement, claiming that he was elsewhere at the time of the robbery.

What are the police now required to do?

A   The victim has already made a positive identification so the man should now be charged.

B   The victim should now be asked to take part in an identification procedure.

C   The police will be required to hold an identification procedure because the officer in charge of the investigation will consider it to be useful.

D   The police should not have shown the victim photographs in batches of 12 so they will not be able to proceed further against the man.

E   The man should now be compelled to take part in an identification procedure.

Answer

Option B is the best answer. The victim has made an identification from viewing the photographs and should now be asked to take part in an identification procedure (Code D, Annex E, para 6). Option A is wrong because a positive identification has not yet been made. Option C is not the best answer because although this may be one of the reasons for conducting an identification procedure the victim must first be asked to take part in such a procedure and in the circumstances of this case, para D 3.12 will be the reason why such a procedure is required. Option D is wrong because the victim must be shown at least 12 photographs at a time (Code D, Annex E, para 4). Option E is wrong because the suspect cannot be compelled to take part in such a procedure.

3 Charging the Suspect

Learning outcomes

By the end of this chapter you will be able to apply relevant core legal principles and rules appropriately and effectively, at the level of a competent newly qualified solicitor in practice, to realistic client-based and ethical problems and situations in the following areas:

- Releasing a suspect under investigation.
- Bailing a suspect before charge.
- Charging a suspect and the role played by the CPS.
- Interviewing and bailing a suspect post-charge.
- Alternatives to charging.

Note that, none of the above outcomes are specifically mentioned in the SRA syllabus, but these cover some fundamental legal principles and rules that a competent, newly qualified solicitor representing clients in the police station would be expected to know. Knowledge of these will also help you to better understand topics that are on the syllabus. As a result, please note there are no sample questions at the end of this chapter.

3.1 Introduction

Once the police have exercised their investigative powers whilst the suspect is detained in the police station (such as interviewing, conducting identification procedures and obtaining forensic evidence) they will then need to determine what step to take next. The decision on what to do next will ultimately be made by the custody officer who has four main options:

(a) release the suspect (either without taking any further action or release under investigation);

(b) release the suspect without charge but on bail whilst the police make further enquiries;

(c) charge the suspect (and either release on bail or keep in custody until the suspect's first court appearance); or

(d) offer the suspect an alternative to charge.

Each of these options will be examined in turn.

3.2 Release under investigation

If, having investigated the offence, the police determine that the suspect did not in fact commit the crime (or there is insufficient evidence against the suspect and it is unlikely that any further evidence will be obtained), the custody officer should release the suspect without charge and without any requirement that the suspect return to the police station at a later date. This means that, from the suspect's point of view, the matter is closed, although there is nothing to prevent the police from re-arresting the suspect at a later date should any further evidence come to light which implicates the suspect. This is sometimes referred to as 'NFA', where the police release the suspect having decided to take *no further action*.

Another very common scenario is that, after exercising their investigative powers in the police station, the police will then need to make further enquiries before deciding whether to charge a suspect or to pass their file to the CPS to determine if there is sufficient evidence to charge the suspect. In such circumstances the police will normally release the suspect on bail under s 47(3)(b) (see **3.3** below).

However, ss 52–67 of the Policing and Crime Act 2017 amended PACE 1984 and effectively introduced a presumption against pre-charge bail. So, where the police had insufficient evidence upon which to charge and where any further investigation was likely to take longer than 28 days to conclude, the police would then release the suspect under investigation (RUI). This power has proved to be controversial, because suspects, victims and witnesses were often left in limbo for lengthy periods of time not knowing what was going to happen to the case.

In light of growing concerns about the use of RUI, the Home Office in February 2020 published a consultation to review the law on pre-charge bail, with proposals including reform that would remove the presumption against pre-charge bail and/or increase the period of pre-charge bail to either 60 or 90 days from the initial 28-day period. This has now been achieved by s 45 and Sch 4 of the Police, Crime, Sentencing and Courts Act 2022 which amends PACE 1984 and establishes a neutral position within the legislation, by removing the presumption against pre-charge bail. Custody officers are now able to authorise the first period of pre-charge bail to a period of three months in standard police cases. Further extensions in these cases will require approval from an officer of the rank of Inspector or above to six months, and a Superintendent or above is required to authorise any extension to nine months. Judicial approval will then be sought to extend beyond nine months (see **3.3** below).

The removal of the presumption against pre-charge bail had led to an increase in the number of those placed on bail and a decrease in the number of those subject to the RUI process.

Schedule 4 also introduced a three-hour pause on the detention clock where an individual has been arrested for breach of pre-charge bail conditions or failure to answer bail.

Finally, note that where the suspect is released without bail (RUI), the police may re-arrest the suspect where new evidence comes to light or an examination or analysis of existing evidence has been made which could not reasonably have been made before the suspect's release.

3.3 Bail before charge

There has never been a presumption against pre-charge bail if the case has been submitted to the CPS for a charging decision (see below).

Pre-charge bail may also be granted where the custody officer is satisfied that releasing the suspect on bail is necessary and proportionate in all the circumstances (having regard, in particular, to any conditions of bail which would be imposed) – under s 47(3)(b). Where it is necessary and proportionate to bail the suspect, a maximum period of three months (starting from the day after the day that the suspect was arrested) applies. This initial period of three months can now be extended for up to six months, if authorised by an officer of inspector rank, and a further extension may then be authorised up to a maximum period of nine months if authorised by an officer of superintendent rank or above. Any further extension can only be granted by a magistrates' court up to a maximum period of 18 months (although for some cases this could be up to 24 months) (PACE 1984, ss 47ZD–47ZG).

Before a suspect is released on pre-charge bail, the investigating officer is under a duty to seek the views of the victim (where this is reasonably practicable) about any relevant bail conditions that might be imposed and to inform the custody officer of these before the custody officer then decides whether to grant bail and, if so, what bail conditions should be imposed (PACE 1984, s 47ZZA).

Where a suspect is released on bail, details of the time and date when the suspect needs to re-attend the police station will be contained in a written bail notice given to the suspect by the police.

When the suspect answers their bail, the police may:

(a) release them without charge (if, after making further enquiries, the police have insufficient evidence to charge);

(b) exercise further investigative powers (such as re-interviewing the suspect or conducting an identification procedure);

(c) release the suspect again on bail if their further enquiries are incomplete (but subject to the maximum periods referred to above) or, having completed their enquiries, they wish to pass their file to the CPS for advice; or

(d) charge the suspect (if, after making further enquiries, the police now have sufficient evidence to charge).

If the suspect fails to answer bail at the police station, they may be arrested without warrant (s 46A). Although failing to answer bail at the police station is technically a criminal offence, it is very rare in practice for the police to charge a suspect with this offence.

The police may impose conditions on bail granted to a suspect whilst the police make further enquiries into the alleged offence (s 47(1A)). The police may, for example, impose a condition of residence or a condition preventing a suspect from entering a certain area or contacting or communicating with named people such as the complainant or prosecution witnesses. The police may arrest without warrant a suspect who breaches such conditions.

3.3.1 Release on bail (or detain in custody) whilst the file is passed to the CPS

The Police and Justice Act (PJA) 2006 made significant changes to the procedure for deciding whether and with what offence a suspect should be charged. The Act created a new s 37B, which provides that in cases other than straightforward ones, it is for the CPS to determine whether the suspect should be charged and, if so, with what offence.

So when the police believe there is sufficient evidence to charge a suspect (particularly in contested or more serious cases), they will send the case papers to the CPS for it to determine whether or not to charge, and if so with what offence(s).

The CPS will apply a two-part test to determine whether or not the suspect should be charged:

(a) there must be sufficient evidence to provide a *'realistic prospect of conviction'*; and

(b) if there is sufficient evidence, the CPS will then need to determine if it is in the *'public interest'* to charge the suspect, or whether the matter should be dealt with other than by way of charge (see **3.7** below).

In urgent or very straightforward cases, advice from the CPS can be given from a CPS lawyer at the police station or by telephone (especially if it is out of hours). In other cases, it can take several weeks for the CPS to review a file, and the police will therefore need to release the suspect on bail under s 47(3)(b) whilst this is done. As with releasing the suspect on bail whilst the police make further enquiries, the suspect will be required to re-attend the police station at a future time and date and will be given a notice to this effect. When the suspect answers their bail, the police may:

(a) charge the suspect (if the CPS found there was sufficient evidence to charge and a charge was in the public interest);

(b) exercise further investigative powers if the CPS considered that further evidence was needed (eg re-interviewing the suspect or obtaining more evidence from witnesses);

(c) release the suspect without charge (if the CPS found there was insufficient evidence to charge); or

(d) deal with the matter other than by way of a charge if the CPS found there was sufficient evidence to charge the suspect, but a charge was not in the public interest (see **3.7** below).

The police may impose conditions on a suspect who is released on bail pending consultations with the CPS (s 47(1A)). For example, conditions may be imposed requiring a suspect to reside at a particular address, not to enter a specified area or not to contact specified persons.

✪ Example

Karl is arrested on suspicion of inflicting grievous bodily harm following a fight that took place outside a public house. It is alleged that he has a vendetta against the complainant, and this is not the first time an incident between the two has taken place outside this public house. Karl claims he was acting in self-defence. The police refer the file to the CPS to determine whether and if so, what charge Karl should face. Karl is released on bail whilst the CPS reviews the file. The police impose conditions on the bail granted to Karl, requiring him not to contact or communicate with the complainant and not to go within a 400-metre radius of the public house.

If the suspect fails to answer bail at the police station, or the police reasonably suspect that the suspect has broken any conditions attached to bail, they may be arrested without warrant (s 46A). Failing to answer bail at the police station is a criminal offence, although it is rare in practice for the police to charge a suspect with this offence.

3.4 The decision to charge

If the police consider that they have sufficient evidence to charge the suspect, they will either charge or pass the case papers to the CPS for it to determine what the appropriate charge should be (see **3.3** above).

The usual practice will be for the police to refer the case to the CPS for it to determine the appropriate charge. However, the police will still decide on the appropriate charge themselves in minor cases, particularly if the offence is summary-only and it is expected that the suspect will enter a guilty plea.

When a decision has been made to charge a suspect, the suspect will be formally charged at the police station. In accordance with para 16.2 of Code C, the suspect must be cautioned on charge and anything the suspect says in response to the charge should be written down.

The suspect should also be given a written notice (the 'charge sheet') which gives the particulars of the offence. Paragraph 16.3 of Code C states:

> As far as possible the particulars of the charge shall be stated in simple terms, but they shall also show the precise offence in law with which the detainee is charged.

In certain circumstances, a suspect against whom there is sufficient evidence to bring a charge may be offered an alternative means of having the matter disposed of. These alternatives are described at **3.7** below.

3.5 Interviewing after charge

A suspect who has been charged cannot be interviewed further by the police about the offence for which they have been charged, unless the interview is necessary:

(a) to prevent or minimise harm or loss to some other persons, or the public;

(b) to clear up an ambiguity in a previous answer or statement; or

(c) in the interests of justice for the suspect to have put to him, and to have an opportunity to comment on, information concerning the offence which has come to light since he was charged (Code C, para 16.5).

If the police do interview a suspect after they have been charged, the suspect must be cautioned before any interview takes place. The wording of the caution is the 'old' caution which was used prior to the court being given the power under the CJPOA 1994 to draw an adverse inference from a suspect's silence at the police station. The wording of the caution will be:

> You do not have to say anything, but anything you do say may be given in evidence.

This means that the suspect may remain silent in the interview and not have any adverse inference drawn from that silence at trial. Before the interview, the suspect must also be reminded of their right to legal advice.

3.6 Bail after charge

3.6.1 When may the police deny bail to a suspect?

When a suspect is charged at the police station, the custody officer must then decide:

(a) whether to keep the person in police custody until they can be brought before a magistrates' court, or to release them; and

(b) if the latter, whether to release them on bail with conditions or without conditions (s 38(1)).

Section 38(1)(a) provides that only if one or more of certain circumstances are satisfied may bail be denied to a suspect who has been charged with an offence:

(1) Where a person arrested for an offence ... is charged with an offence, the custody officer shall, subject to section 25 of the Criminal Justice and Public Order Act 1994, order their release from police detention, either on bail or without bail, unless:

In summary, where the custody officer has reasonable grounds:

- to doubt the name or address provided is the suspect's proper name or address or where such name or address cannot be confirmed;

- to believe that the person arrested will fail to appear in court to answer bail;

- to believe that the detention of the person arrested is necessary to prevent them from committing an offence;

- to believe that detention of the person is necessary to enable a sample to be taken;

- to prevent them from causing physical injury to any other person or from causing loss of or damage to property;

- to prevent them from interfering with the administration of justice or with the investigation of offences or of a particular offence; and

- to believe that the detention of the person arrested is necessary for their own protection.

⭐ *Example 1*

Tariq is charged with burglary. He has several previous convictions for failing to attend court to answer bail. The custody officer may refuse bail as he would have reasonable grounds for believing that Tariq would fail to appear in court if he were granted bail.

⭐ *Example 2*

Meghan is charged with theft. She has numerous previous convictions for theft and related offences, including several offences that were committed whilst she was on bail in the course of previous proceedings. The custody officer may refuse bail with reasonable grounds for believing that Meghan may commit further offences whilst on bail.

3.6.2 Conditional bail

If the custody officer decides to grant bail to a suspect who has been charged, they must then decide whether it is necessary to impose conditions on that bail (PACE 1984, s 47(1A)). Conditions may be imposed only if they are necessary:

(a) to prevent the suspect from failing to surrender to custody;

(b) to prevent the suspect from committing an offence whilst on bail;

(c) to prevent the suspect from interfering with witnesses or otherwise obstructing the course of justice (whether in relation to themselves or another person); or

(d) for the suspect's own protection or, if the suspect is a child or young person (ie 17 or under), for their own welfare or in their own interests (Bail Act 1976, s 3A(5)).

The custody officer may impose most of the same types of condition which a magistrates' court could impose on bail granted to a defendant (see **Chapter 7**), although the custody officer cannot impose a condition that a suspect reside at a bail hostel, undergo medical examination or see their legal adviser. The custody officer may, for example, impose conditions requiring the suspect:

(a) to reside at a particular address;

(b) not to speak to or contact any witnesses;

(c) not to enter a particular area or set of premises; or

(d) to observe a curfew at night between specified hours.

A suspect who wishes to vary conditions imposed on bail which the police have granted may either:

(a) ask the custody officer who imposed the conditions (or another custody officer at the same police station) to vary the conditions (Bail Act 1976, s 3A(4)); or

(b) make an application to the magistrates' court for the conditions to be varied (Magistrates' Courts Act 1980, s 43(B)(1) and CrimPR, r 14.6).

3.6.3 When will the suspect make their first appearance at court?

3.6.3.1 Suspects granted bail by the police

If a suspect is granted bail by the police after being charged, the date of their first appearance in the magistrates' court is likely to be within one to two weeks of being charged (s 47(3A)).

3.6.3.2 Suspects denied bail by the police

If the police refuse to grant bail to a suspect after they have been charged, the suspect will be kept in police custody (unless they are a juvenile – see **Chapter 4**) and must be brought before the magistrates' court as soon as is practicable, and in any event not later than the first sitting of the court after they are charged with the offence (s 46(2)). In practice this means that the suspect will normally appear before the court within 24 hours of being charged. There are remand courts that sit on Saturdays, but not on Sundays.

⭐ *Example 1*

Bill has been charged on Tuesday evening and refused bail by the police following charge. Bill will need to be produced before the next available magistrates' court, which here will be on Wednesday morning.

⭐ *Example 2*

Bill has been charged on Friday evening and refused bail by the police following charge. Bill will need to be produced before the next available magistrates' court, which here will be on Saturday morning, as the court will be required to convene a remand court to deal with Bill (and any other prisoners who have been charged and refused bail).

⭐ *Example 3*

Bill has been charged on Saturday evening and refused bail by the police following charge. Bill will need to be produced before the next available magistrates' court, which here will be on Monday morning, as remand courts are not convened on a Sunday.

3.6.4 Breaching police bail (after charge)

If a suspect has been bailed to attend court following charge, s 7(3) of the Bail Act 1976 gives a police officer the power to arrest that person where they reasonably believe either that the person is unlikely to surrender to custody, or that the person has breached, or is likely to breach, their bail conditions. A person who is arrested under s 7 must be brought before a magistrates' court within 24 hours. The magistrates will determine if there has been a breach of bail conditions (usually by hearing evidence from the arresting officer and the defendant) and, if so, whether they should grant bail to the defendant or remand in custody. Breach of bail conditions is not in itself a criminal offence, although a defendant who has breached police bail may experience difficulties in persuading the magistrates to grant bail subsequently (see **7.8**).

3.7 Alternatives to charging

It is not inevitable that a suspect against whom there is sufficient evidence to bring a charge will always be charged with an offence. Where the suspect is aged over 17, rather than charging them, it may be possible to deal with the matter in one of the following ways:

(a) an informal warning

(b) a penalty notice

(c) a formal caution

(d) a conditional caution.

Each of these is briefly examined below.

3.7.1   Informal warnings

In minor cases the police have always had discretion to release a suspect without charge but to give an informal warning about their future conduct. An informal warning will not appear on a defendant's criminal record if they are later charged with another offence.

3.7.2   Penalty notices

The police may issue a penalty notice to dispose of minor offences without the need for the offender to go to court. Fixed penalty notices (FPNs) are used for minor road traffic offences, and for offences such as littering and dog fouling. Penalty notices for disorder (PNDs) may be used for anti-social behaviour, such as being drunk and disorderly. The receipt of a FPN is not a criminal conviction. The use of PNDs has recently been expanded to cover a wider range of offences (for example, first-time offenders who have committed a minor shoplifting offence or criminal damage).

3.7.3   Simple cautions

Instead of giving an informal warning, the police (in conjunction with the CPS) may instead decide to issue a simple caution. The giving of simple cautions was originally developed for cases involving juveniles but can now be used only for adult offenders. Although criminal records are kept of cautions, a simple caution is not the same as a criminal conviction. If a defendant who has received a caution is later convicted of a separate offence, the caution may be mentioned to the court when the court is considering what sentence to pass.

Cautions are usually given in the police station by a police officer of at least the rank of inspector. The offender must sign a form acknowledging that they agree to the caution and admit the offence for which the caution is being given. Before a caution is given, three conditions must be satisfied:

(a) sufficient evidence must have been collected to have justified a prosecution;

(b) there must be clear and reliable evidence of a voluntary admission by the offender that they have committed the offence;

(c) the offender must agree to being cautioned, having been made aware that the caution might be raised in court were they to be convicted of a later offence.

Section 17(2) of the Criminal Justice and Courts Act 2015 restricts the use of simple cautions for indictable-only offences (offences which, if committed by an adult, are triable only on indictment in the Crown Court). A defendant must not be given a simple caution for such an offence unless a police officer of at least the rank of superintendent determines that there are exceptional circumstances relating to the defendant or the offence, and the CPS agrees that a caution should be given.

In addition, under s 17(3), a defendant must not be given a simple caution for an either-way offence that has been specified by the Secretary of State unless a police officer of at least the rank of inspector determines that there are exceptional circumstances relating to the offender or the offence.

The either-way offences that have so far been specified by the Secretary of State are summarised as follows:

•   offensive weapon and bladed article offences;

•   carrying a firearm in a public place;

- child cruelty;

- sexual offences against children (including those relating to child prostitution and pornography);

- sex trafficking offences;

- indecent and pornographic images of children;

- importing, exporting, producing, supplying and possessing with intent to supply to another Class A drugs.

Further, s 17(4) restricts the use of simple cautions for repeat offending. A defendant must not usually be given a simple caution if in the two years before the offence was committed the defendant has been convicted of, or cautioned for, a similar offence.

3.7.4 Conditional cautions

One of the principal goals of the Criminal Justice Act (CJA) 2003 is to achieve 'restorative justice'. This is best described as bringing offenders and their victims into some form of contact, with a view to an agreement being reached as to what the offender should do to make reparation for the crime they have committed. The intention is to make an offender appreciate the effect their crime has had upon the victim, and to improve victim satisfaction with the criminal justice process. Conditional cautions must be seen against this backdrop.

Conditional cautions do not replace the system of police cautioning detailed above. However, in contrast to formal cautions, they have a statutory basis and may be given only with the approval of the CPS.

Under s 22 of the CJA 2003, a conditional caution can be given to a person aged 18 or over, provided that the following five requirements are satisfied:

(a) there must be evidence that the offender has committed an offence;

(b) a relevant prosecutor or an authorised person must determine that there is sufficient evidence to charge the offender with the offence, and that a conditional caution should be given to the offender in respect of that offence;

(c) the offender must admit that they committed the offence;

(d) the effect of the conditional caution must be explained to the offender, and they must be warned that any failure to comply with any of the conditions attached to the caution may result in them being prosecuted for the offence itself; and

(e) the offender must sign a document containing the details of the offence, an admission that they committed the offence, their consent to a conditional caution and the conditions attached to the caution (CJA 2003, s 23).

Section 25 of the CJA 2003 provides that if an offender fails 'without reasonable excuse' to comply with any conditions attached to the caution, he may be arrested and prosecuted for the original offence and the document he has signed may be used in evidence against him (ie as evidence that he admits having committed the offence).

The conditions that are likely to be attached to cautions will be geared either towards rehabilitating the offender, or towards the offender making reparation to his victim.

3.7.4.1 Disadvantages of accepting a (conditional) caution

A client who accepts a caution will not be prosecuted for the offence. They must, however, be told about the following potential disadvantages in accepting a caution:

(a) a caution is a formal recorded admission of guilt which will form part of an offender's criminal record and may affect how they are sentenced should they re-offend in future;

(b) the client will almost certainly lose the opportunity of receiving a caution on a subsequent occasion;

(c) the existence of the caution will be disclosable should the client apply for certain types of employment (particularly entry to a profession);

(d) if the offence is sexual, the client will also be placed on the sex offenders register; and

(e) the police may retain fingerprints and other identification data taken from the client (a record of cautions is usually kept for a minimum of five years).

A client should accept a caution only if they accept their guilt and there is sufficient evidence against them. If there is insufficient evidence, the CPS may choose not to prosecute. A solicitor should not advise a client to accept a caution as a matter of convenience, simply to dispose of the case.

3.7.5 Commencing a case other than by charge (CrimPR, Parts 4 and 7)

For some offences (particularly summary-only offences including many road traffic offences), a suspect may not have been arrested by the police and may not even have needed to attend the police station. An alternative method of commencing criminal proceedings exists for such offences.

The CJA 2003 has put in place arrangements for commencing prosecutions in this type of case. Under these arrangements, a relevant prosecutor can now send to the person a document called a 'written charge', which charges that person with the offence (CJA 2003, s 29(1)). The prosecutor must also send the person charged a document called a 'requisition' or single justice procedure notice. The requisition requires that the person appear before a magistrates' court at a given time and place to answer the charge (CJA 2003, s 29(2)).

Interestingly, this has also become a fairly common way to commence proceedings where the suspect has been RUI by the police once they have concluded their investigation and this procedure is therefore also being used in practice for more serious offences.

Summary

In this chapter you have considered when and how the police will charge a suspect and other issues related to this. Notably:

- *Releasing a suspect under investigation.* If further investigation is going to take longer than 28 days, the police will now generally release a suspect under investigation (RUI), although remember this will no longer be the starting point once s 45 of the Police, Crime, Sentencing and Courts Act 2022 comes into force.

- *Bailing a suspect before charge.* This will usually only be possible where the investigation will be completed within 28 days (but see s 45 above which will remove the presumption against bail and how this period will be extended to either 3, 6 or 9 months). It does enable the police to impose conditions on such a suspect's police bail.

- *Charging a suspect and the role played by the CPS.* There is an obligation on the police to consider charging a suspect once they have sufficient evidence to charge. However, in many cases the police will first have to obtain advice from the CPS on charge. The CPS will base their advice on a dual *evidence* and *public interest test*.

- *Interviewing and bailing a suspect post-charge.* Generally, this is not allowed. Where in the limited circumstances it is, the defendant has an absolute right to remain silent.

- *Alternatives to charging.* Even where a suspect admits their involvement in an offence, charging the suspect is not the only way the matter may be dealt with. Alternatives include an informal warning; a penalty notice; a formal caution; and a conditional caution.

Figure 3.1 Flowchart – Procedure at the police station

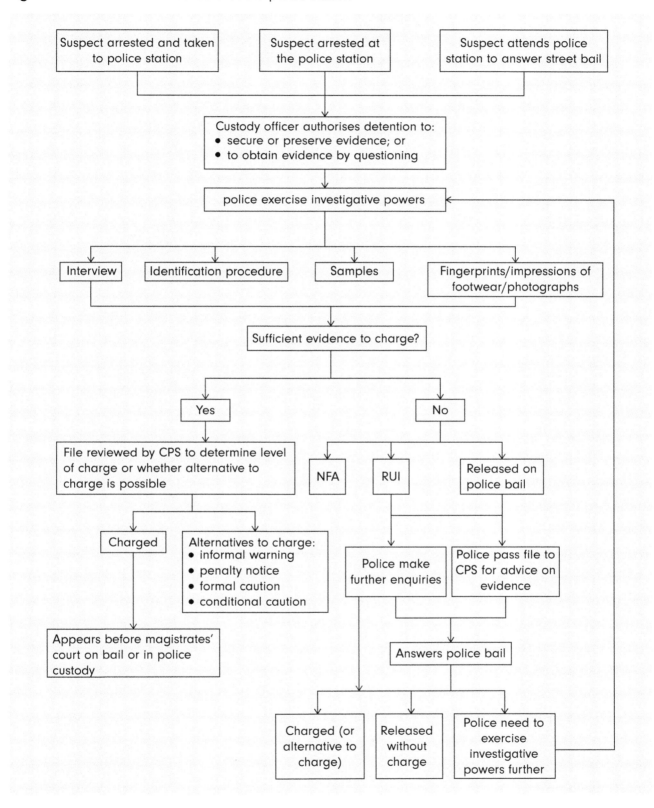

4 Representing Vulnerable Clients

Learning outcomes

By the end of this chapter you will be able to apply relevant core legal principles and rules appropriately and effectively, at the level of a competent newly qualified solicitor in practice, to realistic client-based and ethical problems and situations in the following areas:

- The additional matters which must be taken into account when representing a vulnerable person (including a juvenile) who has been arrested and detained at the police station.

- The role of an appropriate adult at the police station.

- The role of a legal adviser when representing a vulnerable client.

- Identification procedures involving vulnerable clients.

- Charging a juvenile.

- The alternatives to charging a juvenile suspect.

- The power of the police to refuse to grant bail to a juvenile suspect who has been charged with a criminal offence.

4.1   Introduction

A solicitor will often be called to the police station to represent an individual who falls within one of several special categories of suspect, all of whom can be described as potentially vulnerable, and to whom specific rules apply. These categories are:

(a) juveniles – suspects who are aged between 10 and 17 inclusive (although para 1.5 of Code C provides that the police should treat anyone who *appears* to be under 18 as a juvenile in the absence of clear evidence to the contrary);

(b) suspects who suffer from a mental health condition or mental disorder, although para 1.4 of Code C provides that if the police suspect that someone suffers from such a condition, then in the absence of any clear evidence to dispel such suspicion, they should treat that person as suffering from such a condition (see para 1.13(d) of Code C for a more detailed analysis of such a vulnerable person);

(c) suspects who are deaf, unable to speak or blind; and

(d) suspects who cannot speak or understand English.

This chapter will concentrate in particular on the specific rules that apply to juveniles, but there will also be some mention, where applicable, of these other groups of vulnerable suspects.

Paragraph 3.20A of Code C requires that arrangements must be made for ensuring that a girl under the age of 18, whilst detained in a police station, is under the care of a woman (see Code C, Notes for Guidance, para 3G, and the Children and Young Persons Act 1933, s 31).

4.1.1   Informing the person responsible for the juvenile's welfare

All suspects who have been arrested and detained at the police station have the right to have a person informed of their arrest under s 56 (see **1.3.2** above) and the right to receive free and independent legal advice from a solicitor under s 58 (see **1.3.1** above). This right applies to adult and juvenile suspects alike.

In addition, however, if a juvenile has been arrested, the custody officer must, if practicable, find out the person responsible for their welfare (Code C, para 3.13). That person may be:

(a) the juvenile's parent or guardian;

(b) if the juvenile is in local authority or voluntary organisation care, the person appointed by that authority or organisation to have responsibility for the juvenile's welfare (Children and Young Persons Act 1933, s 34(8)); or

(c) any other person who has, for the time being, assumed responsibility for the juvenile's welfare.

That person must be informed as soon as practicable that the juvenile has been arrested, why they have been arrested and where they are being detained. Unlike ss 56 and 58, this right cannot be delayed.

Moreover, if a juvenile is known to be the subject of a court order under which a person or organisation is given any statutory responsibility to supervise or monitor them (for example, a supervision order), reasonable steps must also be taken to notify that person or organisation. The person notified is known as the 'responsible officer' and will usually be a member of a Youth Offending Team (Code C, para 3.14).

4.1.2   Where the suspect doesn't speak or understand English or has a hearing or speech impediment

Where a suspect either doesn't speak or understand English or has a hearing or speech impediment, the custody officer must obtain an interpreter or someone able to assist the suspect with communication (Code C, para 3.12).

4.1.3   Where the suspect is blind or suffers from a serious visual impairment

Where a suspect is either blind or suffers from a serious visual impairment, the custody officer must ensure there is someone (not involved in the investigation) such as an appropriate adult, relative, solicitor or someone likely to take an interest in their welfare, to help them check any documentation (Code C, para 3.20).

4.2   The appropriate adult

4.2.1   Who may be an appropriate adult?

The 'appropriate adult' is a person who attends the police station to provide support and assistance to a juvenile (or suspect with a mental health condition or mental disorder). There is a hierarchical order the police should follow when contacting an appropriate adult for a juvenile, as follows:

(a) The police should initially attempt to contact the juvenile's parent or guardian (or a representative from the local authority where the juvenile is in local authority care) to act as an appropriate adult.

(b) If no one in (a) is available, the police should then ask a social worker from the local authority to act as an appropriate adult.

(c) If a social worker is not available, the police should finally contact another responsible adult who is aged 18 or over and not connected to the police (Code C, para 1.7). This may, for example, be an aunt or uncle, or a grandparent. Although the adult must be aged 18 or over, the police may consider that an adult who is only just 18 or over may not be sufficiently responsible to fulfil the role.

An appropriate adult for a suspect with a mental health condition or mental disorder will be:

- a relative, guardian or other person responsible for that person's care or custody;

- someone experienced in dealing with vulnerable people; or

- some other responsible adult.

A solicitor should never be an appropriate adult, because support and assistance from an appropriate adult is in addition to any legal advice a suspect receives from his solicitor at the police station. Other persons who should not fulfil the role of appropriate adult include:

- police officers or persons employed by the police;

- an interested party such as the victim of the offence, another suspect, a potential witness or anyone else involved in the investigation (this would, for example, prevent a juvenile's mother acting as appropriate adult if the juvenile has been arrested on suspicion of assaulting her, as she would be the victim);

- a person, such as a parent or social worker, to whom the juvenile has made admissions prior to that person being asked to attend the police station to fulfil the role of an appropriate adult; and

- an estranged parent (but only when the juvenile expressly and specifically objects to the presence of such a person).

✪ Example

Fay, aged 14 years, has been arrested and detained at the police station on suspicion of causing damage to a mobile phone belonging to her father following an argument. Fay lives with her father. She is estranged from her mother who she has not seen for over a year, even though she lives nearby. Fay tells the custody officer that she wants her father to attend as her appropriate adult as she does not know any other responsible adult who would be able to attend. When asked by the custody officer, she objects to her mother attending.

In these circumstances the custody officer will have to contact a social worker from the local authority to attend as Fay's appropriate adult. Despite Fay's request, her father cannot act as appropriate adult as he is the 'victim' of the offence and Fay has specifically said she doesn't want her mother attending. Usually a juvenile cannot determine who their appropriate adult will be, but because she is 'estranged' from her mother, Fay's views must be respected. That would mean the only other person who would appear to be eligible would be a social worker.

4.2.2 What is the role of the appropriate adult?

The Home Office has produced a document entitled *Guide for Appropriate Adults* that will be issued to an appropriate adult upon their arrival at the police station. The guidance can be found on the Home Office website: **www.homeoffice.gov.uk**.

The guidance provides that the appropriate adult has 'a positive and important role', and that the appropriate adult is not at the police station simply to act as an observer but rather to ensure that the suspect 'understands what is happening to them and why'. The key roles and responsibilities of an appropriate adult are:

(a) to support, advise and assist the suspect, particularly when the suspect is being questioned;

(b) to ensure that the suspect understands their rights whilst at the police station, and the role played by the appropriate adult in protecting those rights;

(c) to observe whether the police are acting properly, fairly and with respect for the rights of the suspect; and

(d) to assist with communication between the suspect and the police.

The guidance makes it clear that it is not the role of the appropriate adult to provide the suspect with legal advice, and any conversations the appropriate adult has with the suspect are not covered by legal privilege (see also Code C, Note for Guidance 1E).

Code C, para 6.5A provides that an appropriate adult should consider whether legal advice from a solicitor is required. Even if the juvenile or mentally vulnerable suspect indicates that they do not want legal advice, the appropriate adult has the right to ask for a solicitor to attend if this would be in the best interests of the suspect. However, the suspect cannot be forced to see the solicitor if they are adamant that they do not wish to do so.

The custody officer should explain a juvenile's rights whilst at the police station in the presence of the appropriate adult, or repeat those rights in the presence of the appropriate adult if they have already been explained to the juvenile before the appropriate adult arrived at the police station (Code C, para 3.17).

4.3 Role of the legal representative/solicitor

The vulnerable person's solicitor also needs to ensure that the appropriate adult is aware of their role and must ensure that the appropriate adult understands that it is not their role to help the police. The solicitor should also make it clear to the appropriate adult that, whilst they are there to help the suspect understand what the police are doing, they should not answer questions on behalf of the suspect, particularly in an interview situation. The appropriate adult should, however, intervene in an interview if they consider that the vulnerable person has not understood a question which has been asked and that clarification of the question is necessary.

4.4   Interviewing vulnerable suspects

Paragraph 10.12 of Code C provides that if a juvenile or suspect with a mental health condition or mental disorder is cautioned in the absence of the appropriate adult, this caution must be repeated in the appropriate adult's presence.

Similarly, they must not normally be interviewed, or asked to provide or sign a written statement under caution or record of interview, in the absence of the appropriate adult (Code C, para 11.15).

When an appropriate adult is present in an interview, they must be informed by the interviewing officer that they are not there simply to act as an observer, and that the purpose of their presence in the interview is to:

(a)   advise the person being interviewed;

(b)   observe whether the interview is being conducted properly and fairly; and

(c)   facilitate communication with the person being interviewed (Code C, para 11.17).

The appropriate adult's presence at the police station (and particularly during the interview) is necessary to help the suspect cope with the demands of custody and questioning, and to appreciate the seriousness of the situation.

Paragraph 11.17A of Code C provides that an appropriate adult may be required to leave the interview if their conduct is such that the interviewer is unable properly to put questions to the suspect. This will include situations where the appropriate adult's approach or conduct prevents or unreasonably obstructs proper questions being put to the suspect or the suspect's responses from being recorded (see Code C, Notes for Guidance, para 11F).

If the interviewing officer considers an appropriate adult is acting in such a way, they will stop the interview and consult an officer not below superintendent rank, if one is readily available, and otherwise an officer not below inspector rank, not connected with the investigation. After speaking to the appropriate adult, the officer consulted must remind the adult that their role under para 11.17 does not allow them to obstruct proper questioning and give the adult an opportunity to respond.

The officer consulted will then decide if the interview should continue without the attendance of that appropriate adult. If they decide that it should, another appropriate adult must be obtained before the interview continues, unless the provisions of Code C, para 11.18 apply.

The Notes for Guidance to Code C clarify the role an appropriate adult should play in an interview. Paragraph 11C states that:

> Although juveniles ... are often capable of providing reliable evidence, they may, without knowing or wishing to do so, be particularly prone in certain circumstances to provide information that may be unreliable, misleading or self-incriminating. Special care should always be taken when questioning such a person, and the appropriate adult should be involved if there is any doubt about a person's age, mental state or capacity. Because of the risk of unreliable evidence it is also important to obtain corroboration of any facts admitted whenever possible.

4.5   Identification procedures

In addition to the requirements imposed by Code C, if the police require a juvenile (or someone suffering from a mental health condition or mental disorder) to take part in an identification procedure, or to obtain other forensic evidence such as samples, fingerprints or an impression of their footwear, they must comply with additional provisions in Code D.

Paragraph 2.12 of Code D provides that where any procedure in Code D requires a person's consent (for example, if a suspect is asked to consent to taking part in an identification procedure), the following conditions apply:

(a) if the suspect is a juvenile aged 14 or over, consent must be obtained both from the juvenile and from the juvenile's parent or guardian;

(b) if the suspect is a juvenile aged under 14, consent must be obtained from the juvenile's parent or guardian (rather than from the juvenile);

(c) If the suspect is suffering from a mental health condition or mental disorder, then the consent must be given in the presence of the appropriate adult.

4.6 Charging juveniles

The focus will now only be on juvenile suspects. Once the police have conducted their investigations, they will need to decide what the next steps in the case will be. The range of options open to the police is the same as for adult suspects. However, in relation to the refusal of bail after charge, in addition to the considerations in s 38(1)(a), the custody officer may also deny the juvenile bail if they have reasonable grounds for believing that the juvenile ought to be detained in their own interests.

On charge, the written notice (the 'charge sheet'), which gives the particulars of the offence with which the suspect has been charged, should be given to the appropriate adult (Code C, para 16.3).

4.6.1 Juveniles refused bail after charge

If the custody officer denies bail after charge to a juvenile, the suspect will normally be remanded into the care of the local authority rather than at the police station pending their first appearance before the youth court. The only two situations when a juvenile may be kept in police custody after charge are:

(a) if it is impracticable to move the suspect to local authority accommodation; or

(b) if the juvenile is aged at least 12, there is no secure local authority accommodation available and keeping them in other local authority accommodation would not be adequate to protect the public from serious harm from them (s 38(6)).

Note: 'Secure accommodation' is accommodation provided for the purpose of restricting liberty (Children Act 1989, s 25(1)).

If either of these criteria is satisfied and the juvenile is detained at the police station, para 8.8 of Code C provides that the juvenile must be kept separate from adult suspects and must not be detained in a cell unless it is not practicable to supervise the juvenile other than in a cell. The suspect will normally be kept in a juvenile detention room.

The guidance notes to Code C provide that, unless one of the conditions in s 38(6) is satisfied, neither a juvenile's behaviour nor the nature of the offence provides grounds for the custody officer to decide that it is impracticable to arrange the juvenile's transfer to local authority care (Code C, Notes for Guidance, para 16D). This paragraph also states that the lack of secure local authority accommodation does not make it impracticable to transfer the juvenile unless the juvenile is aged 12 or over and the local authority accommodation would not be adequate to protect the public from serious harm from the juvenile.

⭐ *Example*

Yassin, aged 11 years, has been arrested, detained and charged with attempted murder. There is no local authority secure accommodation available. The custody officer therefore believes that if remanded into the care of the local authority before his first court appearance, the public would not be properly protected from serious harm from Yassin.

In such circumstances, the custody officer would still be required to remand Yassin into local authority care (and not keep him detained at the police station), because Yassin is not aged 12 years or over and the lack of secure accommodation would not make it impracticable to transfer Yassin.

4.7   Alternatives to charging juveniles

The Legal Aid, Sentencing and Punishment of Offenders (LASPO) Act 2012 deals with out-of-court disposal systems available in respect of juveniles under 18 years of age. The decision to authorise a youth caution or youth conditional caution (see below) will be dependent on the severity of the offence. Indictable-only offences will be referred to the CPS; first-time summary and either-way offences can be decided by the police; second and subsequent offences will be by a joint decision from the police, following assessment by the Youth Offending Team.

4.7.1   Community resolution

This is the starting point for out-of-court disposals. It is a non-statutory disposal for the resolution of a minor offence or anti-social behaviour incident through informal agreement between the parties involved. It is primarily aimed at first-time offenders where there has been an admission of guilt, and where the victim's views have been taken into account. It will not form part of the offender's criminal record retained by the police.

4.7.2   Youth cautions

Section 66ZA of the Crime and Disorder Act (CDA) 1998 sets out the circumstances in which a youth caution can be offered, namely where:

(a)   there is sufficient evidence to charge the offender with an offence;

(b)   the offender admits that they committed the offence; and

(c)   the police do not consider that the offender should be prosecuted or given a youth conditional caution in respect of the offence, ie it is not in the public interest to deal with the matter in another way.

A youth caution given to a person aged 17 or under must be given in the presence of an appropriate adult.

In determining whether a caution is available the police must also take into account the seriousness of the offence.

4.7.3   Youth conditional cautions

These were introduced by s 48 of the Criminal Justice and Immigration Act 2008, which inserted s 66G into the CDA 1998. The requirements that must be met before a youth conditional caution may be given are:

(a)   there is sufficient evidence against the offender to provide a realistic prospect of conviction;

(b)   it must be determined that a youth conditional caution should be given to the offender;

(c) the offender admits to having committed the offence;

(d) the effect of the youth conditional caution must be explained to the offender and they must be warned that failure to comply with any of the conditions may result in prosecution for the original offence (where the young person is aged 16 years or under, the explanation and warning must be given in the presence of an appropriate adult); and

(e) the offender must sign a document containing details of the offence, their admission, consent to be given to a youth conditional caution and details of the conditions attached.

The type of conditions that can be attached to a youth conditional caution must have one or more of the following objectives in mind – rehabilitation, reparation and punishment. All rehabilitative, reparative and punitive conditions must be capable of being completed within 16 weeks of the date of the original offence where it is a summary-only offence. A period of longer than 16 weeks from the date the conditional caution is administered may be suitable for an offence triable either way or an indictable-only offence, depending on the facts of the particular case, but it must not exceed 20 weeks.

4.7.4 The effect of youth cautions and youth conditional cautions

A solicitor advising a client at the police station needs to identify the circumstances in which the client may be eligible to receive a youth caution or a youth conditional caution, and to be able to advise the client of the consequences of accepting such cautions. The solicitor must also ensure that they do not persuade a client to agree to such cautions when the client is adamant that they did not commit the offence. A client should not be allowed to admit to something they have not done simply because this may appear to be an easy short-term option.

The advantages of a client accepting such cautions are that:

(a) this avoids the client being charged with the offence and having to appear at the youth court;

(b) such cautions are not criminal convictions.

There are, however, consequences of accepting such cautions which must also be pointed out to the client:

(a) A record of such cautions will be retained by the police; this includes having fingerprints, photographs and DNA samples taken.

(b) Although not a conviction, as an admission of guilt the caution will form part of the client's criminal record retained by the police and may be referred to if an employer makes a Criminal Records Bureau check. In addition, the fact that a caution has already been issued will be taken into consideration before a decision is made regarding a future offending disposal.

(c) It may also need, in certain circumstances, to be disclosed to an employer or prospective employer.

(d) The police must refer the client to the appropriate Youth Offending Team who will assess the client and must arrange for them to participate in a rehabilitation programme (unless it is inappropriate to do so).

(e) Failure to comply with any conditions imposed under a conditional youth caution can result in prosecution for the original offence.

(f) Any youth cautions given and/or any report on a failure by a person to participate in a rehabilitation programme may be cited in criminal proceedings similar to how a conviction may be cited.

(g) If the offence is covered by Part 2 of the Sexual Offences Act 2003, the client will be placed on the sex offenders register.

Summary

In this chapter you have considered the additional safeguards given to vulnerable suspects and the types of suspect likely to enjoy such additional protection. Notably:

- *Who may be described as a vulnerable suspect.* This includes juveniles (aged 10 to 17); those suffering from a mental health condition or mental disorder; those who do not speak or understand English or have a hearing or speech impediment; and those who are either blind or have a severe visual impairment. In relation to each type of vulnerable suspect, who needs to be contacted by the custody officer and what they need to be told.

- *The appropriate adult.* Including who can be an appropriate adult and the role this person is required to take at the police station.

- *The role of the legal representative/solicitor.* In relation to the vulnerable suspect and the appropriate adult.

- *Identification procedures involving vulnerable suspects.* Including who is required to provide consent under Code D for a range of identification procedures.

- *Charging a juvenile.* Including when and how bail may be refused based on the age of the juvenile.

- *The alternatives to charging a juvenile suspect.* Including the use of community resolution, youth cautions and youth conditional cautions and the consequences of receiving any of these.

Sample questions

Question 1

A 16-year-old girl has been arrested and is being interviewed about her suspected involvement in relation to an allegation of burglary of shop premises. Her mother is present as the appropriate adult. During the course of the interview, the mother keeps interrupting the interviewing officer, stopping them from asking proper questions of the girl. The interviewing officer stops the interview and speaks to the custody sergeant who listens to a recording of the interview and then reminds the appropriate adult of her role and gives her an opportunity to respond. The custody sergeant then authorises the removal of the girl's mother as appropriate adult and contacts a social worker to continue to act as appropriate adult for the girl.

Have the police acted correctly when removing the girl's mother from acting as appropriate adult?

A   Yes, because the mother has prevented the interviewing officer from putting proper questions to the girl.

B   Yes, because the girl still has an appropriate adult attending to support, advise and assist her.

C   Yes, the custody sergeant followed the correct procedure before authorising the removal of the girl's mother.

D   No, because the custody sergeant is not of the correct rank of officer to make such an authorisation.

E   No, because the mother's role is not just to act as an observer, she is entitled to intervene during the interview.

Answer

Option D is the best answer. Although the mother has prevented the interviewing officer from putting proper questions to the suspect (option A) and the suspect still has an appropriate adult attending to support, advise and assist her (option B) and the custody sergeant followed the correct procedure before authorising the removal of the suspect's mother (option C), such a removal can only be authorised by an officer not below the rank of superintendent, or if such an officer is not available, an officer not below the rank of inspector, so option D is the best answer. Although option E is correct in that the mother's role is not just to act as an observer and she is entitled to intervene during the interview, she is not entitled to prevent the interviewing officer from putting proper questions to the suspect (see Code C, para 11.17 and 11.17A).

Question 2

A boy, aged 13 years, has been arrested on suspicion of robbery. He denies any involvement in the offence and claims that a witness who has recognised him is mistaken. The police propose to carry out a video identification procedure and the solicitor representing the boy advises him and his appropriate adult, a local authority social worker, to agree to take part in the procedure. The boy refuses to give his consent to such a procedure, but the appropriate adult does give her consent and when the boy's mother is contacted, she also gives her consent.

Can the police now lawfully carry out an identification procedure?

A   Yes, because the relevant consent from the boy's parent has been given.

B   No, because consent must be given by the appropriate adult and the boy.

C   Yes, because consent is not required to carry out a video identification procedure.

D   Yes, because the boy's solicitor has advised the boy to consent to the video identification procedure.

E   No, because the parent and the boy must both give their consent.

Answer

Option A is the best answer. Where a juvenile suspect is under 14 years of age, only the consent of the parent (or guardian) is required (Code D, para 2.12). Option B is therefore wrong, as the suspect's consent and the appropriate adult's consent (where this person is not also the parent or guardian) are not required. Option C is not the best answer because although consent is not required to carry out a covert video identification procedure, most video identification procedures are not covert and do require consent. Option D is wrong because although the solicitor's advice will be important in practice, it is not a requirement of Code D. Option E would have been correct had the juvenile suspect been aged 14 years or over, where both the parent/guardian and the suspect must give their consent.

Question 3

A boy, aged 10 years, has been charged with rape, it being alleged that he raped his younger sister. There is no local authority secure accommodation available. The boy's behaviour whilst detained at the police station has given the custody officer genuine concern that if released from the police station the boy will interfere with witnesses. The custody officer also believes that keeping the boy in other local authority accommodation would not be adequate to protect the public from serious harm from the boy.

Where can the custody officer authorise the boy to be remanded following charge?

A   The boy can be remanded at the police station, but he should be detained in a juvenile detention room.

B   The boy can be remanded at the police station, but he must be kept separate from adult suspects and must not be detained in a cell unless it is not practicable to supervise him.

C   The boy can only be remanded to other local authority accommodation because he is under the age of 12.

D   The boy must be released on either unconditional or conditional bail.

E   The boy can only be remanded on bail if it is impracticable to move him to local authority accommodation.

Answer

Option C is the correct answer. The key point to spot here is that the boy is only aged 10 and therefore under the age of 12. Had the boy been aged 12 or over, then s 38(6) provides that the lack of secure local authority accommodation does not make it impracticable to transfer a juvenile to local authority accommodation unless a juvenile is aged 12 or over and the local authority accommodation would not be adequate to protect the public from serious harm from the juvenile. So options A and B may have been correct had the boy been older. Option D is wrong because although the custody officer may remand the boy on either unconditional or conditional bail, the boy may also be remanded into the care of the local authority (which is most likely on these facts). Option E is wrong for the same reason.

PART 2
THE PROCEDURES AND PROCESSES INVOLVED IN CRIMINAL LITIGATION AND THE LAW OF EVIDENCE

5 First Hearings Before the Magistrates' Court

SQE1 syllabus

This chapter will enable you to achieve the SQE1 Assessment Specification in relation to Functioning Legal Knowledge concerned with the following procedures and processes:

- classification of offences;
- applying for a representation order;
- procedural overview – what will happen at the hearing;
- the role of the defence solicitor at the hearing.

Note that, for SQE1, candidates are not usually required to recall specific case names or cite statutory or regulatory authorities. These are provided for illustrative purposes only unless otherwise stated.

Learning outcomes

By the end of this chapter you will be able to apply relevant core legal principles and rules appropriately and effectively, at the level of a competent newly qualified solicitor in practice, to realistic client-based and ethical problems and situations in the following areas:

- The matters which will be dealt with at a first hearing in the magistrates' court based on the classification of the offence.
- The forms of public funding available to a defendant and applying for a representation order.
- What will happen at the first hearing.
- The role played by the defendant's solicitor at the first hearing.

5.1 Introduction

All defendants, no matter the charge, who are aged 18 or over, will make their first court appearance before the magistrates' court. If the defendant is charged with an offence triable only on indictment, the magistrates will immediately send the case to the Crown Court under s 51 of the Crime and Disorder Act (CDA) 1998. Defendants aged 17 and under will usually be dealt with in the youth court (see **Chapter 13**).

This chapter concentrates on adult defendants who are charged with an either-way offence or a summary offence. It describes what happens when the defendant makes their initial appearance at court and the role played by the defence solicitor at this stage in obtaining funding for the case, finding out details of the prosecution case against their client and advising the client as to their plea.

Between April and December 2007, the implementation of CJSSS – 'Criminal Justice: Simple, Speedy, Summary' - was rolled out in England and Wales. The idea of CJSSS was to speed up proceedings before magistrates' courts and to deal with cases as quickly as possible:

Some key principles of CJSSS are as follows:

(a) There is a common presumption that a plea will be entered at the first hearing.

(b) For guilty pleas which will be sentenced in the magistrates' court it is expected that sentence should take place on the same day unless a more detailed pre-sentence report is required.

(c) For not guilty pleas, it is expected that the trial issues should be identified, and a trial date fixed within six to eight weeks.

(d) The CPS should provide sufficient information at the first hearing to ensure the hearing is effective.

This is still the common approach taken by magistrates' courts and adopted in the Criminal Practice Direction VI, at para 24C.9, which provides that when considering an application for an adjournment, the court 'must have regard to the need for expedition. Delay is generally inimical to the interests of justice and brings the criminal justice system into disrepute. Proceedings in a magistrates' court should be simple and speedy.'

5.2 Classification of offences

All criminal offences fall into one of three categories of offence:

- those triable only on indictment;
- those triable either way; and
- those triable only summarily.

Note though that where an Act refers to the phrase 'indictable offence' without any further qualification, this is actually referring to the first two above classifications which, in the case of an adult, either *must* or *may* be tried in the Crown Court on indictment.

5.2.1 Offences triable only on indictment

These are the most serious form of criminal offence and must be dealt with by the Crown Court (you may sometimes see these referred to as 'indictable-only offences'). Although a defendant charged with an offence triable only on indictment will make their first appearance before the magistrates' court, the magistrates will immediately send the case to the Crown Court under s 51 CDA 1998.

Examples of such offences include murder, manslaughter, causing grievous bodily harm/wounding with intent, rape, robbery, aggravated burglary, blackmail, kidnap and conspiracy.

5.2.2 Either-way offences

Either-way offences can be dealt with either by the magistrates' court or by the Crown Court. A defendant charged with an either-way offence will make their first appearance before the magistrates' court, and if the defendant indicates a not guilty plea, the magistrates will then decide whether to keep the case before them or send the case to the Crown Court for trial if it is too serious for them to deal with. If the magistrates do decide to keep the case before them, the defendant then has the right to elect trial by a judge and jury in the Crown Court or consent to summary trial (see **Chapter 6**).

Examples of either-way offences include theft, fraud, most forms of burglary, handling stolen goods, going equipped to steal, inflicting grievous bodily harm/wounding, assault occasioning actual bodily harm, sexual assault, affray, threats to kill, criminal damage, dangerous driving, possession of an offensive weapon, possession/possession with intent to supply and supply of controlled drugs.

5.2.2.1 Low-value shop theft

Section 22A of the Magistrates' Courts Act 1980 makes 'low-value shoplifting' a summary offence. 'Low-value shoplifting' means an offence under s 1 of the Theft Act 1968 in circumstances where the value of the stolen goods does not exceed £200. (**Note**: if the defendant is charged at the same time with more than one allegation of shop theft then the 'aggregate' value must be under £200 for it to be treated as a summary offence.)

Low-value shoplifting offences will be treated as summary-only unless an adult defendant enters a plea of not guilty when they will still be given the opportunity to elect trial in the Crown Court.

The offence therefore attracts a maximum penalty of six months' custody when sentenced in the magistrates' court. If an adult defendant pleads guilty to an offence of low-value shoplifting, they cannot be committed to the Crown Court for sentence.

⭐ *Example*

George is arrested and charged with three allegations of theft from shops. The value of the goods alleged to have been stolen are £75, £50 and £100 respectively. George intends to plead guilty to all three allegations. Although each theft relates to a value under £200, the aggregate value comes to £225 and so George's case will not be treated as 'low-value shoplifting'. This means that these offences will be dealt with as either-way offences. So, if for example, George has a bad criminal record for similar offending he could be committed to the Crown Court for sentence. Consequently, George could be imprisoned for more than six months – R v Daniel Harvey [2020] EWCA Crim 354 (see **Chapters 6** *and* **11**).

5.2.2.2 Criminal damage

Although criminal damage is an either-way offence, where the value of the property damaged is less than £5,000 this will also be treated as a summary offence (Magistrates' Court Act 1980, s 22(1)) unless the damage was caused by fire.

5.2.3 Summary offences

Summary offences are the least serious form of criminal offence and as a general rule may only be dealt with by the magistrates' court.

Examples of summary offences include common assault, ss 4 and 5 of the Public Order Act 1984, taking a vehicle without consent and most road traffic offences.

5.3 Public funding available to a defendant and applying for a representation order

For defendants without sufficient means, defence solicitors will normally make applications on behalf of their client for the client's case to receive public funding from the Legal Aid Agency (LAA). The public funding of a defendant's legal representation in a criminal case is specifically provided for by Article 6(3) of the European Convention on Human Rights (ECHR), which states that defendants who do not have sufficient means to pay for legal assistance should receive this free from charge when this is in the *interests of justice*.

In order to obtain public funding for their clients, a firm of solicitors must have a contract with the LAA to represent defendants in criminal proceedings. This is known as a 'general criminal contract'.

5.3.1 Work done at the police station

The first advice solicitors normally provide to their clients will be at the police station. All persons attending at the police station (whether under arrest or attending voluntarily) are entitled to free legal advice, regardless of their means. Work done by a solicitor at the police station will be claimed as a fixed fee under the Police Station Advice and Assistance Scheme. There is just one fixed payment for every police station case regardless of how many attendances and how long the legal adviser was in attendance at the police station (although special provision is made for cases that are either of the most serious type or are very time-consuming). Non-solicitors (such as trainees) can attend the police station and charge for this work as long as they are either accredited or probationary police station representatives.

Most criminal defence solicitors will be members of duty solicitor schemes for a given police station. These solicitors have their names entered on a rota, and they may be called out to attend the police station if they are 'on duty' and the person who has been arrested does not have their own solicitor.

5.3.2 Work done after the client is charged

5.3.2.1 The duty solicitor scheme

The duty solicitor scheme operates in the magistrates' court in a similar way to the scheme at the police station. Solicitors who are members of a court duty scheme will again have their names on a rota. On the day when it is their turn to attend court as the duty solicitor, the particular solicitor will be available to advise any defendants who do not have their own solicitor but who require legal advice and/or representation. The duty solicitor will claim their costs in attending court from the LAA under the Advocacy Assistance (Court Duty Solicitor) Scheme.

5.3.2.2 Applying for a representation order

A defendant who wishes to apply for criminal legal aid in the magistrates' court must satisfy two tests:

(a) the *interests of justice test* – the defendant must show that it is in the interests of justice that they receive public funding to cover the cost of their legal representation; and

(b) the *means test* – the defendant must demonstrate that their finances are such that they are unable to pay for the cost of their legal representation.

In order to apply for legal aid in the magistrates' court, the defendant must submit an online application form (Form CRM14 – Application for Legal Aid in Criminal Proceedings). Unless the defendant automatically satisfies the means test (see below), they must also submit a financial statement (Form CRM15), together with any supporting evidence.

The interests of justice test

Legal aid will be granted by the magistrates' court only if it is in the interests of justice for a defendant to have their legal costs paid from public funds. This ensures compliance with Article 6(3)(a) of the ECHR.

The factors that are taken into account in deciding whether a defendant can satisfy the interests of justice test are set out in Sch 3, para 5(2) to the Access to Justice Act 1999:

In deciding what the interests of justice consist of in relation to any individual, the following factors must be taken into account:

(a) whether the individual would, if any matter arising in the proceedings is decided against them, be likely to lose their liberty or livelihood or suffer serious damage to their reputation;

(b) whether the determination of any matter arising in the proceedings may involve consideration of a substantial question of law;

(c) whether the individual may be unable to understand the proceedings or to state their own case;

(d) whether the proceedings may involve the tracing, interviewing or expert cross-examination of witnesses on behalf of the individual; and

(e) whether it is in the interests of another person that the individual be represented.

These factors are repeated in Form CRM14. A solicitor completing Form CRM14 must discuss each factor with their client and, if that factor is relevant to the client's case, tick the appropriate box. Full details in support must then be provided. Further guidance on what might be said about each factor is set out below:

> *It is likely that I will lose my liberty if any matter in the proceedings is decided against me.*

This is relevant if the defendant is charged with an offence which is likely to result in a custodial sentence if they are convicted. This may either be because the offence itself is a serious offence and/or because the defendant has a bad criminal record which will be regarded as an aggravating factor, making the present offence more serious. A solicitor can find out the likely sentence for the offence their client has been charged with by consulting the Sentencing Guidelines (see **Chapter 11**). The solicitor will effectively be presenting the prosecution case against their client 'taken at its most serious' in order to justify why their client should receive public funding for their case. The solicitor will need to refer to any factual allegations made by the prosecution which aggravate the seriousness of the offence, and will also need to make reference to any previous convictions the defendant may have for the same or similar types of offence. Such previous convictions will be taken into account by a sentencing court and are likely to lead to the court imposing a more severe sentence than if the defendant had no previous convictions.

This factor is also relevant if, regardless of the sentence which the court is likely to impose if the defendant is convicted, it is likely that the defendant will be refused bail in the proceedings and will be remanded in custody whilst the case is ongoing (see **Chapter 7**).

> *I have been given a sentence that is suspended or non-custodial. If I break this, the court may be able to deal with me for the original offence.*

This will be relevant if the defendant is subject to for example, a suspended sentence of imprisonment in respect of a previous offence (see **Chapter 11**) and commits a further offence during the period of the suspension. There is a statutory presumption that a defendant who is convicted of a further offence during the period of suspension will have their earlier sentence activated and so will go to prison (CJA 2003, Sch 12, para 8).

It is likely that I will lose my livelihood.

This will usually be relevant if the defendant intends to plead not guilty and is in employment and a conviction is likely to lead to the loss of that employment. It will always apply to any defendant in employment who is likely to face a prison sentence if convicted, but can also be relevant for other defendants who are not likely to receive a prison sentence but have particular types of job which may be lost in the event of conviction. For example, the defendant may be a bus driver charged with a road traffic offence (such as dangerous driving), which will result in their disqualification from driving if they are convicted. Alternatively, the defendant may be a teacher charged with common assault (since a conviction for an offence of violence will preclude a defendant from working with children in the future). This is also relevant for a defendant who is in a position of trust at work and who may lose their job if convicted of an offence involving dishonesty (such as an employee of a bank accused of theft).

The remaining factors (unless otherwise stated) will only be applicable where the defendant intends to plead not guilty:

It is likely that I will suffer serious damage to my reputation.

'Serious' damage will occur when the disgrace of a conviction is more than the direct effect of the sentence received and will result in the defendant losing their reputation for honesty or trustworthiness. This will only apply to defendants who either have no previous convictions or convictions for very minor offences. If the defendant has no previous convictions and has a position of standing or respect in the community (such as a vicar, local councillor or school governor), a conviction for any criminal offence, even if the offence is relatively minor, may cause serious damage to their reputation.

A substantial question of law may be involved (whether arising from an act, judicial authority or other source).

This is relevant where either the prosecution evidence is in dispute, or the defendant wishes to adduce evidence which the CPS may argue is inadmissible. Examples of when this may arise are:

(a) if there is disputed identification evidence and the court needs to apply the Turnbull guidelines to such evidence (see **Chapter 9**);

(b) if there is a possibility that the court may draw adverse inferences under ss 34, 36 or 37 of the CJPOA 1994 from the defendant's refusal to answer questions at the police station (see **Chapter 9**);

(c) if either the prosecution or the defence are seeking to persuade the court to admit hearsay evidence under s 114 of the CJA 2003 (see **Chapter 9**);

(d) if the defence are seeking to use ss 76 or 78 of PACE 1984 to argue that a confession made (or allegedly made) by the defendant should be excluded (see **Chapter 9**); and

(e) if the prosecution want to adduce at trial evidence of the defendant's previous convictions under s 101 of the CJA 2003, or either party is seeking to adduce bad character evidence of any other person under s 100 of the same Act (see **Chapter 9**).

I may not be able to understand the court proceedings or present my own case.

This factor may apply to a defendant who intends to plead guilty or not guilty. Reasons which may prevent the defendant from being able to understand the court proceedings or present their case include:

(a) mental or physical disability;

(b) poor knowledge of English (particularly relevant for defendants from overseas);

(c) age (a defendant who is particularly young or old); and

(d) vulnerability (a defendant who is emotionally immature or otherwise vulnerable).

Witnesses may need to be traced or interviewed on my behalf.

This will be relevant where a defendant wishes to call a witness in support of their case, such as a witness who can support a defence of alibi or, for a defendant charged with assault, a witness who will say that the defendant was acting in reasonable self-defence. Such witnesses will need to be traced and a statement taken from them. This may also be important if the defendant needs to call expert evidence in support of their defence (for example, a forensic scientist in a murder case). The defendant will need to explain why they require legal representation to trace or interview such witnesses.

The case involves expert cross-examination of a prosecution witness (whether an expert or not).

This will be relevant if a witness needs to be cross-examined to determine a question of law or to decide on the admissibility of a particular piece of evidence, or if the evidence given by the witness is complex or technical. For example, if the defendant's solicitor is attempting to persuade the court to exclude a confession their client made when interviewed at the police station (on the basis that the confession was made only as a result of improper conduct by the police), it may be necessary to cross-examine the interviewing officer to establish that the Codes of Practice issued under PACE 1984 were breached. Only a person with legal expertise could properly conduct such a cross-examination. Similarly, only someone with a detailed knowledge of the law concerning disputed visual identification evidence could properly conduct a cross-examination of a prosecution witness who claims to have identified the defendant as the person who committed the offence when the defendant disputes this identification.

This factor will also be relevant if the prosecution seeks to rely on any expert evidence, such as evidence from a forensic scientist. If the contents of the evidence to be given by the forensic scientist are disputed, this will require expert cross-examination to cast doubt upon the expert's conclusions.

It is in someone else's interests that I am represented.

This factor will apply when it would be inappropriate for a defendant to represent themself because they would then need to cross-examine prosecution witnesses in person. For example, where a defendant is charged with a sexual or violent offence, it would be inappropriate for the defendant to cross-examine in person the complainant in such a case. It would also be inappropriate for a defendant to cross-examine a child witness in person (particularly if the defendant were charged with having abused the child). Note that this factor should not be used to argue that legal representation is in the general interests of the defendant's family or the court.

Any other reasons.

This is designed to cover any matters not falling under any of the above headings. The guidance notes suggest that further details should be given here if the defendant is likely to receive, for example, a 'demanding' community sentence if convicted. To determine if this is likely, the solicitor will need to consult the relevant section of the Magistrates' Court Sentencing Guidelines. Details should also be provided under this heading if a defence witness requires skilful examination-in-chief in order to bring out their evidence in a way which is most favourable to the defendant.

It is also common practice when using this factor to state that the defendant intends to enter a not guilty plea, since a defendant who is pleading not guilty is likely to need much more in the way of legal advice than a defendant who intends to plead guilty, particularly if the charge is a serious one and the case is likely to be tried in the Crown Court.

The means test

The following defendants will receive criminal legal aid automatically without needing to satisfy the means test:

(a) applicants who receive income support, income-based jobseeker's allowance, guaranteed state pension credit, income-based employment and support allowance or universal credit; and

(b) applicants who are under the age of 18.

Those applicants who do not automatically satisfy the means test must complete Form CRM15. They will also be required to supply to the court the necessary evidence to substantiate their financial details as given on Form CRM15. This will include items such as pay slips, tax returns (if the applicant runs their own business), bank statements, other tax forms, mortgage statements or rental/tenancy agreements and proof of childcare costs.

Upon receipt of Form CRM15, an initial means test to determine whether the applicant is financially eligible for legal aid will then be applied. The means test considers the applicant's income and expenses, but not the applicant's capital.

The purpose of the full means test is to calculate the applicant's disposable income. This is done by deducting the following items from the applicant's gross annual income:

(a) tax and national insurance

(b) annual housing costs

(c) annual childcare costs

(d) annual maintenance to former partners and any children and

(e) an adjusted annual living allowance.

An applicant does not have the right to appeal against a refusal of legal aid because of a failure to satisfy the means test. If, however, an applicant does not satisfy the means test but can demonstrate that they genuinely cannot fund their own defence, the applicant may ask that their entitlement to criminal legal aid be reviewed on the grounds of hardship by completing an application for review on the grounds of hardship (Form CRM16).

If a defendant qualifies for legal aid in the magistrates' court, they will not be required to contribute to their defence costs. To put this another way, in the magistrates' court, legal aid is either free or not available. Whereas in the Crown Court, legal aid may also be available but subject to the defendant paying a contribution towards their legal aid costs.

5.3.2.3 The scope of a representation order

If a defendant satisfies both the interests of justice test and the means test, the magistrates' court will grant a criminal defence representation order and the order will be sent to their solicitor.

The representation order granted to a defendant for a summary-only matter, or an either-way matter which is dealt with by the magistrates' court, will cover all the work done by the solicitor in connection with those proceedings in the magistrates' court, and may be extended to cover an appeal to the Crown Court against conviction and/or sentence. If, for an either-way matter, the magistrates decline jurisdiction or the defendant elects trial in the Crown Court (see **Chapter 6**), the representation order will extend automatically to cover the proceedings in the Crown Court. A representation order granted in respect of an offence that is triable only on indictment will cover proceedings in both the magistrates' court and the Crown Court.

For either-way offences, where a defendant has failed the magistrates' court means test and the case is subsequently committed to the Crown Court, funding will not start until the day after the sending hearing and will only cover work done in the Crown Court, and only if the defendant passes the means eligibility test in the Crown Court.

A defendant whose application for legal aid is refused under the interests of justice test may appeal against this decision either by adding further details to their original Form CRM14 and resubmitting this, or by requesting an appeal. There is no right of appeal against the refusal of legal aid as a result of a failure to satisfy the means test (although the defendant may ask that their application be reviewed on the grounds of hardship – see above).

At the conclusion of the case, the defence solicitor will then claim costs incurred under the representation order from the LAA.

 Example

Darren has been arrested on suspicion of theft from his employer, it being alleged that he stole a significant amount whilst in a position of a high degree of trust. At the police station he receives advice from Uzmar, the duty solicitor. Darren denies the allegation. During interview, it becomes apparent the prosecution will seek to rely on a disputed item of hearsay evidence. Following interview, Darren is RUI. He is also subsequently dismissed from his employment. After a number of weeks, Darren is eventually prosecuted for the offence. Darren has been unable to find employment and by the time his case gets to court he is in receipt of universal credit. Darren maintains his innocence; he intends to plead not guilty and he instructs Uzmar to represent him.

Darren's entitlement to publicly funded advice and representation:

- *At the police station Darren is entitled to free legal advice from Uzmar (even though at that point he was still in paid employment).*

- *At court, he is likely to be eligible for a representation order. Uzmar will complete an online application form (CRM14) setting out why it is in the interests of justice that Darren is granted legal aid. Based on the limited information we have so far, the factors will be:*

  - *'It is likely that I will lose my liberty if any matter in the proceedings is decided against me.'*
  - *'It is likely that I will suffer serious damage to my reputation.'*
  - *'A substantial question of law may be involved (whether arising from an act, judicial authority or other source).'*

- *As Darren is in receipt of universal credit, he will automatically satisfy the means test, but will need to have provided details of his National Insurance number so that this can be verified.*

5.4 Procedural overview – what will happen at the first hearing

What happens at the first hearing is determined by a number of things, including:

(a) the classification of the offence (see above);

(b) the plea the defendant enters in respect of summary or either-way offences;

(c) the level of detail provided by the CPS of the prosecution case; and

(d) whether public/private funding has been secured.

Given the aims of CJSSS (see above), the magistrates will be keen to progress the case at the first hearing. This means that the CPS should make sufficient disclosure at the first hearing to enable the defendant to enter a plea; and the defence should be prepared and ready to do so. This will depend on the defendant's solicitor having had the opportunity to discuss the details of the prosecution case with the defendant, and to advise on the strength of the prosecution case and the plea the defendant should enter (see Chapter 6).

There will be rare occasions when the defendant is not in a position to enter a plea, for example, there may be times when funding issues have not been finalised and financial details remain outstanding, or where the prosecution has not been able to disclose any of their evidence and so the case needs to be adjourned.

If the case is adjourned, the magistrates will consider whether the defendant should be granted bail or remanded in custody prior to the next hearing (see **Chapter 7**).

5.4.1 Summary offences

The defendant will usually be required to enter a plea. If the defendant pleads guilty, a representative from the CPS will then tell the magistrates the facts of the case and if relevant, hand in the defendant's record of previous convictions. If the defendant is legally represented, their solicitor will then give a plea in mitigation on the defendant's behalf. The magistrates will then either sentence the defendant straight away or adjourn the case if they want to obtain any reports (such as a pre-sentence report from the Probation Service) before sentencing the defendant.

The magistrates may also need to adjourn the case if the defendant pleads guilty but disputes the specific factual allegations made by the CPS. In such a situation, a separate hearing (called a 'Newton hearing' – see **Chapter 11**) will be necessary to determine the factual basis upon which the defendant will be sentenced. The sentencing procedure in the magistrates' court is described in more detail in **Chapter 11**.

If the defendant is pleading not guilty, the court will then fix a date for the defendant's trial to take place and will issue case management directions with which both the prosecution and defence must comply before trial. Details of the directions the court will make are given in **Chapter 8**.

Whether the defendant is pleading guilty or not guilty, if the case is adjourned, the magistrates will need to determine whether the defendant should be released on bail or remanded in custody prior to the next hearing (see **Chapter 7**).

5.4.2 Either-way offences

If the offence is an either-way matter and the defendant enters a guilty plea, the magistrates will then need to determine whether they should sentence the defendant, or whether the defendant should be committed to the Crown Court for sentence because the magistrates' sentencing powers are insufficient. The case may then need to be adjourned either for the magistrates to obtain a pre-sentence report from the Probation Service before sentencing the defendant, or, if the magistrates have decided to commit the defendant to the Crown Court to be sentenced, for the sentencing hearing at the Crown Court to take place.

If the defendant enters a not guilty plea, before going any further, the magistrates must determine whether the defendant is to be tried in the magistrates' court or in the Crown Court. This is known as the 'plea before venue and allocation procedure' (see **Chapter 6**).

If the case is to be adjourned, the magistrates will need to determine whether the defendant should be released on bail or remanded in custody prior to the next hearing (see **Chapter 7**).

5.4.3 Offences triable only on indictment

An adult defendant charged with an offence triable only on indictment will be sent straight to the Crown Court for either trial or sentence following a preliminary hearing in the magistrates' court, pursuant to s 51(1) of the CDA 1998.

For such offences, the defendant's case will therefore always have to be adjourned, so the magistrates will need to determine whether the defendant should be released on bail or remanded in custody prior to the next hearing which will take place in the Crown Court.

5.5 The role of the defence solicitor at the first hearing

The solicitor's role at this stage involves taking the following steps:

(a) obtaining funding from the LAA to pay for the work they will do on their client's behalf (unless the client is paying for their legal costs privately);

(b) obtaining details of the prosecution case from the CPS (for summary and either-way offences);

(c) taking a statement from the client;

(d) advising the client on the strength of the prosecution evidence and the plea the client should enter (for summary and either-way offences); and

(e) in the case of an either-way offence where the client is indicating a not guilty plea, informing the client that their case may be dealt with either by the magistrates' court or by the Crown Court, and advising the client about the advantages and disadvantages of each court; and

(f) making an application for bail, where necessary (see **Chapter 7**).

Part (a) has already been considered in this chapter. Parts (b) to (e) will be considered in more detail in **Chapter 6**.

Summary

In this chapter you have considered what happens when a defendant first appears in the magistrates' court. Notably:

- *How the classification of offence impacts on this procedure.* There are three main classifications. Namely, offences which are only triable on indictment, those that are triable either-way and those triable only summarily.

- *The public funding which may be available for a defendant and the relevant criteria for eligibility to receive such funding.* In the police station, all suspects, regardless of their means, are eligible for free, independent legal advice. At court, only those defendants who do not have sufficient means to pay for legal assistance will be eligible for publicly funded legal representation when it is in the *interests of justice* to do so. This interests of justice test focuses on a combination of criteria relating to both the case and the defendant.

- *What will happen at the first hearing?* This will depend on the classification of the offence and the defendant's plea. Offences which are only triable on indictment will be immediately sent to the Crown Court. For summary-only offences, the defendant will be expected to enter a plea and the case will then either be adjourned for a trial to take place, or where a guilty plea is entered, the defendant will be sentenced for the offence. For either-way offences, the court will first conduct a plea before venue hearing at which the defendant will indicate their plea. As with a summary-only offence, if the defendant indicates a guilty plea, they will then be sentenced. If, however, the offence is too serious for the magistrates' court's sentencing powers, the defendant will be committed to the

Crown Court for sentence. If the defendant indicates a not guilty plea, allocation will then be considered (see **Chapter 6**).

- *The defence solicitor's role at this hearing.* The solicitor will obtain publicly funded representation for their client if this is available and for either-way and summary-only offences, they will obtain initial details of the prosecution case before then advising their client on plea. For either-way offences they will also advise clients who are indicating a not guilty plea which trial venue will be the best for them if they are given a choice. If the case is not concluded at the first hearing, they may also need to make a bail application on their client's behalf.

Sample questions

Question 1

A man is due to appear in the magistrates' court charged with an offence of assault occasioning actual bodily harm. It is alleged that he headbutted the victim causing the victim a fractured nose following a neighbour dispute. The man intends to plead guilty. The man is currently the subject of a suspended sentence of imprisonment for an offence of theft. The man is currently unemployed and in receipt of universal credit. The man is widowed and the sole carer for his three young children.

Will the man be entitled to receive publicly funded legal representation at court?

A   Yes, because it will be in the interests of his children that he is represented as he is their sole carer and he automatically satisfies the means test.

B   Yes, because it will be in the interests of justice as it is likely that he will lose his liberty and he automatically satisfies the means test.

C   Yes, because he will lose his liberty if he is convicted, subject to him satisfying the means test by completing a means form.

D   No, because it will not be in the interests of the victim that he is represented as he is pleading guilty, so the man will not need to cross-examine the victim.

E   No, because he will not necessarily lose his liberty if he is convicted, although he does automatically satisfy the means test.

Answer

Option B is the correct answer. The man is '*likely*' to lose his liberty because of the seriousness of the offence itself and also because he is subject to a suspended sentence of imprisonment which is likely to be activated when he pleads guilty to the present offence. The man automatically satisfies the means test as he is in receipt of universal credit. Option A is wrong because although '*It is in someone else's interests that I am represented*' is capable of being a reason to grant legal aid under the interests of justice test, this should not be used to argue that legal representation is in the general interests of the defendant's family. Option C is wrong, because although it is (highly) likely the man will lose his liberty, it is not certain that he will and moreover, he will not need to complete a means form as he automatically satisfies the means test as he is in receipt of universal credit. Option D is not the best answer, because although it is correct to say that it will not be in the interests of the victim that he is represented as he is pleading guilty, so the man will not need to cross-examine the victim, the interests of justice test is still satisfied (see option B). Option E is not the best answer, because although he will not necessarily lose his liberty if he is convicted, it is still '*likely*' that he will.

Question 2

A woman is to appear in the magistrates' court charged with an offence of criminal damage by arson. It is alleged that she set fire to her ex-partner's garden shed following a breakdown of their relationship. £2,000 worth of damage was caused. The woman will plead guilty to this offence.

Which of the following best describes what will happen when she appears in court?

A   The woman will plead guilty and the magistrates will then sentence her since the value of the property damaged is under £5,000.

B   The woman will be expected to enter her plea and the magistrates will then have to decide on allocation as this is an either-way offence.

C   The woman will plead guilty and the court will then adjourn the case for the preparation of a pre-sentence report.

D   The woman will not be asked to indicate her plea as arson is an offence that can only be tried on indictment so her case will be immediately sent to the Crown Court.

E   The woman will be expected to indicate her plea and she will either be sentenced by the magistrates' court or committed to the Crown Court for sentence.

Answer

Option E is the best answer. Criminal damage of property under £5,000 is treated as a summary-only offence, unless the damage was caused by fire (Magistrates' Court Act 1980, s 22(1)), in which case it is an either-way offence. For these reasons, options A and D are wrong. Option B is wrong because although it is an either-way offence, an allocation hearing will only take place where a defendant indicates a not guilty plea (see **Chapter 6**). Option C is not the best answer, because although the court may adjourn the case for a pre-sentence report, it will not definitely do this and it may even commit the woman to the Crown Court if in light of all the other circumstances the magistrates' court decides that its sentencing powers are inadequate.

Question 3

A man has been charged with robbery. It is alleged that he stole a jacket valued at £75 from his victim and assaulted him at the same time, in order to steal the jacket. The victim suffered no physical injuries as a result of the robbery. The man intends to plead not guilty to this allegation.

Where will the man's trial take place?

A   The trial may take place in either the magistrates' court or the Crown Court depending on whether or not the magistrates accept jurisdiction to deal with the case.

B   The trial is likely to take place in the magistrates' court as the item stolen is valued at under £200 and because the man suffered no physical injury.

C   The trial will take place in the Crown Court as this is an offence that is only triable on indictment.

D   The trial may take place in either the magistrates' court or the Crown Court depending on whether or not the man consents to summary trial or elects trial on indictment.

E   The trial must take place in the magistrates' court as the item stolen is valued at under £200 and because the victim suffered no physical injury.

Answer

Option C is the correct answer. Robbery is an offence that can only be tried on indictment regardless of the value of the goods that were stolen or whether or not the victim suffered any physical harm. Options B and E are therefore wrong. Option A is wrong because the magistrates will not be required to decide whether or not they accept jurisdiction to deal with the case and Option D is wrong because the man will not get a choice on where his trial will take place.

6 Plea Before Venue and Allocation of Business Between the Magistrates' Court and Crown Court

SQE1 syllabus

This chapter will enable you to achieve the SQE1 Assessment Specification in relation to Functioning Legal Knowledge concerned with the following procedures and processes:

- advising the client on trial venue;
- procedure on defendant entering plea;
- procedure ss 19–20 and s 22A Magistrates' Courts Act 1980;
- sending without allocation s 50A Crime and Disorder Act 1998.

Note that, for SQE1, candidates are not usually required to recall specific case names or cite statutory or regulatory authorities. These are provided for illustrative purposes only unless otherwise stated.

Learning outcomes

By the end of this chapter you will be able to apply relevant core legal principles and rules appropriately and effectively, at the level of a competent newly qualified solicitor in practice, to realistic client-based and ethical problems and situations in the following areas:

- The obligations on the CPS to provide to the defendant's solicitor the details of the case against the defendant.
- The matters to be taken into account when the defendant's solicitor advises their client on the plea to be entered.
- The matters to be taken into account by the defendant's solicitor when advising their client whether, if given the choice, to elect trial in the Crown Court or consent to summary trial.
- The procedure which is followed at the plea before venue and allocation hearing.
- How either-way offences can be sent to the Crown Court without an allocation hearing.

6.1 Introduction

This chapter continues on from Chapter 5 – what happens at a defendant's first court appearance in the magistrates' court. The focus of this chapter though is on either-way offences. It describes the obligation on the CPS to provide initial details of the prosecution case (IDPC) and advising the client as to their plea and, if given the choice, trial venue. It will then examine the procedure that takes place to determine whether an either-way offence will ultimately be dealt with by the magistrates' court or by the Crown Court. This is sometimes referred to collectively as the mode of trial procedure.

6.2 Prosecution obligation to provide IDPC

If the solicitor has represented their client at the police station, they may have some knowledge as to what the prosecution case against the client is and what evidence the CPS has to support their case. They are unlikely, however, to have seen copies of the witness statements which the police have obtained. It is vital for the defendant's solicitor to see all the prosecution evidence as soon as possible after the defendant has been charged, so that they may give timely advice to the defendant on their plea, which in part will be based on the strength of the case against them, and take instructions on what the prosecution witnesses are saying.

6.2.1 Contents of IDPC (CrimPR, Part 8)

A defendant is entitled to receive IDPC (CrimPR, r 8.2) for all offences (ie summary only, either-way and offences triable only on indictment). In practice, this will be provided in a digital format. The defence solicitor will either contact the CPS in advance of the first hearing with a Unique Reference Number which will be on the charge sheet and the CPS will email the solicitor the IDPC via its Criminal Justice Secure Mail account, or the material will be accessed directly on the Common Platform. This is a digital case management system that allows all parties in criminal cases to access case information including IDPC.

For clients seen in court for the first time, the solicitor may have to phone a centralised CPS number on the day, and the CPS will then email the papers through to the solicitor there and then if the information is not available on the Common Platform.

Part 8 of the CrimPR has been amended to include a provision that where the CPS wishes to introduce information contained in a document that the defence is entitled to and that document/information has not been made available to the defence, the court must not allow the prosecutor to introduce that information unless the court first allows the defendant sufficient time to consider it (CrimPR, r 8.4).

IDPC includes the following:

(a) where the defendant was in police custody for the offence charged immediately before the first hearing in the magistrates' court:

    (i) a summary of the circumstances of the offence; and

    (ii) the defendant's criminal record, if any; or

(b) in all other cases:

    (i) a summary of the circumstances of the offence;

    (ii) any account given by the defendant in interview, whether contained in that summary or in another document;

(iii) any written witness statement or exhibit that the prosecutor has available and considers material to plea, or to the allocation of the case for trial or to sentence;

(iv) the defendant's criminal record, if any; and

(v) if available, a victim impact statement.

The Criminal Practice Direction, para 3A.12 expands the list of material which is expected to be served for cases where the defendant has been released on bail after being charged and where the prosecutor does not anticipate a guilty plea at the first hearing.

It states that in such cases (regardless of whether they are to be heard in the magistrates' court or the Crown Court), unless there is good reason not to do so, the prosecution should make available the following material in advance of the first hearing in the magistrates' court:

(a) a summary of the circumstances of the offence and any account given by the defendant in interview;

(b) statements and exhibits that the prosecution has identified as being of importance for the purpose of plea or initial case management, including any relevant CCTV that would be relied upon at trial and any Streamlined Forensic Report;

(c) an indication of any medical or other expert evidence that the prosecution is likely to adduce in relation to a victim or the defendant;

(d) any information as to special measures, bad character or hearsay, where applicable (see **Chapter 9**).

6.3   Advising a client on plea and trial venue

6.3.1   Advising on plea

After the solicitor has obtained details of the prosecution case, the defendant's solicitor will then need to take further instructions from their client. The following matters will have to be discussed:

(a) The client's response to the prosecution case. Each prosecution witness statement needs to be discussed with the client and an accurate note taken of any points of dispute. This note should then be added to the client's statement. The solicitor should also listen to the record of the audibly recorded interview to check that the transcript which has been provided is accurate. If the client made any admissions when interviewed, the solicitor needs to take instructions from the client – are the admissions correct, or did the client make admissions because of the manner in which the interview was conducted or just to get out of the police station as quickly as possible? Does the client come across well on the audio recording (in which case, should the solicitor ask for the interview to be played out at trial rather than the transcript being read out)? Are there grounds on which an application may be made to the court to exclude the interview record from being used in evidence at trial? (See **Chapter 9**.)

(b) The strength of the prosecution case. Whilst it is the client's decision as to the plea they will enter, if the prosecution case is overwhelming, the solicitor should inform the client of this and remind the client that they will be given credit for entering an early guilty plea when they are subsequently sentenced (see **Chapter 11**).

(c) Whether it is necessary to obtain any further evidence in support of the defendant's case. For example, in light of the prosecution evidence which has been disclosed, the client may recall the identity of other witnesses who could give evidence on their behalf.

(d) Where the client has been charged with an either-way offence and is pleading not guilty, if given the choice, whether they should elect to be tried in the magistrates' court, or before a judge and jury in the Crown Court (see below).

The ultimate decision the client will need to take once the CPS has disclosed details of its case is what plea to enter. This is the client's decision, not the solicitor's. As mentioned in (b) above, as part of the duty to act in the best interests of the client, the solicitor should give the client their view of the strength of the evidence against them. It is also appropriate for the solicitor to advise the client that, when it comes to sentencing, the client will receive a reduced sentence for entering an early guilty plea.

6.3.2 Advising on trial venue

If the magistrates consider that an either-way case is suitable for summary trial, the defendant will then have a choice as to whether they want the trial to take place in the magistrates' court or the Crown Court. The defendant's solicitor must advise them about the factors in favour of each venue.

6.3.2.1 Factors in favour of the Crown Court

Greater chance of acquittal

Statistically, more defendants are acquitted following a jury trial in the Crown Court than are acquitted following a trial before a bench of magistrates or a district judge in the magistrates' court. Juries are perceived to be more sympathetic to defendants than 'case-hardened' magistrates. In particular, if the prosecution case includes evidence from police officers who often give evidence before the same magistrates' court, it is felt that a defendant will get a fairer hearing in the Crown Court where the jurors are hearing from each of the witnesses for the first time. Magistrates may be predisposed to favour the evidence of police officers from whom they may have heard evidence in previous cases, whereas jurors are perhaps more likely to question the testimony of police officers whose evidence is disputed by the defendant. Similarly, if the defendant has several previous convictions before the same magistrates' court, the magistrates may be aware of such convictions and may be prejudiced against the defendant.

Better procedure for challenging admissibility of prosecution evidence

The procedure for deciding the admissibility of disputed prosecution evidence is better for the defendant in the Crown Court than in the magistrates' court. In the Crown Court, when a dispute over the admissibility of a piece of prosecution evidence (such as a confession) arises, the jury will be asked to leave the court room and the judge will conduct a mini-trial to decide whether or not the evidence should be admitted. This mini hearing is known as a *voir dire* (or a 'trial within a trial'). Only if the judge decides that the evidence is admissible will the jury ever hear about it. If the judge rules the evidence to be inadmissible, the evidence will not be placed before the jury.

Were such a situation to arise in the magistrates' court because the magistrates are responsible for determining both matters of law and matters of fact, the magistrates themselves would need to determine whether the evidence was admissible. If the magistrates decided that a piece of prosecution evidence was inadmissible, when considering their verdict, the magistrates would then need to set to one side their knowledge of the existence of that piece of evidence. There is a risk that such knowledge would remain in the back of their minds and affect their decision as to the defendant's guilt or innocence.

(Although the Crown Court remains the better venue for determining the admissibility of disputed items of prosecution evidence, most magistrates' courts do now attempt to determine issues of admissibility of evidence at pre-trial hearings rather than at the hearing itself. Such hearings will take place before a different bench of magistrates from the bench who hear the trial, so there is no risk that the defendant will be prejudiced at trial by the magistrates being aware of any item of prosecution evidence which has been found to be inadmissible.)

More time to prepare the case for trial

If the case against the defendant is complex, as the case will take longer to get to trial in the Crown Court, there will be more time to prepare the defence case. This is also relevant if there are a large number of potential witnesses for the defence who need to be interviewed.

6.3.2.2   Factors in favour of the magistrates' court

Limited sentencing powers

The biggest advantage in electing summary trial is the limited sentencing powers the magistrates' court has. The maximum sentence which the magistrates may impose is 12 months' imprisonment for an either-way offence (see **Chapter 11**). The sentencing powers available to a Crown Court judge are much greater.

However, even if the defendant is tried before the magistrates' court, the magistrates retain the power to commit the defendant to the Crown Court for sentence if, during or after the trial, facts emerge that make the offence more serious than it appeared at the allocation hearing and so render the magistrates' sentencing powers inadequate (if, for example, the defendant is convicted at trial and the magistrates then find that they have numerous previous convictions for the same type of offence).

Speed and stress

A trial in the magistrates' court takes place much sooner than a trial in the Crown Court. This may be significant for a defendant who needs their case to be concluded relatively quickly, such as a defendant who has been offered employment in another part of the country or overseas. This will also be a very important consideration for a defendant who has been denied bail and is remanded in custody prior to trial.

Cases in the magistrates' court are also less stressful for defendants. The procedure in the magistrates' court is less formal than and not as intimidating as the Crown Court (for example, the judge and the advocates in the Crown Court wear wigs and gowns, whereas the magistrates and the advocates in the magistrates' court do not). This may be significant for a defendant who has never previously been charged with an offence, and who is likely to be intimidated by the greater formality of the Crown Court. This is, however, unlikely to be a significant consideration for a defendant with numerous previous convictions who is no stranger to the criminal courts.

Prosecution costs

If a defendant is convicted in either the magistrates' court or the Crown Court, they are likely to be ordered to make a contribution towards the costs incurred by the CPS in bringing the case against them. Such costs are likely to be higher in the Crown Court because of the greater amount of work that goes into preparing a case for trial in the Crown Court (such as the need to instruct counsel).

Defence costs

If granted legal aid in the magistrates' court, a defendant is not required to contribute towards his defence costs.

In the Crown Court, all legal aid applications are subject to a financial eligibility test. If a defendant is eligible for legal aid (ie has a household disposable income currently under £37,500), a means test will consider their income and capital assets, and they may be liable for income contributions towards costs either during the proceedings or at the end of the case.

If the defendant funds their case privately, proceedings before the magistrates' court will be significantly cheaper than in the Crown Court.

No obligation to serve defence statement

A defendant pleading not guilty in the Crown Court is effectively obliged to serve on both the Crown Court and the prosecution a defence statement under ss 5, 6 and 6A of the Criminal Procedure and Investigations Act 1996 (see **Chapter 8**). The giving of a defence statement will provide the prosecution with much more information about the defence case.

In the magistrates' court there is no obligation on the defendant to provide a defence statement either to the court or to the CPS. The giving of such a statement in the magistrates' court is entirely optional, and in practice is very rarely done.

6.3.3 Professional conduct

Occasionally a client will tell their solicitor that they are guilty of the offence but nevertheless intend to enter a not guilty plea at court. This will raise issues of professional conduct for the solicitor who, whilst under a duty to act in their client's best interests, is under an overriding duty not to mislead the court (SRA Code of Conduct, para 1.4). In such circumstances the client has two options – to plead guilty, or to plead not guilty. To comply with their duty to act in the client's best interests, the solicitor will need to advise the client of the benefits were the client to enter a guilty plea, and of the limitations on the solicitor's ability to continue representing the client were they to enter a plea of not guilty.

6.3.3.1 Benefits of pleading guilty

The solicitor should advise the client that, were they to plead guilty, the client will receive a reduction in their sentence from the court for entering an early guilty plea (see **Chapter 11**).

6.3.3.2 Limitations if the client pleads not guilty

If the client insists on maintaining a not guilty plea, they must be advised that the solicitor may still represent them at trial but that the solicitor is limited in what they can do on the client's behalf because of their overriding duty not to mislead the court. At trial, the solicitor would be able to cross-examine prosecution witnesses and put the prosecution to proof of their case, since this would not involve misleading the court (although, in cross-examining the prosecution witnesses, the solicitor would need to be careful not to assert any positive defence that they know to be false). Similarly, the solicitor would be able to make a submission of no case to answer at the end of the prosecution case and to ask the magistrates to dismiss the case, as again this would not involve misleading the court. Such a submission could be made if the prosecution failed to discharge their evidential burden to show that the defendant had a case to answer (see **Chapter 9**).

The defendant's solicitor would, however, be unable to continue acting for the defendant if the submission of no case to answer was unsuccessful and the defendant then insisted on entering the witness box to give evidence which the solicitor knew to be false. In this situation, the defendant's solicitor could not be a party to misleading the court and would need to withdraw from the case. The solicitor would nevertheless still owe a duty of confidentiality to their client and so could not indicate to the court the reason for their withdrawal from the case. A common euphemism that defence solicitors use in such situations is to tell the court that they are withdrawing from the case 'for professional reasons'.

✪ Example

Joe is charged with theft from a store. The evidence against him consists only of identification evidence from a member of the store's security staff. Joe admits his guilt to his solicitor but enters a not guilty plea, believing that the case may be discharged if the evidence given by the identification witness at court is unconvincing. Joe's solicitor is entitled to cross-examine this witness at trial to cast doubt on the evidence he gives. For example, the witness may have caught only a fleeting glimpse of Joe from a long distance away and may admit under cross-examination that he cannot be certain of the identification he has made. If the evidence given by this witness is unconvincing, Joe's solicitor will then be able to make a submission of no case to answer at the conclusion of the prosecution case and ask the magistrates to dismiss the case. If, however, the magistrates decline to dismiss the case and Joe then insisted on giving evidence in his own defence, his solicitor would need to withdraw from the case so as not to be a party to the court being misled. The solicitor would tell the court that they could not continue to act in the case for 'professional reasons' so as not to breach their duty of confidentiality to Joe.

6.4 Procedure on defendant indicating plea (for either-way offences)

The procedure that will take place for an either-way offence when the defendant appears before the magistrates' court is as follows:

(a) The charge will be read out to the defendant by the court's legal adviser, who will also check that the defendant's solicitor has received IDPC.

(b) The legal adviser will then tell the defendant that they may indicate to the court how they would plead if the matter were to proceed to trial (the defendant is under no obligation to indicate their plea). The legal adviser will also tell the defendant that if they indicate a guilty plea, they will then be treated as having pleaded guilty before the magistrates, who may either sentence them or commit them to the Crown Court to be sentenced if they consider their own sentencing powers to be inadequate.

(c) The legal adviser will then ask the defendant to indicate their plea.

6.4.1 Indicating a guilty plea

If the defendant indicates a guilty plea, they are treated as having been tried summarily and convicted. The CPS representative will then outline the facts of the case to the magistrates and tell them about any previous convictions the defendant may have. The defendant's solicitor will then give a plea in mitigation on the defendant's behalf.

At this point the magistrates will need to decide if their sentencing powers are sufficient to deal with the case, or if the defendant should be sentenced by a Crown Court judge who has greater sentencing powers. The maximum sentence a magistrates' court may pass is six months' imprisonment for a defendant who is convicted of one either-way offence (note that this maximum period was extended to 12 months but has now been reduced again to six months (Sentencing Act 2020, s 224)) and up to a total of 12 months' imprisonment for two or more either-way offences.

The magistrates will determine whether their sentencing powers are sufficient by assessing the overall seriousness of the offence, looking at the guideline sentence in the Magistrates' Court Sentencing Guidelines and considering whether there are any aggravating or mitigating factors present which make the offence either more or less serious.

If the magistrates decide that their sentencing powers are sufficient, they will then either sentence the defendant straight away, or adjourn the case for a pre-sentence report before sentencing the defendant (the magistrates will also need to adjourn the case if they consider that a 'Newton hearing' is necessary – see **Chapter 11**). If the case is adjourned for sentence, the defendant will be released on bail or remanded in custody prior to the sentencing hearing.

If the magistrates decide that their sentencing powers are insufficient, they will commit the defendant to Crown Court for sentence pursuant to s 3 of the Powers of Criminal Courts (Sentencing) Act 2000. This section allows the magistrates to commit the defendant to Crown Court for sentence if they consider that the offence (or, if there is more than one offence, the combination of the offences) is so serious that the Crown Court should have the power to deal with the defendant as if they had been convicted at a Crown Court trial.

If the defendant is committed to the Crown Court for sentence, they will be remanded either in custody, or on bail. In most cases where a defendant pleads guilty at the plea before venue hearing and is committed to the Crown Court for sentence, the magistrates will not alter the position as regards bail or custody. Thus, when a defendant who has been on bail enters a guilty plea, the magistrates are likely to grant them bail, even if they anticipate that the defendant will receive a custodial sentence at the Crown Court. If a defendant who has been in custody enters a guilty plea at the plea before venue hearing, they are likely to remain in custody prior to the sentencing hearing at the Crown Court (*R v Rafferty* [1999] 1 Cr App R 235).

6.5 Procedure ss 19–20 and s 22A Magistrates' Courts Act 1980

If the defendant indicates a not guilty plea to an either-way offence in the following circumstances, the court shall send the defendant to the Crown Court for trial (CDA 1998, s 50A(3)(b)):

(a) the defendant is sent to the Crown Court for trial for a related offence;

(b) the defendant is charged jointly with another adult defendant who is sent to the Crown Court for trial for a related offence;

(c) the defendant is charged jointly, or charged with a related either-way offence, with a youth defendant who is sent to the Crown Court for trial.

In all other cases where a not guilty plea is indicated (or where the defendant refuses to enter a plea, as they are entitled to do), the court must determine whether the offence appears more suitable for summary trial or trial on indictment, ie make a decision as to allocation (Magistrates' Courts Act 1980, s 19(1)).

6.5.1 Allocation

A flowchart summarising the plea before venue, allocation and sending procedure is set out below.

The procedure, which is set out in the amended ss 19 and 20 of the Magistrates' Courts Act 1980, is as follows:

(a) The prosecution will inform the court of the facts and the defendant's previous convictions (if any) (s 19(2)(a)).

(b) The magistrates shall consider:

(i) any representations made by the prosecution or defence, as to whether summary trial or trial on indictment would be more suitable (s 19(2)(b)); and

(ii) whether the sentence which they would have power to impose for the offence would be adequate (s 19(3)(a)); and

(iii) the Allocation Guideline issued by the Sentencing Council. The Allocation Guideline states that, in general, either-way offences should be tried summarily unless it is likely that the court's sentencing powers will be insufficient. In addition, it states that the court should assess the likely sentence in the light of the facts alleged by the prosecution case, taking into account all aspects of the case, including those advanced by the defence. The magistrates will do this by considering the Magistrates' Court Sentencing Guidelines (MCSG) for the relevant offences.

(c) In considering the adequacy of its sentencing powers when dealing with two or more offences, the court should consider its potential sentencing powers in the light of the maximum aggregate sentence the magistrates could impose for all the offences taken together, if the charges could be joined in the same indictment or arise out of the same or connected circumstances (s 19(4)).

(d) If the court decides that the offence appears more suitable for trial on indictment, the defendant is sent forthwith to the Crown Court (Magistrates' Courts Act 1980, s 21).

(e) If the court decides that the case is more suitable for summary trial, it must explain to the defendant that:

   (i)   the case appears suitable for summary trial;

   (ii) they can consent to be tried summarily or choose to be tried on indictment; and

   (iii) if they consent to be tried summarily and are convicted, they may be committed to the Crown Court for sentence (Magistrates' Courts Act 1980, ss 20(1) and (2)).

(f) At this stage, the defendant may request an indication of sentence, ie an indication of whether a custodial or non-custodial sentence would be more likely if they were to be tried summarily and plead guilty. It should be no more specific than that (Magistrates' Courts Act 1980, ss 20(3)–(7) and 20A; CrimPR, Part 9). Under s 20A(1) of the Magistrates' Court Act 1980, where the case is dealt with in accordance with s 20(7), no court (whether a magistrates' court or not) may impose a custodial sentence for the offence unless such a sentence was indicated in the indication of sentence referred to in s 20. Further, s 20A(3) states that, subject to subsection (1), an indication of sentence shall not be binding on any court (whether a magistrates' court or not), and no sentence may be challenged or be the subject of appeal in any court on the ground that it is not consistent with an indication of sentence.

(g) The court may, but need not, give an indication of sentence. It would appear that the court cannot give an indication of sentence unless the defendant requests one. If the court gives an indication of sentence, the court should ask the defendant whether they want to reconsider the earlier indication of plea that was given.

(h) If the defendant indicates that they want to plead guilty, they are treated as if they had been tried summarily and pleaded guilty. In these circumstances, an indication of a non-custodial sentence will generally prevent a court from imposing a custodial sentence for the offence.

(i) If the defendant does not change their plea to guilty, the indication of sentence shall not be binding on any court, and in these circumstances no sentence may be challenged or be the subject of appeal in any court because it is not consistent with an indication of sentence. Equally, an indication of a custodial sentence does not prevent the court from imposing a non-custodial sentence.

(j) Where the court does not give an indication of sentence, whether requested to do so or not, or the defendant does not indicate that they want to reconsider the indication of plea or does not indicate that they would plead guilty, the court must ask the defendant whether they consent to summary trial or wish to be tried on indictment (Magistrates' Courts Act 1980, s 20(8) and (9)).

(k) If the defendant consents to summary trial, the court shall proceed to summary trial (Magistrates' Courts Act 1980, s 20(9)(a)).

(l) Under s 25 of the Magistrates' Court Act 1980, the prosecution (not the defence) are allowed to make an application, before summary trial begins and before any other application or issue in relation to the summary trial is dealt with, for an either-way offence allocated for summary trial to be sent to the Crown Court for trial. The court may grant the application only if it is satisfied that the sentence which a magistrates' court would

99

have power to impose for the offence would be inadequate. Where there is a successful application by the prosecution for the offence to be tried on indictment, the case will be sent forthwith to the Crown Court for trial.

(m) If the defendant does not consent to summary trial, they must be sent forthwith to the Crown Court for trial (Magistrates' Courts Act 1980, s 20(9)(b)).

⭐ *Example*

Caitlin has been charged with an offence of fraud by false representation and granted unconditional bail by the police. It is alleged that she tried to claim a refund on items from a shop that she claimed she had purchased when in fact she had not. The relevant items are valued at £1,500. Caitlin has a previous conviction from two years ago for benefit fraud. Caitlin intends to plead not guilty and is represented by her solicitor, Halim. Before her first appearance in the magistrates' court, Caitlin is granted legal aid and Halim obtains IDPC from the CPS. Halim obtains Caitlin's instructions on the prosecution evidence in advance of her first court appearance. Based on Caitlin's instructions, Halim advises her to plead not guilty and to elect trial in the Crown Court, if she is given the choice.

When Caitlin appears in court, the court's legal adviser first checks with Halim whether he is in receipt of IDPC and Halim confirms he is and that he has also taken his client's instructions on this and the case is ready to proceed to plea before venue. The legal adviser then reads out the charge and asks Caitlin to indicate her plea, explaining that if she indicates a guilty plea, she will then be treated as having pleaded guilty and the magistrates may then either sentence her or commit her to the Crown Court to be sentenced if they consider their own sentencing powers to be inadequate.

Caitlin indicates a not guilty plea. The prosecutor then informs the court about the facts of the case and also indicates which trial venue she believes to be most suitable. Halim is then invited to make representations as to which court he believes to be most suitable. In light of these submissions the magistrates will then decide whether or not to accept jurisdiction based on whether their sentencing powers would be sufficient to sentence Caitlin if she were convicted. In deciding this, the court will have regard to the Allocation Guideline issued by the Sentencing Council and the MCSGs for Fraud by False Representation. (Note the MCSGs recommend a starting point sentence for this type of fraud as a medium level community sentence with a sentence range from a fine up to 26 weeks in custody.)

The magistrates therefore decide the case is suitable to be tried in the magistrates' court. Caitlin is told this and also told that she can therefore consent to summary trial or elect trial on indictment in the Crown Court. She is also warned that if she consents to be tried summarily and is convicted, she may be committed to the Crown Court for sentence. Caitlin tells the court that she wants to be tried in the Crown Court. The case is then sent to the Crown Court and Caitlin is granted bail (which is not opposed by the prosecution) to attend her plea and trial preparation hearing in the Crown Court on a given date.

Note: where the court is dealing with two or more defendants charged with the same offence, if one of the defendants elects trial in the Crown Court, *all* of the defendants will be sent to the Crown Court for their joint trial regardless of the other defendant(s)'s decision on venue (CrimPR, r 9.2(6)(a)).

Figure 6.1 Flowchart – Plea before venue, allocation and sending procedure

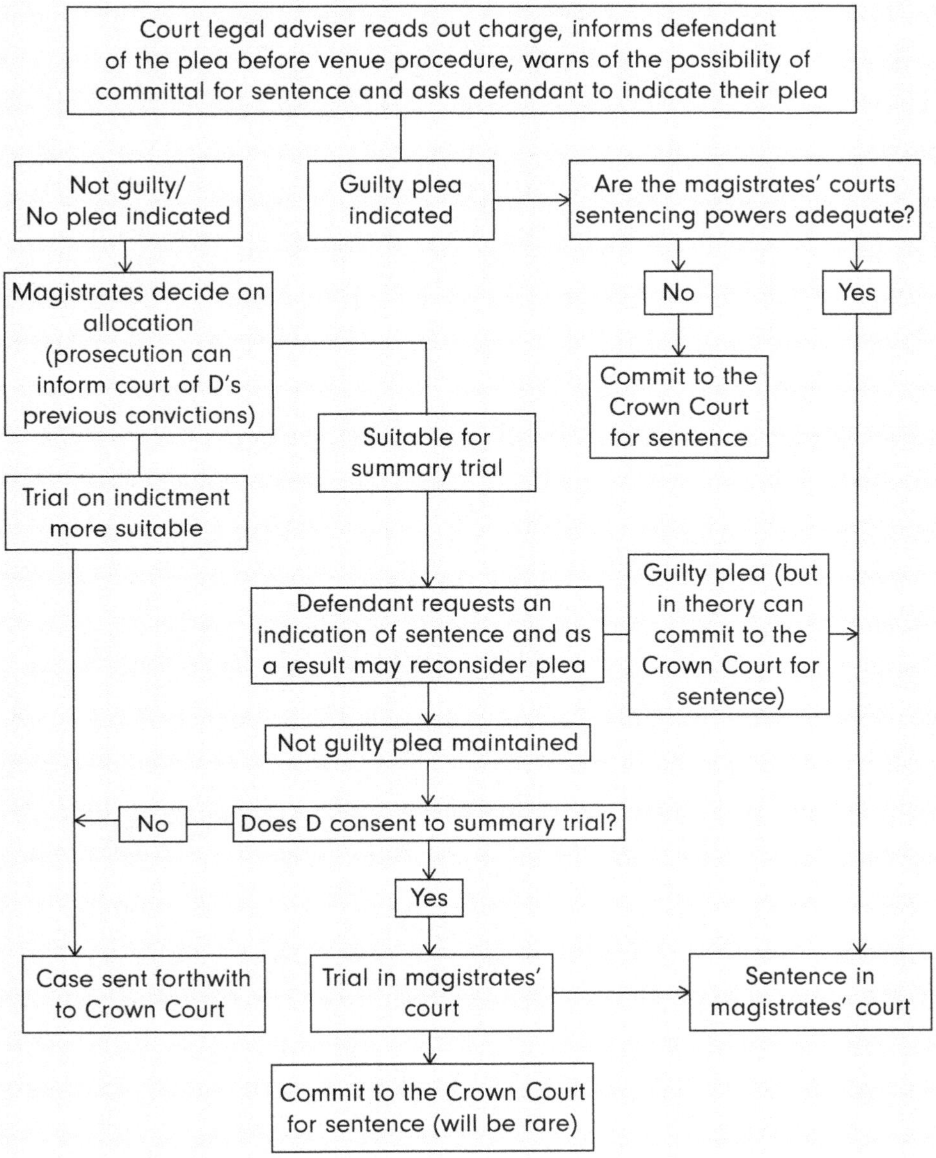

```
┌──────────────────────────────────────────────────────────────┐
│  Court legal adviser reads out charge, informs defendant       │
│  of the plea before venue procedure, warns of the possibility  │
│  of committal for sentence and asks defendant to indicate      │
│  their plea                                                    │
└──────────────────────────────────────────────────────────────┘
```

Not guilty/
No plea indicated

Guilty plea
indicated

Are the magistrates' courts
sentencing powers adequate?

No

Yes

Magistrates decide on
allocation
(prosecution can
inform court of D's
previous convictions)

Commit to the
Crown Court
for sentence

Suitable for
summary trial

Trial on indictment
more suitable

Defendant requests an
indication of sentence and as
a result may reconsider plea

Guilty plea (but
in theory can
commit to the
Crown Court for
sentence)

Not guilty plea maintained

No   Does D consent to summary trial?

Yes

Case sent forthwith
to Crown Court

Trial in magistrates'
court

Sentence in
magistrates' court

Commit to the Crown Court
for sentence (will be rare)

6.5.2   Different pleas at the plea before venue hearing

Occasionally a defendant who is charged with more than one either-way offence will indicate different pleas at the plea before venue hearing. The defendant may indicate a plea of guilty to one offence, but a plea of not guilty to the other. In such circumstances, the magistrates will proceed with the allocation hearing in respect of the offence to which the defendant has indicated a not guilty plea.

If, at the allocation hearing, the magistrates accept jurisdiction (and the defendant does not elect trial at the Crown Court), the magistrates will either sentence the defendant immediately for the offence to which they have pleaded guilty, or adjourn sentence until the end of the trial of the offence to which they have entered a not guilty plea.

If, at the allocation hearing, the magistrates decline jurisdiction (or the defendant elects trial at the Crown Court), the magistrates will send the offence to which the defendant has entered a not guilty plea to the Crown Court for trial. In this situation, the magistrates will then have a choice as to what to do with the offence to which the defendant has pleaded guilty. They may either sentence the defendant themselves or commit the defendant to the Crown Court for sentence.

6.6 Sending without allocation – s 50A Crime and Disorder Act 1998

In certain circumstances, either-way offences will be sent straight to the Crown Court in accordance with s 50A of the CDA 1998. These circumstances are as follows:

(a) Where notice, in serious or complex fraud cases, has been given by the DPP under s 51B of the 1998 Act. Notice is given to the court that the evidence is sufficient to put a person on trial for the offence, and the evidence reveals a case of fraud of such seriousness or complexity that the management of the case should without delay be taken over by the Crown Court.

(b) Where a notice, in certain cases involving children, has been served under s 51C of the CDA 1998. Notice is given to the court that the evidence is sufficient to put a person on trial for the offence, a child will be called as a witness and that for the purpose of avoiding any prejudice to the welfare of the child, the case should be taken over and proceed without delay by the Crown Court. The offences to which this procedure applies include assault or threat of injury to a person, child cruelty, certain sexual offences, kidnapping, false imprisonment and child abduction.

(c) Where there is an either-way offence related to an offence triable only on indictment, or one covered by a notice under s 51B or s 51C of the CDA 1998, in respect of which the same defendant is being sent to the Crown Court. Where a defendant is sent to the Crown Court for trial for an offence triable only on indictment, or for an offence in respect of which notice has been given under ss 51B or 51C of the CDA 1998, the court must at the same time send the defendant for trial for any either-way offence which appears to the court to be related (s 50A(3)(a)). However, where the defendant appears on the related either-way charge on a subsequent occasion, the court may send them for trial.

(d) Where there is an either-way offence related to an offence triable only on indictment, or one covered by a notice under s 51B or s 51C of the CDA 1998, in respect of which another defendant is being sent to the Crown Court (s 50A(3)(a)).

Summary

In this chapter you have considered what will happen where a defendant, who is charged with an either-way offence, makes their first appearance in the magistrates' court. Notably:

* *Prosecution obligation to provide IDPC.* Based on the information contained in the IDPC, the solicitor will take their client's instructions and then advise them on plea and venue.

* *Advising a defendant on trial venue.* Where a client has decided to plead not guilty, the solicitor will explain the advantages of each venue to their client and which of these they believe to the best venue for them. Ultimately, the client will need to decide where they want to be tried (if given the choice).

* *Procedure on defendant indicating plea.* This will depend on the plea indicated by the defendant and whether the magistrates' court believes it has sufficient powers of sentence to deal with the defendant if they indicate a guilty plea or are convicted following a trial.

- *Procedure ss 19–20 and s 22A Magistrates' Courts Act 1980*. Where the defendant indicates a not guilty plea, this part of the hearing focuses on the allocation decision, where the magistrates' court first decides if they have sufficient sentencing powers to deal with the case. If the court believes that its powers are inadequate, they will send the defendant to the Crown Court. If they believe they have sufficient powers, the defendant will then be given an unfettered choice as to trial venue (unless there is a co-accused who elects trial on indictment).

- *Sending without allocation – s 50A Crime and Disorder Act 1998*. This is possible in a limited number of circumstances, including serious/complex fraud cases; some cases involving children and an either-way offence linked to an offence triable only on indictment.

Sample questions

Question 1

A defendant has been jointly charged with an offence of affray. At his first court appearance in the magistrates' court his solicitor advises him on plea and trial venue before his case is called on. The defendant intends to indicate a not guilty plea and decides to consent to summary trial if he is given the choice.

Which of the following best describes whether the defendant's trial will take place in the magistrates' court?

A   If both defendants consent to summary trial, the trial must take place in the magistrates' court.

B   If the defendant consents to summary trial, the trial is likely to take place in the magistrates' court regardless of the other defendant's decision.

C   If the magistrates decide the offence to be more suitable for summary trial and both defendants consent to summary, the trial will take place in the magistrates' court.

D   If the defendant consents to summary trial, the trial is likely to take place in the magistrates' court even if the other defendant elects trial on indictment.

E   If the magistrates decide the offence to be more suitable for trial on indictment and the other defendant also consents to summary trial, the trial will take place in the magistrates' court.

Answer

Option C is the best answer. CrimPR, r 9.2(6)(a) provides that where the court is dealing with two or more defendants charged with the same offence, if one of the defendants elects trial in the Crown Court, *all* of the defendants will be sent to the Crown Court for their joint trial regardless of the other defendant(s)'s decision on venue. The trial will therefore only take place in the magistrates' court if the magistrates decide the offence to be more suitable for summary trial and *both* defendants consent to summary trial. Option A is not the best answer because it fails to deal first with the magistrates accepting jurisdiction. Options B and D are wrong because both defendants have to consent to summary trial. Option E is wrong because if the magistrates decide the offence to be more suitable for trial on indictment, the case must be sent to the Crown Court for trial and the defendants will not get a choice.

Question 2

A man has been charged with an offence of rape and sexual assault in relation to the same complainant. Both are alleged to have occurred within a few days of each other. The man intends to plead not guilty to both charges and wants to know which court or courts will deal with these cases.

Which of the following best describes the advice the man should be given?

A   Both cases are likely to be tried in the Crown Court as rape is triable only on indictment.

B   The rape charge will be dealt with in the Crown Court and the sexual assault charge may be dealt with in the Crown Court if the magistrates decide their powers of punishment are inadequate to deal with it.

C   The rape charge will be dealt with in the Crown Court and the sexual assault charge will only be dealt with in the Crown Court if the man elects trial on indictment.

D   Both cases will be tried in the Crown Court as both charges relate to indictable offences.

E   Both cases will be tried in the Crown Court as the sexual assault charge is related to the rape charge.

Answer

Option E is the best answer. The either-way offence (sexual assault) relates to an offence triable only on indictment (rape) because they are alleged to have taken place over a similar time period and both relate to the same complainant (CDA 1998, s 50A(3)(a)). Consequently, the sexual assault charge will be sent to the Crown Court without an allocation hearing by virtue of s 50A CDA 1998. So, option A is wrong because both cases *will* be tried in the Crown Court, as opposed to being *likely* to be tried there. Options B and C are wrong because there will be no allocation hearing. Option D is not the best answer because although both offences are *indictable offences*, the reason they will be both dealt with in the Crown Court is because the either-way offence is related to the offence that can only be tried on indictment.

Question 3

A woman appears in the magistrates' court charged with an offence of assault occasioning actual bodily harm and an offence of theft. At the plea before venue hearing she indicates a not guilty plea to the assault matter and a guilty plea in relation to the theft matter. The magistrates accept jurisdiction to deal with the assault, but the woman elects trial on indictment.

Which court will sentence the woman for the offence of theft?

A   The magistrates' court will sentence the woman for the offence of theft as they have already accepted jurisdiction to deal with the assault matter.

B   The magistrates' court will have a choice to either sentence the woman for the offence of theft or to commit her to the Crown Court to be sentenced there.

C   The woman will be able to choose which court she is sentenced by.

D   The Crown Court will sentence the woman after her trial for the assault matter has been concluded.

E   The Crown Court will sentence the woman before her trial for the assault matter takes place.

Answer

Option B is the best answer. In this situation, the magistrates have a choice as to what to do with the offence to which the defendant has pleaded guilty. They may either sentence the defendant themselves or commit the defendant to the Crown Court for sentence. This will often depend on whether the two offences are linked or not. If they are not, the magistrates' court may be more likely to sentence the offender, whereas if they are linked, the magistrates may be more likely to send them both up to the Crown Court to be dealt with. Option A is therefore wrong as accepting jurisdiction to deal with the assault matter will not necessarily have any bearing on their decision to sentence for the theft. Option C is wrong, because a defendant will never be able to choose which court sentences her for an either-way offence. This decision will always be for the magistrates' court to take. Options D and E are wrong because although the theft offence could be committed to the Crown Court for sentence, this will not necessarily be the case.

7 Bail

SQE1 syllabus

This chapter will enable you to achieve the SQE1 Assessment Specification in relation to Functioning Legal Knowledge concerned with the following procedures and processes:

- the right to bail and exceptions;
- conditional bail;
- procedure for applying for bail;
- further applications for bail;
- appeals against decisions on bail;
- absconding and breaches of bail.

Note that, for SQE1, candidates are not usually required to recall specific case names or cite statutory or regulatory authorities. These are provided for illustrative purposes only unless otherwise stated.

Learning outcomes

By the end of this chapter you will be able to apply relevant core legal principles and rules appropriately and effectively, at the level of a competent newly qualified solicitor in practice, to realistic client-based and ethical problems and situations in the following areas:

- Remand periods and custody time limits which apply in the magistrates' court.
- The presumption in favour of bail which applies to most types of defendant and the exceptions to the right to bail.
- The difference between the grounds on which bail may be refused by the court and the factors to be taken into account in deciding whether those grounds are satisfied and the conditions which may be attached to a grant of bail.

- Making an application for bail and when further applications for bail may be made to the magistrates' court if the initial application is unsuccessful.

- Appealing to the Crown Court against a bail decision by the magistrates' court.

- The consequences for a defendant who fails to answer their bail, or who breaches any conditions attached to their bail.

7.1 Introduction

Many criminal cases are unlikely to be completed on the first occasion on which the defendant appears before the magistrates' court. This will only usually happen in the case of a straightforward summary or either-way offence where the defendant pleads guilty and the magistrates sentence them immediately (see **6.4** above). In any other type of case there will need to be one or more adjournments before the case is concluded.

7.2 Remands and custody time limits

When a case is adjourned by the court, the defendant will be remanded. So, a 'remand' is an adjournment where the court will want to ensure that the defendant attends the next hearing. A defendant may be remanded in one of three ways:

(a) a remand in custody;

(b) a remand on bail with conditions attached to that bail; or

(c) a remand on unconditional bail.

7.2.1 Remands before conviction

7.2.1.1 Remands in custody

The basic rule

The basic rule is that a defendant may not be remanded in custody for more than eight clear days at a time. However, if the defendant's case is still in the magistrates' court, where there are successive remands in custody, the defendant needs to be brought before the court on every fourth remand, provided they have consented to this and have legal representation. In addition, the court may remand a defendant in custody for up to 28 days if:

(a) it has previously remanded them in custody for the same offence; and

(b) they are before the court; and

(c) it can set a date to remand them to on which it expects the next stage of the proceedings to take place.

⭐ *Example*

Aiden is charged with theft. He is refused bail by the police and appears before a Saturday morning remand court in custody on 3 April. Aiden's solicitor makes an application for bail which is refused. Aiden is remanded in custody by the magistrates for six days and so appears before the court again on Friday, 9 April. At the hearing on 9 April the prosecution provides initial details of the prosecution case to the defence and Aiden indicates a not guilty plea at the plea before venue hearing. The magistrates accept jurisdiction and Aiden consents to summary trial. Aiden's solicitor makes another bail application and the magistrates refuse bail again and remand Aiden in custody for 28 days until 7 May when a case management hearing will take place. The magistrates are able to do this because Aiden is before the court, he has previously been remanded in custody and the next stage of proceedings (the case management hearing) can take place at the next hearing. (In practice, the hearing on 9 April will usually be conducted by live video link with the prison or remand centre where Aiden is being held, rather than Aiden being brought to court.)

Custody time limits (CrimPR, r 14.18 and r 14.19)

Time limits exist to ensure that defendants who are remanded in custody have their cases brought promptly to trial (Prosecution of Offences (Custody Time Limits) Regulations 1987 (SI 1987/299)). The overall maximum period of remand in custody (normally referred to as the custody time limit) in the magistrates' court is 70 days before trial for an either-way offence and 56 days before trial for a summary-only offence. However, if the case involves an either-way offence and the allocation hearing takes place within 56 days, the custody time limit for the either-way offence is reduced to 56 days.

The prosecution may apply to the court to extend the custody time limit, although for an application to be successful the prosecution will need to show on the balance of probabilities that there is good and sufficient cause to do this and that it has acted with due diligence and expedition (Prosecution of Offences Act 1985, s 22). The application may be made orally or in writing, although a written notice of intention must be served on the court and the defendant not less than two days before the hearing in the magistrates' court. Unless the prosecution makes a successful application to extend the custody time limit, once the time limit has expired, the defendant must be released on bail until his trial. If the magistrates grant a prosecution application to extend the custody time limit, the defendant has a right of appeal to the Crown Court. Similarly, the prosecution may appeal to the Crown Court against the magistrates' refusal to extend the custody time limit.

Where will the defendant be kept whilst in custody?

Defendants who are remanded in custody will normally be kept at a prison or remand centre. However, s 128(7) of the Magistrates' Courts Act 1980 allows a magistrates' court to remand a defendant to police custody for up to three days if this is necessary for the purposes of making enquiries in relation to offences other than the offence for which the defendant has been charged. The CPS is likely to apply for such a remand when a defendant has been arrested and charged for one offence, but the police suspect their involvement in other matters about which they wish to interview them. A defendant made subject to such a remand must be brought back before the magistrates as soon as the need to make enquiries has ceased. Whilst they are at the police station, the defendant is entitled to the same rights as if they had been arrested and detained prior to charge (for example, the right to free legal advice; see **1.3.1** above).

7.2.1.2   Remands on bail

A defendant who is on bail may be remanded prior to conviction for any period of time, subject to the defendant's consent.

7.2.1.3   Remands after case committed or sent to Crown Court

A defendant who is committed to the Crown Court for sentence, or whose case is sent to the Crown Court for trial, may be remanded in custody or on bail until the case comes before the Crown Court.

7.2.2   **Remands after conviction**

Following conviction, a defendant may be remanded in custody before sentence (usually for the preparation of pre-sentence reports; see **Chapter 11**) for successive periods of not more than three weeks. If the defendant is remanded on bail, this may be for successive periods of not more than four weeks.

7.3 The right to bail

The substantive law concerning the grant or refusal of bail is contained predominantly in the Bail Act 1976. The procedural rules which are relevant to the issue of bail are found in Part 14 of the CrimPR.

Under s 4 of the Bail Act 1976, there is a presumption that bail will be granted to the following types of defendants (unless one or more exceptions apply):

(a) all defendants prior to conviction;

(b) defendants who have been convicted if their case has been adjourned for the court to obtain reports before sentencing (see **Chapter 11**); and

(c) defendants who are appearing before the court for breach of a community sentence.

The presumption in favour of bail does not apply to defendants:

(a) who have been committed to the Crown Court for sentence (see **Chapter 6**); or

(b) who are appealing against conviction or sentence (see **Chapter 12**).

The only other limitation on the presumption that bail will be granted is in respect of defendants charged with the most serious types of offence. Under s 25 of the CJPOA 1994, if the defendant is charged with one of a number of specified offences or has previously been convicted of any of these specified offences, a court may grant bail to that defendant only if exceptional circumstances exist. The specified offences are:

(a) murder

(b) attempted murder

(c) manslaughter

(d) rape

(e) attempted rape

(f) a number of other serious sexual offences.

✪ Example

David has been charged with an offence of rape and appears before the magistrates' court from police custody following charge. David has a previous conviction five years ago for attempted rape. Because David has a previous conviction for a s 25 offence and has now been charged with another s 25 offence, he loses the presumption in favour of bail under s 4 of the Bail Act 1976. This will mean that he can still apply for bail, but the impact of s 25 effectively means he will now bear the burden of persuading the court why they should grant bail (no doubt with stringent bail conditions attached) rather than the prosecution being required to persuade the court why the normal right to bail should be withheld.

Where a defendant is charged with murder and makes an application for bail, s 115 of the Coroners and Justice Act 2009 (which has amended the power in s 25 of the Criminal Justice and Public Order Act 1994) states that only a Crown Court judge may grant bail. The magistrates' court must transfer the defendant to the Crown Court (in custody). A Crown Court judge must then, within 48 hours, make a decision as to whether to grant bail. Section 114(2) of the Coroners and Justice Act 2009 provides that bail may not be granted, in these circumstances, unless the court is of the opinion that there is no significant risk of the defendant committing, whilst on bail, an offence likely to cause physical or mental injury to another.

7.3.1 Exceptions to the right to bail

7.3.1.1 'No real prospect of custody' restriction

The exceptions to the presumption in favour of bail in relation to imprisonable offences are set out in paras 2 to 7 of Part 1 of Sch 1 to the Bail Act 1976 (see **7.3.1.2**).

However, there is a restriction on the exceptions applying in relation to bail in proceedings where:

(a) the defendant has attained the age of 18;

(b) the defendant has not been convicted of an offence in those proceedings; and

(c) it appears to the court that there is *no real prospect* that the defendant will be sentenced to a custodial sentence in the proceedings.

In such circumstances, a magistrates' court will not have power to remand a defendant in custody before his case is dealt with.

7.3.1.2 Offences triable only on indictment and either-way imprisonable offences

Paragraphs 2 to 7 of Part 1 of Sch 1 to the Bail Act 1976 provide the relevant law, including:

2. (1) The defendant need not be granted bail if the court is satisfied that there are substantial grounds for believing that the defendant, if released on bail (whether subject to conditions or not) would:

(a) fail to surrender to custody, or

(b) commit an offence while on bail, or

(c) interfere with witnesses or otherwise obstruct the course of justice, whether in relation to himself or any other person.

3. The defendant need not be granted bail if the court is satisfied that the defendant should be kept in custody for their own protection or, if they are a child or young person, for their own welfare.

5. The defendant need not be granted bail where the court is satisfied that it has not been practicable to obtain sufficient information for the purpose of taking the decisions required by this Part of this Schedule for want of time since the institution of the proceedings against them.

6. The defendant need not be granted bail if, having previously been released on bail in, or in connection with, the proceedings, the defendant has been arrested in pursuance of section 7.

6ZA. If the defendant is charged with murder, the defendant may not be granted bail unless the court is of the opinion that there is no significant risk of the defendant committing, while on bail, an offence that would, or would be likely to, cause physical or mental injury to any person other than the defendant.

The most common grounds upon which the CPS normally objects to bail being granted to a defendant are those set out in para 2(1) above, namely, that there are *substantial grounds* for believing that the defendant will, if released on bail:

(a) fail to surrender to custody;

(b) commit an offence whilst on bail; or

(c) interfere with a witness in the case (or otherwise obstruct the course of justice).

Note therefore that this is a high threshold. It will not be satisfied if the court only believes the defendant *may* do any of these three things.

In deciding whether any of these grounds is satisfied, the court must take into account the following factors (Bail Act 1976, Sch 1, Pt 1, para 9):

(a) the nature and seriousness of the offence (and the probable sentence the defendant will receive for it);

(b) the character, antecedents, associations and community ties of the defendant;

(c) the defendant's record in respect of previous grants of bail in criminal proceedings; and

(d) the strength of the evidence against the defendant.

The nature and seriousness of the offence and the probable method of dealing with the defendant for it (and the strength of the evidence against the defendant)

These two factors are often linked. They are most likely to be relevant to a prosecution argument that there are substantial grounds for believing that the defendant would fail to surrender to custody if they were to be granted bail. If the defendant has been charged with a serious offence that is likely to result in a prison sentence if they are convicted and the evidence against the defendant is strong, the CPS may argue that the defendant will fail to surrender to custody (usually referred to as absconding) to avoid such a fate.

 Example

> *Bilal pleads not guilty to a charge of wounding with intent. The prosecution allege that Bilal attacked his victim with a hammer in an unprovoked assault, causing the victim to suffer head injuries from which he will never fully recover. They also claim there is compelling CCTV evidence showing that Bilal attacked the victim in this way. This is a serious offence and, if convicted, Bilal will receive a lengthy prison sentence. The prosecution will argue that Bilal should be denied bail as there are substantial grounds for believing that, if granted bail, Bilal will fail to surrender to custody. The factors they will rely on to support this is that if Bilal is convicted, the court will deal with the matter by way of a lengthy custodial sentence, and Bilal will abscond to avoid being sent to prison. Moreover, the CCTV evidence against Bilal is very strong and so he will almost certainly be convicted.*

The defendant's character, antecedents, associations and community ties

Character and antecedents

The reference to a defendant's character and antecedents is a reference to the defendant's previous convictions. A defendant's criminal record may be raised by the CPS when bail is being considered, to argue that there are substantial grounds for believing that the defendant will commit further offences if they are released on bail. This is likely to be relevant if the defendant has a history of committing the same (or similar) types of offence as that with which they have been charged. It will also be an argument raised by the prosecution if the reason for the defendant's previous offending is ongoing (such as a serial shoplifter who steals to fund a drug addiction), or if the defendant has previously committed offences whilst on bail.

 Examples

> *Claire pleads not guilty to a charge of shoplifting. Claire has 10 previous convictions for the same type of offence within the last three years. Claire's previous offences were committed to obtain money to support her heroin addiction (which is ongoing). The CPS will argue that Claire should be denied bail as there are substantial grounds for believing that, if granted bail, Claire will commit further offences. The factor it will rely on to support this is that Claire's character and antecedents indicate that she commits this type of offence on a regular basis to support her ongoing drug addiction.*

> *Damien pleads not guilty to a charge of theft. Damien's list of previous convictions reveals that he has twice been convicted of other property-related offences which were committed whilst he was on bail for other matters. The CPS will argue that Damien should be denied bail as there are substantial grounds for believing that, if released on bail, Damien will commit further offences. The factor it will rely on to support this is that Damien's previous convictions show a history of offending whilst on bail.*

> *Ethan pleads not guilty to a charge of assault occasioning actual bodily harm. Six months previously, Ethan was convicted of unlawful wounding and received a sentence of 12 months' imprisonment, suspended for two years. The evidence against Ethan in*

respect of the current charge is strong, consisting of good quality identification evidence and a confession Ethan is alleged to have made when first arrested. The CPS will argue that Ethan should be denied bail as there are substantial grounds for believing that, if released on bail, Ethan would fail to surrender to custody. The factor it will rely on to support this is that Ethan's antecedents show he is subject to a suspended sentence of imprisonment which is likely to be activated if Ethan is convicted of the current offence. Ethan is also likely to be convicted because of the strength of the evidence against him.

Associations

The reference to the defendant's associations may be relevant to a prosecution argument that, if released on bail, there are substantial grounds for believing that the defendant will commit further offences.

For example, if a defendant is known to associate with other criminals, or is alleged to be a member of a criminal gang, the CPS may use this to suggest there are 'substantial grounds' to believe that they may commit further offences if released on bail.

The CPS may also suggest that a defendant's associations are relevant if a witness is known to the defendant and there is a fear that the defendant may attempt to interfere with the witness. This often arises in the case of domestic assaults when the victim is a relative of the defendant and there is a fear that the defendant may put pressure on the victim to 'change their story'.

 ### Examples

Fariq pleads not guilty to a charge of armed robbery of a bank. The CPS alleges that Fariq is a member of a criminal gang responsible for several similar armed robberies. None of the other members of the gang have as yet been identified or arrested by the police, and none of the proceeds from the bank robberies have been recovered. The CPS will argue that Fariq should be denied bail as there are substantial grounds for believing that, if released on bail, Fariq would commit further offences. The factor it will rely on is that Fariq's associations include membership of a gang responsible for a series of armed robberies, the other members of which are still at large.

Gavin pleads not guilty to a charge of sexual assault. The CPS alleges that Gavin sexually assaulted his 11-year-old daughter (who lives at the same address as Gavin). In her statement to the police, Gavin's daughter has said that Gavin has threatened to 'shut her up' unless she changes her story. The CPS will argue that Gavin should be denied bail on the basis that there are substantial grounds for believing that, if granted bail, Gavin will attempt to interfere with a witness. The factor it will rely on to support this is that Gavin is closely associated with his alleged victim. Gavin and his victim share the same home, and the victim has already indicated that he has attempted to persuade her to change her story.

Community ties

The strength or otherwise of a defendant's community ties will be relevant to an argument that there are substantial grounds for believing that the defendant will fail to surrender to custody if released on bail. If, for example, the defendant is unemployed, has no relatives in the local area, has lived in the area only for a short time or is of no fixed abode, the CPS may argue that there is nothing to keep them in the area and nothing to prevent them from absconding.

 ### Example

Harry pleads not guilty to a charge of possession of Class A drugs. Harry is unemployed and lives alone in bedsit accommodation. Harry has no family or known friends in the local area, and most of his relatives are known to live some 200 miles away. Harry moved

to the area only some three months ago. The CPS will argue that Harry should be denied bail as there are substantial grounds for believing that, if granted bail, Harry will fail to surrender to custody. The factor it will rely on to support this is Harry's lack of community ties, because Harry appears to have nothing to tie him to the local area.

The defendant's record in relation to previous grants of bail

If a defendant has previous conviction(s) for the offence of absconding (ie failing to answer their bail – see **7.8** below), the CPS is likely to raise this to suggest that there are substantial grounds for believing that the defendant will fail to surrender if they are granted bail in the current proceedings.

⭐ *Example*

Ivan pleads not guilty to a charge of affray. Ivan has three previous convictions for failing to answer bail in relation to other public order offences with which he was charged. The CPS will argue that Ivan should be denied bail as there are substantial grounds for believing that, if granted bail, Ivan will fail to surrender to custody. The factor it will rely upon to support this is that Ivan's record in relation to previous grants of bail shows that he has a history of failing to answer his bail.

7.3.1.3   Summary-only imprisonable offences

Note that similar, but not identical, grounds and factors for refusing bail apply to these type of summary offences.

Section 52 of and Sch 12 to the Criminal Justice and Immigration Act (CJIA) 2008 have amended the law on bail in respect of summary-only imprisonable offences.

Bail for these offences may be refused only on one or more of the following grounds:

(a)   failure to surrender (if the defendant has previously failed to surrender);

(b)   commission of further offences (if the instant offence was committed on bail);

(c)   fear of commission of offences likely to cause another person to suffer or fear physical or mental injury;

(d)   defendant's own protection (or welfare if a youth);

(e)   defendant serving custody;

(f)   fear of failure to surrender, commission of offences, interference with witnesses or obstruction of justice (if the defendant has been arrested for breach of bail in respect of the instant offence); and

(g)   lack of sufficient information.

7.3.1.4   Non-imprisonable offences

It is extremely rare for a defendant charged with a non-imprisonable offence not to be granted bail, as there are only very limited circumstances in which the CPS would ever oppose the grant of bail to such a defendant.

Under Sch 1, Pt II to the Bail Act 1976, the court may refuse bail to a defendant charged with a non-imprisonable offence only if:

(a)   the defendant was granted bail in previous criminal proceedings but failed to answer this bail and the court believes that, if granted bail in the current proceedings, the defendant would again fail to surrender to custody;

(b)   the defendant needs to be kept in custody for his own protection or, in the case of a defendant under 18 years of age, for his own welfare;

(c) the defendant is currently serving a custodial sentence in respect of a separate offence; or

(d) the defendant was granted bail at an earlier hearing in the same proceedings, but has been arrested either for failing to answer his bail or for breaking any conditions of his bail, and the court is satisfied that there are substantial grounds for believing that, if released on bail, the defendant would fail to surrender to custody, commit an offence or interfere with witnesses or otherwise obstruct the course of justice.

7.4 Conditional bail

When a defence advocate is making an application for bail on behalf of their client, they will normally invite the magistrates to consider granting conditional bail to their client if the magistrates are not minded to grant bail on an unconditional basis.

A court has the power to grant bail to a defendant subject to the defendant complying with one or more conditions that the court attaches to that bail. Section 3(6) of the Bail Act 1976 requires that such conditions must be necessary to:

(a) prevent the defendant from absconding;

(b) prevent the defendant committing a further offence whilst on bail;

(c) prevent the defendant interfering with witnesses or obstructing the course of justice;

(d) ensure that the defendant makes himself available for the purpose of obtaining medical or other reports;

(e) ensure that the defendant keeps an appointment with his solicitor; or

(f) ensure the defendant's own protection or, in the case of a defendant aged under 18, for his own welfare or in his own interests.

The most common conditions that the court may impose are set out in the table below.

Condition	Bail ground aimed at overcoming	Key points
Sureties	Absconding	A surety is a person who enters into what is termed a 'recognisance' of money and is under an obligation to use every reasonable effort to ensure that the defendant attends court. If the defendant fails to answer their bail at the next hearing, the court must declare the immediate and automatic forfeiture of the recognisance. The court will order the surety to appear before the court to explain why they should not pay over the sum. The court will then determine whether some or all of the surety should be paid. A court is unlikely to accept as a surety a person who has a criminal record, who lives a long distance from the defendant or who has no financial means. As a matter of professional conduct, a solicitor should never stand surety for a defendant.

(continued)

(*continued*)

Condition	Bail ground aimed at overcoming	Key points
Security	Absconding	The defendant will be required to deposit a sum of money (or goods) with the court. If the defendant fails to attend court to answer their bail, they will forfeit the security they have given.
Reporting to a police station	Absconding and committing offences on bail	The court orders the defendant to report to their local police station on a regular basis (on specified day(s) and time) so the police may ensure that the defendant remains in the local area.
Residence	Absconding and committing offences on bail	The court requires the defendant to reside at a specified address. The police will often check that such a condition is being complied with by visiting the address late at night or early in the morning.
Curfew	Committing offences on bail	The court requires a defendant to remain at their place of residence between certain specified hours (for example, between 8 pm and 7 am). The police may visit the residence during these hours to check that the defendant is there. To support conditions of residence and curfew, the court may order that the defendant be electronically monitored (commonly referred to as 'tagging').
Non-communication with prosecution witnesses	Committing offences on bail and interfering with a witness	This condition not only covers direct face-to-face contact with the witnesses, but also indirect contact such as through a third party or contacting the witnesses by telephone or in writing or through any other means such as social media.
Restriction on entering specified areas	Committing offences on bail and interfering with a witness	This prevents the defendant from entering a geographical area or town, for example where a prosecution witness resides, or where the defendant habitually commits offences in the same place or type of place, such as theft from a shopping centre or committing assaults in a city centre.
Attending appointments with his solicitor or the Probation Service		Requires a defendant to keep in regular touch with his solicitor to ensure that the case is not delayed because the defendant has failed to provide their solicitor with prompt instructions.
Surrender of passport	Absconding	Requires a defendant to surrender their passport. Only likely to be appropriate in serious cases where the defendant is known to have substantial financial assets or criminal contacts outside the UK.

Figure 7.1   Will the defendant be granted bail?

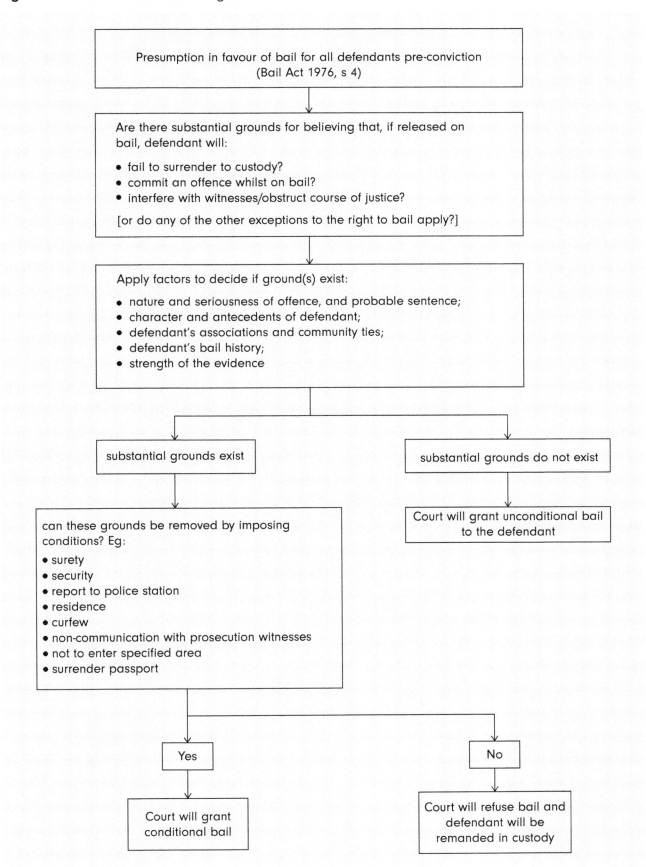

7.5   Procedure for applying for bail

If the CPS objects to bail being granted, the following procedure will take place at court:

(a) The CPS representative must, as soon as practicable, provide the defendant's solicitor, and the court, with all of the information in its possession which is material to what the court must decide (CrimPR, r 14.5(2)).

(b) The CPS representative will state its objection to bail and apply to the magistrates for the defendant to be remanded in custody. If relevant, they will hand the magistrates a list of the defendant's previous convictions and then outline the grounds on which the prosecution objects to bail being granted. The CPS representative will support these grounds by citing the relevant details of the case and applying the factors referred to at **7.3.1.2** above.

(c) The defendant's solicitor will then make an application for bail on their client's behalf. They should take each of the prosecution grounds for objecting to bail in turn and respond to these, applying, where appropriate, the same factors. The defendant's solicitor may suggest appropriate conditions, which the magistrates may impose if they are not prepared to grant unconditional bail.

(d) The magistrates may hear evidence from other persons in support of the defendant's application for bail, such as a prospective employer if the defendant has recently been offered employment, or a person who is prepared to provide the defendant with accommodation if the defendant is currently of no fixed abode.

(e) The magistrates will then decide whether to remand the defendant in custody or on bail. If the magistrates grant bail to the defendant, they will specify any conditions on that bail which they consider necessary. If bail is granted subject to a surety, the court will hear evidence on oath from the surety to ensure that they are suitable to act in that capacity.

A record of the magistrates' decision will be made and a copy of this given to the defendant. If the magistrates refuse bail or grant bail subject to conditions, reasons for the refusal or reasons for the conditions must also be recorded and a copy given to the defendant (this is known as a 'certificate of full argument'). If the CPS opposed bail but bail is granted by the magistrates, a record must be made of the reasons for granting bail and a copy given to the CPS upon request.

A flowchart showing the procedure at a contested bail application is set out below.

Figure 7.2 Contested bail application procedure

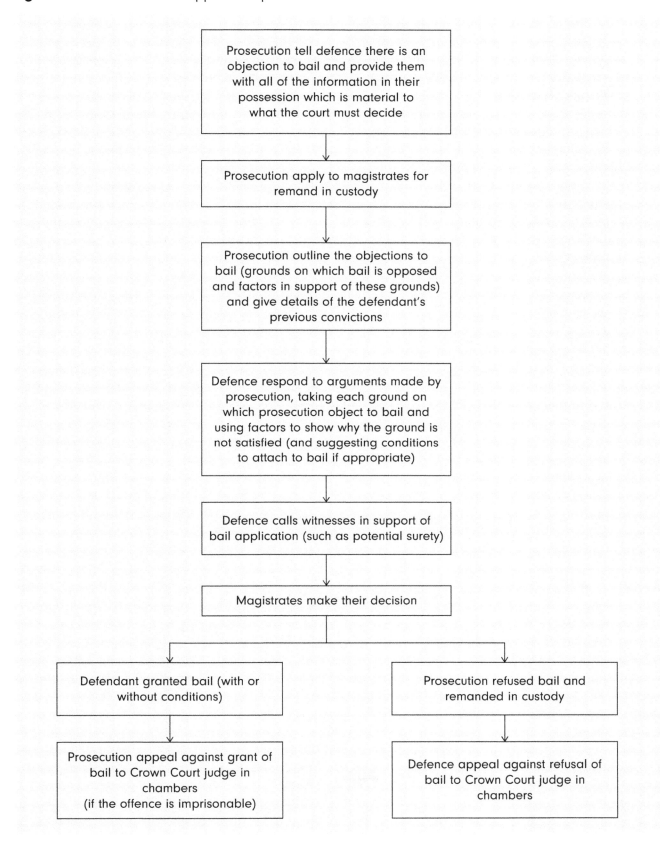

7.6 Further applications for bail

If bail is refused, the magistrates are under a duty to consider the question of bail at any subsequent hearing if the defendant is still in custody and the presumption in favour of bail (see **7.3** above) still applies. However, this does not mean that the defendant's solicitor is permitted to make a full bail application at each subsequent hearing.

At the first hearing after the hearing at which the court refused to grant bail, the defendant's solicitor is permitted to make a full application for bail using any argument as to fact or law, even if they used the same arguments in their first unsuccessful application. At any subsequent hearing, the court need not hear arguments as to fact or law which it has heard previously (Bail Act 1976, Sch 1, Pt IIA).

Thus, a defendant who is refused bail is entitled to have their advocate make one further full bail application in the magistrates' court, but if this is refused, the advocate may make a further bail application only if they are able to raise a *new* legal or factual argument as to why bail should be granted.

 Example

> *Johan makes his first appearance before the magistrates on 14 May. His advocate makes a full application for bail, but this is refused, and Johan is remanded in custody for seven days. When Johan appears before the court again on 21 May, his advocate may make a further full application for bail using any argument as to fact or law, whether or not this argument was used in the bail application made on 14 May. If the magistrates refuse bail on 21 May, Johan's advocate can make a further application for bail only if she can raise a new argument that she has not used previously. For example, a potential surety might have become available, or Johan might have been offered employment.*

Note: such further applications will only be possible in the magistrates' court if the defendant's case is still in that court. If the defendant has been sent or transferred to the Crown Court, any further bail applications will have to be made in that court.

7.7 Appeals against decisions on bail

7.7.1 Appeals by the defendant (CrimPR, r 14.8)

A defendant who is refused bail by the magistrates' court (or who has been refused an application to vary a bail condition) may appeal against this decision to the Crown Court provided the magistrates have issued the 'certificate of full argument' referred to in **7.5** above. Although a defendant may make an appeal to the Crown Court after the magistrates have made an initial refusal of bail, for tactical reasons most defence solicitors will usually delay making an appeal to the Crown Court until they have made two full applications for bail before the magistrates' court. Delaying an appeal until after the second full application before the magistrates maximises the number of potentially successful applications for bail which the defendant will be able to make.

To appeal, the defendant's solicitor must complete a notice of application (on the prescribed form) as soon as practicable after the magistrates' court's decision. This notice needs to be sent to the Crown Court and magistrates' court and also served on the CPS (and any surety affected or proposed). The notice of application will specify the decision the defendant wants the Crown Court to make (eg to grant bail or vary a bail condition) and each offence the defendant has been charged with. The notice should also explain why the Crown Court should grant bail (ie set out the arguments for why bail should be granted or conditions varied) as well as explaining any further information or legal argument that has come to light, if any, since the magistrates' decision. The notice should also set out any suggested conditions to bail.

If the prosecution oppose the appeal, they must notify the Crown Court and the defence at once of the reasons why they are opposing the appeal.

Unless the Crown Court otherwise directs, the appeal should be heard as soon as practicable and in any event no later than the business day after it was served, although note that the Crown Court can vary these time limits.

The appeal will then be heard before a Crown Court judge in chambers, so will normally take place shortly after the notice of application has been sent to the Crown Court. The judge will need to have the following documents before them when considering the application:

(a) the notice of application;

(b) the 'certificate of full argument'; and

(c) a record of the defendant's previous convictions (if applicable).

At the hearing in chambers, the judge will hear representations from the CPS and the defendant's advocate. The judge may refuse the defendant's appeal or grant it, with or without bail conditions. If the judge grants bail, a copy of the judge's order will need to be sent to the prison or remand centre where the defendant is being held so that the defendant may be released from custody.

7.7.2 Appeals by the prosecution (CrimPR, r 14.9)

If the magistrates grant bail to a defendant who has been charged with an imprisonable offence, s 1 of the Bail (Amendment) Act 1993 gives the CPS the right to appeal against this decision to a Crown Court judge in chambers.

Essentially the main requirements contain three sets of deadlines to follow:

*   Oral notice must be given by the prosecutor at the end of the hearing during which the court granted bail; and before the defendant is released from custody.

*   This notice must be confirmed in writing and served on the defendant not more than 2 hours after telling the court of the decision to appeal.

*   The Crown Court must hear the appeal as soon as possible and in any event not later than 2 business days after the appeal notice was served (and this takes place as a re-hearing).

The defendant will therefore be remanded in custody by the magistrates until the appeal is heard. The Code for Crown Prosecutors provides that this power should be used 'judiciously and responsibly', and so the power to appeal is not to be used merely because the Crown Prosecutor disagrees with the decision: 'it should only be used in cases of grave concern.'

7.8 Absconding and breaches of bail

7.8.1 Failing to surrender (absconding)

7.8.1.1 What steps will the court take if the defendant fails to surrender?

A defendant who is granted bail (either by the police after they have been charged, or by the court following a hearing) is under a duty to surrender to the court at the time and place appointed for the next hearing. If the defendant fails to attend court to answer their bail at the appointed time and date, the magistrates will issue a warrant for their arrest (Bail Act 1976, s 7(1)). The warrant will either be backed with bail (which means that the police, having arrested the defendant, will then release them again pending their next court appearance), or, as is much more common, not backed with bail. If the warrant is not backed with bail, the police must arrest the defendant and then keep them in police custody until they can be brought before the court. The defendant will be brought before the magistrates' court at the next hearing.

Note: if the defendant is arrested after the court has finished sitting on a Friday, then a specially arranged remand court will be convened on the Saturday morning. No such courts will sit on a Sunday, so a defendant arrested later on a Saturday will be kept in custody until the following Monday morning.

7.8.1.2   What will happen when the defendant appears before the court?

A defendant who has been charged by the police and bailed to appear before the magistrates' court will be in breach of police bail if they fail to attend court at the appointed date and time. When that defendant is arrested and brought before the court, whether they are charged with failing to surrender to custody under ss 6(1) or (2) of the Bail Act 1976 (see below) is a matter for the CPS.

If, however, the defendant has already made an appearance before the court and been granted bail by the court, the decision to commence proceedings against them for failing to surrender will be made by the court rather than the CPS because the defendant will be in breach of court bail.

7.8.1.3   Offences with which the defendant may be charged

The Bail Act 1976 creates two offences with which a defendant who fails to surrender to custody at the appointed time and date may be charged:

(a) If the defendant fails without reasonable cause to surrender to custody, they will be guilty of the offence of absconding, contrary to s 6(1).

In R v Scott [2007] All ER (D) 191 (Oct) the Court of Appeal held that a judge had correctly put a charge of failing to surrender to a defendant who arrived at court half an hour late for a hearing.

(b) If the defendant did have a reasonable cause for failing to surrender, they will still be guilty of an offence under s 6(2) unless they surrendered to custody *as soon as it was reasonably practicable* for them to do so.

⭐ *Example*

Kevin is unable to answer his bail because he is injured in a road traffic accident and has to go to hospital. Kevin will still be guilty of an offence under s 6(2) unless he answers his bail as soon as reasonably practicable after he has been discharged from hospital.

7.8.1.4   Consequences of failing to surrender

If the defendant does not have a reasonable excuse for absconding, the court may either sentence him immediately or adjourn sentence until the conclusion of the substantive proceedings. The Sentencing Council has published a definitive guideline on failure to surrender to bail. This suggests that sentence should be imposed 'as soon as practicable' but, depending on the facts of the case, this could be immediately or at the end of the substantive case.

Even if the magistrates decide not to impose a separate penalty for the absconding offence, they may decide to refuse the defendant bail in the substantive proceedings, or grant bail but with a much more stringent package of conditions.

The court may be persuaded to make a further grant of bail to the defendant if their failure to surrender was the result of a genuine misunderstanding, or if the defendant voluntarily surrendered to custody. The defendant is unlikely to be granted bail again, however, if they wilfully failed to surrender and had to be arrested by the police.

7.8.2   Breaching bail

A defendant who breaches any bail conditions other than a condition to attend the next court hearing (for example, a defendant who fails to comply with a curfew, a condition of residence or a condition not to contact a prosecution witness) does not commit a criminal offence by breaching such conditions. However, a defendant who breaches their bail conditions is likely to have their bail reviewed by the magistrates, who may decide that the failure to comply with the conditions requires a remand in custody.

Section 7(3) of the Bail Act 1976 empowers a police officer to arrest a person who has been bailed to attend court (either by the police following charge, or by the court at a previous hearing) if the officer reasonably believes that the person:

(a) is not likely to surrender to bail; or

(b) has broken, or is likely to break, their bail conditions.

A defendant who is arrested will be detained in police custody and must then be brought before the magistrates' court within 24 hours. The magistrates' court will then decide whether to remand the defendant in custody, or whether to grant bail with or without conditions pending the next substantive hearing in the case.

The magistrates will adopt a two-stage approach:

(a) The court will first determine if there has been a breach of the bail conditions previously imposed. In practice the defendant will often admit the breach because there will usually be compelling evidence available to prove this. However, if the defendant does not admit to breaching their bail conditions, the magistrates will have to decide whether or not there has been a breach. Although it is possible that oral evidence from both the police officer who arrested the defendant and the defendant will be given to determine whether a breach has occurred, usually the court will rely on the witness statements from the prosecution and only the defendant is likely to give oral evidence.

(b) If the magistrates determine that there has been a breach of bail conditions, they will decide whether the defendant should be remanded in custody or on bail pending the next hearing (unless the case can be disposed of at that hearing). So, a defendant who has breached their bail conditions without good reason is likely to be remanded in custody, although the magistrates may be persuaded to make a further grant of bail but with more stringent conditions attached to it.

⭐ Example

The police charge Liam with affray following an incident at a city centre pub and release him on conditional bail pending his first appearance before the magistrates' court one week later. The condition is that Liam does not enter a defined area in the city centre. The following day Liam attends the birthday party of a friend at another pub. This pub is within the area Liam is prohibited from entering, although Liam genuinely thought that it was outside this area. Liam is arrested for breaching his bail condition and is brought before the magistrates' court within 24 hours. Liam accepts that he breached his bail condition but explains that he made an honest mistake. Liam makes an application for bail and this is opposed by the CPS. The magistrates nevertheless decide to grant bail to Liam, although this is made subject to more onerous conditions. In addition to keeping out of the city centre, the magistrates impose an additional condition that Liam is not to enter any public house.

Summary

In this chapter you have considered what the law says about bail along with some important practice and procedural requirements, notably:

* *The right to bail and exceptions.* The right to bail (or presumption in favour of bail) is contained in s 4 of the Bail Act 1976 and the exceptions are set out in Part 1 of Sch 1 to the Bail Act 1976.

- *Conditional bail.* Bail may be granted unconditionally, or with a range of conditions where the court believes it necessary under s 3(6) of the Bail Act 1976 to prevent the defendant from doing a number of things, including failing to surrender, committing offences on bail or interfering with witnesses.

- *Procedure for applying for bail at a contested bail hearing.* The prosecution will start by outlining their objections to bail, identifying the relevant ground(s) they are relying on and applying the relevant factors to support that ground(s). The defence will then try to counter these objections and will usually suggest a package of realistic conditions in support of their application for bail.

- *Further applications for bail.* A defendant is entitled to make two full applications for bail before the magistrates' court using any argument as to fact or law. If bail is refused, then the defendant may only make a further bail application if they can raise new legal or factual arguments as to why bail should be granted.

- *Appeals against decisions on bail.* Both the defence and prosecution can appeal against bail decisions made in the magistrates' court. Such appeals are before a Crown Court judge in chambers.

- *Absconding and breaches of bail.* There are two offences of absconding, namely failing without reasonable cause to surrender to custody (Bail Act 1976, s 6(1)) and having a reasonable cause for failing to surrender but then failing to surrender as soon as it was reasonably practicable to do so (Bail Act 1976, s 6(2)). Breaching a bail condition is not an offence, but it does provide the police with a power of arrest under s 7 of the Bail Act 1976 and to bring the defendant before the magistrates' court. The court will then have to decide whether or not to grant bail or remand the defendant in custody if the case is further adjourned and not dealt with on that day.

Sample questions

Question 1

A solicitor is representing a defendant at his first appearance in court. The defendant has been charged with inflicting grievous bodily harm. It is alleged he punched the victim, fracturing his jaw. The defendant claims he was acting in self-defence. The defendant does not know the victim. The defendant has no previous convictions for violence. His last conviction was 18 months ago when he received a sentence of imprisonment of six months, suspended for two years, for burglary. The defendant has three previous convictions for failing to surrender to custody for a range of dishonesty offences. The defendant is presently of no fixed abode.

Which of the following best explains the ground on which the prosecution is likely to object to bail being granted to the defendant?

A   There are substantial grounds to believe that the defendant will fail to surrender to custody.

B   The defendant may commit an offence whilst on bail given his antecedent history.

C   The nature and seriousness of the offence with which the defendant has been charged.

D   There are substantial grounds to believe the defendant will interfere with a key prosecution witness.

E   The defendant's character, antecedents, associations and community ties.

Answer

Option A is the best answer. This is the only ground on these facts for refusal of bail given that the defendant is presently subject to a suspended sentence of imprisonment which is likely to be activated if he is convicted. Moreover, he appears to have poor community ties as we are told he is of no fixed abode and he also has a number of previous convictions for absconding. All of the other options are either not grounds for refusing bail or do not apply to these facts. To refuse bail on the ground of committing further offences, there must be 'substantial grounds to believe' that he will commit offences whilst on bail. The fact that he 'may' is not sufficient and in any event, there is no evidence that he has committed offences whilst on bail in the past, so option B is not the best answer. Option C is wrong because it is not a ground for refusal of bail at all; it is a factor for the court to take into account when considering the grounds, as is option E. Option D is not the best answer because there are no substantial grounds to believe that the client will interfere with a prosecution witness. We are told that the defendant does not know the victim, nor is there any suggestion that he has made threats to interfere with this witness or has ever done so in the past (see Bail Act 1976, Sch 1).

Question 2

A solicitor attends the cells in the magistrates' court to speak to his client who has been remanded in custody on his first appearance in court. The defendant's case has been sent to the Crown Court for a plea and trial preparation hearing (PTPH), and the defendant wants to know whether he can make a further bail application in the magistrates' court.

Can the defendant make a further bail application in the magistrates' court?

A   Yes, because he is entitled to make a further bail application relying on the same facts and arguments as before.

B   Yes, because he is entitled to make a further bail application but only if he can refer to 'new argument'.

C   Yes, because he is entitled to make two full bail applications before the magistrates' court.

D   No, because his case has now been sent to the Crown Court and so his best option is to appeal against the bail decision to the Crown Court.

E   No, because his case has now been transferred to the Crown Court and so he can now only apply for bail at the PTPH.

Answer

Option D is the best answer. At the first hearing after the hearing at which the magistrates refused to grant bail, the defendant's solicitor is allowed to make a full application for bail using any argument as to fact or law, even if they used the same arguments in the first unsuccessful bail application. However, options A and C would not be available because we are told that the defendant's case has now been sent to the Crown Court and so the magistrates' court will no longer have jurisdiction to hear a further bail application. Option B is wrong because the requirement for new argument only applies after two full bail applications have been made (Bail Act 1976, Sch 1, Pt IIA). Although option E is technically correct, it will be much quicker to make a bail appeal before a judge in chambers in the Crown Court rather than waiting some time for the PTPH in the Crown Court.

Question 3

A man has been charged with an offence of burglary and bailed to attend the magistrates' court in two weeks' time. The police attach a bail condition which requires the man to report to his local police station on a daily basis between the hours of 5 pm and 7 pm. The man obtains employment which requires him to work away from home and he forgets to report to his local police station between the allotted times on two consecutive days.

What will happen to the man as a result of breaching his bail condition?

A   The man is likely to be arrested for breaching his bail condition, but he has a reasonable excuse for breaching it if he can provide evidence of his present employment status.

B   The man is likely to be arrested for breaching his bail condition and bailed to attend the magistrates' court to answer for this breach.

C   The man is likely to be arrested for breaching his bail condition and will be detained in police custody and must then be brought before the magistrates' court within 24 hours although he does not commit an offence by breaching this condition.

D   The man will be given a formal warning for breaching his bail condition and any further breach will result in his arrest and production before the magistrates' court to answer the breach.

E   The man will be arrested for breaching his bail condition and will be detained in police custody and must then be brought before the magistrates' court within 24 hours. He also commits an offence by breaching this condition.

Answer

Option C is the best answer. Although breaching a bail condition (whether imposed by the police or the court) does not amount to a criminal offence, it will almost certainly result in his arrest and he will then be detained in police custody and must be brought before the magistrates' court within 24 hours. The magistrates' court will then decide whether to remand the man in custody, or whether to grant bail with or without conditions pending his next substantive hearing.

Option A is wrong because this would not amount to a reasonable excuse. Option B is wrong because the man would be unlikely to be bailed as a result of breaching this condition. The police will usually let the magistrates' court decide what to do in such circumstances. Option D is wrong because breach of bail is not something that would trigger the issuing of a formal warning. Option E is wrong because breaching this type of a bail condition does not amount to a criminal offence.

8 Case Management and Pre-trial Hearings

SQE1 syllabus

This chapter will enable you to achieve the SQE1 Assessment Specification in relation to Functioning Legal Knowledge concerned with the following procedures and processes:

- magistrates' court case management directions;
- plea and trial preparation hearing (PTPH);
- disclosure – prosecution, defence and unused material.

Note that, for SQE1, candidates are not usually required to recall specific case names or cite statutory or regulatory authorities. These are provided for illustrative purposes only unless otherwise stated.

Learning outcomes

By the end of this chapter you will be able to understand and apply the following law, practice and procedure on:

- What happens at a case management hearing in the magistrates' court.
- The procedure by which an offence triable only on indictment or an either-way offence gets to trial in the Crown Court.
- What happens at a preliminary hearing and the plea and trial preparation hearing (PTPH) in the Crown Court.
- The disclosure obligations imposed on the CPS in respect of any unused material in its possession.
- The circumstances in which a defence statement may or must be given.

8.1 Introduction

Prior to the Criminal Procedure Rules (CrimPR) coming into effect, there were no standard, uniform case management directions that the magistrates' court or Crown Court would give in order to ensure that the CPS and the defendant's solicitor were properly prepared for trial. The CrimPR have introduced this system, with a formal set of case management directions with which the parties must comply. These directions include an obligation on the prosecution to disclose their unused material to the defence who in turn may be required to provide the prosecution with a defence statement.

8.2 Magistrates' court case management directions

After a defendant has entered a not guilty plea to a summary offence, or has pleaded not guilty to an either-way offence and has consented to a trial in the magistrates' court (see **Chapter 6**), the magistrates will fix the date when the defendant's trial is to take place. The magistrates will also give a series of directions that the CPS and the defendant's solicitor must comply with prior to the trial. This part of the chapter will look at the steps which the defendant's solicitor needs to take in order to prepare their client's case for trial. These steps include obtaining evidence from witnesses other than the defendant and obtaining details of any 'unused' material the CPS has which may undermine the case for the prosecution or assist the defence case.

8.2.1 Case management hearing

The court will give case management directions usually at the same hearing at which the defendant enters their plea of not guilty (and, for an either-way offence, after the plea before venue/allocation hearing), or sometimes at a subsequent hearing. The hearing at which case management directions are given is referred to in the Rules as a case management hearing, although some courts call this a pre-trial review.

The case management directions are standard directions, although the court may vary them if necessary. The directions allow the parties eight weeks to prepare the case for trial (or 14 weeks when expert evidence is required). There is a standard form used to record these directions called the Magistrates' Court Trial Preparation Form. The blank form used to record the directions is reproduced at **8.5** below. You will see that Parts 1 to 4 of the form require the prosecution and the defence to provide very detailed information about how they will prepare for and conduct the trial. This is to ensure the trial is effective on the date that has been fixed for trial. Part 5 of the form contains all the decisions and directions made by the court.

8.2.2 Additional trial preparation

8.2.2.1 Securing the attendance of a witness at trial

Witnesses who are prepared to give a written statement are often reluctant to attend court to give oral evidence at trial, and a prudent solicitor will secure their attendance by obtaining a witness summons from the magistrates' court. The procedural rules which apply (in the magistrates' court and Crown Court) when an application for a witness summons is necessary are contained in Part 17 of the CrimPR.

The court will issue a witness summons if it is satisfied that the witness can give material evidence in the proceedings and it is in the interests of justice for a summons to be issued (Magistrates' Courts Act 1980, s 97). The defendant's solicitor will usually ask a potential defence witness to confirm in writing that they will attend court. If a negative response is received, or if, as is much more likely, no response is received, the solicitor should then write to the court requesting that it issue a witness summons. The court will issue a witness summons requiring the witness to attend the trial.

8.2.2.2   Defence witness obligations

Under s 6C of the Criminal Procedure and Investigations Act (CPIA) 1996, a defendant must serve on the CPS a notice setting out the names, addresses and dates of birth of any witnesses they intend to call to give evidence. This rule was introduced to enable the CPS to check whether any defence witnesses have previous convictions, although there is nothing to stop the CPS, via the police, interviewing these witnesses (since there is no property in a witness). Should the police wish to interview a defence witness, a code of practice exists which governs the conduct of the interview (CPIA 1996, s 21A).

This obligation is relevant to both the magistrates' court and the Crown Court, and thus exists in addition to the obligation to serve a defence statement (see **8.4** below). The obligation, in effect, exists in relation to all cases where a defendant pleads not guilty in the magistrates' court or any case sent to the Crown Court for trial.

By virtue of the Criminal Procedure and Investigations Act 1996 (Defence Disclosure Time Limits) Regulations 2011 (SI 2011/209), the time limit to comply with s 6C of the CPIA 1996 is 28 days from the date on which the prosecutor complies, or purports to comply, with s 3 of the CPIA 1996.

Failure to comply with these provisions could result in the inference provisions of s 11 of the CPIA 1996 being applicable (see **8.4** below).

Unlike civil proceedings, there is no requirement for a defendant in a criminal case to serve on the CPS copies of the statements taken from the witnesses whom they intend to call to give evidence at trial. The only exception to this is reports from any expert witnesses whom the defendant wishes to call to give evidence at trial. These must be served on the CPS (see below).

8.2.2.3   Expert witnesses

Expert evidence may be required at trial in respect of any technical matter which is outside the competence of the court. Evidence may, for example, be required from a forensic scientist or a medical expert. Expert evidence should be obtained as soon as possible, although if the defendant's case is funded by way of a representation order, the defendant's solicitor should obtain prior authority from the LAA to instruct the expert.

Disclosure obligations

If the defendant's solicitor wishes to call an expert to give evidence at trial, they must serve a copy of the expert's report on the CPS in advance of trial. An expert witness is unlikely to require a witness summons, although the defendant's solicitor must check the expert's availability to attend trial so that the trial can be fixed on a date when the expert is available to attend court.

8.2.2.4   Do all witnesses need to attend the trial?

Some witnesses may give evidence that is not in dispute. For example, in an assault case the CPS may obtain a statement from a doctor who treated the victim for their injuries. If the defendant accepts that they caused these injuries but claims that they were acting in self-defence, there is little point in the CPS having to call the doctor to give evidence if the nature of the injuries is accepted and the doctor's evidence will go unchallenged by the defendant.

Section 9 of the CJA 1967 provides that a written statement from a witness will be admissible at trial (as opposed to the witness having to come to court to give evidence) provided that:

(a) it is signed and dated;

(b) it contains the following declaration:

This statement (consisting of [1] page signed by me) is true to the best of my knowledge and belief and I make it knowing that if it is tendered in evidence I shall be liable to prosecution if I have wilfully stated in it anything which I know to be false or do not believe to be true.

(c) a copy has been served before the hearing on the other parties in the case; and

(d) none of the other parties has objected within seven days.

The statement may only contain matters which would have been admissible if the witness had given oral evidence at court.

'Section 9' witness statements should be used only for evidence which is not in dispute (although the CPS routinely serves the statements of all prosecution witnesses in the form of a s 9 statement). If the party receiving a statement which is served in this form wishes to challenge the admissibility of anything said in the statement, or to cross-examine the maker of the statement, it should object in writing within seven days. Although the CPS is the more likely party to rely on the s 9 procedure, note that either party in criminal proceedings is entitled to use it.

8.2.2.5 Documentary evidence

Documentary evidence which may be used at trial will often take the form of plans or photographs of the place where the alleged crime occurred. Any plans or photographs should be verified by a witness statement from the person who prepared the plan or took the photographs.

8.2.2.6 Obtaining unused material from the CPS

When the police investigate an alleged offence, they will compile a large amount of documentary evidence (for example, witness statements, business records, CCTV footage, forensic evidence, analysis of mobile phone data etc). In the case of summary-only or either-way offences, any evidence obtained which will subsequently be relied upon as part of the prosecution case at trial will be supplied to the defendant's solicitor as part of the initial details of the prosecution case (IDPC).

The remaining material the CPS has in its possession but which it does not propose to rely upon at trial is referred to as 'unused material'. A common example of unused material is a statement taken from a witness whom the police initially think may help the prosecution case, but who in fact does not say anything that assists the case against the defendant. We will look in more detail at the obligations placed on the CPS in relation to such unused material at **8.4** below.

8.3 Plea and trial preparation hearing

We will start this part of the chapter by considering which type of cases will go to the Crown Court and be the subject of a plea and trial preparation hearing (PTPH).

8.3.1 Offences triable only on indictment

In **Chapter 6** we saw that where an adult appears before a magistrates' court charged with an offence triable only on indictment, the court must send them to the Crown Court for trial pursuant to s 51(1) of the CDA 1998:

(i) the either-way or summary offence appears to the court to be related to the offence triable only on indictment; and

(ii) in the case of a summary-only offence, it is punishable with imprisonment, or involves obligatory or discretionary disqualification from driving (CDA 1998, s 51(11)).

⭐ *Example*

Juan is charged with robbery and assault occasioning actual bodily harm. The CPS alleges that Juan attacked his victim to steal the victim's mobile phone and, in the process, struck the victim in the face, causing the victim to sustain a fractured nose. Robbery is an offence triable only on indictment and so must be sent to the Crown Court for trial. Assault occasioning actual bodily harm is an either-way offence. It fulfils the 'requisite conditions' because it is related to the offence triable only on indictment.

If Juan had been charged with common assault (a summary-only offence) instead of assault occasioning actual bodily harm, the 'requisite conditions' would still be satisfied. The common assault charge is related to the offence triable only on indictment, and common assault is punishable by imprisonment.

8.3.1.1   The sending hearing in the magistrates' court

An adult defendant charged with an offence triable only on indictment will be sent straight to the Crown Court for trial following a hearing in the magistrates' court, pursuant to s 51 of the CDA 1998. The purpose of the hearing is to determine whether an offence triable only on indictment is charged and whether there are related offences which should also be sent to the Crown Court.

When the magistrates have determined that the defendant is charged with an offence triable only on indictment, they will set a date for the PTPH at the Crown Court – or a date for a preliminary hearing in the Crown Court if such a hearing is necessary (see below) – and will remand the defendant either on bail or in custody to appear at the Crown Court. Unless a preliminary hearing is to take place at the Crown Court, the magistrates will also give a set of standard case management directions for the CPS and the defendant's solicitor with which they must comply prior to the PTPH taking place. The magistrates will give the defendant a notice specifying the offence(s) for which they have been sent for trial and the Crown Court at which they are to be tried. A copy of the notice will also be sent to the relevant Crown Court (CDA 1998, s 51D).

8.3.2   Either-way offences

8.3.2.1   Cases to which the allocation procedure applies

A defendant charged with an either-way offence who pleads not guilty at plea before venue will be tried in the Crown Court if either the magistrates decline jurisdiction, or the defendant elects Crown Court trial at the allocation hearing (see **Chapter 6**). In such a case the defendant is sent to the Crown Court forthwith, as for offences triable only on indictment (CDA 1998, s 51(1)).

8.3.2.2   Linked summary offences

Just as with offence triable only on indictment, a defendant who is sent for trial in respect of an either-way offence may also be charged with another offence that is summary-only.

If the summary-only offence is common assault, taking a conveyance without consent, driving whilst disqualified or criminal damage, the defendant may be tried for these offences at the Crown Court if the offence is founded on the same facts as the either-way offence, or is part of a series of offences of the same or a similar character (CJA 1988, s 40(1)).

⭐ *Example*

Brett is charged with theft of goods from a motor vehicle and taking a conveyance without consent. The CPS alleges that Brett took a vehicle without the owner's consent and stole a wallet from the vehicle whilst it was in his possession. Brett is sent to the Crown Court for trial on the theft charge after he enters a not guilty plea at the plea before venue hearing and elects Crown Court trial. The summary-only offence of taking a conveyance without consent can also be tried in the Crown Court as it is founded on the same facts as the either-way offence.

In addition to the above, if the magistrates send a defendant for trial for one or more either-way offences, they may also send the defendant for trial in relation to any summary-only offence with which they are also charged if the summary-only offence:

(a) is punishable with imprisonment or disqualification from driving; and

(b) appears to the court to be related to the either-way offence (CDA 1998, s 51).

If the defendant, on conviction for the either-way offence, pleads guilty to the summary-only offence, the Crown Court can sentence for the summary offence, although its sentencing powers are limited to those of the magistrates. If the defendant is acquitted of the either-way offence or pleads not guilty to the summary-only offence, this offence must be remitted back to the magistrates' court for trial.

 Example

Natalie is sent for trial to the Crown Court on a charge of assault occasioning actual bodily harm. She also faces a charge for the summary-only public order offence of using threatening behaviour. Both charges arise out of the same incident. If Natalie is convicted of the assault charge at the Crown Court, she can also be sentenced for the public order offence if she pleads guilty to it. If Natalie is acquitted of the assault charge or pleads not guilty to the public order offence, however, the Crown Court must remit the public order offence back to the magistrates' court for trial.

8.3.3 Preliminary hearings in the Crown Court

The CrimPR contain standard case management directions that the magistrates' court will issue when a case is sent for trial to the Crown Court. In some limited circumstances, however, when an offence triable only on indictment is sent for trial, a preliminary hearing may take place at the Crown Court. If such a preliminary hearing is needed, any directions necessary will be given by the judge at this hearing.

A preliminary hearing will take place for an offence triable only on indictment if:

(a) there are case management issues which the Crown Court needs to resolve;

(b) the trial is likely to exceed four weeks;

(c) it is desirable to set an early trial date;

(d) the defendant is under 18 years of age; or

(e) there is likely to be a guilty plea and the defendant could be sentenced at the preliminary hearing.

A preliminary hearing must take place within 10 business days of the date on which the magistrates send the case to the Crown Court.

8.3.4 The PTPH

For those cases sent to the Crown Court where a preliminary hearing is not required, the first hearing in the Crown Court will be the PTPH. The purpose of the PTPH is to enable the defendant to enter their plea and, if the defendant is pleading not guilty, to enable the judge to give further case management directions for the CPS and the defendant's solicitor to comply with prior to trial.

Where a case has been sent for trial and no preliminary hearing is held, the PTPH should take place within 20 business days after sending.

8.3.4.1   The arraignment

At the start of the PTPH the defendant will be arraigned. This means that the count(s) on the indictment will be put to the defendant who will either plead guilty or not guilty (see **Chapter 10**). If the defendant pleads guilty to some counts but not guilty to others, the jury at the defendant's trial will not be told about the counts to which a guilty plea has already been entered (so they are not in any way prejudiced against the defendant).

It will sometimes be the case that a defendant charged with several counts will agree with the CPS to plead guilty to certain counts if the CPS does not proceed with other counts. If this happens, at the arraignment, the CPS will offer no evidence in respect of these other counts and the judge will order that a verdict of not guilty be entered. The CPS will also offer no evidence at the arraignment if, since the case was sent for trial, further evidence has become available which leads it to conclude that there is no longer a reasonable prospect of securing a conviction. In this case, the judge will again order that a not guilty verdict be entered, and the defendant will be formally discharged.

As an alternative to offering no evidence, the CPS may ask that a count 'lie on the court file'. This may happen when there are several counts on the indictment and the CPS evidence in respect of each count is strong. If the defendant is prepared to plead guilty to the more serious counts, the CPS may agree to lesser counts being left on the file. In such a case a not guilty verdict will not be entered and (in theory) with the leave of the court the CPS may be allowed to re-open the case at a later date.

8.3.4.2   Guilty pleas

If the defendant pleads guilty at the PTPH, the judge will either sentence immediately or, if necessary, adjourn sentence for the preparation of pre-sentence reports, such as medical reports or reports from the Probation Service. The judge may also need to adjourn the case if the defendant pleads guilty but disputes the specific factual allegations made by the prosecution witnesses. In such a situation a separate hearing (called a 'Newton hearing' – see **Chapter 11**) will be necessary to determine the factual basis on which the defendant will be sentenced. If the case is adjourned, the defendant will either be released on bail or remanded in custody pending either the sentencing hearing or the Newton hearing.

8.3.4.3   Indication of sentence

Following the judgment of the Court of Appeal in *R v Goodyear* [2005] EWCA Crim 888, a judge is now permitted at the PTPH to give a defendant an advance indication of the likely sentence they would receive if they were to enter a guilty plea at that stage. The defendant must specifically ask for such an indication. If the judge gives an indication and the defendant then enters a guilty plea, the indication given by the judge will be binding. In practice, 'Goodyear' indications are quite common.

8.3.4.4   Not guilty pleas

If the defendant pleads not guilty at the PTPH, the judge will then consider if any further directions are necessary to prepare the case for trial (over and above those given by the magistrates' court when the case was sent to the Crown Court). To determine whether further directions may be necessary, the judge will require the prosecution and defence advocates present at the PTPH to be in a position to supply the following information:

(a)   a summary of the issues in the case;

(b)   details of the number of witnesses who will be giving oral evidence at trial and the estimated length of the trial;

(c)   whether the transcript(s) of the defendant's police station interview(s) require(s) editing;

(d)   whether a defence statement has been served and, if so, whether there is any issue as to the adequacy of the statement;

(e) whether the prosecution will be serving any additional evidence;

(f) whether there is any dispute as to the adequacy of disclosure of unused material by the prosecution;

(g) whether any expert evidence is to be called and, if so, whether any additional directions are needed in respect of this;

(h) whether any further directions are necessary concerning hearsay or bad character evidence;

(i) whether special measures are required for any witnesses;

(j) any facts which can be formally admitted;

(k) any points of law or issues concerning the admissibility of evidence which are likely to arise at trial;

(l) dates of availability to attend trial of the witnesses and the advocates.

8.3.4.5   Listing the case for trial

At the PTPH, the judge will give any further case management directions that are necessary in the light of the above information disclosed by the parties, and then either fix a date for the defendant's trial or place the case in the 'warned list'. The warned list is a list of cases awaiting trial that have not been given a fixed date for the trial to start. If a case is placed in the warned list, the Crown Court will contact the defendant's solicitor to let them know that the case has been listed for trial shortly before the date when the trial is due to start.

At the conclusion of the PTPH, the defendant will either be released on bail, or remanded in custody pending his trial.

8.3.4.6   Change of plea

A defendant who initially enters a not guilty plea may, at the discretion of the judge, change this to a guilty plea at any time before the jury return their verdict. This is likely to happen if a defendant admitted their guilt but pleaded not guilty in the hope that a successful submission of no case to answer could be made at the end of the prosecution case but before the defendant needed to give evidence. If the submission is unsuccessful, the defendant will change his plea to guilty. A defendant may also change their plea to guilty during the trial if the judge makes a ruling on a point of law or the admissibility of a piece of evidence which deprives the defendant of a defence on which they wanted to rely.

8.4   Disclosure – prosecution, defence and unused material

The disclosure obligations with which both the CPS and the defendant must comply in a case before the magistrates' court or the Crown Court are contained in the CPIA 1996.

To supplement these statutory provisions there is also a 'Judicial Protocol on the Disclosure of Unused Material in Criminal Cases and Attorney-General's Guidelines on Disclosure' along with a 'National Disclosure Improvement Plan' produced jointly by the police and the CPS. These set out the principles to be applied to disclosure and the expectations of the court, its role in disclosure, particularly in relation to case management, and the consequences if there is a failure by the prosecution or defence to comply with their disclosure obligations. This chapter will just be focussing on the key provisions contained in the CPIA 1996.

8.4.1   Initial prosecution duty of disclosure

Just as in the magistrates' court, the CPS is required to serve on the defendant all the evidence on which it wishes to rely at trial to prove the defendant's guilt.

In addition to this evidence, the prosecution will also have a quantity of 'unused material', such as statements from witnesses whom the CPS does not intend to call to give evidence at trial. The CPS is required to retain this material and, in the event of the defendant entering a not guilty plea, the CPS must disclose any such material to the defendant if the material satisfies the test set out in s 3 of the CPIA 1996. Section 3 provides that such material must be disclosed if it *'might reasonably be considered capable of undermining the case for the prosecution ... or of assisting the case for the accused'*. Examples of the types of material that require disclosure include:

(a) records of the first description of a suspect given to the police by a potential eyewitness if that description differs from that of the defendant;

(b) any information provided by the defendant which indicates an innocent explanation for the offence;

(c) material casting doubt on the reliability of a witness (eg previous convictions);

(d) material casting doubt on the reliability of a confession; and

(e) any statements from witnesses which appear to support the defendant's account.

⭐ Example

Mahmood is charged with assaulting Selim. Mahmood denies the offence and claims that Selim threw the first punch, and that he was acting only in self-defence. The CPS serves on Mahmood's solicitor several statements from eyewitnesses who state that Mahmood threw the first punch. The CPS also has a statement from another witness who says that Selim threw the first punch. The CPS does not intend to rely on evidence from this witness at trial, but it is under an obligation to serve a copy of the statement on Mahmood's solicitor. The statement undermines the prosecution case that Mahmood threw the first punch and assists Mahmood's case that he was acting in self-defence after being attacked.

The case management directions referred to above give time limits as to when the prosecution must make initial disclosure of any unused material in their possession which satisfies the test in s 3 of the CPIA 1996. The CPS usually sends to the defendant's solicitor a schedule of all the non-sensitive unused material in its possession, together with copies of any items on the schedule which satisfy the test in s 3.

The duty of disclosure on the CPS is ongoing, and so the CPS must apply this test to any further material it receives after making initial disclosure (CPIA 1996, s 7A). The CPS must also consider the need to make further disclosure in the light of any information received from the defence about the nature of the defence case (see below).

If the defendant's solicitor considers that the disclosure made by the CPS is incomplete, they will request disclosure of any 'missing' items when drafting the defence statement (see below).

Should the CPS refuse to supply to the defendant's solicitor items which the solicitor has requested, the solicitor may apply to the court to request the specific disclosure of such items under s 8(2) of the CPIA 1996. Such an application may be made only if the defendant has provided a defence statement.

8.4.1.1 Can the prosecution withhold disclosure of unused material?

In addition to having non-sensitive items of unused material, the CPS may also have 'sensitive' items which it does not wish to disclose. Examples include:

(a) material relating to matters of national security or intelligence;

(b) material relating to the identity of police informants or undercover police officers;

(c) material revealing techniques and methods relied upon by the police (eg covert surveillance techniques used); and

(d) material relating to a child witness (such as material generated by a local authority social services department).

If such material satisfies the test for disclosure to the defence in s 3 of the CPIA 1996 (see above), the CPS can withhold the material only if it is protected by 'public interest immunity'. It is the decision of the court as to whether disclosure can be avoided on the grounds of public interest immunity (*R v Ward* [1993] 1 WLR 619). The CPS must therefore make an application to the court for a finding that it is not obliged to disclose the relevant material. The relevant procedural rules which must be followed when a public interest immunity application is made to the court are set out in Part 15 of the CrimPR and this type of an application will often be made ex parte (ie without notice to the defence).

It is usual, when drafting a defence statement (see below), to ask the CPS if a schedule of sensitive materials has been prepared and, if so, whether the CPS has made any application to the court for an order that it is not obliged to disclose the existence of such material.

8.4.2   Defence disclosure

Once the CPS has made its initial disclosure of unused material, the onus switches to the defendant's solicitor. In the magistrates' court, if the defendant enters a not guilty plea, and decides to serve a defence statement (sometimes referred to as a 'Defence Case Statement' or DCS), they should do so within 10 business days of the CPS making initial disclosure of any unused material it has. The defence statement will be served on the CPS and a copy of the statement sent to the court. In the Crown Court, the time period is extended to 20 business days from service of unused material by the prosecution (Criminal Procedure and Investigations Act 1996 (Defence Disclosure Time Limits) Regulations 2011 (SI 2011/209)). If the case is particularly complex and 10/20 days will be insufficient, the defendant may apply to the court for a longer period within which to serve the defence statement. In a case involving two or more co-accused, s 5A of the CPIA 1996 allows the court to make an order that a copy of the defence statement made by each defendant is to be served on the other defendants in the case. The requirements for the contents of a defence statement are set out below.

Section 5 of the CPIA 1996 sets out the obligation on the defence to provide a defence statement. This is referred to by s 5 as '*Compulsory disclosure*'. This obligation applies only to a defendant facing a trial in the Crown Court and not the magistrates' court. This obligation is enforced in the Crown Court by the court being able to draw an adverse inference against the defendant if a defence statement is not provided.

For a case in the magistrates' court, the defendant's solicitor should consider serving a defence statement on the CPS only if they think that the CPS will, in the light of the information disclosed in the statement, be in a position to disclose additional unused material that may *assist* the defence case. Such a situation is likely to arise only if the defence statement contains additional details about the defence of which the CPS was previously unaware.

In reality, it is extremely rare for a defence statement to be served on the prosecution in the magistrates' court. The possible advantage of gaining additional disclosure from the CPS is heavily outweighed by the disadvantage of giving away too many details of the defence case to the CPS prior to the trial when there is no obligation to do so.

8.4.2.1   Contents of the defence statement

The contents of the defence statement are prescribed by s 6A of the CPIA 1996, as amended by s 60 of the CJIA 2008. The defence statement must be a written statement which:

(a) sets out the nature of the defence, including any particular defences on which the defendant intends to rely (for example, alibi or self-defence);

(b) indicates the matters of fact on which the defendant takes issue with the prosecution and why they take such issue;

(c) sets out particulars of the matters of fact on which the defendant intends to rely for the purposes of their defence;

(d) indicates any points of law (including any point as to the admissibility of evidence) that the defendant wishes to take at trial, and any legal authority on which the defendant intends to rely for this purpose; and

(e) in the case of an alibi defence, provides the name, address and date of birth of any alibi witness, or as many of these details as are known to the defendant.

The defence are also under a continuing duty to update the defence statement if the details to be given under any of the above points should change before trial (if, for example, a witness comes forward who is able to support an alibi given by the defendant and whose existence was unknown at the time the initial defence statement was prepared) (CPIA 1996, s 6B(3)).

8.4.2.2   Obtaining the defendant's approval of the defence statement

Section 6E of the CPIA 1996 provides that defence statements will be deemed to be given with the authority of the defendant unless the contrary is proved. A defendant's solicitor should therefore ensure that the defendant sees and approves a copy of the defence statement before this is served. As the defence statement will usually be drafted by the defendant's solicitor, the usual practice will be for the defendant's solicitor to sign the original statement which is served, and for the defendant to sign a copy of the statement which will be kept on the solicitor's file.

8.4.2.3   When may the court draw an adverse inference?

Defence statements are effectively obligatory for defendants pleading not guilty in the Crown Court because, if there are any 'faults' in disclosure given by the defence, the court may draw an adverse inference from this when determining the defendant's guilt (CPIA 1996, s 11). These faults include:

(a) failing to provide a defence statement at all;

(b) late service of the defence statement;

(c) serving a defence statement that is incomplete;

(d) serving a defence statement which is not consistent with the defence put forward at trial; and

(e) failing to update a defence statement.

If any of these faults occurs the court or, with leave, any other party (such as the prosecution or any co-accused) may make such comments as appear appropriate, and the court or jury may draw such inferences as appear proper when deciding whether the defendant is guilty.

⭐ *Example 1*

Amanda is charged with theft. Her case is sent for trial to the Crown Court. She enters a not guilty plea at the PTPH. Amanda fails to serve a defence statement on the CPS. At her trial Amanda raises the defence of alibi and claims that the prosecution witness who identified her as the person who committed the theft is mistaken. As Amanda failed to serve a defence statement setting out this defence, the trial judge or, with leave, the prosecution, may comment on this and the jury may draw such inferences as appear proper (which is likely to be an adverse inference).

Example 2

> *Javed is charged with unlawful wounding. His case is sent for trial to the Crown Court. At the PTPH he enters a not guilty plea. In his defence statement, Javed claims that he was not present at the time of the alleged incident and raises the defence of alibi. At his trial, Javed accepts that he was present at the time of the incident and instead raises the defence of self-defence. As there is a disparity between what was said in his defence statement and the defence he is now raising at trial, the judge or, with leave, the prosecution, may comment on this and the jury may draw such inferences as appear proper (which is likely to be an adverse inference).*

8.4.3 Further disclosure obligations on the prosecution

The only 'reward' for a defendant who provides a defence statement is that the CPS must review its initial disclosure of unused material and determine if there is any further unused material in its possession which, in light of the matters contained in the defence statement, might now be deemed capable of *undermining* the case for the prosecution or of *assisting* the case for the defendant (CPIA 1996, s 7A).

 Example

> *Sergio is jointly charged with Philip with the production of cannabis at premises owned by Philip. Sergio's defence is that he knows nothing about the production of cannabis at the premises and was employed by Philip at the premises solely to clean and valet cars. The CPS is not aware that this is the basis of Sergio's defence because he refused to answer any questions when interviewed at the police station. As part of their investigations, the police recover from the premises a number of documents, including receipts for various items of car-cleaning equipment. The CPS does not intend to use these receipts in evidence and is not under an initial duty to disclose such documents to Sergio's solicitor, because the documents neither undermine the prosecution case nor assist the case for the defence (because there has been no indication as to what the defence case is).*
>
> *Sergio's solicitor subsequently serves a defence statement on the CPS stating that Sergio knew nothing about the premises being used for the production of cannabis and confirming that Sergio was employed at the premises solely to valet cars. The CPS is under a continuing duty of disclosure and so, in the light of the defence statement, it must now disclose the receipts to Sergio's solicitor, as the receipts assist Sergio's defence that he had an innocent explanation for being at the premises.*

8.4.3.1 Can the defence challenge the prosecution failure to provide unused material?

Section 8(2) of the CPIA 1996 enables a defendant who has provided a defence statement to make application to the court if the CPS has failed to comply with its continuing duty of disclosure in light of the matters contained in the defence statement. The defendant may ask the court for an order that the CPS disclose material provided the defendant has reasonable cause to believe that there is prosecution material which should have been, but has not been, disclosed. The defendant will only be allowed to make such an application if they have set out in detail in their defence statement the material which they consider the CPS has in its possession which it has not subsequently disclosed. The procedure to be followed when such an application is made is contained in Part 15 of the CrimPR.

A flowchart summarising the disclosure obligations imposed on both the CPS and the defendant in both the Crown Court and the magistrates' court is provided at **8.6** below.

8.5   Magistrates' court trial preparation form

Figure 8.1   Magistrates' court trial preparation form

.... Magistrates' Court

Preparation for effective trial
Criminal Procedure Rules Parts 1 & 3

■ This form:
  ● collects information about the case that the court will need to arrange for an effective trial: CrimPR rules 3.2 and 3.3
  ● records the court's directions: CrimPR rule 3.5.

■ After the court gives directions for trial, if:
  ● information about the case changes, or
  ● you think another direction is needed
  you must tell the court at once: CrimPR 1.2(1) & 3.12.

■ If the defendant pleads not guilty, and the court requires:
  ● the prosecutor must complete Parts 1, 2 and 4
  ● the defendant must complete Parts 1, 3 and 4
  ● the court will record directions in Part 5.

■ See also the:*
  ● notes for guidance on using this form
  ● directions about intermediaries and ground rules hearings
  ● standard trial preparation time limits at the end of this form

Court contact details can be found at: https://courttribunalfinder.service.gov.uk/search/

Address	Phone
	Fax
Email	

Part 1: to be completed by the prosecutor and the defendant (or defendant's representative)

| **Defendant** | |
| **Offence(s)** | |

| **Police / CPS URN** | | **Date of first hearing** | |

1   Prosecution contact details

Prosecuting authority		Phone
	Email	
	Contact for this case:	

2   Defendant's contact details

Defendant	Address	Phone
		Mobile
	Email	

3   Defendant's trial representative**

No legal representative   ☐
OR
Representation is: legal aid granted   ☐
Defendant's representative to complete   legal aid applied for   ☐
                                               privately funded   ☐

Lawyer(s) / firm		Phone
		Ref
	Email	
	Address	
	Contact for this case:	

*This form and those notes and directions are at: https://www.gov.uk/government/publications/preparation-for-trial-in-a-magistrates-court.
**This means the defendant's legal representative for the whole trial, not a person appointed only to cross-examine a witness under CrimPR Part 23.

(continued)

Figure 8.1 *(continued)*

Part 2: to be completed by the prosecutor

4   Case management information

4.1   **Evidence**
Does the prosecutor intend to serve more evidence?   ☐ Yes ☐ No
If yes, give details:

4.2   **Disclosure of unused prosecution material**
Has the initial duty of disclosure of unused prosecution material been complied with?   ☐ Yes ☐ No
If yes, when?   If not, anticipated date for service

4.3   **Investigation**
Are there any pending enquiries or lines of investigation?   ☐ Yes ☐ No
If yes, give details (including likely timescale):

4.4   **Modern Slavery Act**
Is there any suggestion that the defendant has been a victim of slavery or exploitation?   ☐ Yes ☐ No
If yes, give details including the date of any reference to the national referral mechanism:

4.5   **Prosecution case**
The prosecution will rely on: defendant's admissions in interview   ☐
Tick / delete as appropriate   defendant's failure to mention facts in interview   ☐
                                      [a summary] [a record] of the defendant's interview   ☐
                                      expert evidence   ☐
                                      hearsay evidence   ☐
                                      bad character evidence   ☐
                                      [CCTV] [electronically recorded] evidence   ☐
                                      [diagram] [sketch map] [photos]   ☐

4.6   **Display equipment**
What equipment (live link or other media player, etc.) will the prosecutor need in the trial courtroom?
The prosecutor must make sure that any electronic media can be played in the courtroom.

4.7   **Points of law**
Does the prosecutor presently expect the case to involve a complex, novel or unusual point of   ☐ Yes ☐ No
law and / or fact? If so what?

5   Applications for directions

5.1   **Prosecution witness requiring assistance, special measures, etc.**
Are there any prosecution witness requirements that may make special measures, reasonable   ☐ Yes ☐ No
adjustments or other support appropriate? If yes, give details in Part 4.

5.2   **Ground rules for questioning**
Does the prosecutor want the court to arrange a discussion of ground rules for questioning?   ☐ Yes ☐ No
*If an intermediary is appointed, the court must discuss ground rules with the intermediary and
advocates. A discussion may be helpful in other cases.*

5.3   **Variation of standard directions**
Does the prosecutor want the court to vary a standard trial preparation time limit or make any   ☐ Yes ☐ No
other direction? If yes, give details:

Figure 8.1 (*continued*)

Part 3: to be completed by the defendant (or defendant's representative)

6   Advice on plea and absence

Credit for guilty plea; trial in absence
Does the defendant understand that:

(a) they will receive credit for a guilty plea?   ☐ Yes ☐ No
     A guilty plea may affect the sentence and any order for costs

(b) the trial and sentencing, if convicted, can go ahead even if they do not attend?   ☐ Yes ☐ No
     CrimPR rule 24.12

7   Partial or different guilty plea

7.1   **Mixed pleas**
If more than one offence is alleged, does the defendant want to plead guilty to any of them?   ☐ Yes ☐ No ☐ N/A
If yes, which offence(s)?

7.2   **Basis of plea**
Does the defendant want to plead guilty, but not on the facts alleged?   ☐ Yes ☐ No
If yes, provide a written note of the facts on which the defendant wants to plead guilty.

7.3   **Different offence**
Does the defendant want to plead guilty, but to a different offence?   ☐ Yes ☐ No
If yes, what offence?

8   Case management information

Initial details of the prosecution case should have been served: CrimPR rule 8.2. Questions 8.1, 8.2, 8.3 and 8.4 are to help the court find out what is in dispute and give appropriate directions for trial. Tick and give details as appropriate.

8.1   **(a) presence**
The defendant was present at the scene of the offence alleged

☐ Not disputed.   ☐ Disputed.   ☐ Irrelevant in this case
If disputed, explain what is in dispute:

(b) involvement
The defendant [[carried out] [took part in] the conduct alleged] [drove the vehicle involved]

☐ Not disputed.   ☐ Disputed.   ☐ Irrelevant in this case
If disputed, explain what is in dispute:

(c) injury / loss / damage
[Nature of injury] [extent of loss or damage] alleged by the prosecution

☐ Not disputed.   ☐ Disputed.   ☐ Irrelevant in this case
If disputed, explain what is in dispute:

(d) identification
The defendant was correctly identified

☐ Not disputed.   ☐ Disputed.   ☐ Irrelevant in this case
If disputed, explain what is in dispute:

Page 3

(*continued*)

Figure 8.1 (*continued*)

(e) lawful arrest
The defendant was arrested lawfully

☐ Not disputed.   ☐ Disputed.   ☐ Irrelevant in this case
If disputed, explain what is in dispute:

(f) interview
The defendant's interview [summary] [record] is accurate

☐ Not disputed.   ☐ Disputed.   ☐ Irrelevant in this case
If disputed, explain what is in dispute:

(g) fingerprints / DNA
[Fingerprint] [DNA] evidence

☐ Not disputed.   ☐ Disputed.   ☐ Irrelevant in this case
If disputed, explain what is in dispute by reference to the expert evidence summary:

(h) scientific evidence
[Medical] [identification of drug] [other scientific] prosecution evidence

☐ Not disputed.   ☐ Disputed.   ☐ Irrelevant in this case
If disputed, explain what is in dispute by reference to the expert evidence summary:

(i) alcohol / drug testing procedure
The [alcohol] [drug] testing procedure was carried out correctly

☐ Not disputed.   ☐ Disputed.   ☐ Irrelevant in this case
If disputed, explain what is in dispute:

(j) disqualification / court order (e.g. restraining order)
The defendant was [disqualified from driving] [subject to the court order specified] at the time
of the offence alleged

☐ Not disputed.   ☐ Disputed.   ☐ Irrelevant in this case
If disputed, explain what is in dispute:

(k) continuity
Exhibits and samples were collected and delivered as stated by the prosecution (i.e. continuity)

☐ Not disputed.   ☐ Disputed.   ☐ Irrelevant in this case
If disputed, explain what is in dispute:

(l) anticipated defence(s) - *Tick as appropriate*
The defendant is likely to rely upon: self-defence   ☐
       reasonable excuse   ☐
       slavery or exploitation   ☐
       another statutory defence   ☐

If there is any suggestion that the defendant has been a victim of slavery or exploitation, give
details including the date of any reference to the national referral mechanism. If any other
defence is anticipated, give an outline.

OR - Irrelevant in this case   ☐

Page 4

142

Figure 8.1 (*continued*)

8.2 **Admissions**

Can any facts which are not in dispute be recorded in a written admission? ☐ Yes ☐ No

If yes, a written admission made by the defendant and the prosecutor [is set out here and signed at the end of this form] [is attached] [will be served later].
Undisputed facts can be admitted by reference to a statement accepted in paragraph 8.1, e.g. "I admit 8.1(a)and (e)." Facts which are admitted are evidence: CrimPR rule 24.6 & Criminal Justice Act 1967, s.10.

8.3 **Issues**

What are the real issues in this case? Explain:

(a) what particular facts are in dispute, if any, in addition to those identified in paragraph 8.1?

(b) what matters of law are in dispute, if any?

8.4 **Points of law**

Does the defendant presently expect the case to involve a complex, novel or unusual point of law and / or fact? If so what? ☐ Yes ☐ No

8.5 **Defence statement**

Does the defendant presently intend to give a defence statement? *Giving a defence statement* ☐ Yes ☐ No
is voluntary, but if one is given it must include the information collected in paragraphs 8.1 and 8.3 and must include particulars of facts relied on by the defence.

8.6 **Display equipment**

What equipment (live link or other media player, etc.) will the defendant need in the trial courtroom? *The defendant must make sure that any electronic media can be played in the courtroom.*

9 Applications for directions

9.1 **Variation of standard directions**

Does the defendant want the court to vary a standard trial preparation time limit or make any other direction? ☐ Yes ☐ No
If yes, give details:

9.2 **Defendant or defence witness requiring assistance, special measures, etc.**

Are there any defendant or defence witness requirements that may make special measures, reasonable adjustments or other support appropriate? If yes, give details in Part 4. ☐ Yes ☐ No

9.3 **Ground rules for questioning**

Does the defendant want the court to arrange a discussion of ground rules for questioning? ☐ Yes ☐ No
If an intermediary is appointed, the court must discuss ground rules with the intermediary and advocates. A discussion may be helpful in other cases.

9.4 **Trial in Wales**

If the trial will take place in Wales, does the defendant wish to speak Welsh (whether the defendant is likely to give evidence or not)? *See also paragraphs 11, 12.3 and 12.5.* ☐ Yes ☐ No

Page 5

(*continued*)

Figure 8.1 (*continued*)

Defendant's name:

Part 4: to be completed by the prosecutor, the defendant (or the defendant's representative) and the court

10 Prosecution witnesses. *If this information changes, you must tell the court at once: CrimPR rule 1.2(1) & 3.12.*

| Name of witness | Prosecutor to complete | | | | Defendant to complete | Both parties to complete | | Tick if live link ordered | For the court |
	Tick if under 18	If trial in Wales Tick if witness wishes to give evidence in Welsh	Other language(s) - interpreter needed? If so, specify language and dialect.	Special or other measures e.g. live link needed? If so, specify.**	What disputed issue in the case makes it necessary for the witness to give evidence in person?	Tick if attendance proposed P D			Evidence to be read ('R') or time required per witness EinC X-exam
1)	☐	☐				☐	☐	☐	
2)	☐	☐				☐	☐	☐	
3)	☐	☐				☐	☐	☐	
4)	☐	☐				☐	☐	☐	
5)	☐	☐				☐	☐	☐	
6)	☐	☐						☐	

11 Expected defence witnesses. *If this information changes, you must tell the court at once: CrimPR rule 1.2(1) & 3.12.*

| Name of witness | Defendant to complete | | | | Why is it necessary for the witness to give evidence in person? | Both parties to complete | | Tick if live link ordered | For the court |
	Tick if under 18	If trial in Wales Tick if witness wishes to give evidence in Welsh	Other language(s) - interpreter needed? If so, specify language and dialect.	Special or other measures e.g. live link needed? If so, specify.**		Tick if attendance proposed D P			Evidence to be read ('R') or time required per witness EinC X-exam
1)*	☐	☐				☐	☐	☐	
2)	☐	☐				☐	☐	☐	
3)	☐	☐				☐		☐	

*If the defendant is likely to give evidence, list him or her as the first expected defence witness.   **Special or other measures may include screens, evidence by live link or in private, video recorded evidence, intermediary, breaks in examination or other measures to accommodate disability.   They may increase the time needed for the witness. In some cases, the defendant may not be allowed to cross-examine a prosecution witness.

Figure 8.1 (*continued*)

Defendant's name:

Part 5: record of court's decisions and directions for effective trial

12   **Directions for trial:** *The court must actively manage the case by giving any direction appropriate to the needs of that case as early as possible: CrimPR rule 3.2(3). Complete or delete the following as appropriate*

12.1   **Service of evidence.** The prosecutor must serve any further evidence by: *(date)*

12.2   **Disclosure.** If the initial duty of disclosure has not been complied with, the prosecutor must comply by: *(date)*

12.3   **Witnesses & evidence.** Part 4 of this form indicates which witnesses are to give oral evidence, with time estimates, and which witnesses' evidence is to be read. The court expects evidence to be given as indicated in that Part. A party who wants to use electronic media, etc. must check <u>before</u> the trial that it can be played in the courtroom.
    Trial in Wales. If the trial will take place in Wales, and if the defendant (whether they give evidence or not) or any witness, wishes to speak Welsh, then (i) a Welsh speaking judge / magistrates and legal adviser should be arranged if possible, and (ii) a Welsh language interpreter is required for anyone who does not speak Welsh.

12.4   **Securing attendance** *CrimPR Part 17; rule 3.8(3).* [Witness summons / warrant] [other steps to secure attendance] for:
                   (name)
                   (name)

12.5   **Interpretation ordered**
    Witness name / defendant   Language   To be arranged by

               Court staff ☐ Prosecutor ☐ Defendant ☐

               Court staff ☐ Prosecutor ☐ Defendant ☐

12.6   **Special measures, reasonable adjustments or other support**
    Witness name / defendant   Type of special measure, adjustment or other arrangement

12.7   **Prohibited cross-examination** *CrimPR Part 23*

    ☐ The defendant may not cross-examine the following witness(es) except through a lawyer:
                                 (name(s) of witness(es))
    The following directions apply for as long as the defendant has no legal representative for the trial:
    ☐ the defendant to give notice of his/her appointment of a lawyer to cross-examine the witness(es) by: *(date)*
    If the defendant gives no such notice by that date then either:
    ☐ the court appoints   *(name of lawyer)* to cross-examine the witness(es); or
    ☐ the court directs the appointment for that purpose of a lawyer to be selected at a later date.

12.8   **Directions for intermediary's report and ground rules.** The directions at page 8 apply.

12.9   **Standard trial preparation directions.** The standard trial preparation time limits at page 9 apply [except] [with these variations]:

12.10   **Other directions**:

    *After the court gives directions for trial, if information about the case changes, or you think another direction is needed, **you must tell the court and the other party or parties at once**: CrimPR rules 1.2(1) & 3.12.*

Arrangements for trial

Trial date:	Trial time:	Trial Venue:
Custody time limit expires:	Court category:	
Total estimated trial length:	hours:minutes	
Including evidence and submissions:	Deliberations and decision:	
A detailed trial timetable must be considered and attached if necessary: CrimPR rules 3.8 & 3.13		

Signed: Prosecution:	Defence:	Court:	
Completed on:	*(date)*		

Page 7

(continued)

145

Figure 8.1 (*continued*)

Directions for intermediary's report and ground rules

Intermediary's report *CrimPR rule 18.32*

a.   Intermediary's report to be delivered to the court by: *(date)*
b.   The court will determine the application for an intermediary by: *(date)*

Ground rules hearing *CrimPR rule 3.9*

c.   The court will discuss ground rules for questioning on: *(date)*
If an intermediary is appointed for a witness or for the defendant, the court must discuss the ground rules for questioning with the intermediary and the advocates before the witness or defendant gives evidence. Sufficient time must be allowed for this.

Ground rules: witness(es) *CrimPR rules 3.8(7), 3.9*

d.   The following ground rules will apply for the questioning of   .... (name of witness(es)):
(a) clear and simple language to be used;
(b) no tagged questions;
(c) no multiple questions;
(d) no questions to be repeated unless not heard or not understood;
(e) the witness must be allowed to answer one question before another is asked;
(f) questions to be asked in cross-examination to be submitted by: *(date)*;
(g) other ground rules:

Ground rules: defendant *CrimPR rules 3.8(7), 3.9*

e.   The following ground rules will apply for the questioning of the defendant:
(a) clear and simple language to be used;
(b) no tagged questions;
(c) no multiple questions;
(d) no questions to be repeated unless not heard or not understood;
(e) the defendant must be allowed to answer one question before another is asked;
(f) questions to be asked in cross-examination to be submitted by: *(date)*;
(g) other ground rules:

Page 8

Figure 8.1 (*continued*)

Standard trial preparation time limits

The court can vary any of these time limits. Time limits marked * are not prescribed by rules or other legislation.
The total time needed to comply with all these time limits is 6 weeks (9 weeks if paragraph m applies).

Written admissions (Criminal Procedure Rules, r.24.6; Criminal Justice Act 1967, s.10)

a. The parties must serve any written admissions of agreed facts within **10 business days.***

Defence statement (Criminal Procedure Rules, r.15.4; Criminal Procedure and Investigations Act 1996, s.6)

b. Any defence statement must be served within **10 business days** of the prosecutor complying with the initial duty of disclosure.

Defence witnesses (Criminal Procedure and Investigations Act 1996, s.6C)

c. Defence witness names, etc. must be notified within **10 business days** of the prosecutor complying with the initial duty of disclosure.

Application for disclosure (Criminal Procedure Rules, r.15.5; Criminal Procedure and Investigations Act 1996, s.8)

d. The defendant must serve any application for an order for prosecution disclosure as soon as reasonably practicable after the prosecutor complies with the initial duty of disclosure.* *Under s.8 of the Criminal Procedure and Investigations Act 1996, no such application may be made unless a defence statement has been served.*

e. The prosecutor must serve any representations in response within **10 business days after that.**

Witness statements (Criminal Procedure Rules, r.16.4; Criminal Justice Act 1967, s.9)

f. The defendant must serve any defence witness statement to be read at trial at least **10 business days before the trial.***

g. Any objection to a witness statement being read at trial must be made within **5 business days of service of the statement.** *This does not apply to the statements listed in Part 4.*

Measures to assist a witness or defendant to give evidence (Criminal Procedure Rules, rr.18.3, 18.13, 18.17, 18.22, 18.26)

h. Any [further] application for special or other measures must be served within **20 business days.**

i. Any representations in response must be served within **10 business days after that.**

Cross-examination where defendant not represented (Criminal Procedure Rules, rr.23.2, 23.4, 23.7)

j. The defendant must serve notice of any representative appointed to cross-examine within **5 business days.***

k. The prosecutor must serve any application to prohibit cross-examination by the defendant in person as soon as reasonably practicable.

l. Any representations in response must be served within **10 business days after that.**

Expert evidence (Criminal Procedure Rules, rr.19.3, 19.4)

m. If either party relies on expert evidence, the directions below apply.
  (i) The expert's report must be served within **20 business days.***
  (ii) A party who wants that expert to attend the trial must give notice within **5 business days after (i).***
  (iii) A party who relies on expert evidence in response must serve it within **10 business days after (ii).***
  (iv) There must be a meeting of experts under rule 19.6 within **10 business days after (iii).***
  (v) The parties must notify the court **immediately after (iv)** if the length of the trial is affected by the outcome of the meeting.*

Hearsay evidence (Criminal Procedure Rules, rr.20.2, 20.3)

n. The prosecutor must serve any notice to introduce hearsay evidence within **20 business days.**

o. The defendant must serve any notice to introduce hearsay evidence as soon as reasonably practicable.

p. Any application to determine an objection to hearsay evidence must be served within **10 business days of service** of the notice or evidence.

Bad character evidence (Criminal Procedure Rules, rr.21.2, 21.3, 21.4)

q. The prosecutor must serve any notice to introduce evidence of the defendant's bad character within **20 business days.**

r. Any application to determine an objection to that notice must be served within **10 business days after that.**

s. Any application to introduce evidence of a non-defendant's bad character must be served within **10 business days** of prosecution disclosure.

t. Any notice of objection to that evidence must be served within **10 business days after that.**

Previous sexual behaviour evidence (Criminal Procedure Rules, rr.22.2, 22.3, 22.4, 22.5)

u. The defendant must serve any application for permission to introduce evidence of a complainant's previous sexual behaviour within **20 business days** of prosecution disclosure.

v. The prosecutor must serve any representations in response within **10 business days after that.**

Point of law, including abuse of process etc. (Criminal Procedure Rules, rr.3.3, 3.12)

w. Any skeleton argument must be served at least **10 business days before the trial.***

x. Any skeleton argument in reply must be served within **5 business days after that.***

Trial readiness (Criminal Procedure Rules, rr.3.3, 3.12)

y. The parties must certify readiness for trial at least **10 business days before the trial,*** confirming that witnesses due to give evidence in person will do so and confirming the trial time estimate.

January 2023

8.6 Disclosure flowchart (magistrates' court and Crown Court)

Figure 8.2 Disclosure flowchart (magistrates' court and Crown Court)

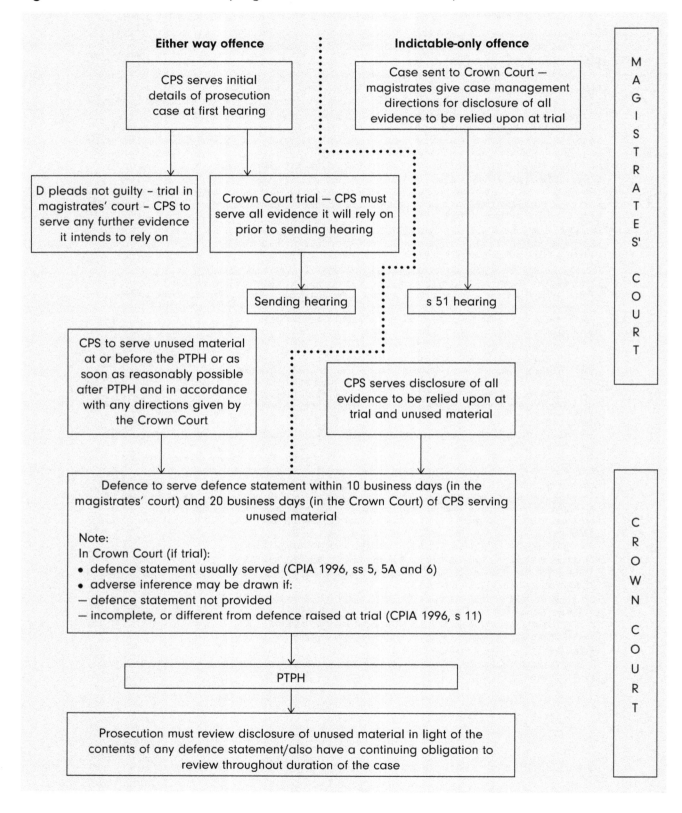

Summary

In this chapter you have considered what the law, practice and procedure says about the case management directions that the magistrates' court and Crown Court give in order to ensure that the CPS and the defendant's solicitor are properly prepared for trial. This includes an obligation on the prosecution to disclose their unused material to the defence who may in turn be required to serve a defence statement on the prosecution and the court. Notably:

- *The magistrates' court case management directions.* The court will give case management directions usually at the same hearing at which the defendant enters their plea of not guilty. These are standard directions, which can be varied if necessary. They require the parties to provide very detailed information about how they will prepare for and conduct the trial.

- *The Plea and Trial Preparation Hearing* (PTPH). For those cases sent to the Crown Court where a preliminary hearing is not required, the first hearing will be the PTPH. The PTPH enables the defendant to enter their plea and, if the defendant is pleading not guilty, to enable the judge to give further case management directions for the CPS and the defendant's solicitor to comply with prior to trial.

- *Disclosure – prosecution, defence and unused material.* As well as providing the defence with all the evidence they intend to rely on at trial, the CPS also has a continuing obligation to disclose any of its unused material in its possession that *'might reasonably be considered capable of undermining the case for the prosecution ... or of assisting the case for the accused'.* This duty of disclosure is subject though to withholding sensitive information, where the court has granted an application for public interest immunity. The defence disclosure obligations are much more limited, but there is an obligation in the Crown Court for the defence to provide a defence statement. Failure to provide such a statement may lead to the drawing of adverse inferences.

Sample questions

Question 1

A solicitor is representing a defendant at his first appearance in the magistrates' court. The defendant has been charged with offences of rape (an offence that can only be tried on indictment) and sexual assault (an either-way offence). It is alleged that he sexually assaulted the victim before he then raped her the following week. The defendant intends to plead not guilty to both allegations.

Will both offences be sent to the Crown Court for trial?

A   Yes, because the defendant is pleading not guilty to both allegations.

B   No, because the sexual assault allegation can only be tried in the magistrates' court.

C   No, because the defendant may elect trial for both allegations in the magistrates' court or the Crown Court.

D   Yes, because the sexual assault allegation is related to the rape allegation which must be sent to the Crown Court for trial.

E   Yes, because the sexual assault allegation is punishable with imprisonment and is related to the rape allegation which must be sent to the Crown Court for trial.

Answer

Option D is the best answer. This is because rape is an offence triable only on indictment and sexual assault is an either-way offence. Where an adult appears before a magistrates' court charged with an offence triable only on indictment, the court must send the defendant to the Crown Court for trial pursuant to s 51(1) of the CDA 1998 for that offence; and for any either-way offence (or summary offence) with which they are charged which fulfils the 'requisite conditions'. Here the 'requisite conditions' are that the either-way offence appears to the court to be related to the offence triable only on indictment. Given that both allegations relate to the same victim and they are alleged to have taken place within a week of each other, they will be regarded as related to each other. Although sexual assault is also an imprisonable offence, option E is not the best answer because this is only a requirement for a summary-only offence. Option A is not the best answer, because the defendant will not be asked to indicate his plea to either of these matters in this case (he would have been asked to indicate his plea to the allegation of sexual assault if he had not also been charged with rape, an offence that can only be tried on indictment). Option B is not correct as sexual assault is an either-way offence. Option C is not correct because rape is not an either-way offence and so he will never be given the choice to elect where his trial takes place.

Question 2

A defendant has been charged with an offence of burglary that took place at office premises in the city centre. As part of the investigation the police have a witness statement from a neighbour of the defendant claiming she saw the defendant in his back garden at the time the burglary took place. However, she tells the police that she is not prepared to give evidence about this as she does not like her neighbour. The prosecution does not believe the neighbour is telling the truth and does not intend to call her as a witness at the defendant's trial in the magistrates' court.

Which of the following best describes whether the prosecution will be required to disclose the existence of the neighbour's witness statement to the defence?

A   The prosecution will be required to disclose this material as part of the initial details of the prosecution case.

B   The prosecution will not be required to disclose this witness statement because the trial is taking place in the magistrates' court and not the Crown Court.

C   The prosecution will be required to disclose this witness statement because it provides the defendant with an alibi defence.

D   The prosecution will not be required to disclose this witness statement because it is sensitive material and subject to public interest immunity as the neighbour does not want to testify at trial.

E   The prosecution will be required to disclose this witness statement because it might reasonably be considered capable of undermining the case for the prosecution.

Answer

Option E is the best answer. Section 3 CPIA 1996 provides that such unused material must be disclosed to the defence if it 'might reasonably be considered capable of undermining the case for the prosecution'. Arguably this witness statement might also reasonably be considered capable of assisting the case for the accused, but we are not told what defence the defendant is raising and, in any event, this is not one of the options available. Option A is not correct because this witness statement will not be provided as IDPC, as we are told the prosecution will not be calling this witness to give evidence. The obligation to disclose unused prosecution material applies to trials in the magistrates' court and Crown Court, so option B is not correct. Option C is not the best answer, because although this may support the defendant's defence of alibi, we do not know whether the defendant is raising such a defence and in any event, this does not set out the test for disclosure in s 3. Option D is not correct because a witness's unwillingness to testify does not make it sensitive material that may be eligible for a public interest immunity application.

Question 3

A man is facing trial in the Crown Court for an offence of wounding. The prosecution has provided disclosure of their non-sensitive, unused material which might reasonably be considered capable of undermining their case or of assisting the case for the defendant.

What obligation, if any, is now on the defendant to make disclosure of his defence to the prosecution?

A   The defendant is required to serve a defence statement. This obligation will be enforced by the court by drawing an adverse inference against the defendant if the statement is not provided.

B   The defendant may serve a defence statement but cannot be obliged to do so. Failure to provide the statement means the prosecution will not be required to review their initial disclosure and determine if there is any further relevant unused material in its possession.

C   The defendant is not required to serve a defence statement on the prosecution as this would violate the defendant's right to a fair trial and his presumption of innocence.

D   The prosecution cannot insist on the defendant providing a defence statement, but the court is likely to make an award of costs against the defendant for failing to provide one.

E   The defendant is not required to serve a defence statement but there are good tactical reasons for serving one. This includes placing an obligation on the prosecution to then provide disclosure of their sensitive, unused material.

Answer

Option A is the best answer. Section 5 of the CPIA 1996 sets out the obligation on the defence to provide a defence statement. This is referred to as 'compulsory disclosure' where a defendant is facing trial in the Crown Court (as opposed to the magistrates' court where there is no such obligation). This obligation is enforced in the Crown Court by the court being able to draw an adverse inference against the defendant if a defence statement is not provided.

Option B is wrong, although this would be correct if the man's trial were taking place in the magistrates' court. Option C is wrong because the obligation to provide a defence statement does not violate his right to a fair trial, nor his presumption of innocence. Option D is correct to the extent that the prosecution cannot insist on the defendant providing a defence statement, but the court would not make an award of costs against the defendant for failing to do so. Option E is wrong because the defendant is required to serve this statement. Moreover, this would not trigger an obligation on the prosecution to then provide disclosure of their sensitive, unused material. Such material will never be disclosed if the prosecution makes a successful public immunity interest application to withhold its disclosure.

Principles and Procedures to Admit and Exclude Evidence

SQE1 syllabus

This chapter will enable you to achieve the SQE1 Assessment Specification in relation to Functioning Legal Knowledge concerned with the following procedures and processes:

- burden and standard of proof;

- visual identification evidence and Turnbull guidance;

- inferences from silence ss 34, 35, 36, 37, 38 Criminal Justice and Public Order Act 1994;

- hearsay evidence:
  - definition
  - grounds for admitting hearsay evidence

- confession evidence:
  - definition
  - admissibility
  - challenging admissibility ss 76 and 78 PACE 1984

- character evidence:
  - definition of bad character
  - the 7 gateways s 101(1) Criminal Justice Act 2003
  - procedure for admitting defendant's bad character
  - court's powers to exclude defendant's bad character
  - bad character of a person other than the defendant

- exclusion of evidence:
  - scope and application of s 78 PACE and the right to a fair trial.

Note that, for SQE1, candidates are not usually required to recall specific case names or cite statutory or regulatory authorities. These are provided for illustrative purposes only unless otherwise stated.

Learning outcomes

By the end of this chapter you will be able to understand and apply the following law, practice and procedure on:

- The burdens and standards of proof that operate in a criminal case.

- What is meant by disputed visual identification evidence and when the admissibility of such evidence may be excluded.

- What the Turnbull guidelines are and when they will be relevant and how they are applied in court.

- When an 'adverse inference' may be drawn against a defendant who exercises their right to remain silent.

- The meaning of hearsay evidence and when it may be admitted at trial.

- What is meant by confession evidence and the rules on admissibility of such evidence.

- The meaning of evidence of bad character and the rules and procedure on the admissibility of such evidence.

- The admissibility of improperly obtained evidence and the right of the accused to a fair trial.

9.1 Introduction

The law of evidence has a number of purposes, including the laying down of rules, establishing principles and determining the exercise of discretions in relation to what is admissible for the purposes of establishing facts in issue at trial. It also regulates the ways in which such matters can be put before the court and determines how a judge may, or must, comment on the evidence. It also establishes who should prove disputed issues of fact and the standard of proof such a party must meet in order to prove these.

There are two basic requirements which need to be satisfied if the jury or the magistrates are to take a piece of evidence into account in deciding what the facts in issue are:

(a) evidence must be relevant to the facts in issue in the case; and

(b) evidence must be admissible. This means that the rules which comprise the law of evidence must allow such evidence to be used in a criminal trial.

Evidence that is both relevant and admissible may be either direct evidence of a defendant's guilt, or circumstantial evidence from which a defendant's guilt may be inferred.

 Example

John is charged with the wounding of Liam. The CPS alleges that John stabbed Liam with a knife whilst Liam was drinking in a busy pub. The CPS has an eyewitness who identifies John as the assailant. The CPS also has a letter sent by John to Liam shortly before the stabbing, in which John threatened to 'get even' with Liam following an argument between them over some money. The evidence from the eyewitness will be direct evidence of John's guilt. The letter will be circumstantial evidence, since it is evidence that John had a motive for killing Liam.

9.2   Burden and standard of proof

9.2.1   The legal burden

In all criminal cases, the prosecution will bear the legal burden (sometimes also referred to as the persuasive burden) of proving the defendant's guilt. The standard of proof that the prosecution needs to satisfy in order to do this is to prove beyond a reasonable doubt that the defendant is guilty of the offence with which they have been charged. In other words, the magistrates or jury should convict the defendant only if they are sure of guilt (*Woolmington v DPP* [1935] AC 462).

Occasionally the legal burden of proof will also fall upon the defendant. An example of this is the defendant who pleads not guilty and raises the defence of insanity or duress. A defendant pleading either defence is required to prove those facts. In cases where the defendant bears the legal burden of proof, the standard of proof that is required is proof on the balance of probabilities. This is the lower standard of proof that also applies in civil trials and simply means 'more probable than not'.

A defendant who raises a specific defence (for example, a defendant who claims they have an alibi, or were acting in self-defence), does not have the burden of proving that defence – they only have what is called an evidential burden to raise it. The burden of disproving this then rests with the prosecution (as part of the requirement that the prosecution prove the defendant's guilt beyond a reasonable doubt) to satisfy the magistrates or the jury that the defence is not true (see below).

9.2.2   The evidential burden

9.2.2.1   The burden on the prosecution

At trial, the prosecution will present their case first. At the conclusion of its case, the prosecution must have presented sufficient evidence to the court to justify a finding of guilt and to show that the defendant has a case to answer (this is before the defendant has adduced any evidence). If the prosecution fails to do this, the defendant's solicitor (or counsel) will be entitled to make a submission of no case to answer, and to ask the court to dismiss the case. In such circumstances it is said that the prosecution has not discharged their evidential burden (see the relevant test to apply in *R v Galbraith* [1981] 2 All ER 1060 which we will look at in more detail in **Chapter 10**).

9.2.2.2   The burden on the defence

The defendant is not obliged to place any evidence before the court to show that they are innocent. However, a defendant who is raising a specific defence (for example, alibi or reasonable self-defence) must place some evidence of that defence before the court if they want the magistrates or jury to consider that defence when deciding the verdict. This is the evidential burden that the defendant bears. It is relatively simple for the defendant to satisfy such a burden. All the defendant needs to do is to enter the witness box and give details of this defence. The onus will then fall on the CPS, as part of its legal burden, to prove beyond a reasonable doubt that the defence which has been raised is not true.

✪ *Example*

Arlo is on trial for burglary and raises the defence of alibi, claiming that at the time of the burglary he was at home with his girlfriend. When presenting its case at court, the CPS must first satisfy its evidential burden by presenting sufficient evidence to the court to show that Arlo has a case to answer. Should the CPS fail to do this, Arlo's advocate will make a submission of no case to answer and ask the judge to dismiss the case. If the CPS satisfies its evidential burden, Arlo then bears the evidential burden of placing some evidence of his alibi defence before the court. Arlo will satisfy this burden by entering the witness box and giving details of his alibi. In order to secure a conviction and to satisfy its legal burden, the CPS will then need to prove beyond a reasonable doubt both that Arlo's alibi is untrue, and that Arlo did commit the burglary.

9.3 Visual identification evidence and Turnbull guidance

An important form of evidence relied upon by the prosecution in a criminal trial is visual identification evidence from a witness who claims to have seen the defendant committing the crime. Evidence from eyewitnesses is, however, notoriously unreliable, and the defendant will often dispute the visual identification which the eyewitness claims to have made. In this part of the chapter we will look at the factors the court will take into account in deciding whether disputed, visual identification evidence is admissible and, if it is, how the quality of that evidence should be assessed.

9.3.1 Challenging the admissibility of disputed visual identification evidence

Section 78 of PACE 1984 provides the court with a discretion to exclude evidence upon which the prosecution seek to rely if *'the admission of such evidence would have such an adverse effect on the fairness of proceedings that the court ought not to admit it'*. Section 78 is examined more fully at the end of this chapter. In summary, however, it is commonly raised by the defendant's solicitor when the methods employed by the police to obtain evidence constitute a significant and substantial breach either of PACE 1984, or of the Codes of Practice.

In the context of disputed visual identification evidence, such a situation may occur if the police breach the rules for holding an identification procedure contained in Code D of the Codes of Practice, that we looked at earlier in **Chapter 2**. For example:

(a) at a video identification procedure, the police may breach the requirement that the other images shown to the witness must resemble the suspect in age, general appearance and position in life (Code D, Annex A, para 2);

(b) at an identification parade, the police may breach the requirement that the witnesses attending the parade are segregated both from each other and from the suspect before and after the parade (Code D, Annex B, para 14);

(c) a breach of the Codes of Practice will occur if, whilst the defendant was detained at the police station, the police failed to hold an identification procedure when such a procedure should have been held pursuant to para 3.12 of Code D.

If the defendant's solicitor considers that disputed visual identification evidence upon which the prosecution seek to rely has been obtained following such a significant and substantial breach of Code D, they should initially challenge the admissibility of this evidence, and ask the court to exercise its discretion to exclude the evidence under s 78 of PACE 1984. Only if the court declines to exercise its discretion under s 78 should the solicitor then consider how, in cross-examination, to undermine the quality of the evidence of the original sighting of the defendant which the witness claims to have made, and what representations to make to the court in respect of the Turnbull guidelines (see below).

⭐ Example

Fynn is charged with robbery. Nadia, the victim of the robbery, gives a statement to the police describing the person who robbed her. She comments that she got only a brief glimpse of this person's face, and there are several dissimilarities between the description she gives and the actual appearance of Fynn. Nadia is nevertheless able to pick Fynn out at an identification parade carried out at the police station. The identification parade was carried out in breach of Code D because four of the other participants in the parade did not resemble Fynn and the officers investigating the robbery were present during the parade. Fynn denies taking part in the robbery and claims that Nadia is mistaken (which makes Nadia's evidence disputed visual identification evidence).

At trial, Fynn's advocate will make an application to the court under s 78 PACE 1984, for the identification evidence given by Nadia to be excluded on the basis of the breaches of Code D which occurred when the identification parade took place. Only if this application is unsuccessful will Fynn's advocate then need to consider how in cross-examination to undermine the quality of Nadia's original sighting of the robber, and what representations should be made to the court in respect of the Turnbull guidelines.

9.3.2 The Turnbull guidelines

Special guidelines apply when a witness who gives evidence for the CPS visually identifies the defendant as the person who committed the crime, and the defendant disputes that identification. The guidelines were laid down in the case of *R v Turnbull* [1977] QB 224.

A witness will identify the defendant as the person who committed the offence if:

(a) the witness picks out the defendant informally; or

(b) the witness identifies the defendant at a formal identification procedure at the police station; or

(c) the witness claims to recognise the defendant as someone previously known to them.

Such a witness is known as a 'Turnbull witness'. In all three cases, the Turnbull guidelines will apply only if the defendant disputes the visual identification made by the witness.

 Example

Lewis is on trial for an offence of affray following a public order incident outside a club. A witness called by the CPS tells the court that he saw a man involved in the affray and later identified Lewis as that man at a video identification procedure held at the police station.

(a) If Lewis denies being at the scene of the affray, the Turnbull guidelines will apply.

(b) If Lewis admits to being at the scene of the affray but denies that he was involved in the affray, and suggests that it was somebody else who was also present at the time who was involved in the affray, the Turnbull guidelines are likely to apply (see R v Thornton *below).*

(c) If Lewis admits taking part in the incident but claims that he was only acting in self-defence, the Turnbull guidelines will not apply. In this case Lewis will not be disputing the visual identification evidence given by the witness.

In R v Thornton *(1995) 1 Cr App R 578, there was a public order incident where it was alleged that the accused was one of the aggressors. Although he admitted to being present at the scene, he denied that he had been involved in the fighting and claimed that the witnesses who alleged this were mistaken. The Court of Appeal held that the Turnbull guidelines applied in this case since, on the facts, there were a number of people present who were of a similar description to the accused. However, contrast this decision with the next case.*

In R v McEvoy *[1997] Crim LR 887 there had been a similar public order situation, the only difference being that there was no one else present who could have resembled the accused in height, clothing and hair colour. For this reason, the Court of Appeal concluded that this was not a case where the Turnbull guidelines applied.*

If a witness only gives a description to the court of the person who committed the crime, but there is no direct evidence that it was the defendant (other than the fact that the defendant's physical appearance matches the description given), the Turnbull guidelines will not apply.

⭐ *Example*

Iqbal is on trial for burglary. A witness who saw the burglary tells the court that it was committed by a man who was 'approximately 6ft tall, with brown, spiky hair and a moustache'. Iqbal matches this description, but the witness failed to pick Iqbal out at a video identification at the police station.

The Turnbull guidelines will not apply in this case, because there is no direct visual identification evidence from the witness identifying Iqbal as the person responsible for the burglary, simply evidence of description.

9.3.2.1 The application of the Turnbull guidelines

Assessing the quality of the identification evidence

In the Crown Court, the trial judge is responsible for assessing the quality of the identification evidence given by a witness called by the CPS. The judge must look at the circumstances of the original sighting of the defendant by the witness and determine how strong this evidence is. The original sighting is the sighting of the person who committed the offence made by the eyewitness at the time the offence was committed.

In assessing the quality of this evidence, the trial judge will take into account a number of factors, including the following:

(a) The length of the observation – did the witness see this person for a lengthy period of time, or did they just get a fleeting glimpse?

(b) Distance – was the witness close to this person, or were they some distance away?

(c) Lighting – did the observation happen in daylight or at night? If at night, was there any street lighting? If the observation occurred inside a building, was the building well-lit or was it dark?

(d) Conditions – if the sighting was outside, what were the weather conditions at the time? Was it a clear day, or was it raining or foggy? How many other people were present at the time and did they obstruct the witness's view? Did anything else obstruct the view? If the sighting was in a building such as a pub, did any part of the building (such as a pillar) obstruct the view?

(e) How much of the suspect's face did the witness actually see – did the witness see all of the suspect's face, or merely part of it? Can the witness give a clear description of the suspect's face, or is the description vague and lacking detail?

(f) Whether the person identified was someone who was already known to the witness (a recognition case), or someone the witness had never seen before.

(g) How closely does the original description given by the witness to the police match the actual physical appearance of the defendant? Are there any discrepancies in height, build, hair colour/length or age?

Identification is good quality

If the judge considers the quality of the original sighting made by the eyewitness to be good, when the judge sums up the case to the jury before they retire to consider their verdict, the judge will point out to them the dangers of relying on identification evidence, and the special need for caution when such evidence is relied on. The judge will tell the jury that it is very easy for an honest witness to be mistaken as to identity, and will direct the jury to examine closely the circumstances of the original sighting and take into account the factors listed above when considering the quality of the identification evidence. This is usually referred to as a 'Turnbull warning'.

 Example

Elias is charged with assault occasioning actual bodily harm. The CPS seeks to rely on evidence from an eyewitness to the assault who later picked out Elias at a video identification procedure at the police station. When giving evidence at court, the witness states that he saw the assault take place over a period of 40 seconds. He also says that he had an unobstructed view of the assault from only 5 metres away, and that the assault occurred in daylight when the weather conditions were bright and clear. The judge considers that the quality of the initial sighting by the eyewitness is good. When summing up the case at the end of the trial the judge will give a 'Turnbull warning' to the jury, by warning the jury about relying on identification evidence and will direct them to take into account the factors listed above when considering the quality of the identification evidence.

Identification poor but supported

If the judge considers the quality of the initial sighting by the eyewitness to be poor, but this identification evidence is supported by other evidence, a 'Turnbull warning' similar to that described above should be given to the jury. The judge will again point out the dangers of relying on identification evidence and the special need for caution when the jury are considering such evidence. The judge will also draw to the specific attention of the jury the weaknesses in the identification evidence which has been given.

Supporting evidence means some other evidence which suggests that the identification made by the witness is reliable. The judge will normally warn the jury about the dangers of convicting on the basis of the identification evidence alone and tell the jury to look for other supporting evidence. The jury will be directed to what other evidence may amount to supporting evidence. Examples of supporting evidence include:

(a) a confession made by the defendant;

(b) other evidence placing the defendant at the scene of the offence (such as fingerprints or DNA evidence);

(c) in a theft case, stolen property being found in the defendant's possession;

(d) adverse inferences being drawn from the defendant's silence when questioned at the police station (see later in this chapter).

 Example

Jake is charged with unlawful wounding. The CPS has two items of evidence:

(i) Jake's fingerprints, found on a knife which it is alleged he used as a weapon; and

(ii) evidence from an eyewitness to the wounding who picked Jake out in a video identification procedure at the police station.

When giving evidence at Jake's trial, the eyewitness concedes that the incident occurred at night in an alley where there was no lighting. The eyewitness also says that he only observed the incident briefly and saw only part of the attacker's face.

At the end of the prosecution case, the judge assesses the identification evidence given by the eyewitness as being of poor quality. However, this evidence is supported by Jake's fingerprints on the knife. When summing up the case, the judge will give a 'Turnbull warning' to the jury, by warning the jury about the dangers of relying on identification evidence and the special need for caution when such evidence is being considered. The judge will also point out all the weaknesses in the identification evidence that has been given. The judge will tell the jury about the dangers of convicting on the basis of the identification alone and to look for other supporting evidence. Finally, the judge will explain to the jury what other evidence is capable of amounting to supporting evidence (ie the fingerprints on the knife).

Identification poor and unsupported

If the judge considers the identification evidence to be of poor quality, and it is not supported by any other prosecution evidence, the judge should stop the trial at the end of the prosecution case and direct the jury to acquit the defendant. This will normally follow a submission of no case to answer being made by the defendant's advocate.

 Example

Rebecca is charged with theft. The only evidence called by the CPS is from an eyewitness who picked Rebecca out at a video identification procedure at the police station. When cross-examined at court, the witness concedes that she got only a fleeting glimpse of the person who committed the theft, and that this was from a long distance away at a time when it was raining heavily and a lot of other people were present to obstruct her view. At the end of the prosecution case, Rebecca's counsel will make a submission of no case to answer. If the judge assesses the identification evidence which has been given to be of poor quality and unsupported, the judge will stop the trial and direct the jury to acquit Rebecca.

9.3.3 The Turnbull guidelines in the magistrates' court

In the magistrates' court, the magistrates decide matters of both fact and law, and it will therefore be necessary for the defendant's solicitor to address the magistrates on the Turnbull guidelines during the course of the trial.

If the defendant's solicitor considers that the quality of the identification evidence given by an eyewitness is poor, and the CPS has no other supporting evidence, the solicitor should make a submission of no case to answer at the end of the prosecution case (see **Chapter 10**).

If the identification evidence given by the eyewitness is either good or poor, but supported by other evidence called by the CPS, the defendant's solicitor is unlikely to make a submission of no case to answer. They will instead address the Turnbull guidelines in their closing speech to the magistrates, and will point out that, however strong it might appear, identification evidence from an eyewitness is notoriously unreliable and the magistrates should exercise caution when considering such evidence. The defendant's solicitor will also point out any weaknesses in the identification evidence that has been given.

For a summary of visual identification evidence, see **Figure 9.1** below.

Figure 9.1 Flowchart – Visual identification evidence

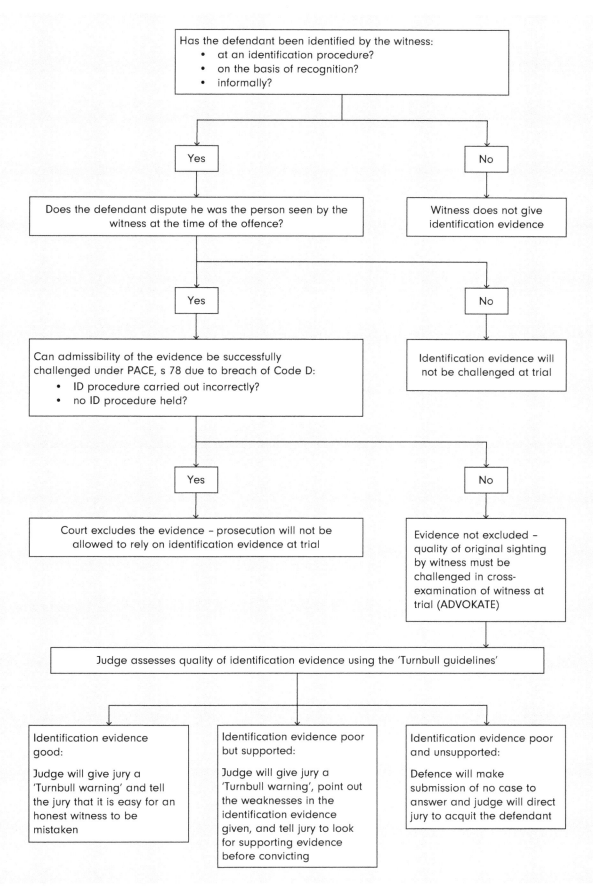

9.4 Inferences from silence – ss 34, 35, 36, 37, 38 Criminal Justice and Public Order Act 1994

9.4.1 The 'right to silence'

Anyone who is arrested on suspicion of having committed a criminal offence has a right to remain silent when interviewed at the police station. However, under the provisions of the Criminal Justice and Public Order Act (CJPOA) 1994, when a defendant's case comes to trial, the court may be allowed to draw what are termed 'adverse inferences' from this earlier silence when being questioned under caution about the offence. We will consider when a court is allowed to draw such inferences, and the potential evidential consequences which may arise at trial when a solicitor advises a client not to answer questions when interviewed at the police station.

9.4.1.1 What is an adverse inference?

The provisions of the CJPOA actually refer to 'proper inferences' being drawn, but the reality is that these are likely to be adverse inferences. The term 'adverse inference' means a court is likely to draw a negative conclusion from the defendant's silence when interviewed at the police station. In other words, the court may hold a defendant's silence against them. The usual inference that the jury or magistrates will draw is one of recent fabrication, namely that the defendant remained silent when interviewed by the police because they had no adequate explanation for their conduct, and that they fabricated the facts which make up their defence at trial after being charged by the police. Alternatively, the court may draw an inference that, even though the defendant did not fabricate this defence after leaving the police station, the defendant did not put the defence forward when interviewed by the police because they did not believe it would stand up to further investigation by the police.

A defendant will not be convicted of an offence if the only evidence against them is an adverse inference under ss 34, 36 or 37 of the CJPOA 1994, because a defendant's silence when interviewed by the police cannot on its own prove guilt (CJPOA 1994, s 38(3)). Before the prosecution may ask the court to draw an adverse inference from a defendant's silence when interviewed by the police, the prosecution must first have adduced other evidence of the defendant's guilt. Such evidence must establish that the defendant has a case to answer and must call for an explanation from the defendant.

Note however that a court is not allowed to draw an adverse inference from a defendant's silence if that silence occurred at a time when the defendant had not been allowed the opportunity to consult a solicitor to obtain independent legal advice (s 58 of the Youth Justice and Criminal Evidence Act 1999). In such circumstances, the defendant is said to have an absolute right to remain silent and the caution given before interview should reflect this. Adverse inferences may therefore only be drawn when a defendant has been given the opportunity to take independent legal advice, even if they decline that opportunity.

9.4.2 Inferences under s 34 CJPOA 1994

Section 34 allows the court or jury to draw an adverse inference from a defendant's silence when the defendant was being questioned or charged at the police station. Section 34 provides:

(1) Where in any proceedings against a person for an offence, evidence is given that the accused:

    (a) at any time before he was charged with the offence, on being questioned under caution by a constable trying to discover whether or by whom the offence had been committed, failed to mention any fact relied on in his defence in those proceedings; or

    (b) on being charged with the offence or officially informed that he might be prosecuted for it, failed to mention any such fact ...

being a fact, which in the circumstances existing at the time the accused could reasonably have been expected to mention ... the court or jury ... may draw such inferences from the failure as appear proper.

✪ *Example*

Ethan is arrested on suspicion of theft. Ethan refuses to answer questions put to him by the police when interviewed at the police station under caution. Ethan is subsequently charged with the theft. At his trial, Ethan raises the defence of alibi, claiming that he was at a friend's house at the time the alleged theft took place. Section 34 allows the court to draw an adverse inference from Ethan's failure to mention his alibi defence when being questioned by the police.

So, the inferences that may be drawn against a defendant need not necessarily arise out of 'no comment' interviews. The terms of s 34 may be satisfied even where a defendant has answered every question put to them, if at trial they raise some other fact in their defence that they did not mention, but could reasonably have been expected to mention, when interviewed.

9.4.2.1 Pre-conditions for the drawing of an adverse inference

There has been a lot of case law on the operation of s 34.

In *R v Argent* [1997] 2 Cr App R 27, the Court of Appeal said that certain conditions had to be satisfied before adverse inferences could be drawn from a defendant's silence in police interview under s 34(1)(a):

(a) the interview had to be an interview under caution;

(b) the defendant had to fail to mention any fact later relied on in his defence at trial;

(c) the failure to mention this fact had to occur before the defendant was charged;

(d) the questioning of the defendant at the interview in which the defendant failed to mention the fact had to be directed to trying to discover whether or by whom the alleged offence had been committed; and

(e) the fact which the defendant failed to mention had to be a fact which, in the circumstances existing at the time, the defendant could reasonably have been expected to mention when questioned.

In *Condron v UK* (2001) 31 EHRR 1, the European Court of Human Rights held that a jury should be directed that an adverse inference from a defendant's silence could be drawn only if the court was satisfied that the real reason for the defendant's silence was that they had no answer to the questions that were being put to them, or no answer that would stand up to scrutiny.

In *R v Betts and Hall* [2001] 2 Cr App R 257, the Court of Appeal stated that if a defendant remained silent during their initial interview at the police station and then answered questions during a subsequent interview, inferences from their failure to answer questions in the first interview might still be drawn at trial.

Note that it is unlikely, in practice, for a court to draw an adverse inference under s 34(1) (b). If a defendant places their factual defence on record when interviewed by the police, a court will not then draw an adverse inference if the defendant says nothing when they are subsequently charged. If, conversely, the defendant remains silent in interview and then raises a defence at trial, the court is very likely to draw an adverse inference under s 34(1)(a).

9.4.2.2 Use of a prepared written statement

A solicitor advising a client at a police station will often advise a client that rather than answering questions in interview, the client should instead hand to the police a written statement, which the solicitor will prepare on the client's behalf. The advantage of this is that it allows the client's version of events to be set out in a clear and logical way. This is particularly useful for a client whom the solicitor feels may not come across well in interview (for example, a client who is distressed, emotional or tired).

In *R v Knight* [2003] EWCA Crim 1977, the Court of Appeal held that the purpose of s 34 was to encourage defendants to make an early disclosure of their defence to the police, not to allow the police to scrutinise and test that defence in interview (although of course the police would be able to investigate the facts of the defence outside the interview by, for example, speaking to witnesses who the defendant said would support their case). Therefore, as long as a written statement which is handed to the police contains all the facts which a defendant later relies on in their defence at court, the court will not be able to draw an adverse inference under s 34 if, having handed in the statement, the defendant then refuses to answer questions from the police based on the contents of that written statement.

In the rare situations when a defence solicitor prepares a written statement for their client but does not hand this in to the police, whilst this will prevent the court at trial from drawing the inference of recent fabrication, it will not prevent the court from drawing an inference that the defendant was not sufficiently confident about their defence to expose this to investigation by the police following the interview.

9.4.2.3 When may a solicitor advise a suspect to remain silent?

The appellate courts have said on a number of occasions it may be appropriate for a solicitor to advise their client to remain silent when interviewed by the police in the following circumstances:

(a) Level of disclosure given by the police – although the police are not under a general duty to disclose to the suspect's solicitor all the details of the evidence which they have obtained against the suspect, the courts have held that if the absence of meaningful disclosure means that a solicitor is unable properly to advise their client, this may amount to a good reason for advising the client to remain silent (*R v Argent* [1997] 2 Cr App R 27; *R v Roble* [1997] Crim LR 449).

(b) Nature of the case – if the material the police have is particularly complex, or relates to events which occurred a long time ago, the solicitor may advise their client to remain silent when it would not be sensible to give an immediate response to the police (*R v Roble* (see above); *R v Howell* [2003] Crim LR 405).

(c) Personal circumstances of the suspect – if the solicitor considers the suspect to be suffering from some form of ill health, the suspect is mentally disordered or vulnerable, is excessively tired or is otherwise confused, shocked or intoxicated, the solicitor would be justified in advising the suspect to remain silent (*R v Howell*, above).

9.4.2.4 Silence on legal advice

Can a defendant avoid an adverse inference by claiming their refusal to answer questions was based on legal advice?

A defendant who at trial claims that the only reason for their silence when interviewed by the police was as a result of legal advice they received from their solicitor will not automatically prevent the court from drawing an adverse inference if they subsequently raise in their defence a fact which they failed to mention at the police station. The European Court of Human Rights has accepted that this does not breach a defendant's right to a fair trial under Article 6 of the ECHR, although the Court has pointed out that legal advice is a fundamental part of the right to a fair trial and, as such, the fact that a defendant was advised by his solicitor to not answer questions in the police station must be given appropriate weight at trial (*Condron v UK* [2000] see above).

In *R v Beckles* [2004] EWCA Crim 2766, the Court of Appeal held that where a defendant explained his reason for silence as being their reliance on legal advice, the ultimate question for the court or jury under s 34 was whether the facts relied on at trial were facts which the defendant could reasonably have been expected to mention in police interview. If they were not, then no adverse inference could be drawn. If the court or jury considered that the defendant genuinely relied on the advice they had received from their solicitor, that would not necessarily be the end of the matter because it still might not have been reasonable for them to rely on the advice, or the advice might not have been the true explanation for this silence.

Following the *Beckles* and *Howell* cases, the jury will now be directed by the trial judge that adverse inferences should not be drawn under s 34 (and ss 36 and 37) if the jury believe that the defendant genuinely and reasonably relied on the legal advice to remain silent.

9.4.2.5 Legal privilege

Conversations between a suspect and their solicitor at the police station are protected by legal privilege. In an interview, the police are not allowed to ask a suspect what advice they received from their solicitor (or, if the police were to ask, the solicitor would instruct the suspect not to answer). At trial, however, a defendant may give evidence which has the effect of waiving such privilege and allowing the prosecution to cross-examine them about the reasons for the legal advice they were given.

If at trial, in order to prevent an adverse inference being drawn by the court, a defendant gives evidence that they remained silent in interview only following advice from their solicitor, this will not in itself waive privilege (*R v Beckles* above). However, if an adverse inference is to be avoided, the court is likely to want to know the reasons for the solicitor's advice. Once a defendant gives this information, legal privilege is said to be waived (*R v Bowden* [1999] 1 WLR 823). This means that if a defendant, when giving evidence-in-chief, gives the reasons for the legal advice they received, the defendant (and conceivably their solicitor, should the solicitor give evidence on the defendant's behalf) may then be cross-examined as to any other reason for the solicitor's decision to advise their client to remain silent. Similarly, the prosecution will be entitled to cross-examine the defendant (and their solicitor) on the instructions which the defendant gave to their solicitor whilst at the police station which led to the solicitor advising them to remain silent in interview.

9.4.2.6 Denial of access to legal advice

Note that an adverse inference cannot be drawn in the following circumstance, according to s 34(2A):

> Where an accused was at an authorised place of detention at the time of the failure, subsection (1) and (2) do not apply if he had not been allowed an opportunity to consult a solicitor prior to being questioned, charged ...

✪ *Example*

Marco has been arrested on suspicion of armed robbery. The police believe that accomplices are still at large and the weapons that were used have not yet been located. Marco requests legal advice on his arrival at the police station, but this is lawfully postponed by a superintendent. When Marco is interviewed, he will be cautioned, but his caution will simply remind him that he has a right to remain silent and will not go on to explain when proper inferences may be drawn if he exercises this right. In other words, Marco has an absolute right to remain silent and must be told that when he is cautioned, and a trial judge will also be required to direct a jury about what such a right actually means where a defendant does remain silent at interview and then subsequently relies on facts they did not mention when first interviewed.

9.4.3 Inferences under s 36 CJPOA 1994

Section 36 allows the court or jury to draw an adverse inference if, when interviewed by the police, the defendant failed to account for the presence of an object, substance or mark.

Section 36 provides:

(1) Where:

    (a) a person is arrested by a constable, and there is:
        (i) on his person; or
        (ii) in or on his clothing or footwear; or
        (iii) otherwise in his possession; or
        (iv) in any place in which he is at the time of his arrest,
        any object, substance or mark, or there is any mark on any such object; and

    (b) that or another constable investigating the case reasonably believes that the presence of the object, substance or mark may be attributable to the participation of the person arrested in the commission of an offence specified by the constable; and

    (c) the constable informs the person arrested that he so believes, and requests him to account for the presence of the object, substance or mark; and

    (d) the person fails or refuses to do so,
        then ... the court or jury ... may draw such inferences from the failure or refusal as appear proper.

⭐ Example 1

Jon is arrested on suspicion of assaulting Fergus. In an interview at the police station, Jon is asked to account for the fact that when he was arrested there was blood on his shirt and his knuckles were grazed. Jon does not reply to this question. Section 36 allows a court to draw an adverse inference from Jon's failure to account for his bloodstained shirt and grazed knuckles.

⭐ Example 2

Rick is arrested on suspicion of the burglary of commercial premises. Entry to the premises was gained by the use of a crowbar to open a window. In an interview at the police station, Rick is asked to account for the fact that when he was arrested, he had in his possession a crowbar. Rick does not reply to this question. Section 36 allows a court to draw an adverse inference from Rick's failure to account for his possession of the crowbar.

Although there is a degree of overlap between ss 34 and 36, note that s 34 will apply only if a defendant raises a fact at trial, which they failed to mention at the police station, whereas s 36 will operate irrespective of any defence put forward. It may apply even if no defence is raised at trial, because the inference arises from the defendant's failure to account for the object, substance or mark at the time of interview. The inference which is likely to arise in such a case is that the defendant had no explanation for the presence of the object, substance or mark, or no explanation that would have stood up to police questioning.

Another important difference from s 34 is that inferences may be drawn under s 36 only if the police officer requesting the explanation for the object, substance or mark has told the suspect certain specified matters before requesting the explanation (this is referred to as a 'special caution'). The suspect must be told:

(a) what the offence under investigation is;

(b) what fact the suspect is being asked to account for;

(c) that the officer believes this fact may be due to the suspect taking part in the commission of the offence in question;

(d) that a court may draw an adverse inference from failure to comply with the request; and

(e) that a record is being made of the interview and that it may be given in evidence if the suspect is brought to trial (PACE 1984, Code C, para 10.11).

9.4.4 Inferences under s 37 CJPOA 1994

Section 37 allows the court to draw an adverse inference if, when questioned at the police station, the defendant failed to account for his presence at a particular place at or about the time the offence was committed.

Section 37 provides:

(1) Where:

(a) a person arrested by a constable was found by him at a place at or about the time the offence for which he was arrested is alleged to have been committed; and

(b) that or another constable investigating the offence reasonably believes that the presence of the person at that place and at that time may be attributed to his participation in the commission of the offence; and

(c) the constable informs the person that he so believes, and requests him to account for that presence; and

(d) the person fails or refuses to do so,

then ... the court or jury ... may draw such inferences from the failure or refusal as appear proper.

 Example

Lance is arrested on suspicion of the burglary of a jewellery shop. Lance is arrested by the police whilst standing outside the jewellery shop, only two minutes after the shop's burglar alarm went off. When interviewed at the police station, Lance is asked to account for his presence near the shop at or about the time of the burglary. Lance does not reply to this question. Section 37 allows the court to draw an adverse inference from Lance's failure to account for his presence near the shop at or about the time of the burglary.

As with s 36, there is some overlap between ss 34 and 37, but whilst s 34 will apply only if a defendant raises a fact which they failed to mention at the police station, in their defence at trial, s 37 will operate irrespective of any defence put forward. It may apply even if no defence is raised at trial, because the inference arises from the defendant's failure to account for their presence at a particular place at or about the time of the offence at the time of interview. The inference which is likely to be drawn in such circumstances is that the defendant has no explanation for their presence at that particular place at or about the time the offence was committed, or no explanation that would have stood up to police questioning.

 Example

Sonia is arrested whilst walking late at night along an alley behind a house which has just been burgled. Sonia is interviewed at the police station and is asked to account for her presence in the alley at or about the time of the burglary. Sonia refuses to answer this question.

If, at her trial, Sonia states that she was walking along the alley because she was taking a shortcut home, s 34 will apply because Sonia did not mention this fact when interviewed at the police station. Whether or not at trial Sonia puts forward an explanation for her presence in the alley, s 37 will apply because Sonia failed to explain the reason for her presence in the alley when she was interviewed at the police station (assuming she was given a 'special caution').

So as with s 36, inferences may be drawn under s 37 only if a suspect has been given the 'special caution'.

Figure 9.2   Flowcharts – Adverse inferences under ss 34, 36 and 37 CJPOA

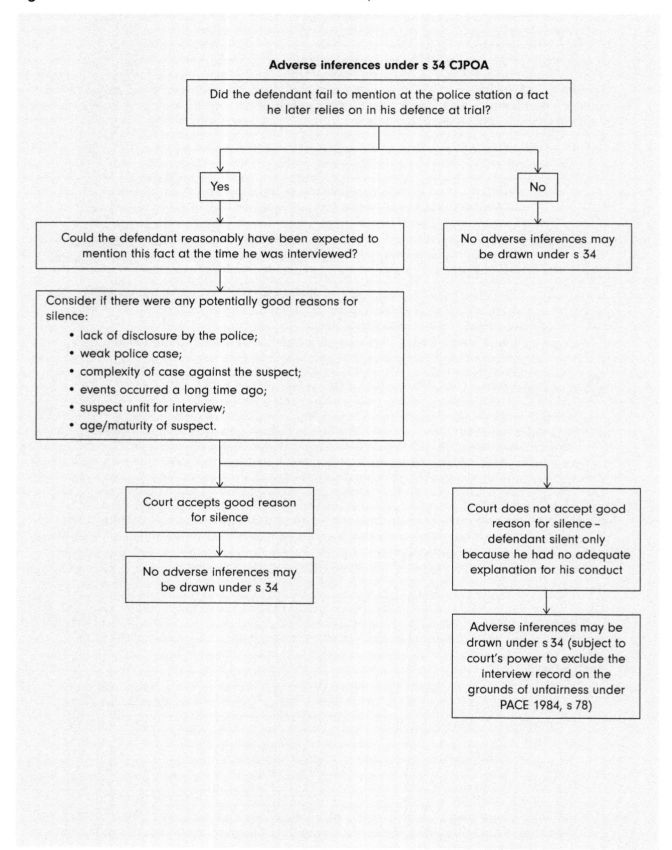

Figure 9.2 (*continued*)

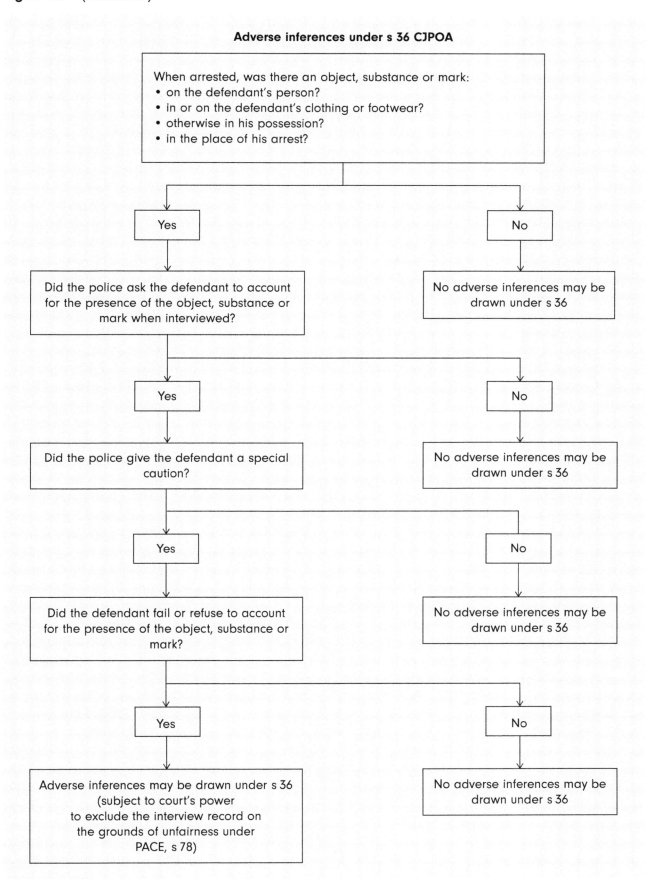

Adverse inferences under s 36 CJPOA

When arrested, was there an object, substance or mark:
• on the defendant's person?
• in or on the defendant's clothing or footwear?
• otherwise in his possession?
• in the place of his arrest?

Yes → Did the police ask the defendant to account for the presence of the object, substance or mark when interviewed?

No → No adverse inferences may be drawn under s 36

Yes → Did the police give the defendant a special caution?

No → No adverse inferences may be drawn under s 36

Yes → Did the defendant fail or refuse to account for the presence of the object, substance or mark?

No → No adverse inferences may be drawn under s 36

Yes → Adverse inferences may be drawn under s 36 (subject to court's power to exclude the interview record on the grounds of unfairness under PACE, s 78)

No → No adverse inferences may be drawn under s 36

(*continued*)

Figure 9.2 (*continued*)

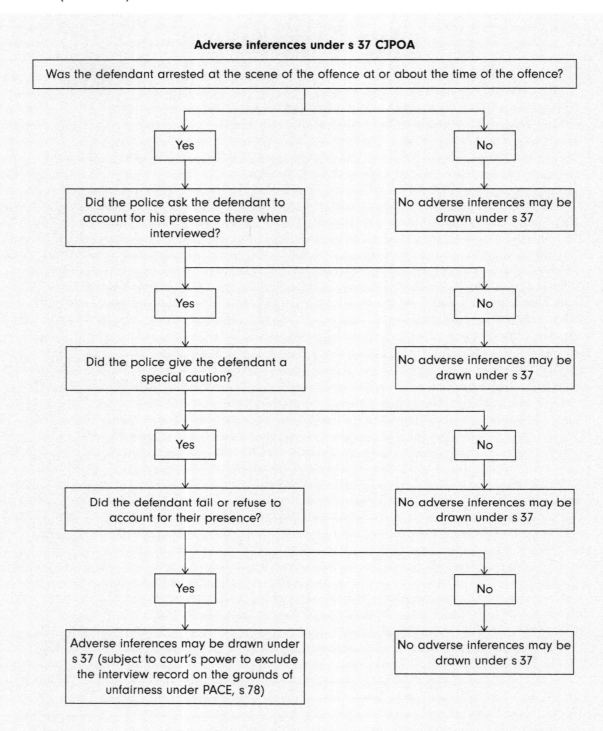

9.4.5 Silence at trial and inferences under s 35 CJPOA

Unless at trial a defendant makes a successful submission of no case to answer at the end of the prosecution case, the defendant will then have the opportunity to put their case before the court. A defendant is not obligated to give evidence on their own behalf at trial. Neither is a defendant obligated to raise any facts in their own defence. The defendant is entitled to remain silent at trial (Criminal Evidence Act 1898, s 1(1)) and simply argue that the CPS has failed to prove guilt beyond a reasonable doubt.

Since the defendant will not be raising any facts in his defence at trial which he did not mention in the police station, no adverse inferences may be drawn under s 34.

However, a defendant who fails to give evidence on his own behalf at trial may be subject to an adverse inference being drawn by the court or jury under s 35 of the CJPOA 1994.

Section 35(2) provides that:

> the court shall, at the conclusion of the evidence for the prosecution, satisfy itself ... that the accused is aware that the stage has been reached at which evidence can be given for the defence and that he can, if he wishes, give evidence and that, if he chooses not to give evidence, or having been sworn, without good cause refuses to answer any question, it will be permissible for the court or jury to draw such inferences as appear proper from his failure to give evidence or his refusal, without good cause, to answer any question.

The effect of s 35 is that, if the prosecution has raised issues which call for an explanation from the defendant, should the defendant then fail to give evidence, the court will be entitled to infer from that failure that the defendant has either no explanation, or no explanation that will stand up to cross-examination.

✪ Example

Marcus is charged with common assault. Marcus pleads not guilty on the basis that he was acting in self-defence. At the end of the prosecution case, Marcus declines to enter the witness box to give evidence on his own behalf. The court is entitled to infer from this that Marcus has no defence to the charge, or no defence that will stand up to cross-examination (in other words, an inference that Marcus is guilty of the offence).

In the combined appeal of *R v Cowan; R v Gayle; R v Ricciardy* [1995] 4 All ER 939, the Court of Appeal stated that the court had to take into account the following matters when considering the application of s 35:

(a) the burden of proof remains on the prosecution throughout;

(b) the defendant is entitled to remain silent;

(c) before drawing an adverse inference from the defendant's silence, the court had to be satisfied that there was a case to answer on the prosecution evidence;

(d) an adverse inference from the defendant's failure to give evidence cannot on its own prove guilt; and

(e) no adverse inference could be drawn unless the only sensible explanation for the defendant's silence was that he had no answer to the case against him, or none that could have stood up to cross-examination.

As with ss 34, 36 and 37, a defendant will not be convicted of an offence if the only evidence against him is an adverse inference from his failure to give evidence in his defence at trial (CJPOA 1994, s 38(3)).

Unlike ss 34, 36 and 37, there is also a limited statutory exception to the drawing of adverse inferences which can be found at s 35(1)(b). This provides the court with a discretion to direct that an adverse inference is not drawn where

> it appears to the court that the physical or mental condition of the accused makes it undesirable for him to give evidence.

Case law suggests that this exception will be applied strictly.

 In R v Friend [1997] Crim LR 817, the accused, a boy aged 14 years at the time of the trial, was convicted of murder. It was said that he had an IQ of a 9-year-old. He didn't give evidence at his trial and the trial judge invited the jury to draw an adverse inference. On appeal, it was argued by the defence that the exception should have applied, and no adverse inference should have been drawn from his refusal to testify. In dismissing the appeal, the Court of Appeal held that although the trial judge had a discretion under s 35(1)(b) to direct that no adverse inference be drawn, this was not one of those where the exception applied. The Court of Appeal indicated the type of circumstances that the statutory exception was aimed at. For example, if giving evidence was likely to trigger an epileptic seizure, or if the accused was schizophrenic and testifying was likely to cause a florid state.

However, Friend's second appeal R v Friend (No 2) [2004] EWCA 2661 saw the Court of Appeal entertain the possibility of widening the availability of this exception. It did so when it quashed the original conviction in light of new expert evidence which concluded that Friend suffered from Attention Deficit Hyperactivity Disorder (ADHD) and, consequently, he was unlikely to have been able to effectively participate in the trial and might have given inconsistent and conflicting evidence.

9.5 Hearsay evidence

We will start by looking at the statutory definition of hearsay evidence provided by the Criminal Justice Act (CJA) 2003, and the various forms of hearsay evidence that are made admissible in criminal proceedings by virtue of the Act before touching on the procedural requirements that must be complied with should any party seek to adduce hearsay evidence at trial.

9.5.1 Definition

A 'hearsay statement' is defined in s 114(1) of the CJA 2003 as 'a statement, not made in oral evidence, that is relied on as evidence of a matter in it'.

 Example

George is charged with handling a stolen bike. At George's trial, the CPS calls Adam to give evidence. Adam tells the court: 'George showed me a bike. He told me he had just been given it by a mate of his who had nicked it from somewhere else.' This will be hearsay evidence because the CPS will rely on the out-of-court statement made by George to Adam to show that he was in possession of a bike which he knew to be stolen. The statement by George is being relied on as evidence of a matter stated in it.

A 'statement' is defined in s 115(2) as 'any representation of fact or opinion made by a person by whatever means; and it includes a representation made in a sketch, photofit or other pictorial form'.

The purpose, or one of the purposes, of the person making the statement must appear to the court to have been to cause another person to believe that the matter, or to cause another person to act (or a machine to operate) on the basis that the matter, is as stated (CJA 2003, s 115(3)).

 R v Knight [2007] All ER (D) 381 (Nov) – the defendant was convicted of various sexual offences committed against a 14-year-old girl. At trial, the girl's aunt was allowed to give evidence of entries she had read in the girl's diaries that detailed the girl's sexual contacts with the defendant. The defendant submitted that such evidence was hearsay

and should not have been admitted. In refusing the appeal, the Court of Appeal held that such evidence was not hearsay, because the girl had not intended other people to read the entries in the diary and it therefore fell outside the scope of s 115.

9.5.1.1 Examples of hearsay evidence in criminal proceedings

Examples of hearsay evidence that commonly arise in criminal proceedings are:

(a) a witness repeating at trial what they had been told by another person;

(b) a statement from a witness being read out at trial instead of the witness attending court to give oral evidence;

(c) a police officer repeating at trial a confession made to them by the defendant;

(d) a business document being introduced in evidence at trial.

9.5.1.2 First-hand and multiple hearsay

Hearsay evidence may be either 'first-hand' hearsay, or 'multiple' hearsay.

⭐ **Example 1**

Jason is on trial for theft. The arresting officer (PC Kalpar) gives evidence that when he arrested Jason, Jason made the following confession: 'Okay, fair enough, it was me. I only did it for drug money.'

This is first-hand hearsay evidence, because PC Kalpar is repeating a statement that he heard Jason make. Details of the contents of Jason's statement did not pass through anyone else before getting to PC Kalpar.

⭐ **Example 2**

Maryam is a bank clerk. She receives a cash deposit of £5,000 from a customer and places this in the bank's safe. She tells Brian, the senior cashier, who in turn tells Emir, the manager. Emir makes a record of the deposit in a ledger. An armed robbery subsequently takes place and the £5,000 is stolen. At the robber's trial, the CPS seeks to use the entry in the ledger to show how much money was in the safe. The entry in the ledger will be multiple hearsay. The details of the amount of money placed in the safe have passed from Maryam to Brian, then from Brian to Emir and then from Emir into the ledger itself.

The circumstances in which a statement containing multiple hearsay is admissible in evidence are more limited than when a statement contains only first-hand hearsay (see below).

9.5.2 Grounds for admitting hearsay evidence

Hearsay evidence will be admissible if it falls within one of four categories. Section 114 of the CJA 2003 states:

(1) In criminal proceedings a statement not made in oral evidence in the proceedings is admissible as evidence of any matter stated if, but only if:

(a) any provision of this Chapter or any other statutory provision makes it admissible,

(b) any rule of law preserved by section 118 makes it admissible,

(c) all parties to the proceedings agree to it being admissible, or

(d) the court is satisfied that it is in the interests of justice for it to be admissible.

9.5.2.1 Hearsay admissible under a statutory provision – s 114(1)(a)

There are a number of statutory provisions contained in the CJA, including:

(a) cases where a witness is unavailable – CJA 2003, s 116;

(b) business and other documents – CJA 2003, s 117;

(c) previous inconsistent statements of a witness – CJA 2003, s 119;

(d) previous consistent statements by a witness – CJA 2003, s 120;

(e) statements from a witness which are not in dispute – CJA 1967, s 9; and

(f) formal admissions – CJA 1967, s 10.

We will just focus on the first two groups.

Cases where a witness is unavailable to attend court

Section 116 of the CJA 2003 provides:

(1) In criminal proceedings a statement not made in oral evidence in the proceedings is admissible as evidence of any matter stated if:

  (a) oral evidence given in the proceedings by the person who made the statement would be admissible as evidence of that matter [ie the statement must be 'first-hand hearsay'],

  (b) the person who made the statement (the relevant person) is identified to the court's satisfaction, and

  (c) any of the five conditions mentioned in subsection (2) is satisfied.

The conditions referred to in s 116(2)(a)–(e) are that:

(a) the relevant person is dead;

(b) the relevant person is unfit to be a witness because of his bodily or mental condition;

(c) the relevant person is outside the United Kingdom and it is not reasonably practicable to secure his attendance;

(d) the relevant person cannot be found, although such steps as it is reasonably practicable to take to find him have been taken;

(e) through fear the relevant person does not give oral evidence in the proceedings, either at all or in connection with the subject matter of the statement, and the court gives leave for the statement to be given in evidence.

✪ Example 1

Zoë witnesses an assault and gives a signed statement to the police describing what she saw. Before the case comes to trial, Zoë is killed in a road traffic accident. Zoë's written statement will be admissible in evidence because she satisfies the condition in s 116(2)(a) and oral evidence given by her of what she saw when the assault occurred would have been admissible at trial.

✪ Example 2

Hafsa witnesses an armed robbery at the bank where she works and provides a witness statement describing what happened and identifying the robbers. Before the case comes to trial, Hafsa is involved in a serious road traffic accident and is placed on a life support machine. Hafsa's witness statement will be admissible in evidence because she satisfies the condition in s 116(2(b) and oral evidence given by her of what she saw when the robbery occurred and her identification of the robbers would have been admissible at trial.

✪ Example 3

Tariq, a serving soldier, witnesses a theft and gives a signed statement to the police describing what he saw. Before the case comes to trial, Tariq is posted abroad. Tariq's written statement will be admissible in evidence because he satisfies the condition in s 116(2)(c) (assuming it is not reasonably practicable to secure his attendance at trial) and oral evidence given by him of what he saw when the theft occurred would have been admissible at trial.

Example 4

Ben lives in a shelter for the homeless. He witnesses a road traffic accident in which a young child is seriously injured. Ben gives a witness statement to the police, and the driver involved in the accident is subsequently charged with dangerous driving. Before the trial takes place, Ben leaves the shelter. Despite making extensive enquiries, the police are unable to locate Ben's current whereabouts. Ben's written statement will be admissible in evidence because the condition in s 116(2)(d) appears to be satisfied and oral evidence given by Ben of what he saw when the accident occurred would have been admissible at trial.

 Example 5

Ava witnesses a murder. She gives a signed statement to the police describing what she saw. Before the case comes to trial, Ava receives several anonymous letters telling her that if she gives evidence at court, her baby son will be killed. Ava refuses to attend court to give oral evidence of what she saw. Ava's written statement may be admissible in evidence. She appears to satisfy the condition in s 116(2)(e) and oral evidence given by her of what she saw when the murder occurred would have been admissible at trial. However, the trial judge will still need to give leave for her written statement to be admitted in evidence, having regard to the matters listed in s 116(4).

Section 116(4) requires the court to give leave only if it considers that the statement ought to be admitted in the *interests of justice* having regard to the contents, to any risk of unfairness (in particular how difficult it would be to challenge the statement) and the fact that (in appropriate cases) a special measures direction could be made.

Remember, s 116 applies only to 'first-hand' hearsay. In other words, a statement can be admissible under this section only if the person who made that statement would have been allowed to give oral evidence at trial of the matters contained in the statement. In the examples given above, the statement of each witness who was unable to come to court to give oral evidence would constitute 'first-hand' hearsay because their evidence had not passed through any other hands and was direct evidence of what they either saw or did. Below is an example of 'second-hand' or multiple hearsay. Such evidence is not admissible under s 116.

 Example

Fozia witnesses an assault. She tells Jenny what she saw when the assault occurred. Jenny then gives a signed statement to the police repeating what she had been told by Fozia. Before the case comes to trial, Jenny is killed in a road traffic accident. Jenny's statement will not be admissible under s 116. Although Jenny satisfies the condition in s 116(2)(a) above, she would not have been allowed to give oral evidence at court as to the contents of her statement because her statement merely repeated what she had been told by Fozia and was itself hearsay. Any evidence given by Jenny would be multiple hearsay and therefore not admissible.

Business and other documents

Section 117 of the CJA 2003 provides:

(1) In criminal proceedings a statement contained in a document is admissible as evidence of any matter stated if:

(a) oral evidence given in the proceedings would be evidence of that matter,

(b) the requirements of subsection (2) are satisfied, and

(c) the requirements of subsection (5) are satisfied, in a case where subsection (4) requires them to be.

The requirements of s 117(2) are that:

(a) the document (or the part of it containing the statement) must have been created or received by a person in the course of a trade, business, profession or other occupation, or as the holder of a paid or unpaid office;

(b) the person who supplied the information contained in the statement (the relevant person) had, or may reasonably be supposed to have had, personal knowledge of the matters dealt with; and

(c) each person (if any) through whom the information was supplied from the relevant person to the person mentioned in paragraph (a) received the information in the course of a trade, business, profession or other occupation, or as the holder of a paid or unpaid office.

The practical effect of s 117 is to make both 'first-hand' and 'multiple' hearsay in certain documents admissible in evidence.

Business records

Section 117 will commonly be used to ensure the admissibility in evidence of business records.

 Example 1

Omar is charged with armed robbery. The CPS alleges that Omar bought the shotgun used in the robbery from a local gun shop two weeks prior to the robbery taking place. The CPS seeks to adduce in evidence a handwritten receipt given to Omar at the time the shotgun was purchased. The receipt was prepared by Neville, the owner of the gun shop.

The receipt will be first-hand hearsay evidence and will be admissible under s 117. The receipt is a statement in a document and was prepared by Neville in the course of his business from information about which he had first-hand knowledge, namely Omar's purchase of the shotgun.

Example 2

Paul deposits £500 in a safe at the bank where he works. He tells Youssef, a clerk at the bank, who records the deposit in a ledger.

The ledger is multiple hearsay, but it will be admissible under s 117. The entry in the ledger is a statement in a document and was created by Youssef in the course of business. The person who supplied the information contained in the ledger (Paul) had personal knowledge of the making of the deposit.

Example 3

Ahmed deposits £1,000 in a safe at the betting shop where he works. He tells Shona, one of his colleagues. Shona passes this information on to Gavin, the owner of the shop, who records the deposit in a ledger.

The entry in the ledger is multiple hearsay, but it will be admissible under s 117. The entry in the ledger is a statement in a document which was created by Gavin in the course of business. The person who supplied the information contained in the ledger (Ahmed) had personal knowledge of the making of the deposit, and the person through whom the information was passed (Shona) received the information in the course of business.

The three above examples illustrate the usual operation of this exception. However, a further layer of requirements applies where a business document has been prepared for the purpose of criminal proceedings.

Statements prepared for use in criminal proceedings

If the statement was prepared for 'the purposes of pending or contemplated criminal proceedings, or for a criminal investigation' (s 117(4)), the requirements of s 117(5) must be satisfied. The requirements of s 117(5) will be satisfied if:

(a) any of the five conditions mentioned in s 116(2) is satisfied (see above); or

(b) the relevant person cannot reasonably be expected to have any recollection of the matters dealt with in the statement (having regard to the length of time since he supplied the information and all other circumstances).

⭐ Example

A burglary occurs at a shop. Charlie, the owner of the shop, prepares a list of all the items taken in the burglary in order to claim on his business insurance policy and to also provide the police with a list of the items stolen. Two years later, the police arrest Niall and charge him with the burglary. At Niall's trial, the CPS seeks to use the list to prove what was taken in the burglary. Charlie is able to attend trial to give evidence but, given the time which has elapsed since the time of the burglary, he is unable to recall all the items contained on the list. The list of stolen items compiled by Charlie is first-hand hearsay and should be admissible in evidence under s 117. The list is a statement in a document. Charlie created the list in the course of his business and the person who supplied the information contained in the list (Charlie) had personal knowledge of the matters dealt with in the list. As the list was compiled for use in contemplated criminal proceedings, one of the requirements in s 117(5) must be satisfied. These requirements are satisfied because, although Charlie can attend court to give oral evidence, due to the time which has elapsed since the list was compiled, he cannot reasonably be expected to have any recollection of the matters dealt with in the statement.

9.5.2.2 Hearsay admissible under a preserved common law exception – s 114(1)(b)

Section 118(1) of the CJA 2003 preserves several common law exceptions to the rule excluding hearsay evidence. The most important exceptions preserved by s 118(1) are:

(a) evidence of a confession or mixed statement made by the defendant; and

(b) evidence admitted as part of the *res gestae*.

Confession evidence

Prior to the enactment of the CJA 2003, evidence that the defendant had made a confession was admissible at common law as an exception to the rule excluding hearsay evidence. This rule was subsequently codified by s 76(1) of PACE 1984, which provides:

> (1) In any proceedings a confession made by an accused person may be given in evidence against him insofar as it is relevant to any matter in issue in the proceedings and is not excluded by the court in pursuance of this section.

Section 118(1) preserves the common law rule that a confession made by a defendant will be admissible in evidence against the defendant, even if the confession is hearsay evidence. This is such an important exception in practice, we will look at it in more detail later in this chapter.

Evidence admitted as part of the *res gestae*

Section 118(1) of the CJA 2003 also preserves the common law rule admitting evidence that forms part of the *res gestae*.

The common law principle of evidence being admitted as part of the *res gestae* provides that a statement made contemporaneously with an event will be admissible as an exception to the hearsay rule because the spontaneity of the statement meant that any possibility of concoction can be disregarded.

🔵 *R v Andrews [1987] AC 281 – the House of Lords held that hearsay evidence of a statement made by a fatally stabbed man soon after he was attacked naming his two attackers was properly admitted as evidence of the truth of the facts he had asserted under the* res gestae *principle. Lord Ackner set out the following criteria (known as the 'Ackner criteria') for the admission of such evidence:*

(1) The primary question which the judge had to ask himself in such a case was: Can the possibility of concoction or distortion be disregard?

(2) To answer that question the judge first had to consider the circumstances in which the particular statement was made in order to satisfy himself that the event was so unusual or dramatic as to dominate the thoughts of the victim so that his utterance was an instinctive reaction to that event thus giving no real opportunity for reasoned reflection.

(3) In order for the statement to be sufficiently spontaneous it had to be so closely associated with the event which had excited the statement that it could fairly be said that the mind of the declarant was still controlled by the event.

(4) Quite apart from the time factor there might be special features in a case which related to the possibility of distortion.

(5) As to the possibility of error in the facts narrated in such a statement: If only the ordinary fallibility of human recollection was relied upon that went to the weight to be attached and not to the admissibility of the statement and was therefore a matter for the jury.

⭐ Example

Jordan is charged with murder. The CPS alleges that Jordan shot his victim with a rifle. Jordan's defence is that the rifle went off by accident as he was examining it. The CPS want to call evidence from a witness who did not see the shooting but did hear the victim scream, 'Don't shoot me Jordan!' immediately before hearing the gun fire. This would be hearsay evidence, but is likely to be admissible as part of the res gestae, *to help prove the shooting was not an accident.*

9.5.2.3 Hearsay admissible by agreement – s 114(1)(c)

If all the parties in the case agree, any form of hearsay evidence may be admissible in evidence.

9.5.2.4 Hearsay admissible in the interests of justice – s 114(1)(d)

This is a 'catch-all' provision, allowing the court to admit hearsay evidence that would not otherwise be admissible if it is in *the interests of justice* to do so. This provision gives the courts a very wide discretion to admit hearsay evidence which is cogent and reliable.

In deciding whether to admit hearsay evidence under s 114(1)(d), the court must have regard to the factors in s 114(2):

(a) how much probative value the statement has (assuming it to be true) in relation to a matter in issue in the proceedings, or how valuable it is for the understanding of other evidence in the case;

(b) what other evidence has been, or can be, given on the matter or evidence mentioned in para (a);

(c) how important the matter or evidence mentioned in para (a) is in the context of the case as a whole;

(d) the circumstances in which the statement was made;

(e) how reliable the maker of the statement appears to be;

(f) how reliable the evidence of the making of the statement appears to be;

(g) whether oral evidence of the matter stated can be given and, if not, why not;

(h) the amount of difficulty involved in challenging the statement; and

(i) the extent to which that difficulty would be likely to prejudice the party facing it.

In assessing these factors, the court will need to have regard to the defendant's right to a fair trial enshrined in Article 6 of the ECHR (see below).

The Court of Appeal considered the application of s 114(1)(d) and s 114(2) in *R v Taylor* [2006] EWCA Crim 260. The court held that to reach a proper conclusion on whether the evidence should be admitted under s 114(1)(d), the trial judge was required to exercise his judgment in the light of the factors in s 114(2), give consideration to them and to any other factors he considered relevant and then to assess their significance and the weight that in his judgment they carried. There is no need, however, for the judge to reach a specific conclusion in relation to all the factors.

Maher v DPP [2006] EWHC 1271 (Admin) – the defendant was convicted of various road traffic offences after crashing her vehicle into another car (owned by X) and then leaving the scene without leaving her contact details. The evidence against the defendant came from a witness who claimed to have seen the accident and left a note attached to X's car giving the registration number of the defendant's car. X's partner saw the note and telephoned the police, who made a record of the registration number on their incident log. The note was subsequently lost. The issue for the Divisional Court was whether the entry in the police log could be admitted as hearsay evidence. The Divisional Court said the entry in the log was admissible under s 114(1)(d). There was nothing to suggest that it was not in the interests of justice to admit the log, and the evidence was substantial and reliable.

R v Z [2009] Crim LR 519 – the appellant appealed against his conviction for a number of sexual offences that were of an historic nature. The relevant prosecution evidence came from a witness who claimed that she had also been raped by the appellant at around the same time as the present case. The witness though refused to give evidence on the basis that she did not want to have to relive that period in her life and that she wanted to put the whole incident behind her. In other words her refusal to testify did not come within any of the recognised exceptions contained in s 116. The Court held that although the interests of justice test under s 114(1)(d) may allow evidence to be adduced which fell outside s 116, such evidence would only usually apply to hearsay evidence which formed part of the incident itself. The witness's apparent untested reluctance to testify did not merit admission under this provision. To do so would wrongly circumvent the provisions of s 116. To admit such evidence would have been extremely prejudicial to the appellant and very difficult for him to properly challenge.

9.5.3 Procedure for admitting hearsay

The procedural rules to be followed should a party seek to rely on hearsay evidence at trial (or to challenge the admissibility of hearsay evidence on which another party seeks to rely) are contained in Part 20 of the CrimPR. These rules do not, however, apply in all cases when a party wishes to use hearsay evidence at trial. The rules in Part 20 only apply to cases where:

(a) it is in the interests of justice for the hearsay evidence to be admissible (s 114(1)(d));

(b) the witness is unavailable to attend court (s 116);

(c) the evidence is multiple hearsay (s 121); or

(d) either the prosecution or the defence rely on s 117 for the admission of a written witness statement prepared for use in criminal proceedings (CrimPR, r 20.2).

For hearsay evidence which is admissible on any other grounds, the procedural rules contained in Part 20 do not apply. If, for example, the defendant made a confession at the time of their arrest, the rules in Part 20 will not apply should the CPS seek to rely on the arresting officer repeating details of that confession when the officer gives evidence at the defendant's trial.

Similarly, the rules in Part 20 will not apply if the hearsay evidence is admissible under any of the preserved common law exceptions to the rule excluding hearsay evidence. The significance of this is that if the hearsay evidence to be adduced at trial does not fall within one or more of the four sections noted at (a) to (d) above, the party seeking to rely on that evidence will not need to serve on the other party notice of its intention to rely on such evidence.

A party wishing to adduce hearsay evidence to which Part 20 applies, or to oppose another party's application to introduce such evidence, must give notice of its intention to do this both to the court and to the other parties in the case (CrimPR, r 20.2). Notice must be given using a set of prescribed forms. As part of the standard directions that will be given in both the magistrates' court and the Crown Court (see **Chapter 6**), the court will impose time limits for the CPS and the defendant to give notice of their intention to adduce hearsay evidence at trial. The relevant time limits are set out in CrimPR, r 20.2(3) (for the CPS) and CrimPR, r 20.2(4) (for the defendant).

However, r 20.5 of the CrimPR allows the court to dispense with the requirement to give notice of hearsay evidence, to allow notice to be given orally rather than in writing, and to shorten or extend the time limits for giving notice.

9.5.3.1 Determining the admissibility of hearsay evidence

When either the CPS or the defendant has made an application to adduce hearsay evidence at trial, and this application is opposed by the other party, the court will usually determine the admissibility of such evidence at a pre-trial hearing. In the magistrates' court, this is likely to be at the case management hearing/pre-trial review, or at a specific pre-trial hearing to resolve disputes about the admissibility of evidence. In the Crown Court, this is likely to be at the PTPH, or at a specific pre-trial hearing (see **Chapter 6**).

9.6 Confession evidence

We will now consider what constitutes a confession and when such evidence is admissible in evidence at trial. We will also look at the circumstances in which confession evidence may be excluded and the procedure to be followed when the defendant challenges the admissibility of confession evidence upon which the CPS seeks to rely.

9.6.1 Definition

A confession is 'any statement wholly or partly adverse to the person who made it, whether made to a person in authority or not and whether made in words or otherwise' (PACE 1984, s 82(1)).

Anything said by a defendant that constitutes an admission of any element of the offence with which they are subsequently charged, or that is in any way detrimental to their case, will satisfy the definition of a confession in s 82(1).

⭐ *Example 1*

Jade is arrested on suspicion of theft from a supermarket. When interviewed at the police station, Jade tells the police: 'Yeah, it was me who nicked the stuff. I wanted to sell it to get money for drugs.' Jade's comments satisfy the definition of a confession in s 82(1) because she has admitted to carrying out the theft and it is therefore 'wholly adverse' to her.

⭐ *Example 2*

PC Nowak is called to a pub where an assault has taken place. On arriving at the pub, PC Nowak obtains a description of the person alleged to have committed the assault.

Shortly after leaving the pub, PC Nowak sees Michael in the street. Michael matches the description of the person who committed the assault. PC Nowak asks Michael if he has been at the pub that evening. Michael replies: 'Yeah, but I only hit him in self-defence.' Although Michael has not admitted to committing the assault, his comments still satisfy the definition of a confession in s 82(1) above. This is because, in the event that Michael is later charged with the assault, the comments he made will be 'partly adverse' to his case. Michael admits to having been at the pub, and also admits to hitting the victim, so this is at least 'partly adverse' to his case.

9.6.2 Admissibility

As we saw earlier, a confession made by a defendant prior to trial will be admissible in evidence at trial by virtue of s 76(1) of PACE 1984:

> In any proceedings a confession made by an accused person may be given in evidence against him insofar as it is relevant to any matter in issue in the proceedings and is not excluded by the court in pursuance of this section.

This means that a confession will be admissible at trial to prove the truth of its contents (ie to prove the defendant's guilt) and is therefore also an exception to the hearsay rule.

 Example 1

Juan is charged with theft. He admits the theft in an audibly recorded interview at the police station. A transcript of the interview is subsequently read out at Juan's trial. The transcript is hearsay evidence, but it will be admissible in evidence by virtue of s 76(1) to prove his guilt.

 Example 2

Ayesha is arrested on suspicion of theft. As she is being arrested, Ayesha tells the arresting officer: 'Okay I did it. You know I only steal because I have no money.'

At Ayesha's trial, the arresting officer repeats the comment made by Ayesha at the time of her arrest. This will be hearsay evidence, but it will be admissible in evidence by virtue of s 76(1) to prove Ayesha's guilt.

 Example 3

Steve is charged with theft. He denied the theft when interviewed at the police station, but later admits to his friend Tianna that he committed the theft. Tianna has provided the CPS with a statement in which she repeats the confession which Steve has made. If Tianna repeats this at court when giving oral evidence, this will be hearsay evidence, but it will be admissible in evidence by virtue of s 76(1) to prove Steve's guilt.

9.6.2.1 Mixed statements

A confession may sometimes also include a statement which is favourable to the defendant. These are referred to as 'mixed statements'. The whole statement will be admissible under s 76(1) as an exception to the rule excluding hearsay evidence.

 Example

Connor is charged with rape. When interviewed at the police station, he says: 'I did have sex with her, but only because she consented.' This is a mixed statement, because Connor makes a confession (admitting to having sexual intercourse with the complainant) but he also makes a statement favourable to his defence (saying that it was consensual). The entire statement will be admissible under s 76(1).

9.6.2.2   Confessions and a co-accused

Is a confession made by a defendant admissible in evidence against a co-defendant?

Any evidence given by a co-defendant at trial which implicates a defendant (including a confession made by the co-defendant) will be admissible in evidence against the defendant. Also, if the co-defendant has pleaded guilty at an earlier hearing and is giving evidence for the prosecution at the trial of the defendant, any evidence given implicating the defendant in the commission of the offence will be admissible in evidence against the defendant.

⭐ Example

Trisha and Matthew are jointly charged with theft. Tricia is to plead guilty and Matthew will plead not guilty. Tricia enters her guilty plea on her first appearance before the court. She then gives a statement to the CPS stating that she and Matthew committed the theft together. As Tricia is no longer being tried with Matthew (because she has pleaded guilty), she will be able to give evidence as a prosecution witness at Matthew's trial. If, when giving evidence, Tricia states that she and Martyn committed the theft together, this confession will be admissible in evidence against Matthew.

The longstanding position at common law has been that a pre-trial confession made by one defendant which also implicates another defendant is admissible only against the defendant who makes the confession. This is also supported by s 76(1) which provides that 'In any proceedings a confession made by an accused person may be given in evidence against *him*' and is silent about its admissibility against anyone else.

9.6.3   Challenging admissibility by s 76 PACE 1984

A defendant who is alleged to have made a confession may challenge the admissibility of this confession at trial by arguing either:

(a)   that they did not make the confession at all, and that the person to whom the confession was made was either mistaken as to what they heard or has fabricated evidence of the confession; or

(b)   that they did make the confession, but it should still not be admitted in evidence.

If the defendant accepts that they made a confession, they will usually challenge the admissibility of the confession under s 76(2) of PACE 1984. This provides that:

> If, in any proceedings where the prosecution proposes to give in evidence a confession made by an accused person, it is represented to the court that the confession was or may have been obtained:
>
> (a)   by oppression of the person who made it; or
>
> (b)   in consequence of anything said or done which was likely, in the circumstances existing at the time, to render unreliable any confession which might be made by him in consequence thereof, the court shall not allow the confession to be given in evidence against him except in so far as the prosecution proves to the court beyond reasonable doubt that the confession (notwithstanding that it may be true) was not obtained as aforesaid.

This means that if a defendant argues that a confession was obtained in the manner or circumstances detailed under paras (a) or (b) above, the court must not allow that confession to be used as evidence by the prosecution, unless the prosecution prove beyond a reasonable doubt that the confession was not so obtained. Even if the court thinks that the confession is true, the court must still rule that the prosecution cannot use the confession in evidence unless the prosecution can prove that the confession was not obtained by oppression or in circumstances which render it unreliable.

⭐ *Example*

> *Jeff is charged with murder. When interviewed at the police station he confessed to having committed the murder. At his trial, Jeff argues that the confession was obtained by oppression and should be ruled inadmissible by the trial judge. The CPS must prove beyond a reasonable doubt that the confession was not obtained by oppression, even if the judge believes the confession to be true. If the prosecution fails to do this, the judge must not allow evidence of the confession to be placed before the jury.*

Oppression

Section 76(8) of PACE 1984 states that 'oppression' includes 'torture, inhuman or degrading treatment, and the use or threat of violence (whether or not amounting to torture)'. In *R v Fulling* [1987] 2 WLR 923, the Court of Appeal said that 'oppression' consisted of 'the exercise of authority or power in a burdensome, harsh or wrongful manner; unjust or cruel treatment of subjects, inferiors, etc; the imposition of unreasonable or unjust burdens'.

A good example of oppression can be seen in the case of *R v Paris* (1993) 97 Cr App R 1999 – in an audibly recorded interview at the police station, the defendant was bullied and hectored into making a confession. The Court of Appeal said that, other than actual physical violence, it would find it hard to think of a more hostile and intimidating approach adopted by interviewing officers.

Unreliability

This tends to be the more common basis upon which the defence will challenge admissibility. For the court to exclude a confession under s 76(2)(b), something must be said or done which, in the circumstances that existed at the time, would render unreliable any confession which the defendant made. In other words, something must have been said or done (usually by the police) which might have caused the defendant to make a confession for reasons other than the fact that they had actually committed the offence and wanted to admit guilt. Although s 76(2)(b) does not require deliberate misconduct on the part of the police, the thing which is said or done will usually involve a breach of Code C of the Codes of Practice to PACE 1984. Examples of the types of breach of Code C which may lead to a confession being excluded on the grounds of unreliability include:

(a) denying a suspect refreshments or appropriate periods of rest between interviews, so that the suspect is either not in a fit state to answer questions properly, or makes admissions in interview simply to get out of the police station as soon as possible or to obtain rest or refreshments (this may be particularly relevant if the suspect is suffering from some form of illness or ailment, even if the police are not aware of this condition);

(b) offering a suspect an inducement to confess, for example, telling a suspect that if they confess they will receive a lesser sentence, suggesting to the suspect that they will be able to leave the police station much more quickly if they admit their guilt, or telling the suspect that they will only be granted police bail if they make a confession;

(c) misrepresenting the strength of the prosecution case, for example by telling a suspect that the prosecution case is much stronger than it actually is and that there is no point in denying guilt;

(d) questioning a suspect in an inappropriate way, for example by repeatedly asking a suspect the same question, or badgering a suspect until they give the answer the officer wants to hear;

(e) questioning a suspect who the police should have known was not in a fit state to be interviewed either because the suspect had consumed drink or drugs, or because the suspect was suffering from some form of medical condition or ailment. The answers given by such a suspect in interview may be unreliable;

(f) threatening a suspect, for example by telling them that they will be kept at the police station until they make a confession, so that the suspect thinks they have no option other than to confess if they want to get out of the police station.

A common example of an argument used to exclude a confession on the unreliability ground under s 76(2)(b) is for a defendant to argue that their confession is unreliable because they were denied access to legal advice at the police station in breach of Code C and s 58 of PACE 1984. A breach of s 58 and Code C will not, however, in itself, automatically lead to the exclusion of the confession. In order for the confession to be excluded, there must be a causal link between the breach and the unreliability of the confession that was subsequently made. The court will need to consider whether if the defendant had been allowed access to legal advice, they would not have made a confession. Therefore, if denial of access to legal advice is relied upon as an argument to exclude a confession under s 76(2)(b), a defendant will find it hard to establish a causal link if they are an experienced criminal who is fully aware of their rights when detained at the police station.

In R v Trussler [1998] Crim LR 446, the defendant was a drug addict who was kept in custody for 18 hours. He was interviewed several times without being given any rest and was denied access to legal advice. His confession was excluded under s 76(2)(b).

In R v Alladice (1998) 87 Cr App R 380, the defendant was denied access to legal advice and confessed to a robbery. When giving evidence at trial, the defendant stated that he knew his rights and that he understood the police caution. The defendant's application to exclude his confession was rejected by the trial judge. Although denying access to legal advice was a serious breach of Code C, there was nothing to suggest that this might have rendered any confession he had made unreliable, because he was fully aware of what his rights were.

9.6.3.1 Can a co-defendant rely on a confession made by another defendant?

Section 76A(1) of PACE 1984 allows a defendant to adduce evidence that a co-defendant has made a confession where both defendants plead not guilty and are tried jointly. Clearly a defendant would only want to do this if the co-defendant's confession doesn't also implicate that defendant.

Under s 76A(2), however, if the co-defendant who made the confession represents to the court that his confession was obtained as a result of oppression, or in circumstances rendering it unreliable (see above), the court must exclude the evidence of the confession (even if the court believes the confession to be true), unless the court is satisfied that the confession was not obtained in such a way. The court need only be satisfied on the balance of probabilities that the confession was not obtained either by oppression or in circumstances rendering it unreliable in order for the confession to be admissible when a co-defendant wants to rely on it as opposed to the prosecution.

✪ *Example*

Bilal and Patrick are jointly charged with common assault. Both are pleading not guilty. When Patrick was interviewed by the police, he confessed to having committed the crime. Under s 76A(1), Bilal is entitled to raise Patrick's confession in evidence at trial to show that it was Patrick rather than he who committed the assault. However, Patrick argues at trial that the confession he made when interviewed was obtained only as a result of threats made by the police to keep him in custody indefinitely until he confessed, and so is unreliable. If Bilal attempts to adduce evidence of Patrick's confession and Patrick challenges the admissibility of this, the court must exclude the evidence of Patrick's confession under s 76A(2) (even if the court believes the confession to be true) unless the court is satisfied by Bilal on the balance of probabilities that the confession was not obtained in circumstances making it unreliable.

9.6.4 Challenging admissibility s 78 PACE 1984

Section 76 of PACE 1984 deals exclusively with the court's power to exclude evidence of a confession made by the defendant. Under s 78, the court has a more general discretion to exclude prosecution evidence. This includes evidence of a confession made by a defendant. Section 78 provides the court with the discretion to exclude confession evidence on which the CPS seeks to rely if the court considers that the admission of the confession would have such an adverse effect on the fairness of proceedings that it ought not to be admitted. Section 78 may be relied on either when the defendant admits making a confession but claims that the confession is untrue, or when the defendant denies making the confession at all.

9.6.4.1 Confessions the defendant accepts having made

When a defendant alleges that the police breached the provisions of PACE 1984 and/or the Codes of Practice in obtaining a confession, the court is only likely to exercise its discretion under s 78 to exclude such evidence if these breaches are both *significant and substantial* (*R v Keenan* [1990] 2 QB 54).

Many of the cases in which the court has exercised this discretion under s 78 are concerned with suspects who have been denied access to legal advice. In *R v Walsh* (1989) 91 Cr App R 161, the Court of Appeal said that in most cases where a defendant had been denied access to legal advice in breach of s 58 of PACE 1984 or the provisions of Code C, this would lead to the court exercising its discretion to exclude any confession that the defendant subsequently made, since allowing the CPS to rely on such evidence would have an adverse effect on the fairness of the proceedings.

There is therefore a degree of overlap between the court's discretion to exclude a confession (which the defendant admits to having made) under s 78, and the duty of the court to exclude a confession under the 'unreliability' ground in s 76(2)(b).

9.6.4.2 Confessions the defendant denies having made

A defendant may sometimes be alleged to have made a confession 'outside' the police station when first approached by the police. If the defendant subsequently denies having made such a confession, its admissibility may be challenged under s 78 (and not under s 76(2)(b)).

For example, a confession allegedly made by the defendant when questioned by the police in an interview 'outside' the police station is likely to be excluded under s 78 if the police breached the provisions of Code C of PACE 1984 by:

(a) failing to make an accurate record of the defendant's comments (Code C, para 11.7(a)), as the police would not then be able to substantiate that such comments were in fact made by the defendant;

(b) failing to give the defendant an opportunity to view the record of his comments and to sign this record as being accurate, or to dispute the accuracy of the record (Code C, para 11.11), as the defendant would then be deprived of the opportunity to challenge the accuracy of the police record; or

(c) failing to put this admission or confession to the defendant at the start of his subsequent interview at the police station (Code C, para 11.4), as the whole point of putting the confession to the defendant at the start of the audibly recorded interview is to ensure that the defendant has the opportunity to confirm or deny 'on the record' what he is alleged to have said.

R v Canale *[1990] 2 All ER 187 – the police alleged that the defendant had made certain admissions to them. The defendant denied making these admissions. The interviewing officer to whom these admissions had allegedly been made failed to make a contemporaneous note of the interviews as required by Code C, and the defendant was therefore denied the opportunity to comment on the accuracy of the record of these interviews. The evidence was excluded by the court under s 78 because its admission would have had such an adverse effect on the fairness of the proceedings.*

9.6.5 Procedure for challenging the admissibility of confession evidence

9.6.5.1 Crown Court

In the Crown Court, the admissibility of disputed confession evidence will be determined by the trial judge in the absence of the jury at a *voir dire* (a trial within a trial). If the confession was made by the defendant in an interview at the police station, the interviewing officer will give evidence as to how the confession was obtained and the defendant will then give their version of events. The audio recording of the interview is also likely to be played. If the confession was made 'outside' the police station, the officer to whom the confession was allegedly made will give evidence, as will the defendant. Prosecuting and defence counsel will then make submissions to the judge on whether or not the confession should be excluded in the light of the evidence given. The judge will then make their ruling.

If the judge rules the confession to be inadmissible, the jury will hear nothing about the confession. If the judge rules the confession to be admissible, the interviewing officer will then give evidence of the confession when giving evidence to the jury. The defendant will still be able to attack the credibility of the confession (either when giving evidence, or when the police officer is being questioned) in an attempt to persuade the jury to attach little or no weight to it.

9.6.5.2 Magistrates' court

In the magistrates' court, a ruling as to the admissibility of the disputed confession will normally be sought when the interviewing officer gives evidence. If the defendant seeks to exclude evidence of the confession under s 76(2) of PACE 1984, the magistrates must also hold a *voir dire*. If the defendant raises submissions under s 76(2) and s 78, both arguments should be dealt with at the same *voir dire*. If the defendant seeks to rely only on s 78, there is no obligation to hold a *voir dire*. In such cases, a challenge to the admissibility of the confession may be left either to the close of the prosecution case (if the defendant's solicitor wishes to make a submission of no case to answer), or to the end of the trial when the defendant's solicitor makes their closing speech.

9.6.6 Evidence obtained as a result of an inadmissible confession

The fact that the court excludes evidence of a confession made by a defendant will not affect the admissibility in evidence of any facts discovered as a result of the confession (s 76(4) PACE 1984) although the CPS will not be able to tell the court that such facts were discovered as a result of a confession made by the defendant.

 Example

Max is charged with murder. As a result of a confession made by him, the police are able to recover the murder weapon with Max's fingerprints on it. The trial judge rules that the confession is inadmissible under s 76(2)(b). The CPS will still be able to adduce evidence as to the finding of the weapon with Max's fingerprints on it even though it will not be able to raise in evidence that this item was discovered as a result of a confession made by Max. This evidence will still be an important piece of circumstantial evidence against Max.

Figure 9.3 Confession evidence flowchart

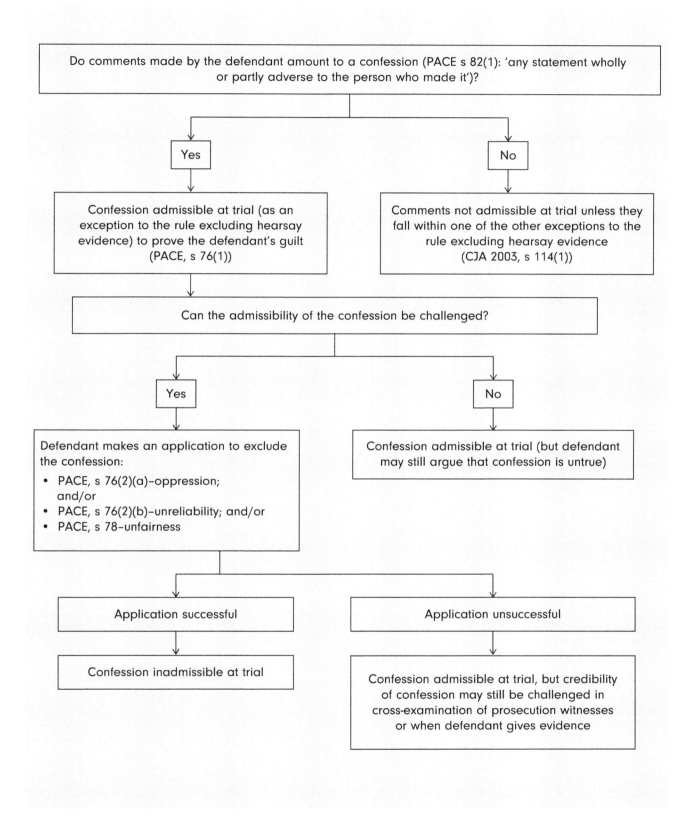

9.7 Character evidence

Defendants in a criminal case will often have previous convictions. We will now examine the circumstances in which such previous convictions may be admitted in evidence at trial. As with hearsay evidence, the admissibility of bad character evidence is governed by the Criminal Justice Act 2003.

9.7.1 Definition of bad character

'Bad character' is defined in s 98 as being 'evidence of, or a disposition towards, misconduct', other than evidence connected with the offence for which the defendant has been charged. 'Misconduct' is defined in s 112 as 'the commission of an offence or other reprehensible behaviour'. Note therefore that misconduct covers more than just the existence of previous convictions.

If the alleged misconduct by the defendant is connected to the offence with which he has been charged, this will not fall within the definition of bad character in s 98, and will therefore be admissible in evidence without needing to consider whether it satisfies the test for admissibility of bad character evidence set out in the CJA 2003.

⭐ *Example*

Sean is charged with the murder of Frank, his father. The CPS alleges that Sean fabricated a will in Frank's name, leaving all Frank's assets to Sean, and that Sean then murdered Frank so that he could take these assets. The allegation that Sean fabricated Frank's will is an allegation of misconduct on the part of Sean. It will not fall within s 98 of the CJA 2003, however, because it is connected to the subsequent murder of Frank. Evidence of the fabrication of the will is therefore admissible without needing to consider whether it satisfies the test for admissibility of bad character evidence set out in the CJA 2003.

9.7.2 The 7 gateways s 101(1) Criminal Justice Act 2003

Evidence of a defendant's bad character may be raised at trial through one or more of the 7 'gateways' which are set out in s 101(1) of the CJA 2003. Section 101 provides that:

(1) In criminal proceedings evidence of a defendant's bad character is admissible if, but only if:

(a) all parties to the proceedings agree to the evidence being admissible,
(b) the evidence is adduced by the defendant himself or is given in answer to a question asked by him in cross-examination and intended to elicit it,
(c) it is important explanatory evidence,
(d) it is relevant to an important matter in issue between the defendant and the prosecution,
(e) it has substantial probative value in relation to an important matter in issue between the defendant and a co-defendant,
(f) it is evidence to correct a false impression given by the defendant, or
(g) the defendant has made an attack on another person's character.

As with the drawing of adverse inferences, a defendant's bad character cannot of itself prove guilt. The prosecution must adduce other evidence to substantiate their case before the jury or magistrates are allowed to take bad character into account.

9.7.2.1 Gateway (a) – all parties to the proceedings agree to the evidence being admissible

If the CPS and the defendant are in agreement that the evidence is admissible, it may be admitted under this gateway.

9.7.2.2 Gateway (b) – the evidence is adduced by the defendant himself or is given in answer to a question asked by him in cross-examination and intended to elicit it

This gateway allows a defendant to introduce evidence of their own bad character. A defendant may do this if, for example they only have very minor previous convictions and do not want the jury or magistrates to think that, because they are not adducing evidence of their own good character, they may have extensive previous convictions. Another example of when a defendant may do this is if they pleaded guilty on previous occasions but are pleading not guilty to the current matter. The defendant may use such convictions to say to the jury that they accept their guilt when they have committed an offence, but on this occasion they are pleading not guilty because they genuinely have not committed the offence charged.

In *R v Paton* [2007] EWCA Crim 1572, the defendant was charged with kidnapping, false imprisonment and firearms offences after he was alleged to have blindfolded and interrogated the manageress of a garden centre about the security systems at the centre, and then locked her in the boot of her car. Various items found in the defendant's car suggested that the defendant had been the kidnapper. The defendant raised evidence of his own bad character by claiming that these items had come from a burglary he had committed on an earlier occasion, and that he was not guilty of the more serious offences charged.

9.7.2.3 Gateway (c) – it is important explanatory evidence

Only the prosecution may adduce evidence of the defendant's bad character under gateway (c). The gateway is, however, likely to be used only in limited circumstances. Evidence is important explanatory evidence if:

(a) without it, the magistrates or jury would find it impossible or difficult properly to understand the case; and

(b) the value of the evidence for understanding the case as a whole is substantial (CJA 2003, s 102) ('substantial' in this context is likely to mean more than merely trivial or marginal).

🖉 *In R v Campbell [2005] EWCA Crim 248, the defendant was convicted of the kidnapping and murder of his 15-year-old niece. The prosecution alleged that the defendant was infatuated with his niece and that his infatuation was partly sexual. The Court of Appeal held that the trial judge had correctly allowed the prosecution to adduce bad character evidence that the defendant had downloaded material from teenage sex sites, because such evidence was necessary to explain the defendant's motive for committing the offence.*

Case law does make it clear that where the evidence is clearly understandable without evidence of bad character, it should not be admitted (see for example R v Davis (2008) 172 JP 358 and R v Broome [2012] EWCA Crim 2879).

If the prosecution can establish that the test for admitting evidence of the defendant's bad character through this gateway is satisfied, the court has no power under the CJA 2003 to prevent the admission of this evidence. The court does, however, retain the discretionary power to exclude such evidence under s 78 of PACE 1984 (see later).

9.7.2.4 Gateway (d) – it is relevant to an important matter in issue between the defendant and the prosecution

In practice this is by far the most important gateway relied on by the prosecution. Important matters in issue between the defendant and prosecution include:

(a) the question whether the defendant has a propensity to commit offences of the kind with which he is charged (except where his having such propensity makes it no more likely that he is guilty of the offence); and

(b) the question whether the defendant has a propensity to be untruthful (except where it is not suggested that the defendant's case is untruthful in any respect) (CJA 2003, s 103(1)).

Only the prosecution may adduce evidence of a defendant's bad character under gateway (d).

Propensity to commit an offence of the kind charged

The CPS may place before the court evidence that a defendant has previous convictions in order to suggest that the defendant has a propensity to commit offences of the kind with which they are currently charged. To place such evidence before the court, the CPS must first satisfy the court that establishing such propensity makes it more likely that the defendant committed the offence.

Section 103(2) of the CJA 2003 states that:

> A defendant's propensity to commit offences of the kind with which he is charged may (without prejudice to any other way of doing so) be established by evidence that he has been convicted of:
>
> (a) an offence of the same description as the one with which he is charged, or
>
> (b) an offence of the same category as the one with which he is charged.

This subsection does not apply in the case of a particular defendant if the court is satisfied that, as a result of the time which has passed since the conviction (or for any other reason), it would be *unjust* for it to be applied (CJA 2003, s 103(3)).

 Example

Josh is on trial for common assault. Josh has a previous conviction for common assault. This conviction occurred 15 years ago. Josh's solicitor will argue that this previous conviction should not be admitted in evidence at Josh's trial to show that Josh has a propensity to commit this type of offence. Given the amount of time that has elapsed since Josh's previous conviction, he will argue under s 103(3) that it would be unjust *for this conviction to be used in the present case.*

Offences of the same description

Two offences will be of the same description as each other if the statement of the offence in a written charge or an indictment would, in each case, be in the same terms (CJA 2003, s 103(4)(a)).

 Example

Pablo is charged with assault occasioning actual bodily harm. He pleads not guilty on the basis that he was acting in reasonable self-defence. He has two previous convictions for the same offence. These will be offences of the same description because they would be described in the same way in a written charge or an indictment. The CPS may therefore attempt to raise these convictions at trial to show that Pablo has a propensity to commit offences of this type.

Offences of the same category

Two offences will be of the same category as each other if they belong to the same category of offences prescribed by the Secretary of State (CJA 2003, s 103(4)(b)). The Secretary of State has so far prescribed two categories of offences which are in the same category:

(a) the sexual offences category, which specifies a number of sexual offences committed against children under 16 years of age; and

(b) the theft category, which includes the following offences:

(i) theft

(ii) robbery

(iii) burglary

(iv) aggravated burglary

(v) taking a motor vehicle or conveyance without authority

(vi) aggravated vehicle taking

(vii) handling stolen goods

(viii) going equipped for stealing

(ix) making off without payment

(x) any attempt to commit any of the above substantive offences

(xi) aiding, abetting, counselling, procuring or inciting the commission of any of the above offences.

 Example

Esme pleads not guilty to a charge of theft. She has two previous convictions for offences of burglary and one previous conviction for handling stolen goods. These will be offences of the same category because they fall within the 'theft category' prescribed by the Secretary of State. The CPS may therefore seek to raise these convictions in evidence to show that Esme has a propensity to commit offences of this type.

May other offences be used to demonstrate such propensity?

Even if an earlier offence is not of the same description or in the same category as the offence charged, evidence of the defendant's conviction for the earlier offence may still be admissible under this gateway if there are significant factual similarities between the offences, since this would fall within the definition of having a propensity to commit offences of the kind with which the defendant is charged.

 In R v Brima [2006] EWCA Crim 408, the Court of Appeal held that previous convictions for assault and robbery which both involved the use of a knife were admissible in the defendant's trial for murder where the defendant was alleged to have stabbed his victim. The convictions demonstrated that the defendant had a propensity to commit violent offences using a knife.

Guidelines

In *R v Hanson, Gilmore & Pickstone* [2005] Crim LR 787, the Court of Appeal set out guidelines for judges or magistrates to consider when the CPS seeks to adduce evidence of a defendant's previous convictions in order to demonstrate his propensity to commit offences of the kind with which he is charged. The court stated as follows:

(a) Three questions need to be considered should the CPS seek to adduce evidence of the defendant's bad character under this part of gateway (d):

(i) Does the defendant's history of offending show a propensity to commit offences?

(ii) If so, does that propensity make it more likely that the defendant committed the current offence?

(iii) If so, is it just to rely on convictions of the same description or category, having in mind the overriding principle that proceedings must be fair?

Only if the answer to each of these questions is in the affirmative should the convictions be allowed in evidence.

(b) Offences which can be relied upon by the CPS to show this propensity may go beyond offences of the same description or of the same category.

(c) The fewer the number of previous convictions the defendant has, the less likely it is that propensity will be established. If the defendant has only one previous conviction of the same description or category, this is unlikely to show propensity unless there are distinguishing circumstances or a tendency towards unusual behaviour. The Court gave examples of unusual behaviour as including fire starting and the sexual abuse of children.

In R v Bennabou [2012] EWCA Crim 3088 the Court of Appeal held that a single conviction for rape ought not to have been adduced as bad character evidence in relation to counts of sexual assault and assault by penetration. The appellant argued that the rape conviction was a single offence committed some eight years before the first of the two offences being tried, and that the circumstances of the earlier offence were markedly different. It was further submitted that even if the previous conviction would otherwise be admissible, it should be excluded in the judge's discretion because its admission would have such an adverse effect on the fairness of the proceedings that it ought not to be admitted (CJA 2003, s 101(3)). The Court of Appeal held that the rape conviction, though technically admissible, should not have been admitted in evidence. It bore some limited similarities in relation to the current offences, but there were also dissimilarities. Accordingly, the probative value of the earlier rape in establishing a relevant propensity was limited. On the other hand, the admission of the evidence must have had a highly prejudicial effect on the fairness of the trial. The court went on to say that it was not suggesting, by saying that the rape conviction was technically admissible, that an offence of rape will always amount to unusual behaviour of the kind referred to in the case of Hanson. Sometimes it may, but it would be wrong to approach any case on the basis that a rape would necessarily attract that description.

Propensity to be untruthful

The CPS may also place before the court evidence of a defendant's previous convictions to show that the defendant has a propensity to be untruthful and therefore that evidence given by the defendant at trial may lack credibility. The CPS will be allowed to do this only if it is suggested that the defendant's case is in any way untruthful (s 103(1)(b)).

In *R v Hanson, Gilmore & Pickstone*, the Court of Appeal held that a defendant's previous convictions will not be admissible to show that the defendant has a propensity to be untruthful unless:

(a) the manner in which the previous offence was committed demonstrates that the defendant has such a propensity (because they had made false representations); or

(b) the defendant pleaded not guilty to the earlier offence but was convicted following a trial at which the defendant testified and was not believed.

Manner in which previous offence was committed

The court drew a distinction between a propensity to be dishonest and a propensity to be untruthful. Only if a defendant's previous convictions demonstrated a propensity to be untruthful will they become admissible under this gateway. The court stressed that the only types of offence that would demonstrate such a propensity were offences where the defendant had actively sought to deceive or mislead another person by the making of false representations. This includes previous convictions for perjury and offences involving an active deception of another (such as fraud by false representation), but not other offences where dishonesty forms part of the mental element of the offence but where the defendant has not actually been untruthful and has not actively deceived anyone. For example, a previous conviction for theft is unlikely to demonstrate a propensity to be untruthful because, unless the defendant had actually sought to mislead or had lied to another person as part of the commission of the theft, although the defendant had acted dishonestly, they had not been untruthful.

 Example

> *Duleep is charged with common assault. The CPS alleges that he punched his victim in the face for no reason. Duleep denies the charge, claiming that he was initially attacked by his victim and that he was acting only in self-defence. Duleep's alleged victim refutes this. Duleep has previous convictions for perjury and fraud by false representation. These are offences which the CPS may attempt to raise in evidence to demonstrate that Duleep has a propensity to be untruthful and therefore show that the victim's evidence at trial is more likely to be truthful than Duleep's.*

Convictions following a not guilty plea

Offences of any description may also fall within this part of gateway (d) if the defendant pleaded not guilty, testified but was convicted following a trial at which the court disbelieved their version of events, since this will demonstrate that the defendant has been found by a court to have been untruthful on a previous occasion.

 Example

> *Kate is charged with common assault. She is pleading not guilty and will raise the defence of alibi at trial. Kate has several previous convictions for various offences. On each occasion she pleaded not guilty and raised the defence of alibi but was convicted following a trial in which her alibi was disbelieved. The CPS may attempt to raise these previous convictions in evidence to show that Kate has a propensity to be untruthful.*

Excluding evidence admitted under gateway (d)

Under s 101(3) of the CJA 2003, the court must not admit this evidence if on an application by the defendant to exclude it, it appears to the court that the admission of the evidence would have *such an adverse effect on the fairness of the proceedings that the court ought not to admit it.*

This is a very similar test that the court applies when deciding whether to exclude unfairly obtained evidence under s 78 of PACE 1984, save that under s 78 the court has a discretion to exclude the evidence if the test is satisfied, whereas under s 101(3) the court must exclude the evidence if the test is satisfied. The courts are most likely to use their powers under s 101(3) in three situations:

(a) when the nature of a defendant's previous convictions is such that the jury are likely to convict a defendant on the basis of these convictions alone, rather than examining the other evidence placed before them, or where the evidence of the previous convictions is more prejudicial than probative (see *R v Bennabou* above);

(b) when the CPS seeks to adduce previous convictions to support a case which is otherwise weak (*R v Hanson, Gilmore & Pickstone* [2005] Crim LR 787);

(c) when the defendant's previous convictions are 'spent'. The Rehabilitation of Offenders Act 1974 provides that after a prescribed period of time, certain convictions are spent. This means that, for most purposes (such as completing an application form for a job), the convicted person is to be treated as never having been convicted of the spent offence. The rehabilitation period varies with the sentence, as follows:

Although the Act specifically does not prevent 'spent' convictions from being admissible in evidence in subsequent criminal proceedings, it is likely that the court will consider exercising its power under s 101(3) in such cases. In particular, s 101(4) provides that when an application to exclude evidence is made under s 101(3), the court must have regard to the length of time between the matters to which that evidence relates and the matters which form the subject of the offence charged.

absolute discharge	None
conditional discharge	None
fine	1 year
community order	1 year
custodial sentence up to 6 months	2 years
custodial sentence between 6 and 30 months	4 years
custodial sentence between 30 months and 4 years	7 years
custodial sentence over 4 years	never spent

Summary of gateway (d)

The prosecution will seek to adduce evidence of a defendant's previous convictions under gateway (d) to demonstrate that:

(a) the defendant has a propensity to commit offences of the kind charged; or

(b) the defendant has a propensity to be untruthful.

Previous convictions showing a propensity to commit offences of the kind charged will be convictions for offences of the same description or category, or convictions for offences where there is a significant factual similarity between the previous conviction and the current offence.

Previous convictions showing a propensity to be untruthful will be convictions for specific offences where a lie has been told (eg fraud by false representation or perjury), or offences where the defendant pleaded not guilty but was convicted following a trial. Offences of dishonesty (such as theft) will not generally show a propensity to be untruthful.

The defendant's solicitor may seek to challenge the admissibility of previous convictions which the prosecution seeks to admit under gateway (d) in two ways:

(a) Arguing that the previous convictions do not actually demonstrate the relevant propensity and so do not satisfy gateway (d). For example:

(i) How many convictions does the defendant have? One conviction is unlikely to show a propensity.

(ii) If the previous convictions are being adduced to show a propensity to commit offences of the same kind:

- do the factual circumstances of the previous convictions differ from the facts of the current offence;

- would it be unjust to rely on them given the time which has elapsed since they occurred
(s 103(3)); or

- does the propensity make it no more likely that the defendant is guilty of the offence?

(iii) If the previous convictions are being adduced to show a propensity to be untruthful, is it not suggested that the defendant's case is in any way untruthful?

(b) If the previous convictions do show the relevant propensity, can the court be persuaded to exercise its power under s 101(3) to exclude the convictions? Arguments that may be raised include:

(i) Would the convictions be more prejudicial than probative? Is there a danger that the defendant would be convicted on the basis of their previous convictions alone, due either to the extent or to the nature of such convictions?

(ii) Are the convictions being used to support a prosecution case that is otherwise weak?

(iii) Are the previous convictions spent?

9.7.2.5 Gateway (e) – it has substantial probative value in relation to an important matter in issue between the defendant and a co-defendant

This gateway may be used by one defendant to admit evidence of another defendant's bad character. It cannot be used by the CPS.

A co-defendant is likely to want to admit evidence of a defendant's bad character to demonstrate that the other defendant has a propensity to be untruthful (and thus to undermine the credibility of the evidence given by that defendant), or to show that the other defendant has a propensity to commit the kind of offence with which they have both been charged (thereby suggesting that it is the other defendant, rather than the co-defendant, who committed the offence).

Propensity to commit offences of the same kind

A co-defendant may therefore want to introduce in evidence the fact that a defendant has previous convictions for offences of the kind with which they have both been charged, in order to show that the defendant has a propensity to commit such offences and is therefore the more likely of the two to have committed the current offence.

A co-defendant who seeks to introduce evidence of a defendant's previous convictions for this purpose will need to demonstrate that such convictions are relevant to an important matter in issue between himself and the defendant, and that the relevance of such convictions is more than merely marginal or trivial.

R v Edwards and Others *[2005] EWCA Crim 3244* – *two defendants (M and S) were jointly charged with wounding with intent to cause GBH. Both defendants entered not guilty pleas, on the basis that they were not involved in the attack on the victim. Neither defendant sought to blame the other for the attack. M had previous convictions for offences of wounding, assault and affray. S made an application under gateway (e) to adduce evidence of these convictions on the basis that they demonstrated a propensity to act in a violent manner. The trial judge granted this application, and M was subsequently convicted. The Court of Appeal upheld the conviction. The court's reasoning was that each defendant's defence was that he was not involved in the violence, and if one defendant has previous convictions for offences of violence, this has a substantial probative value to the issue between them, namely, which of them was in fact responsible for the offence.*

Propensity to be untruthful

Section 104(1) of the CJA 2003 states:

(1) Evidence which is relevant to the question whether the defendant has a propensity to be untruthful is admissible on that basis under section 101(1)(e) only if the nature or conduct of his defence is such as to undermine the co-defendant's defence.

This part of the gateway is most relevant where the defendants enter into what is called a 'cut-throat' defence. This occurs when there are two (or more) defendants jointly charged with an offence, and each defendant pleads not guilty and blames the other(s) as having committed the offence. In such a situation, it will be an advantage for a co-defendant to be able to adduce evidence of his fellow defendant's previous convictions, in order to undermine the credibility of that defendant's evidence and to suggest that their version of events is the more credible.

The most relevant previous convictions of a defendant which a co-defendant will seek to adduce in evidence in order to demonstrate that the defendant has a propensity to be untruthful will be convictions for specific offences which involve the making of a false statement or representation (for example, perjury or fraud by false representation), or convictions for any offence where the defendant was convicted at trial after entering a not guilty plea and testifying but not being believed by the court.

 Example

Murad and Arthur are jointly charged with the burglary of a warehouse. Each pleads not guilty, alleging that the other was solely responsible for carrying out the burglary. Murad has several previous convictions for offences of obtaining property by deception. As Murad's defence (that Arthur carried out the burglary) will clearly undermine Arthur's defence, at trial, Arthur will adduce evidence of Murad's previous convictions to show that Murad has a propensity to be untruthful, and so undermine the credibility of the evidence that Murad gives.

If the co-defendant can establish that the test for admitting evidence of the defendant's bad character through this gateway is satisfied, the court has no power under the CJA 2003 to prevent the admission of this evidence.

9.7.2.6 Gateway (f) – it is evidence to correct a false impression given by the defendant

Only the prosecution may adduce evidence of a defendant's bad character under gateway (f).

A defendant will give a false impression 'if he is responsible for the making of an express or implied assertion which is apt to give the court or jury a false or misleading impression about the defendant'.

A defendant will be treated as being responsible for making such an assertion if the assertion is:

(a) made by the defendant in the proceedings (for example, when giving evidence in the witness box, or in a defence statement served on the CPS);

(b) made by the defendant when being questioned under caution by the police before charge, or on being charged;

(c) made by a witness called by the defendant;

(d) made by any witness in cross-examination in response to a question asked by the defendant that is intended to elicit it; or

(e) made by any person out of court, and the defendant adduces evidence of it in the proceedings (CJA 2003, s 105(2)).

✪ *Example*

Phillip is on trial for common assault. Phillip has several previous convictions for offences involving violence. When the allegation of assault was put to Phillip in interview at the police station, Phillip said: 'I would never do such a thing. I'm a good Christian and I go to church every Sunday.' The CPS will be allowed to correct the false impression given by Phillip in the police interview by adducing evidence of his previous convictions.

If the prosecution can establish that the test for admitting evidence of the defendant's bad character through this gateway is satisfied, the court has no power under the CJA 2003 to prevent the admission of this evidence. The court does, however, retain the discretionary power to exclude such evidence under s 78 of PACE 1984 (see below).

9.7.2.7   Gateway (g) – the defendant has made an attack on another person's character

What constitutes an attack on another person's character?

Under this gateway, a defendant's bad character will become admissible if the defendant makes an attack on any person's character. The attack does not necessarily need to be on the character of a witness for the prosecution who is attending court to give evidence (although commonly it will be). It may be an attack on the character of a person who is dead, or a person whom the CPS does not intend to call to give evidence. Furthermore, the attack on the character of the other person does not necessarily need to take place at trial. The attack may be made when the defendant is being questioned at the police station, or in a defence statement which is served on the CPS.

Only the prosecution may adduce evidence of a defendant's previous convictions under gateway (g).

Evidence attacking another person's character is evidence to the effect that the other person has:

(a) committed an offence (whether a different offence from the one with which the defendant is charged or the same one); or

(b) behaved, or is disposed to behave, in a reprehensible way (CJA 2003, s 106(2)).

Although the courts are likely to find that a defendant who makes an emphatic denial of guilt has not attacked the character of another, it is likely that the courts will give a very wide interpretation to this gateway.

🔖 *In R v Ball [2005] EWCA Crim 2826, the defendant was charged with rape and raised the defence of consent. When interviewed at the police station, the defendant denied the complainant's version of what had taken place, but then went further and made a disparaging remark about the complainant's sexual promiscuity, referring to her as a 'slag'. This imputation was held to be sufficient to enable the CPS to raise at trial evidence of the defendant's previous convictions. The Court of Appeal did say, however, that the defendant's claim that the complainant had fabricated the allegation of rape would not have been sufficient in itself to invoke s 101(1)(g).*

R v Williams *[2007] EWCA Crim 1951 – the defendant was charged with various sexual offences. During cross-examination of the police officers in the case, it was alleged by the defence that the officers had conspired to 'set the defendant up'. The trial judge ruled that this amounted to an attack on the character of the officers under gateway (g), and the prosecution was allowed to adduce evidence of the defendant's previous conviction for indecent assault. The Court of Appeal upheld the judge's ruling – whilst the defendant would not have opened up gateway (g) merely by suggesting that the account of the officers was untrue, to go further and allege a conspiracy was to make a clear attack on the character of the officers.*

Excluding evidence admitted under gateway (g)

As with gateway (d), the court must exclude evidence that would otherwise be admitted under this gateway if, on an application by the defendant, the admission of the evidence would have such an adverse effect on the fairness of the proceedings that the court ought not to admit it (CJA 2003, s 101(3)) (see gateway (d) above).

 Example

Eddie is charged with assault occasioning actual bodily harm following a fight in a pub when he is alleged to have pushed a fellow customer (John) to the ground, causing a gash to John's cheek. Eddie pleads not guilty and elects trial at the Crown Court. In his interview at the police station, Eddie said to the police: 'John has had it in for me ever since I started coming to the pub. He's a troublemaker and a bully and will say anything to get me in trouble.'

This is an attack on John's character which would then allow the prosecution to adduce evidence of Eddie's previous convictions at his trial. Eddie has previous convictions for a number of sexual offences, including sexual assault and gross indecency with children. Although these convictions would be admissible under gateway (g), the trial judge may exercise their power under s 101(3) to prevent the prosecution adducing evidence of these convictions at trial. It is likely that the prejudicial effect of the jury finding out about such convictions would outweigh the probative value of such convictions in determining Eddie's guilt.

9.7.3 Court's powers to exclude defendant's bad character

The court has no power under the provisions of the CJA 2003 to exclude bad character evidence admitted under any gateway other than (d) and (g). Bad character evidence under gateways (a), (b), (c), (e) and (f) is automatically admissible if the requirements for each of these gateways are satisfied.

The court does, however, retain a discretionary power under s 78 of PACE 1984 to exclude evidence on which the prosecution propose to rely if the admission of the evidence would have such an adverse effect on the fairness of the proceedings that it ought not to be admitted. In *R v Highton & Others* [2005] EWCA Crim 1985, the Court of Appeal held that judges should apply the provisions of s 78 when making rulings as to the use of evidence of bad character, and exclude evidence where it would be appropriate to do so under s 78 (so in reality this will apply to bad character evidence which the prosecution seek to adduce under gateways (c) and (f)).

Stopping contaminated case

Section 107 of the CJA 2003 allows a judge in the Crown Court either to direct the jury to acquit the defendant, or to order a retrial in circumstances where evidence of the defendant's bad character is 'contaminated'. Contamination may occur if witnesses have colluded in order to fabricate evidence of the defendant's bad character. Section 107 does not apply to trials in the magistrates' court.

Figure 9.4   Bad character of the defendant

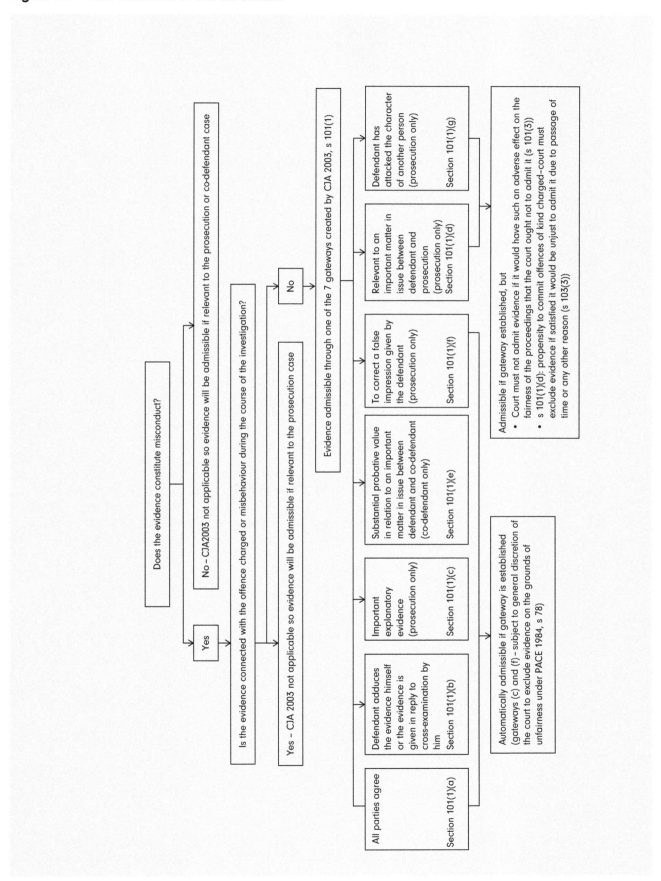

9.7.4 Procedure for admitting evidence of bad character

If the CPS wishes to adduce evidence of the defendant's bad character, notice of this intention must be given both to the court and to the other parties in the case (CrimPR, r 21.4(1) and (2)). A prescribed form must be used, with a written record of the previous convictions the party giving the notice or making the application is seeking to adduce being attached to the form.

As part of the standard directions that will be given in both the magistrates' court and the Crown Court, the court will impose time limits for the parties to serve any notice or make any application to adduce bad character evidence at trial. The relevant time limits are set out in CrimPR, r 21.4.

If a defendant opposes the introduction of evidence of their bad character at trial, the defendant must apply to the court for such evidence to be excluded. The application must be sent both to the court and to the other parties in the case. The time limit for making this application is set out in CrimPR, r 21.4.

9.7.5 Bad character of persons other than the defendant

In contrast to the numerous ways in which a defendant's bad character may now be admissible in evidence at trial, the bad character of *persons other than the defendant* (ie, not just other witnesses in the case) is now admissible only on very limited grounds. These grounds are set out in s 100(1) of the CJA 2003:

(1) ... evidence of the bad character of a person other than the defendant is admissible if and only if—

    (a) it is important explanatory evidence,

    (b) it has substantial probative value in relation to a matter which—

        (i) is a matter in issue in the proceedings, and

        (ii) is of substantial importance in the context of the case as a whole, or

    (c) all parties agree to the evidence being admissible.

In practice, s 100 will commonly be used by the defence when applying to adduce bad character evidence of the complainant, but note that these provisions are much wider than that and can be relied on by both the defence and the prosecution and apply to any witness giving evidence in the case or indeed to any other person, other than the defendant, even if they are not a witness in the case.

9.7.5.1 Section 100(1)(a) – it is important explanatory evidence

This is very similar to gateway (c) for evidence of a defendant's previous convictions (see **9.7.2.3** above). The evidence will be important explanatory evidence only if:

(a) without it, the court or jury would find it impossible or difficult properly to understand other evidence in the case; and

(b) its value for understanding the case as a whole is substantial (s 100(2)).

'Substantial' in this context is likely to mean more than merely trivial or marginal (see **9.7.2.5** above).

This gateway is not relied on very much in practice. The case of *R v Lee* [2012] EWCA Crim 316 emphasises that 'when bad character is admitted it is essential that counsel and the judge focus on the exact basis upon which it is being admitted. A case which is truly one of propensity cannot and must not be dressed up as a case of important explanatory evidence.'

⭐ *Example*

Dean is charged with assaulting Erin, his partner. The prosecution alleges that Dean grabbed Erin by the hair as she was attempting to put George, their baby son, to bed. Erin has a previous conviction for assaulting George after she slapped him repeatedly when he wouldn't stop crying. Dean's defence is that he grabbed Erin by the hair because he thought she was going to assault George. As Erin went to put George to bed, he heard her say: 'For God's sake, will he never shut up!' On hearing this, Dean thought that Erin might assault George again. To explain why he grabbed Erin by the hair, Dean may seek to adduce evidence of Erin's previous conviction for assaulting George.

Note that unlike any of the gateways to s 101, under s 100(4), leave of the court will be required if a party wishes to adduce evidence of the bad character of a person other than the defendant under s 100(1)(a).

9.7.5.2   Section 100(1)(b) – it has substantial probative value in relation to an important matter in issue in the proceedings

Although this ground may apply to any person other than the defendant (and so may apply to a witness for the defence as well as to a witness for the prosecution), it is most likely to arise when the defendant seeks to adduce evidence of the previous convictions of a witness for the prosecution in order to support an allegation that either:

(a)   the witness is lying or has fabricated evidence against the defendant; or

(b)   the witness themselves is either guilty of the offence with which the defendant has been charged or has engaged in misconduct in connection with the alleged offence:

In *R v Weir and Others* [2005] EWCA Crim 2866, the Court of Appeal held that evidence of the bad character of a witness which is adduced under s 100(1)(b) may be used either to show that the witness engaged in misconduct in connection with the offence, or to show that the evidence given by the witness lacks credibility because the witness has a propensity to be untruthful.

In assessing the probative value of the evidence of another person's previous convictions, the court must have regard to:

(a) the nature and number of the events, or other things, to which the evidence relates; and

(b) when those events or things are alleged to have happened or to have existed (s 100(3)).

The term 'substantial' is likely to be construed by the courts as meaning more than merely marginal or trivial (see **9.7.2.5** above).

Credibility as a witness

Previous convictions of a witness for the prosecution which may be used to suggest that the evidence given by the witness lacks credibility may be:

(a) convictions for offences where the witness has made a false statement or representation (such as perjury, fraud by false representation, or theft, where the witness has lied to another person as part of the commission of the theft); or

(b) convictions where the witness has been found guilty of an offence to which they pleaded not guilty but were convicted following a trial at which their version of events was disbelieved.

In *R v Stephenson* [2006] EWCA Crim 2325, the Court of Appeal suggested that previous convictions of a witness which demonstrated a propensity to be dishonest (as opposed to a propensity to be untruthful) may nevertheless be admissible under s 100(1)(b) to undermine the credibility of the witness. Similarly, in *R v Hester* [2007] EWCA Crim 2127, the defendant was charged with blackmail and the prosecution called evidence from a witness who had a previous conviction for burglary. The Court of Appeal held that where credibility is in issue in relation to an important witness, the evidence that the witness had previous convictions for dishonesty offences may be admissible as being relevant to the issue of credibility, whether or not the previous convictions involved untruthfulness.

The decision in *Stephenson* was approved in *R v Brewster* [2011] 1 WLR 601, which said that whether convictions are persuasive as to creditworthiness depends on their nature, number and age, and it was not necessary for the conviction to demonstrate a propensity to untruthfulness.

This represents a different approach to establishing a propensity to be untruthful under s 101(1)(d) (see **9.7.2.4** above).

Misconduct in connection with the current offence or guilty of that offence

The other reason for a defendant wanting to raise the bad character of a person other than themselves is to use such evidence to suggest either that:

(a) the other person has committed some form of misconduct in connection with the current offence (for example, a defendant charged with assault may claim that they were in fact acting merely in self-defence, and that they were in fact attacked by their alleged victim); or

(b) the other person is in fact guilty of the offence with which the defendant has been charged.

Although this ground applies equally to witnesses called either by the defence or by the prosecution, it is likely to be used most regularly by a defendant to suggest that a witness for the prosecution either committed the offence with which the defendant is charged or is guilty of some other form of misconduct in connection with that offence.

Misconduct in connection with the current offence

If it is alleged that evidence of another person's misconduct has probative value because there is a similarity between that misconduct and alleged misconduct in connection with the current offence, the court will have regard to the nature and extent of the similarities and dissimilarities between each of the alleged instances of misconduct (s 100(3)(c)).

 Example

> *Mahmud is on trial for assaulting Bilal. The prosecution alleges that Mahmud punched Bilal in the face. Mahmud denies the offence, claiming that he was in fact attacked by Bilal (who was in a drunken state) after Mahmud had made a provocative remark about Bilal's girlfriend. Bilal has previous convictions for offences of common assault and threatening behaviour. Mahmud will seek to use evidence of Bilal's previous convictions to show that Bilal is more likely to have been the aggressor on this occasion.*
>
> *In deciding whether evidence of Bilal's previous convictions is admissible, the court will have regard to the nature and extent of the similarities and dissimilarities between his previous convictions and the facts of the current offence. The court will want to know if Bilal's previous convictions arose in similar circumstances, and in particular if Bilal committed these offences after any provocation and/or whilst in a drunken state.*

In *R v Bovell* [2005] EWCA Crim 1091, the Court of Appeal held that a judge could admit evidence of previous convictions relied upon to show the propensity of a prosecution witness to commit a particular type of offence if the defendant could show sufficient factual similarities between the earlier offence and the current incident.

Guilty of committing the current offence

If it is alleged that evidence of another person's misconduct has probative value because it is suggested that the person is responsible for having committed the offence with which the defendant has been charged, the court will have regard to the extent to which the evidence shows or tends to show that the same person was responsible each time (s 100(3)(d)).

Example

Nathan is on trial for the burglary of items from a warehouse. One of the witnesses for the prosecution is Jack, the night watchman at the warehouse. Jack claims to have seen Nathan committing the burglary. Nathan denies the offence and alleges that Jack has fabricated evidence against him because he (Jack) was in fact responsible for stealing these items. Jack has two previous convictions for offences of theft. Nathan will seek to use evidence of Jack's previous convictions to show Jack to have been the more likely of the two to have been responsible for the offence. In deciding whether the evidence of Jack's previous convictions are admissible, the court will have regard to the nature and extent of the similarities and dissimilarities between Jack's previous convictions and the facts of the current offence. If the facts of the previous convictions are markedly different, it is unlikely that the court will permit the defendant to raise these convictions at trial (see, eg, R v Gadsby [2005] EWCA Crim 3206).

Witnesses who are not giving evidence

Although the defendant will usually rely upon s 100(1)(b) in respect of a witness for the prosecution who has previous convictions, it may also be used in relation to persons who are not giving evidence in the case.

 Example

Emir is on trial for the unlawful killing of Tariq. It is alleged that Emir stabbed Tariq with a knife. Emir raises the defence of self-defence. He alleges that Tariq attacked him with a knife and that Tariq was stabbed after he (Emir) managed to turn the knife against him. Tariq has a previous conviction for carrying a knife as an offensive weapon. Emir will want to use this previous conviction to support his defence of self-defence. In deciding whether the evidence of Tariq's previous conviction is admissible, the court will have regard to the nature and extent of the similarities and dissimilarities between the facts of Tariq's previous conviction and the facts of the current case. The fact that Tariq will not be a witness in the present case is not a relevant consideration.

Leave of the court

Under s 100(4), leave of the court will also be required if a party wishes to adduce evidence of the bad character of a person other than the defendant under s 100(1)(b).

9.7.5.3   Section 100(1)(c) – all parties to the proceedings agree to the evidence being admissible

If all parties to the case are in agreement, evidence of the bad character of a person other than the defendant will always be admissible.

A flowchart summarising the operation of s 100(1) is set out below.

Figure 9.5   Bad character of persons other than the defendant

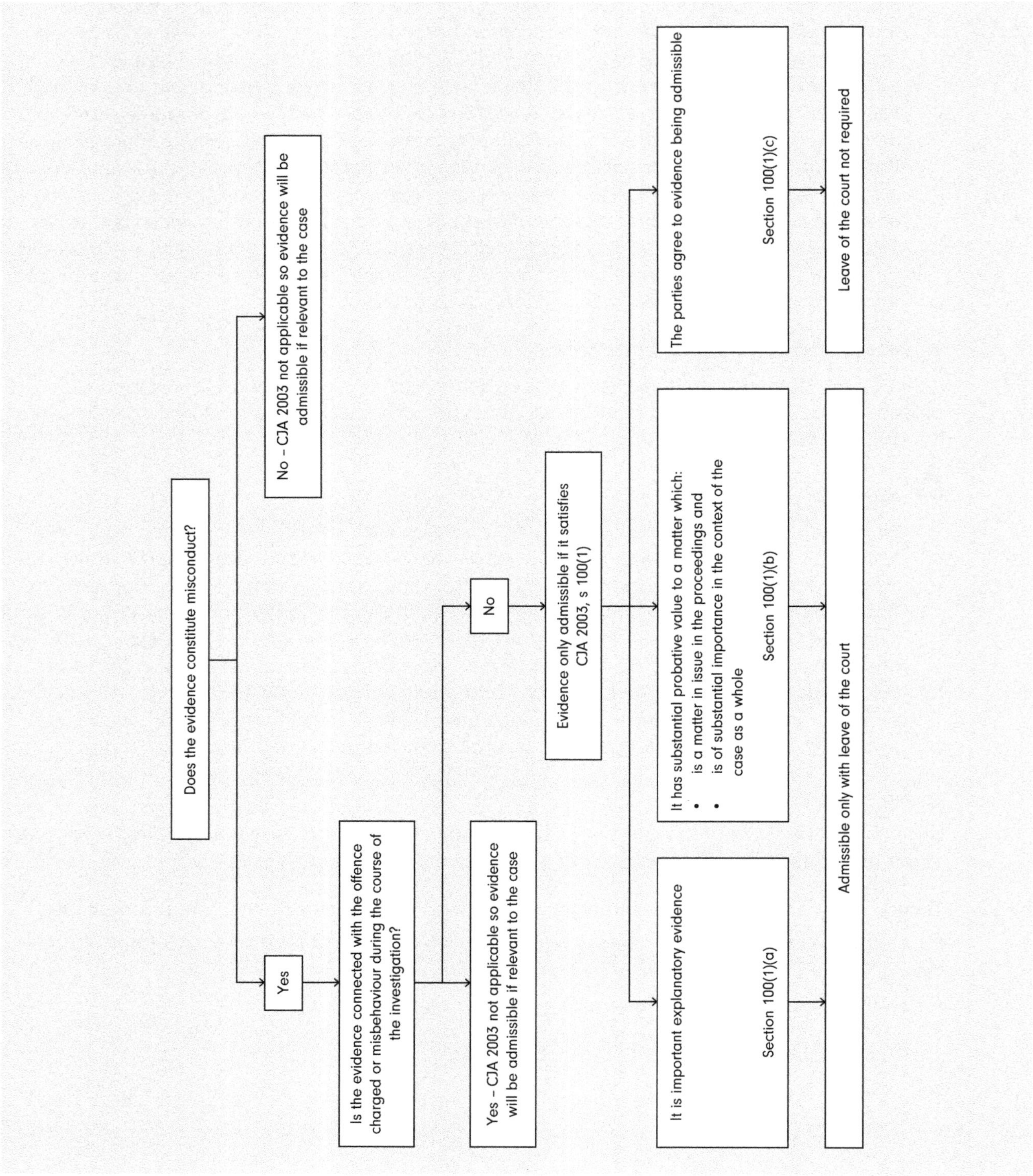

9.8   Exclusion of evidence

We have already identified how the court has a discretion to exclude improperly or unfairly obtained prosecution evidence. Section 78(1) provides:

> In any proceedings a court may refuse to allow evidence on which the prosecution proposes to rely to be given if it appears to the court that, having regard to all of the

circumstances, including the circumstances in which the evidence was obtained, the admission of the evidence would have such an adverse effect on the fairness of the proceedings that the court ought not to admit it.

Case law on s 78 suggests that this section has been interpreted broadly in line with the earlier common law position. The power in s 78 is discretionary, and the court is only likely to exercise its discretion to exclude prosecution evidence under s 78 if there is something unreliable about the evidence which the police have obtained, which in turn means that it would be unfair to allow the CPS to rely on such evidence. If the evidence is relevant to the charge faced by the defendant, and there is nothing in the way in which it has been obtained which casts doubt on its reliability, the evidence is unlikely to be excluded under s 78, even if the police have breached the provisions of PACE 1984 and/or the Codes of Practice when obtaining it.

The courts have said repeatedly that applications by defendants to exclude prosecution evidence under s 78 on the ground that the police have breached PACE 1984 or the Codes of Practice in the obtaining of such evidence, should only be granted if the breaches are *'significant and substantial'* (*R v Keenan* [1990] 2 QB 54).

Common examples of prosecution evidence which a defendant may seek to persuade a court to exclude under s 78 are:

(a) evidence obtained following an illegal search

(b) identification evidence

(c) confession evidence

(d) evidence obtained from the use of covert listening and surveillance devices and

(e) evidence obtained in 'undercover' police operations.

9.8.1 Scope and application of s 78 PACE and the right to a fair trial

Article 6 of the ECHR provides that anyone charged with a criminal offence is entitled to a 'fair' hearing. The appellate courts have held, on several occasions, that the discretion given to a trial judge to exclude evidence under s 78 where the admission of that evidence would otherwise lead to unfairness, ensures that a defendant will receive a fair trial. Similarly, in cases such as *Khan v United Kingdom* [2000] Crim LR 684, the European Court of Human Rights has stated repeatedly that the key question to be answered when determining whether the defendant's rights under Article 6 have been breached is whether the proceedings as a whole were fair. The width of the discretion given to the trial judge by s 78 should ensure that proceedings are conducted in a manner which is fair to the defendant.

Figure 9.6   Operation of s 78 flowchart

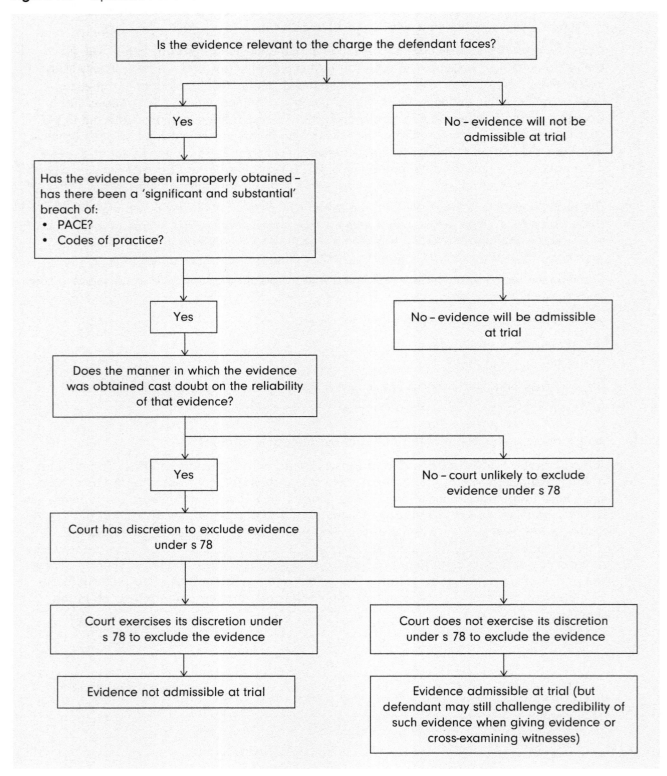

9.8.2 Evidence obtained by entrapment and abuse of process

In *R v Sang* [1980] AC 402 the House of Lords emphasised that there is no defence known as 'entrapment'. Although it is possible to challenge the admissibility of such evidence under s 78, the preferred approach is to invite the court to exercise its common law power to stop the case on the basis that it would represent an abuse of process to allow such a prosecution to continue.

In the combined appeal of R v Loosely; AG's Reference No 3 of 2000 *[2001] UKHL 53, the defendant in the second case had been supplied by undercover officers with cheap cigarettes who in return asked him to supply them with heroin. The defendant did so, but only after considerable persuasion and some apparent difficulty. He then put the undercover officers in touch with his own supplier. The evidence was excluded by the trial judge on the basis that this amounted to an abuse of process by the police. The House of Lords agreed. They found that the police had incited the accused to commit the offence and that the trial judge had been right to stay the proceedings as an abuse of process. In one of the leading judgments, Lord Nicholls stated that every court has an inherent (common law) power and duty to prevent an abuse of process. Entrapment was an instance where such misuse of power could occur and that it was not acceptable for the state to lure individuals into committing unlawful acts and then prosecute them for doing so. In such circumstances, the court's focus should be on the conduct and behaviour of the police. Lord Nicholls went on to set out guidelines for trial judges when deciding whether or not to stay proceedings for an abuse of process:*

(1) The nature of the investigation – the more intrusive the investigation, the harder the courts should scrutinise it.

(2) The nature of the offence. Certain offences can only be committed in a covert way such as drug trafficking and therefore police can only crack them in a covert way.

(3) The nature of the police involvement. For example, how they behaved, how persistent they were in trying to persuade the defendant to take part in the offence, for example did they behave like a 'normal customer' might and no more.

(4) The defendant's criminal record – usually this would not be relevant unless there was evidence of recent similar involvement.

(5) The level and extent of supervision of the undercover officers.

Summary

In this chapter you have considered what the law, practice and procedure say about the principles and procedures to admit and exclude evidence. Notably:

- *The operation of the burden and standard of proof.* Firstly, how the evidential burden operates differently on the prosecution to its operation on the defence. Secondly, how the persuasive burden (legal burden) usually remains with the prosecution throughout the trial and what the standard of proof is in relation to this burden, but how it may also occasionally shift onto the defendant in relation to some specific defences.

- *Visual identification evidence and Turnbull guidance.* What is meant by disputed visual identification evidence and how the defence may first challenge its admissibility where it has been obtained in breach of Code D and if this fails (or is not possible to argue) how the Turnbull guidelines apply to such evidence.

- *The drawing of inferences from silence ss 34, 35, 36, 37, 38 Criminal Justice and Public Order Act 1994.* Although the defendant is said to have a right to silence at both the police station and at court, when and in what circumstances a court may draw (adverse) inferences from the defendant's exercise of this right.

- *The admissibility of hearsay evidence.* What is meant by hearsay and the four general exceptions contained in the CJA 2003 as to when such evidence will be admissible.

- *The admissibility of confession evidence.* Being able to identify when something said or done by a suspect amounts to a confession and how prima facie such evidence is admissible as an exception to the hearsay rule. Then very importantly, how the defence may challenge the admission of such evidence under either s 76(2) and/or s 78 PACE 1984.

- *The admissibility of the defendant's bad character.* Firstly, the meaning of bad character and then how such evidence may be admitted under one of 7 gateways available under s 101(1) of the CJA 2003 and the extent of the court's powers to exclude such evidence.

- *Exclusion of improperly or unlawfully obtained evidence under s 78 PACE and the right to a fair trial.* How s 78 provides the court with a discretion to exclude such prosecution evidence and the relationship between this discretion and the right to a fair trial under Article 6 of the ECHR.

Sample questions

Question 1

A boy, aged 14, has been charged with robbery. The boy does not suffer from any recognised medical condition but his mental age has been assessed as that of a 9-year-old and he is distressed at the prospect of having to testify at trial.

If the boy does not testify, will it be appropriate for an adverse inference to be drawn from his silence at trial?

A   Yes, because an adverse inference will always be drawn if a defendant refuses to testify at trial.

B   Yes, because distress about testifying is not in itself a sufficient reason and will not by itself prevent the drawing of an adverse inference.

C   No, because an adverse inference cannot be drawn against a juvenile with a mental age of a 9-year-old.

D   No, because it appears that the mental condition of the boy makes it undesirable for him to give evidence.

E   Yes, because the court will require the boy to testify to put forward his defence if he is to be acquitted.

Answer

Option B is the best answer because distress about testifying will not be sufficient to engage s 35(1)(b). This exception provides a statutory exception to the drawing of such an adverse inference where 'it appears to the court that the physical or mental condition of the accused makes it undesirable for him to give evidence'.

So Option A is wrong because an adverse inference will not always be drawn where an accused does not testify – option C is wrong because the mental age alone would not be a sufficient reason (see *R v Friend* (1997)). Although option D does correctly state the above statutory exception, on these facts, the boy does not appear to have a medical condition that would make it undesirable for him to testify (contrast that with *R v Friend (No 2)* (2004) where evidence then came to light that the defendant also suffered from ADHD, which was found to be such a medical condition). Option E is wrong because a defendant has a right to remain silent at trial and cannot be convicted on his silence alone. Moreover, the boy does not necessarily need to testify in order to be acquitted.

Question 2

A man has been arrested on suspicion of burglary, it being alleged that he stole some computer equipment from premises he broke into. When interviewed, the man confesses to the offence and also tells the police where the stolen items can be found. These are recovered by the police and the man's fingerprints are found on them. The interview was however, conducted unlawfully and the defence will argue at trial that the confession ought to be excluded on the basis that it was obtained in circumstances rendering it unreliable.

Assuming the man's confession is excluded at trial, which of the following best describes whether the prosecution will be allowed to adduce evidence of the finding of the stolen items?

A   The finding of the items is still relevant and admissible as the exclusion of the confession will not affect the admissibility of this evidence.

B   The finding of these items will still be admissible because the confession was not excluded as a result of oppression.

C   Any evidence resulting from an inadmissible confession will not be admitted at trial.

D   It will always be more prejudicial than probative to allow such evidence to be admitted.

E   The finding of the items will be admissible unless it would have such an adverse effect on the fairness of the proceedings that the court ought not admit it.

Answer

Option A is the statement that best describes the operation of s 76(4) PACE 1984 about the admissibility of relevant facts discovered as a result of an inadmissible confession. Not only is the finding of the stolen items relevant, but more importantly, the man's fingerprints found on the stolen items link him to the burglary.

Option B is wrong because s 76(4) operates regardless of whether the confession is excluded under s 76(2)(a) or (b). Option C is also wrong. Although such evidence coming from an inadmissible confession may not be admitted, this will by no means always be the case. Option D is wrong because although evidence will generally be excluded under the court's common law power (more prejudicial than probative) it will not 'always' be the case. Option E is not the best description because this only sets out the test under s 78 PACE, which is not the only test to apply when determining the admissibility of evidence.

Question 3

A man has been charged with murder. A key prosecution witness has subsequently died, and the prosecution want to adduce her witness statement in the absence of the deceased witness.

What will the prosecution need to establish for the witness statement to be admitted?

A   That she had first-hand knowledge of the matters contained in her witness statement and all reasonable steps have been taken to secure her attendance.

B   That she had first- or second-hand knowledge of the matter contained in her witness statement and she is identified to the court's satisfaction.

C   That she has died and so it is not reasonably practicable to secure her attendance and she is identified to the court's satisfaction.

D   That she had first-hand knowledge of the matters contained in her witness statement and is identified to the court's satisfaction.

E   That she has died, and she had first-hand knowledge of the matters contained in her witness statement and is identified to the court's satisfaction.

Answer

Option E is the correct answer as it identifies the three key requirements needed to adduce such hearsay evidence. Namely, that the witness had first-hand knowledge of the matters contained in her witness statement, she is identified to the court's satisfaction and the relevant prescribed reason under s 116(2) is satisfied. Here (a), that the relevant person is dead.

Option A is wrong because it only refers to one of these requirements and then goes on to mention part of another prescribed reason under s 116(2)(d). Option B is wrong because s 116 only allows first-hand hearsay to be admitted. Option C is wrong because although it does refer to two of the above requirements, it also refers to part of another prescribed reason under s 116(2)(c). Option D is not the best answer because it fails to mention the relevant prescribed reason, namely that the witness is dead.

10 Trial Procedure in the Magistrates' Court and Crown Court

SQE1 syllabus

This chapter will enable you to achieve the SQE1 Assessment Specification in relation to Functioning Legal Knowledge concerned with the following procedures and processes:

- burden and standard of proof;
- stages of a criminal trial, including submission of no case to answer;
- modes of address and court room etiquette;
- difference between leading and non-leading questions;
- competence and compellability;
- special measures;
- solicitor's duty to the court.

Note that, for SQE1, candidates are not usually required to recall specific case names or cite statutory or regulatory authorities. These are provided for illustrative purposes only unless otherwise stated.

Learning outcomes

By the end of this chapter you will be able to apply relevant core legal principles and rules appropriately and effectively, at the level of a competent newly qualified solicitor in practice, to realistic client-based and ethical problems and situations in the following areas:

- How the burden and standard of proof operates in a criminal trial.
- The various stages of a criminal trial, including when and how to make a submission of no case to answer.

- The modes of address and court room etiquette to follow when conducting a criminal trial.

- The difference between leading and non-leading questions and when it is most appropriate to use each type of question.

- The rules relating to competence and compellability of witnesses.

- The operation of the special measure provisions in relation to vulnerable witnesses.

- The solicitor's duty owed to the court.

10.1 Introduction

The process of trials in the magistrates' court and Crown Court are heavily prescribed. This is aimed at ensuring a fair trial for the accused which will culminate in the magistrates/district judge or a jury of peers reaching their verdict. This verdict represents the climax of the trial. It may then result in the passing of a sentence and possibly an appeal against any resulting conviction and/or sentence which we shall look at in the following two chapters.

10.2 Burden and standard of proof

We saw in **Chapter 9** that subject to a few statutory defences (and the common law defence of insanity), the burden of proof remains with the prosecution throughout a criminal trial. This explains why the prosecution must always present their case first and why they must persuade the court beyond a reasonable doubt of the defendant's guilt. We also saw in **Chapter 9** how the evidential burdens operate on both the prosecution and the defence. These help to explain some key features of the trial procedure that we shall be looking at later in this chapter. For example, when and on what basis a submission of no case to answer may be made. It also explains why the defendant is likely to testify at trial, particularly where the defence bear an evidential burden to raise some common defences such as alibi or reasonable self-defence, even if the law of evidence does not require them to prove such defence.

10.3 Stages of a criminal trial, including submission of no case to answer

10.3.1 Trial in the magistrates' court (CrimPR, Part 24)

The normal order of events at a trial in the magistrates' court is as follows:

(a) Opening speech by the solicitor from the CPS.

(b) The prosecution witnesses will then be called in turn to give evidence. Each witness will be examined in chief by the prosecuting solicitor and then cross-examined by the defendant's solicitor. The prosecuting solicitor may then choose to re-examine the witness.

(c) (Possible submission of no case to answer by defendant's solicitor.)

(d) The defence witnesses will then be called in turn to give evidence (with the defendant being called first). Each witness will be examined in chief by the defendant's solicitor and will then be cross-examined by the prosecuting solicitor. The defendant's solicitor may then choose to re-examine the witness.

(e) The prosecuting solicitor may make a closing speech where the defendant is represented, or the defendant has introduced evidence other than his own (whether represented or not).

(f) Closing speech by the defendant's solicitor.

(g) The magistrates retire to consider their verdict.

(h) The magistrates deliver their verdict.

(i) If the defendant is found guilty, the magistrates will then either sentence the defendant immediately, or adjourn sentence until later if they wish to obtain pre-sentence reports on the defendant. If acquitted, the defendant will be formally discharged by the magistrates and told that they are free to go.

10.3.1.1 Opening speech

A trial in the magistrates' court will begin with the advocate from the prosecution giving an opening speech. This does not form part of the evidence on which the magistrates will decide the case and is more a matter of 'setting the scene'. The opening speech will normally begin with the prosecutor telling the magistrates the factual details about the charge which the defendant faces. They will then explain to the magistrates the relevant substantive law and will tell them what the prosecution will need to prove in order to secure a conviction. The prosecutor should remind the magistrates that the prosecution has the burden of proving beyond a reasonable doubt that the defendant is guilty, and that the defendant is entitled to an acquittal unless the magistrates are sure of guilt. The prosecutor will then outline what the prosecution case consists of, telling the court which witnesses they intend to call to give evidence for the prosecution, and summarise briefly the evidence that is to be given by these witnesses. The prosecutor may also refer the magistrates to any points of law which they anticipate may arise during the trial (for example, the Turnbull guidelines if the case consists of disputed identification evidence or ss 76 or 78 of PACE 1984 if there is disputed confession evidence).

10.3.1.2 Prosecution evidence

After completing their opening speech, the prosecutor will call their first witness to give evidence. Unless the witness is a child under the age of 14 (see **10.6** later) such evidence will be sworn evidence which means the witness will either take an oath or affirmation, in which they promise to tell the truth. It is customary for the first prosecution witness to be the complainant. For example, in an assault case, the first prosecution witness is likely to be the person who was injured in the assault. In a theft case, the first prosecution witness is likely to be the person whose property has been stolen. After this person has given evidence, other prosecution witnesses (including any expert witnesses) will be called to testify.

Each prosecution witness will initially be asked questions by the prosecutor. The defendant's solicitor will then have the opportunity to cross-examine the witness. At the end of the cross-examination, the prosecutor may, if they choose, briefly re-examine the witness.

Any prosecution witness who is not being called to give evidence (for example, witnesses who have given a statement under s 9 of the CJA 1967 to which the defence have not objected, or witnesses whose statements are to be read out as hearsay evidence) will have their statements read out to the court by the prosecutor.

If the defendant was interviewed at the police station, either a summary or the full transcript of the interview will be read out to the court, unless the defendant's solicitor objects to this. If the defence solicitor does object (if, for example, the summary does not include points made by the defendant in support of their defence), the audio recording of the interview will be played to the court.

10.3.1.3 Arguments on points of law

During the presentation of their case, the prosecutor may seek to place evidence before the court which the defendant's solicitor considers to be inadmissible. A common example of this is when the prosecution seek to adduce evidence that the defendant made a confession, and the defendant's solicitor seeks to challenge the admissibility of this confession under s 76 of PACE 1984 on the basis that the confession was obtained in circumstances rendering it unreliable. Another example is if the prosecution seek to adduce evidence that the defendant was visually identified by a witness following an identification procedure, and the defendant's solicitor seeks to challenge the admissibility of this evidence under s 78 of PACE 1984 on the basis that the identification procedure was not carried out in accordance with the requirements of Code D. Another example is if the prosecution wants to adduce evidence of the defendant's bad character and the defence solicitor challenges its admissibility (see **Chapter 9** for the relevant law and legal arguments in relation to all of these examples).

If such a situation arises, the magistrates will normally hold a hearing called a *voir dire* to determine the admissibility of the particular piece of evidence in dispute. Such hearings are also often referred to as 'a trial within a trial'.

A *voir dire* will involve witnesses giving evidence on matters relevant to the admissibility of the evidence (for example, in the case of a disputed confession made in the context of an interview at the police station, both the police officer who conducted the interview and the defendant are likely to give evidence). After the witnesses have given evidence, the prosecutor and the defendant's solicitor will make legal submissions as to the admissibility of the disputed evidence.

If the magistrates decide that the evidence is inadmissible, the prosecutor will not be allowed to make any further reference to such evidence during the course of the trial. If the evidence is ruled to be admissible, it may then be produced by the prosecutor as part of the prosecution case (although the defendant's solicitor will still be entitled to attempt to undermine the reliability or cogency of such evidence during the trial).

 Example

> *Ryan is charged with theft. In an audibly recorded interview at the police station he confessed to the theft, and the CPS wishes to adduce evidence of this at Ryan's trial. Ryan's solicitor challenges the admissibility of the confession, arguing that it was obtained in circumstances which make it unreliable. The basis of this argument is that Ryan claims that he confessed only after being told by the interviewing officer that he was going to be kept at the police station until he made a confession. At the* voir dire, *the magistrates are likely to hear evidence from Ryan and the interviewing officer, and they will also read a transcript of the interview or have the recording of the interview played out. Submissions will also be made by the prosecutor and Ryan's solicitor. At the conclusion of the* voir dire, *the magistrates decide that the confession is inadmissible. This means that the prosecutor cannot use the confession as part of their case against Ryan.*

The difficulty faced by the defendant's solicitor when conducting a *voir dire* in the magistrates' court is that the magistrates decide matters of both law and fact. This means that even if the magistrates decide that a piece of prosecution evidence is inadmissible, the magistrates will still be aware of the existence of that item of evidence. This situation will not arise in a Crown Court trial where the judge will conduct a *voir dire* in the absence of the jury, who will therefore never hear about any prosecution evidence which the judge rules to be inadmissible. The absence of a satisfactory procedure for dealing with the question of the admissibility of disputed prosecution evidence in a magistrates' court trial is one reason why a defendant may elect trial in the Crown Court when charged with an either-way matter (see **Chapter 6**).

As an alternative to holding a separate 'trial within a trial', the magistrates may sometimes hear the disputed evidence as part of the trial itself, and then consider the question of the admissibility of such evidence either when the defendant's solicitor makes a submission of no case to answer at the conclusion of the prosecution case (see below), or when the defence makes their closing submissions at the end of the trial.

To overcome problems at trial with magistrates being aware of the existence of an item of prosecution evidence, even if they have decided that such evidence is inadmissible, many magistrates' courts now hold pre-trial hearings to determine the admissibility of disputed evidence. Pre-trial hearings will be held before a different bench of magistrates to the bench which ultimately conducts the trial, thus ensuring that the magistrates who actually decide the case need never be aware of items of evidence which are inadmissible.

10.3.1.4 Submission of no case to answer

When presenting the prosecution case, the prosecutor bears an evidential burden. This burden is to present sufficient evidence to the court to justify a finding of guilt (see **Chapter 9**). If the prosecutor fails to satisfy this burden, the defendant's solicitor should make a submission of no case to answer at the conclusion of the prosecution case, asking the magistrates to dismiss the case. The leading authority on the relevant test to apply is set out in *R v Galbraith* [1981] 2 All ER 1060.

A submission of no case to answer will be made by the defendant's solicitor if either:

(a) the prosecution has failed to put forward evidence to prove an essential element of the alleged offence; or

(b) the evidence produced by the prosecution has been so discredited as a result of cross-examination, or is so manifestly unreliable, that no reasonable tribunal could safely convict on it.

✪ Example 1

Harvinder is charged with the theft of a bicycle. In presenting their case, the prosecutor fails to produce evidence that the bicycle belonged to another person. Proving that the item stolen belonged to another person is an essential element in the offence of theft. Harvinder's solicitor should therefore make a submission of no case to answer and request that the magistrates dismiss the case.

✪ Example 2

Lee is charged with assault occasioning actual bodily harm following an incident outside a nightclub. The victim of the alleged assault claims that he was the subject of an unprovoked attack by Lee, whom he did not know before the incident. The defence case is that Lee only used reasonable force to defend himself. The prosecution case is based solely on evidence from the complainant. In cross-examination by Lee's solicitor, this evidence is shown to be unreliable. The complainant accepts that in fact he threw the first punch and he also admits that he knew Lee before the incident, because his ex-girlfriend left him to go out with Lee. He also admits that he exaggerated the extent of his injuries. At the conclusion of the prosecution case, Lee's solicitor will make a submission of no case to answer on the basis that the prosecution evidence is so manifestly unreliable that the court cannot safely convict on it.

In practice it is usually difficult to make a successful submission of no case to answer, because not much prosecution evidence is actually required to get past this halfway stage.

This can be seen from the following case.

215

In R v Sardar [2016] EWCA Crim 1616 the accused was charged with murdering a US soldier in Iraq from an improvised explosive device (IED). Sir Brian Leveson applied the test in Galbraith and in doing so relied on a passage from King CJ's judgment in Questions of Law Reserved on Acquittal (No 2 of 1993) (1993) 61 SASR 1. Namely, where there is direct evidence capable of proving the charge, then there will always be a case to answer, no matter how weak or tenuous this appears. If the case depends on circumstantial evidence, there will only be no case to answer where the evidence is not capable in law of supporting a conviction. So in a case where the prosecution is solely relying on circumstantial evidence, if all the prosecution evidence was accepted and all the inferences favourable to the prosecution were drawn from this evidence, if a reasonable mind could still not reach a conclusion of guilt beyond a reasonable doubt, or exclude other hypotheses consistent with innocence, then the prosecution will not have discharged their evidential burden. In this case, the circumstantial evidence was that the accused was in the region at the time. He was in possession of information about terrorism and bomb-making equipment and his fingerprints were found on other, similar IEDs which had been deployed in the same narrow geographical area during the same time period. On this evidence, it was held that he was rightly found to have a case to answer.

If the magistrates accept a submission of no case to answer, the charge against the defendant will be dismissed. If the magistrates reject the submission of no case to answer, the defendant may then present their case and call witnesses. The fact that the prosecution has satisfied their evidential burden does not mean that the prosecution is entitled to a conviction at that stage. This is because the court will not yet have heard either from the defendant, or from any witnesses the defendant wishes to call in support of their defence.

10.3.1.5 The defence case

A defendant is a competent witness for the defence but is not compellable. This means that a defendant can give evidence on his own behalf, but he is not obliged to do so (Criminal Evidence Act 1898, s 1(1)). Prior to the trial taking place, the defendant's solicitor should always discuss with the defendant whether or not they should give evidence in their own defence. A defendant may be reluctant to give evidence, particularly if they are young or nervous, or if they fear that their 'story' will not stand up to cross-examination by the prosecutor.

In the normal course of events, it will be necessary for the defendant to give evidence (assuming there has not been a successful submission of no case to answer). For example, a defendant who is raising a defence such as self-defence or alibi has the evidential burden of placing some evidence of this defence before the court. The simplest way to discharge this burden is for the defendant to give evidence. Similarly, if the prosecution has adduced evidence of a confession made by the defendant, and the defendant disputes the truth of this confession, the defendant will need to give evidence to explain why he made a false confession.

A defendant who answered questions (or provided a prepared written statement) at the police station will also have the credibility of this evidence enhanced if they go into the witness box at trial and repeat what they said at the police station. A defendant who does this will enable their solicitor, when giving their closing speech, to say that the defendant has put forward a consistent defence since first being arrested and questioned.

In addition to the above, we also saw in **Chapter 9** as a result of s 35 of the CJPOA 1994, a defendant who fails to give evidence on their own behalf at trial is likely to find that the court will draw an adverse inference from such failure.

The effect of s 35 is that, if the prosecution has raised issues which call for an explanation from the defendant, should the defendant then fail to give evidence, the court will be entitled to infer from that failure that the defendant has either no explanation, or no explanation that will stand up to cross-examination.

 Example

Lloyd is charged with common assault. Lloyd pleads not guilty on the basis that he was acting in self-defence. At the end of the prosecution case, Lloyd declines to enter the witness box to give evidence on his own behalf. The court is entitled to infer from this that Lloyd has no defence to the charge, or no defence that will stand up to cross-examination (in other words, an inference that Lloyd is guilty of the offence).

Figure 10.1   Flowchart – Will the defendant need to testify?

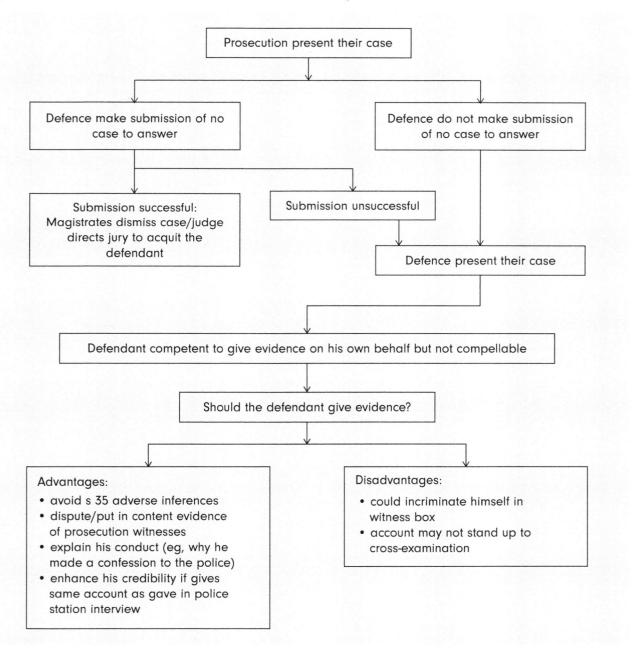

10.3.1.6 Order of defence witnesses

If a defendant is to give evidence on their own behalf, they must be called first before any other witnesses for the defence (unless the court 'otherwise directs' (PACE 1984, s 79)). The rationale behind this rule is that the defendant will be in court throughout the proceedings. Therefore, if other defence witnesses were to give evidence before the defendant, the defendant would have the opportunity to hear what they said and how they were cross-examined. They could then tailor their own testimony to take account of the comments made by the other defence witnesses. All other witnesses (for either the prosecution or the defence) are not allowed in court until they have testified.

Defence witnesses will give evidence in the same way as prosecution witnesses. Each defence witness will be examined in chief by the defendant's solicitor and will then be cross-examined by the prosecutor. The defendant's solicitor will then have the opportunity to re-examine their witness.

10.3.1.7 Closing speeches

It used to be the case that the prosecution was not thought to have a right to make a closing speech in a magistrates' court trial. HM Crown Prosecution Service Inspectorate asked the Criminal Procedure Rules Committee to clarify the position in relation to r 37. As a result, a new rule was added (r 24.3(g) to (h)) which now expressly recognises the prosecution's right to make such a speech. Guidance suggests though that this right should only usually be exercised in more complex cases where it will be of assistance to the court. Where this right is exercised, then as with trials in the Crown Court, the defence will always make their closing speech after the prosecution closing speech.

In fact, the defendant's solicitor has a choice in the magistrates' court as to whether to make an opening or a closing speech. In practice, solicitors representing the defendant will nearly always choose to make a closing speech, given the tactical importance of having the last word after all the evidence has been presented to the court. Like the prosecution opening speech, the defence closing speech is not itself evidence. It does, however, allow the defendant's solicitor to sum up the case from the defence point of view, to point out all the weaknesses in the prosecution case and to remind the court of all the points in favour of the defendant.

Although there is no set format for making a closing speech, the following points should be borne in mind:

(a) The closing speech should be kept short and to the point. Closing speeches that are too long often have little impact on the magistrates.

(b) The defendant's solicitor must always remind the magistrates that the CPS bears the burden of proving beyond a reasonable doubt that the defendant is guilty of the offence with which he is charged. The magistrates should be told that the defendant is entitled to an acquittal unless they are sure that the defendant is guilty. The defendant does not need to prove that they are innocent. All they need to do to secure an acquittal is to demonstrate that the prosecution has failed to prove its case beyond a reasonable doubt.

(c) The defendant's solicitor should refer back to the opening speech made by the prosecutor, in which the prosecutor set out what they were going to prove. The defendant's solicitor should point out each and every area where the prosecution case has 'come up short'. The defendant's solicitor should place particular emphasis on the factual weaknesses or discrepancies in the prosecution case.

(d) The defendant's solicitor may also need to cover evidential issues during the closing speech. If, for example, the prosecution has relied upon disputed identification evidence, the defendant's solicitor will need to give a Turnbull warning to the magistrates. Alternatively, if the prosecution has been allowed to rely on disputed confession evidence, the defendant's solicitor should seek to undermine the credibility of such evidence. If the evidence of the defendant's bad character has emerged at trial, the defendant's solicitor will need to downplay the significance of such evidence.

(e) The closing speech is all about persuasion. In other words, the defendant's solicitor should 'show' the magistrates how to find the defendant not guilty. It is often a sensible tactic to conclude the closing speech by listing all the weaknesses of the prosecution case (and the strengths of the defence case), and then invite the magistrates to conclude that the only possible verdict is one of not guilty.

10.3.1.8 The verdict

The magistrates will normally retire to consider their verdict. Most trials in the magistrates' court will be before a bench of three magistrates. The magistrates may make their decision by majority. There does not need to be unanimous agreement on the verdict. When the magistrates return to court after deciding upon the verdict, the defendant will be asked to stand and will be told by the chairperson of the bench that they have been found either not guilty or guilty.

If the defendant is found guilty, the magistrates will move on to consider the sentence to be imposed. The magistrates will either sentence the defendant immediately or adjourn the case if they wish to obtain medical or other reports before passing sentence. If the defendant is sentenced immediately, their solicitor will deliver a plea in mitigation to the magistrates prior to sentence. If the magistrates adjourn the case before passing sentence, they will need to consider whether the defendant should be granted bail or remanded in custody prior to the sentencing hearing. A defendant who has been found guilty following a trial in the magistrates' court has the right to appeal against the conviction and/or sentence to the Crown Court. The procedure for doing this is described in **Chapter 12**.

If the defendant is acquitted by the magistrates, they will be formally discharged and told that they are free to go.

Figure 10.2 Flowchart – Trial procedure in the magistrates' court

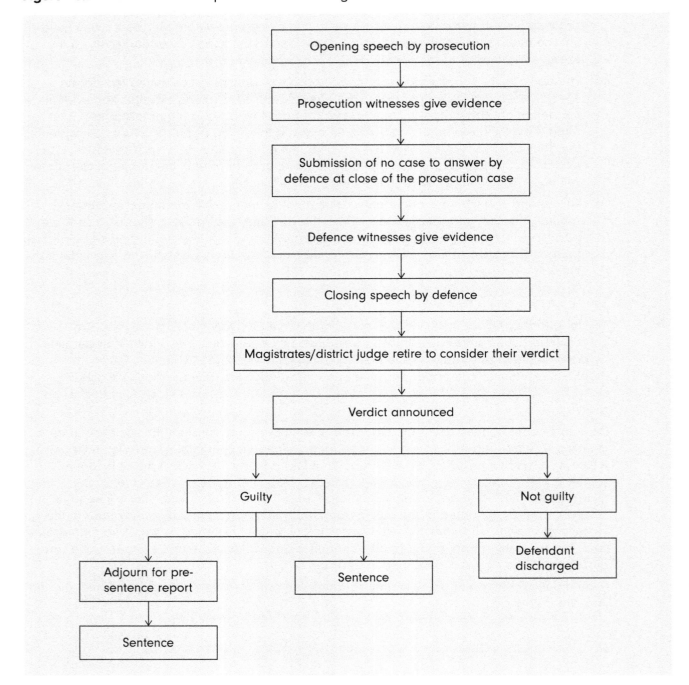

10.3.2 Trial in the Crown Court

We have seen in the magistrates' court the magistrates decide matters of both fact and law. In a Crown Court trial, these functions are split between the judge and the jury. The jury (made up of 12 members of the public) will decide any matters of fact which are in dispute and will ultimately decide upon the defendant's guilt or innocence. The judge will resolve any disputes that arise over points of law during the course of a trial, and will direct the jury as to the relevant law which they must apply to the facts of the case when they retire to consider their verdict. Although the judge will also sum up for the jury the evidence which they have heard before the jury retire to consider their verdict, the jury are solely responsible for deciding what the true facts of the case are. The judge will also be responsible for sentencing the defendant in the event of a finding of guilt by the jury.

The advocates appearing on behalf of the prosecution and defence will either be solicitors who have obtained their higher rights of audience qualification or barristers.

10.3.2.1 Change of plea from guilty to not guilty

Rule 25.5 of the CrimPR sets out the procedure to be followed if a defendant who has pleaded guilty wants to change his plea to not guilty. The defendant must apply, in writing, as soon as practicable after becoming aware of the grounds for making such an application to change a plea of guilty (eg if the defendant had misunderstood the prosecution case). A very similar procedure applies to changing plea in the magistrates' court (r 24.10).

10.3.2.2 Order of events

The procedure at a trial in the Crown Court is very similar to that in the magistrates' court, but with some important differences, many of which are due to the split functions between the trial judge and the jury referred to above. The order of events is as follows:

(a) The jury will be sworn in (commonly referred to as being 'empanelled'). The jury will comprise a randomly selected panel of 12 members of the public between the ages of 18 and 75, whose names are on the electoral roll for the local area and who have resided in the UK for at least five years. Certain persons are ineligible for jury service (for example, anyone suffering from a mental disorder), and certain classes of people are disqualified from being jurors (for example, anyone currently on bail in criminal proceedings and many who have previous convictions for which they have served a custodial sentence (Juries Act 1974, s 1)).

Note that the defendant will usually have already been arraigned and entered their not guilty plea(s) at the PTPH (see **Chapter 8**). If for some reason this has not yet taken place, the arraignment will usually occur before the jury is empanelled so that the jury is not prejudiced by hearing the defendant plead not guilty to some of the offences on the indictment and guilty to others. The court clerk will then inform the jury what counts on the indictment to which the defendant has pleaded not guilty but will not say anything about the guilty pleas.

(b) The prosecutor will then give an opening speech to the jury, explaining what the case is about and what evidence the prosecution intends to call. The opening speech will usually contain the following elements:

(i) the legal elements of the offence(s) on the indictment;

(ii) an outline of the evidence the prosecutor intends to call; and

(iii) an explanation of the operation of the burden and standard of proof in a criminal case

The prosecutor may also highlight to the jury any points of law that they anticipate may arise during the case and possible defences open to the defendant.

(c) Each prosecution witness will then be called in turn to give evidence in just the same way as in the magistrates' court, starting with the complainant. Each witness will be examined in chief by the prosecutor, cross-examined by the defence advocate and then (if necessary) re-examined by the prosecutor. The prosecutor will read out the statements of any witness whose evidence has been accepted by the defendant under the s 9 CJA 1967 procedure without the witness who gave the statement being required to attend court in person. The prosecutor will also read out the statement of any witness whose evidence is to be admitted as hearsay evidence.

(d) If any disputes as to points of law or arguments as to the admissibility of evidence arise, a hearing known as a 'voir dire' (or a 'trial within a trial') will take place in the absence of the jury. Such hearings normally arise in the context of disputes as to the admissibility of a piece of evidence upon which the prosecution seek to rely (for example, a disputed

221

confession). It is normal practice for the defence to notify the prosecutor prior to the trial of any items of prosecution evidence of which they will seek to challenge the admissibility at trial. Often the issue is dealt with at a hearing prior to the trial date and the judge may rule on the admissibility then; at times it is dealt with on the day of trial prior to the jury being 'empanelled'. Where it is not resolved before the start of the trial, the prosecutor, having advance notice of the issue, will not mention these items of evidence during their opening speech.

When the relevant point is reached during the presentation of the prosecution case, the judge will ask the jury to retire and will then conduct the *voir dire*. The judge will hear evidence from witnesses, and then legal submissions from both parties' advocates about the item of evidence in dispute. The judge will then make their ruling. If the judge rules that a particular piece of evidence is inadmissible, the jury will never hear about that piece of evidence. If the judge rules that the evidence is admissible, the party wishing to rely on that evidence (usually the prosecution) may then raise it during the trial. It will still be open to the other party (usually the defence) to attempt to undermine the reliability or cogency of that evidence either when cross-examining the witness giving the evidence, or when examining-in-chief their own witnesses.

(e) At the conclusion of the prosecution case, defence counsel may make a submission that there is no case for the defendant to answer. This submission will be made to the judge in the absence of the jury. The test which the judge will apply in deciding whether there is a case to answer is the same 'Galbraith test', which we looked at for summary trials.

(f) If the submission of no case to answer is successful, the jury will be asked to return, and the judge will instruct them to return a verdict of not guilty. If the submission of no case to answer is unsuccessful, the judge may allow the defendant to change their plea from not guilty to guilty at this stage. A defendant may wish to do this if, for example, they have admitted their guilt to their solicitor but put the prosecution to proof of their case. A defendant may also wish to change their plea to guilty at the end of the prosecution case if the trial judge has made a ruling on a point of law, or on the admissibility of a piece of evidence, which deprives the defendant of a defence upon which they had hoped to rely.

(g) If the submission of no case to answer is unsuccessful (and the defendant does not seek to change his plea), or no submission is made, the defence advocate will then present the defendant's case. If the defence intend calling a witness or witnesses in addition to the defendant, defence counsel is entitled to make an opening speech to the jury. They are not entitled to do this if only the defendant is to give evidence. If there is more than one defendant, each defendant will present their case in turn. The order in which this is done will follow the order in which the defendants' names appear on the indictment.

(h) Witnesses for the defence will then be called to give evidence. The defendant will be called first (assuming they are to give evidence). Should the defendant fail to give evidence, the judge will direct the jury that they may draw an adverse inference from such silence under s 35 of the CJPOA 1994 (see **Chapter 9**). Each defence witness will be examined in chief by the defence advocate, cross-examined by the prosecutor and then (if necessary) re-examined by the defence advocate.

(i) At the conclusion of the defence case, both prosecuting and defence advocates will deliver a closing speech to the jury. The prosecutor will give their closing speech first, followed by the defence.

(j) Before the jury retire to consider their verdict, the judge will then give their 'summing up' to the jury. The summing up has two parts, namely directions on the law and a summary of the evidence.

When the judge directs the jury on the law, they will cover three areas:

(i)   the burden and standard of proof;

(ii) the legal requirements of the offence; and

(iii) any other issues of law and evidence that have arisen during the trial (for example, a Turnbull warning in the case of disputed identification evidence, or a direction as to the drawing of adverse inferences under ss 34 to 37 of the CJPOA 1994).

A very common ground of appeal raised by defendants following conviction at a trial in the Crown Court is that the judge has misdirected the jury on a point of law or evidence.

When the judge gives the jury a summary of the evidence, they will provide the following:

(i)   a succinct summary of the issues of fact that the jury has to decide;

(ii) an accurate and concise summary of the evidence and arguments raised by both prosecution and defence; and

(iii) a correct statement of the inferences the jury is entitled to draw from their conclusions about the facts.

At the end of the summing up, the judge will tell the jury to appoint a foreman and will instruct them to retire to consider their verdict and to reach a unanimous conclusion.

(k) The jury will then retire to consider their verdict. The deliberations of the jury are private and must remain completely secret. The jurors are permitted to consider only the evidence they have heard at trial when deciding their verdict and are not permitted to discuss the case with anyone other than their fellow jurors. The jury must decide their verdict unanimously, although a majority verdict of 11:1 or 10:2 will be accepted if, after at least 2 hours and 10 minutes, unanimity is not possible (Juries Act 1974, s 17). If the case was lengthy or in any way complex, the judge is likely to wait much longer than this minimum period before telling the jury that they are prepared to accept a majority verdict.

If any jurors have been discharged during the trial then the majority verdict requirements reflect this, so where there were only 11 jurors, the majority must be 10:1. If there were only 10 jurors, it must be 9:1 and where there are only nine jurors then only a unanimous verdict is acceptable.

(l) If the jury cannot reach a majority verdict within a reasonable time, the judge will discharge the jury. The prosecution is then likely to request a retrial before a new jury.

(m) If the jury finds the defendant not guilty, the defendant will be discharged by the judge and told that they are free to go. If the defendant's case was not funded by way of a representation order, the judge will usually order that their legal costs be paid from central funds (ie by the state).

(n) If the jury finds the defendant guilty, the judge will then proceed to sentence the defendant. The judge will either sentence the defendant immediately, or, if necessary, adjourn sentence so that pre-sentence reports can be obtained (see **Chapter 11**). If the judge adjourns sentence, they will remand the defendant either on bail or in custody. Although there is a presumption in favour of bail for a defendant who has been convicted but not yet sentenced, if the sentencing hearing has been adjourned so that pre-sentence reports may be prepared, a defendant who has been convicted of a serious offence is very unlikely to be granted bail before sentence. The judge is likely to refuse the defendant bail on the grounds either that the defendant will fail to surrender to custody, or that it would be impractical to prepare the report unless the defendant is in custody. The procedure for sentencing a defendant is described in **Chapter 11**.

A flowchart summarising the above is set out below.

Figure 10.3 Flowchart – Trial procedure in the Crown Court

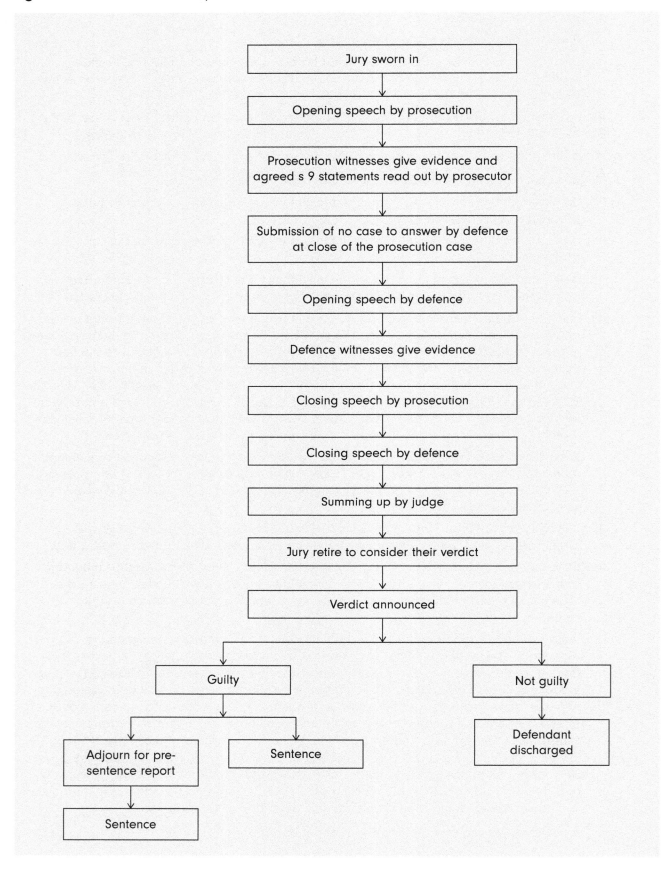

10.4 Modes of address and court room etiquette

A trial in the magistrates' court will normally be conducted before a bench of three magistrates. Traditionally magistrates were addressed collectively as 'Your Worships', although it is now more common for remarks to be addressed to the chairperson of the bench of magistrates, using 'Sir' or 'Madam' as appropriate. If the trial takes place before a district judge, 'Sir' or 'Madam' should be used. If the trial takes place in the Crown Court, the normal form of address to the judge is 'Your Honour'.

When referring to an opposing advocate it is courteous to refer to them as 'my friend' or, if the other advocate is a barrister, 'my learned friend'.

On entering or leaving court, it is customary to bow to the judge or magistrates (in fact this is linked to the Royal Coat of Arms which will usually be positioned behind where they sit and recognises that justice stems from the Crown and that the law courts are part of the Royal Court). Similarly, all those in court will be required to stand up when the judge or magistrates enter or leave the court.

Another important feature of being a criminal advocate is that when you address the court or are examining witnesses, the default position is that you are required to stand up if the proceedings are taking place in open court, which most criminal proceedings are. However, there are now a number of occasions when advocate will usually remain seated:

- when representing a juvenile client in the youth court;
- where a defendant appears via videolink from prison;
- where a witness appears via secure link, normally because of special measures (see **10.7**);
- where witnesses are located far from court (especially police officers) and need to give evidence via videolink;
- where an advocate has requested to appear over videolink (the court videolink facility is called CVP or Cloud Video Platform);
- when making a bail appeal before a judge in chambers in the Crown Court (see **Chapter 7**).

Finally, you should not eat food when in court and any electronic devices such as mobile phones or tablets must be turned off (or placed on silent mode). You would be committing an offence and also be in contempt of court if you were to take pictures, video or audio record court proceedings.

10.5 Difference between leading and non-leading questions

At **10.3** above we described the procedure that is followed during a trial, including advocates examining witnesses. We will now consider some advocacy techniques dealing with the use of leading and non-leading questions and when they should be used.

10.5.1 Examination-in-chief

The purpose of examination-in-chief is to allow a witness to 'tell their story'. The advocate conducting the examination-in-chief should ask questions which enable the witness to repeat the version of events which that witness has provided earlier in their witness statement.

The difficulty with conducting an examination-in-chief is that the advocate is not allowed to ask leading questions. Leading questions are questions which are suggestive of the answer.

⭐ *Example*

Ewan is called as a prosecution witness. He is to testify to the fact that at 2 pm on 5 June he saw Grant steal a tin of baked beans from Sainsbury's.

The prosecuting solicitor cannot say to Ewan: 'Did you see Grant steal a tin of baked beans from Sainsbury's at 2 pm on 5 June?' because this is a leading question.

Instead of asking such a leading question, the advocate conducting the examination-in-chief should use 'open' questions to elicit the information from the witness.

⭐ *Example*

Continuing with the example above, the prosecutor could elicit the information from Ewan in the following way:

Q   *Where were you on 5 June at about 2 pm?*

A   *I was in Sainsbury's.*

Q   *What did you see when you were in Sainsbury's?*

A   *I saw Grant pick up a tin of baked beans and put them in his jacket pocket.*

Q   *What happened next?*

A   *I saw Grant walk out of the shop without paying for the tin of baked beans.*

The use of non-leading, open questions enables the witness to place their account before the court in their own words. Such questions usually start with words such as:

*   Who...?
*   What...?
*   When...?
*   Where...?
*   How...?

10.5.2 Cross-examination

Cross-examination of a witness called by the other party has three main purposes:

*   to enable the party conducting the cross-examination to put their case to the witness;
*   to undermine the credibility of the evidence which that witness has just given in examination-in-chief; and
*   to obtain favourable evidence from the witness that supports your case.

'Putting your case' means suggesting to a witness that the version of events which that witness has just put forward in examination-in-chief is incorrect and suggesting an alternative version of events. It is always necessary for an advocate to put their client's version of events to a witness in cross-examination. For example, in an assault case where the defendant is claiming they acted only in self-defence, the defendant's solicitor must, when cross-examining the alleged victim of the assault, put to the victim that they (the victim) attacked the defendant first and that the defendant was acting only in self-defence. If the defendant's solicitor fails to put to the witness that the defendant was acting in self-defence, the defendant will then not be entitled to enter the witness box and say that they were acting in self-defence.

Cross-examination will usually be done by asking a witness 'closed' or leading questions. This is to try and keep better control of what the witness will say and generally can be answered with a 'yes'/'no' or provide the witness with the required answer.

⭐ *Example*

Q   *Mr Barnard, you told the court that you spent the evening of 14 December at a club?*

A   *Yes.*

Q   *You had quite a bit to drink, didn't you Mr Barnard?*

A   *I wouldn't say I had that much.*

Q   *Well according to your witness statement you had seven pints to drink. Is that correct?*

A   *Yes.*

Q   *That's quite a lot isn't it Mr Barnard?*

A   *I suppose so.*

10.5.3   Re-examination

At the end of the cross-examination, the party who called the witness may, if they choose, briefly re-examine their witness. Such re-examination should only be in relation to matters that have arisen in cross-examination and as with examination-in-chief, only open, non-leading questions are allowed.

It would be normal to re-examine a witness to clarify any confusion which may have arisen following cross-examination and/or to try and repair damage caused by such cross-examination.

10.6   Competence and compellability

10.6.1   The general rule

All persons are competent to give evidence at a criminal trial.

Section 53 Youth Justice and Criminal Evidence Act (YJCEA) 1999 provides a uniform test that applies to all criminal proceedings:

>   (1)   At every stage in criminal proceedings all persons are (whatever their age) competent to give evidence.

All competent persons are also compellable. This means that a witness can be compelled to testify by the court issuing a witness summons. Failure to attend court in such circumstances amounts to contempt of court. If, having come to court, the witness refuses to answer questions, this will again be contempt of court which can result in imprisonment either under the general law of contempt or under a specific statute such as s 97 Magistrates' Courts Act 1980.

10.6.2   Exception to the general rule on competence

Section 53 goes on to provide:

>   (3)   A person is not competent to give evidence in criminal proceedings if it appears to the court that he is not a person who is able to:
>
>   (a)   understand questions put to him as a witness; and
>
>   (b)   give answers to them which can be understood.

Issues relating to credibility and reliability are therefore not relevant to this test. Section 53(3) is solely concerned with understanding.

Two groups of witnesses in particular may fall within this exception.

227

10.6.2.1 Children

Sometimes a child might not have the level of understanding that is required by this test. It is important to note though that a child's age is not determinative. The appellate courts have on a number of occasions emphasised that the only issue is whether the witness is able to give intelligible testimony. So even very young children may be competent if they have sufficient intelligence.

 In R v Barker [2010] EWCA Crim 4 a conviction of rape was upheld based in part on the evidence of the complainant who had been aged three at the time of the incident and aged four-and-a-half when she gave evidence at trial. The Court of Appeal took the view that the child had been a 'compelling as well as competent witness', but emphasised that the test for competency required a judgment from the trial judge that is specific to the particular witness.

For child witnesses, there is a linked question. Should the child give sworn or unsworn evidence? The answer to this is very straightforward and provided by s 55. Namely, that 'the witness may not be sworn ... unless he has attained the age of 14'.

So where a witness is over 14, they will generally give sworn evidence if 'he has sufficient appreciation of the solemnity of the occasion and of the particular responsibility to tell the truth which is involved in taking the oath' and this will be presumed to be the case unless there is evidence to show the contrary.

Example

Noah is aged seven years and is the victim and key prosecution witness in an allegation of sexual assault by his grandfather. Noah will be a competent witness on behalf of the prosecution assuming he is intelligent enough to understand questions put to him and to give answers which can be understood. Because Noah is under 14 years, he will give unsworn evidence.

10.6.2.2 Those with a defective intellect

Where a potential witness is suffering from a defective intellect, they may be able to give unsworn evidence in criminal proceedings provided they can satisfy the basic test for competence (see above). Where there is such an issue with this type of a witness then it is for the judge to decide whether a person whose capacity is challenged is competent.

10.6.3 Exceptions to the general rule on compellability

We have seen under the general rule that all persons are competent to give evidence at a criminal trial and all competent persons are also compellable. However, there are some qualifications to the rule on compellability when dealing with the accused and the spouse of the accused.

10.6.3.1 The accused

As a witness for the Crown

In general, an accused is not a competent witness for the Crown. The rule is however much more important where there are several co-accused because the same rule prevents the Crown from calling one co-accused to testify against another. Section 53(4) YJCEA 1999 states 'A person charged in criminal proceedings is not competent to give evidence in the proceedings for the prosecution'.

In four situations the prosecution may however be allowed to call a co-accused and these are recognised by s 53(5):

1. The Attorney-General may file a *nolle prosequi* (a formal notice abandoning the prosecution).

2. An order may be made for separate trials but note that in such a case, a co-accused from the first trial may be called at the second, but not vice versa.

3. The accused may be formally acquitted, for example if the prosecution offers no evidence.

4. The accused may plead guilty and may then give evidence for the Crown against a co-accused; it is usually considered desirable that the accused should be sentenced first before giving evidence.

As a witness for a co-accused

A co-accused is competent but not compellable.

In his own defence

A defendant is competent to give evidence in his own defence but never compellable. Remember though that adverse inferences may be drawn where an accused chooses not to testify (CJ&PO Act 1994, s 35).

10.6.3.2 The spouse of the accused

Assuming the spouse is not also an accused, the question of their competence is dealt with by s 80 PACE 1984.

For the Crown

The spouse of an accused is only compellable for the Crown in the limited class of cases referred to in ss (3). This sets out certain offences which are regarded as 'specified offences', which will then make the spouse compellable. For any other offence, the spouse cannot be compelled to testify for the Crown, but they may still choose to do so.

The two categories of specified offences that would make a spouse compellable are:

*   where the offence charged involves an assault on or injury or threat of injury to the spouse or a person who was under 16; or

*   where the charge is a sexual offence, or such an attempted offence involving a person under 16 or aiding and abetting such offences.

⭐ Example

John has been charged with assaulting his daughter Mia, aged 16. This was witnessed by Belinda, John's wife and mother of Mia. Since the incident, John and Belinda have reconciled and Belinda no longer wants to testify against John.

Although Belinda is a competent witness for the prosecution, she cannot be compelled to testify, because this case does not come within s 80 PACE 1984. Belinda could have been compelled by the prosecution to testify had Mia been aged under 16 or had Belinda also been a victim of the assault.

The same rule also applies where same sex couples have taken part in a formal civil partnership ceremony. They will be treated just the same as if they were spouses.

(i)   For the accused

A spouse is compellable.

(ii)   For a co-accused

The spouse is only compellable in the same limited class of specified offences that apply to the prosecution under ss (3) above.

(iii)   Where spouses are co-accused then one is never compellable for the other.

Note that s 80(5) provides that if spouses are no longer married at the date of the trial it is as if they were never married for the purpose of establishing their compellability.

⭐ *Example*

Hassan has been charged with an offence of fraud. At the time of the alleged offence he was married to Brianna and the prosecution would like to call her to testify against Hassan, as it is believed she can provide crucial evidence to establish his guilt. Brianna is not prepared to testify against Hassan, even though they have since separated and are no longer living together.

In these circumstances the prosecution cannot compel Brianna to testify against Hassan because they are still married. Moreover, the offence is not one of those limited offences identified in ss (3) where Briana could have been compelled to testify. Had she and Hassan divorced before the date of the trial then she could have been compelled and if she was still reluctant to do so, the prosecution would have been able to serve a witness summons on her.

10.7 Special measures

Sections 16 to 33 of the Youth Justice and Criminal Evidence Act (YJCEA) 1999 introduced a number of 'special measures' which are available to assist witnesses (other than the defendant) who might otherwise have difficulty in giving evidence in criminal proceedings, or who might be reluctant to do so. The following categories of witness may apply to the court for the assistance of special measures to help them give evidence in court (ss 16 and 17 YJCEA 1999):

(a) children aged under 18;

(b) those suffering from a mental or physical disorder, or having a disability or impairment that is likely to affect their evidence;

(c) those whose evidence is likely to be affected by their fear or distress at giving evidence in the proceedings;

(d) complainants in sexual offences;

(e) those who are witnesses in specified gun and knife crimes (YJCEA 1999, Sch 1A).

Witnesses who are alleged to be the victims of sexual offences will automatically be considered eligible for special measures under (c) above when giving evidence, unless the witness tells the court that he or she does not want such assistance. In all other cases, it is for the court to determine whether a witness falls into any of these categories.

We saw in **Chapter 9** that under s 116(2)(e) of the CJA 2003, a witness who is fearful about having to give evidence at trial may, with the leave of the court, have their written statement read out to the court rather than having to attend court in person to give oral evidence. If leave is granted, the defendant will be deprived of the opportunity to cross-examine the witness on their account. Thus, before giving leave, the trial judge should assess whether the fears of the witness may be allayed by the use of special measures to enable the witness to give evidence. If special measures are used, the defendant will not then be deprived of the opportunity to cross-examine the witness.

The types of special measure which may be used are:

(a) screens, to ensure that the witness does not see the defendant;

(b) allowing a witness to give evidence from outside the court by live television link, and where appropriate, allowing a witness supporter to accompany the witness whilst giving evidence;

(c) clearing people from the court so evidence can be given in private;

(d) in a Crown Court case, the judge and barristers removing their wigs and gowns;

(e) allowing a witness to be examined in chief before the trial and a video recording of that examination-in-chief to be shown at trial;

(f) allowing a witness to be cross-examined (and re-examined) before the trial and a video recording of this to be shown at trial;

(g) allowing an approved intermediary (such as an interpreter or speech therapist) to help a witness communicate when giving evidence at the court; and

(h) allowing a witness to use communication aids, such as sign language or a hearing loop.

Where special measures are employed, s 32 of the 1999 Act obligates the trial judge to warn the jury that the fact that special measures have been used should not in any way prejudice them against the defendant or give rise to any suggestion that the defendant has behaved in any way improperly towards the witness.

Although a defendant is not eligible to take advantage of these special measure provisions, s 33A of the 1999 Act allows a defendant whose ability to participate effectively as a witness in court is compromised by reason of their mental disorder, impaired intellectual ability or social functioning, to give evidence by video link.

10.8 Solicitor's duty to the court

A solicitor representing a defendant at a trial before the magistrates is under a duty to say on behalf of their client what that client would properly say, were they to have the necessary skills and knowledge to do this. In other words, it is the duty of the defence solicitor to act in their client's best interests and to ensure that the prosecution discharges the onus placed upon it to prove the defendant's guilt. Therefore, even if a client admits their guilt to the solicitor, it would still be appropriate for the solicitor to put the prosecution to proof of its case if the solicitor considered that case to be weak.

The defendant's solicitor nevertheless is required to act in a way that upholds the constitutional principle of the rule of law, and the proper administration of justice (Principle 1 SRA Code of Conduct), and also remains under an overriding duty not to mislead the court (under Standard 2 of the SRA Code of Conduct). They cannot therefore say anything in their client's defence which they know to be untrue.

The defendant's solicitor also owes a duty of confidentiality to their client (under Standard 6.3 of the SRA Code of Conduct). This means that if the defendant's solicitor has to cease to act for their client, the defence solicitor must not tell the court why they are ceasing to act. A defence solicitor who withdraws from acting in such circumstances will tell the court that they are no longer able to act for their client for 'professional reasons'.

The detailed rules of professional conduct with which a solicitor must comply when acting as an advocate (whether for the prosecution or the defence) are contained in Standard 2 of the SRA Code of Conduct.

10.8.1 Preparing the defendant to give evidence

Prior to the trial, the defendant's solicitor must tell their client what is likely to happen at the trial. If the client is to give evidence in their own defence, it is a sensible step to supply the client with a copy of their witness statement, so that they can read it before the trial commences. The client will not be able to refer to their witness statement when giving evidence, but it is useful for them to be able to refresh their memory as to what they first told their solicitor about the offence.

The defendant's solicitor should be careful, however, not to 'coach' their client (or indeed any other defence witness). Advocates in the magistrates' court or Crown Court (whether representing the prosecution or the defence) should not rehearse or coach witnesses in relation to their evidence, or in the way in which that evidence should be given.

Summary

In this chapter you have considered a range of matters relating to trials that take place in the magistrates' court and the Crown Court. Notably:

- *The burden and standard of proof.* How the burden and standard of proof operates at a criminal trial in both the magistrates' court and Crown Court.

- *The order of events in a criminal trial.* An outline of the sequence of events at a summary trial in the magistrates' court and comparing and contrasting this with the relevant procedure at a trial on indictment in the Crown Court.

- *Trial court advocacy.* Some basic advocacy skills including modes of address and appropriate court room etiquette.

- *Competence and compellability.* Some rules relating to competence and compellability of witnesses, especially in relation to child witnesses, the accused and the spouse of the accused.

- *Special measures.* The operation of the special measure provisions for vulnerable witnesses including children and victims of sexual offences and offences of violence.

- *The solicitor's duty to the court.* The duties owed by a solicitor to their client and their overriding duty owed to the court.

Sample questions

Question 1

A solicitor is representing a defendant at trial in the magistrates' court on a charge of assault occasioning actual bodily harm. When testifying, the complainant states that she was punched by the defendant following an argument but she did not give any evidence about the nature of her injuries and the prosecution did not adduce any medical evidence to establish what injuries she suffered. No other prosecution evidence is adduced to establish the complainant did suffer actual bodily harm although there is independent evidence to help prove the defendant did punch the complainant.

Will the defence be likely to succeed in a submission of no case to answer at the end of the prosecution case?

A   Yes, because the evidence produced by the prosecution is so manifestly unreliable, that no reasonable tribunal could safely convict on it.

B   No, because the prosecution has produced direct and independent evidence that the complainant was assaulted.

C   No, because the complainant has testified to say that she was assaulted by the defendant.

D   Yes, because the prosecution has failed to put forward evidence to prove an essential element of the alleged offence.

E   No, because there is circumstantial evidence to help prove that an assault took place.

Answer

Option D is the best answer. According to the test in *R v Galbraith*, a submission of no case to answer should succeed where either the prosecution has failed to put forward evidence to prove an essential element of the alleged offence, or the evidence produced by the prosecution has been so discredited as a result of cross-examination, or is so manifestly unreliable, that no reasonable tribunal could safely convict on it. We are told that the prosecution has adduced evidence that there was an assault and there is nothing to suggest that this evidence is manifestly unreliable, so option A is wrong. However, the prosecution does not appear to have adduced any evidence that the complainant suffered actual bodily harm as a result of this assault. So, option D is the correct explanation as to why a submission ought to succeed.

Options B and C are therefore wrong because these explanations would only help prove one element of the offence and not that the victim suffered actual bodily harm from the assault. Option E is wrong because although circumstantial evidence is capable of establishing a case to answer, we are not told about any such evidence in this case.

Question 2

Three defendants have been charged with robbery. One defendant, a woman, admits that she acted as a look-out and intends to plead guilty to being an accomplice to the robbery when she appears in the Crown Court. This woman is also prepared to give evidence for the prosecution implicating her co-accused, who are both men and whom she claims were responsible for carrying out the robbery.

Which of the following best describes whether the woman will be a competent and compellable witness for the prosecution assuming that she is sentenced before the date of the trial of the two men?

A   The woman is both competent and compellable because she has pleaded guilty and so she has been severed from her co-accused.

B   The woman is both competent and compellable because all persons are competent to give evidence and competent persons are also compellable.

C   The woman is competent to give evidence for the prosecution, but she cannot be compelled to do so as she is also a co-accused.

D   The woman is not competent to give evidence for the prosecution because she is still an accomplice even if she has pleaded guilty.

E   The woman is not competent to give evidence for the prosecution as she has a purpose of her own to serve in testifying for the prosecution.

Answer

Option A is the best answer. Although the general rule is that all persons are competent and compellable, this rule is subject to some important exceptions. One such exception is in relation to an accused, who is neither a competent nor compellable witness for the prosecution – see 53(4) YJ&CE Act 1999. However, this is subject to four exceptions, which are recognised by s 53(5), including where an accused is severed from their co-accused by pleading guilty. This means they can give evidence for the Crown against a co-accused (in such circumstances it is usually considered desirable that the accused is sentenced first before giving evidence). So, option A is correct and option D is wrong.

Option B is not the best answer because this only states the general rule and does not adequately explain why the woman has become competent and compellable. Option C is wrong because once the woman becomes competent, she also becomes compellable. Option E is wrong as the woman is now competent. If she did have a purpose of her own to serve in testifying against her co-accused, this would not stop her from being a competent witness, but it may require the judge to give a warning to the jury to treat her evidence with some caution (this is known as a corroboration warning but is beyond the SQE1 syllabus).

Question 3

A solicitor represented a new client in the magistrates' court at a trial for burglary. The prosecution case was on the basis that the defendant was someone of good character. The magistrates convicted the defendant. After the trial, the client instructs her solicitor that she wants to appeal against her conviction. The client also confides in her solicitor by telling him that the police got her name wrong when they charged her. Had she been prosecuted under her correct name the prosecution would have discovered that she had a number of previous convictions for dishonesty offences including three similar offences for burglary. The client is adamant that she does not want the court or the prosecution to learn of her correct name.

What should the solicitor now do in light of this information?

A   The solicitor can continue to act for the client, but he must not make any reference to the client's name or her good character at the appeal hearing.

B   The solicitor can continue to act for the client as he has an overriding duty to act in the client's best interests.

C   The solicitor should withdraw from acting for the client, but he cannot tell the court or the prosecution why.

D   The solicitor should withdraw from acting for the client because he has breached his overriding duty to the court.

E   The solicitor should withdraw from acting for the client and must inform the court of the client's true name otherwise he will be complicit in misleading the court.

Answer

Option C is the best answer. The solicitor can no longer act for the client because to do so would be knowingly misleading the court now that the solicitor is aware of the client's true name. However, the solicitor could not tell the court or the prosecution why, because to do so would be breaching his duty of confidentiality to the client.

Option A is wrong because the solicitor would have to give the client's name to lodge an appeal and would also be misleading the court when appealing under a false name. Especially so in a case like this where the prosecution would have been likely to make a bad character application had they known of the client's correct name. Option B is wrong, because although it is correct to say that the solicitor has a duty to act in the client's best interests, this is not his overriding duty. Option D is wrong, because although his overriding duty is to the court, the solicitor has not yet breached this as he was unaware of the client's true name at the time of the trial. However, the solicitor would now breach it if he continued to act for the client knowing that the court and prosecution will be misled at the appeal. Option E is wrong, because if the solicitor tells the court why he is withdrawing, he will be breaching his duty of confidentiality to the client.

11 Sentencing

SQE1 syllabus

This chapter will enable you to achieve the SQE1 Assessment Specification in relation to Functioning Legal Knowledge concerned with the following procedures and processes:

- role of sentencing guidelines;
- determining seriousness (aggravating and mitigating facts);
- concurrent and consecutive sentences;
- mitigation;
- types of sentence;
- Newton hearings.

Note that, for SQE1, candidates are not usually required to recall specific case names or cite statutory or regulatory authorities. These are provided for illustrative purposes only unless otherwise stated.

Learning outcomes

By the end of this chapter you will be able to apply relevant core legal principles and rules appropriately and effectively, at the level of a competent newly qualified solicitor in practice, to realistic client-based and ethical problems and situations in the following areas:

- How an offender will be sentenced based on the sentencing guidelines issued by the Sentencing Council.
- The use of aggravating and mitigating facts to help determine the seriousness of an offence.
- When a sentencing court will use concurrent and consecutive sentences and what these mean to the overall custodial sentence to be served.
- The use of mitigation in sentencing procedure.

- The range of sentences available to a sentencing court including custodial sentences, suspended sentences and community orders.
- What is meant by a Newton hearing and when such a hearing will be used.

11.1 Introduction

The law on sentencing was overhauled by the Criminal Justice Act 2003 and then underwent further reform by the Legal Aid, Sentencing and Punishment of Offenders Act 2012. More recently it was the subject of a consultation paper and draft Sentencing Bill by the Law Commission who recommended that the law on sentencing be simplified and rewritten. The Commission described their Bill as a 'clean sweep', replacing all procedural law on sentencing with a new and simplified Sentencing Code. This Code is part of the Sentencing Act 2020 and came into force at the start of December 2020. It consolidates the existing sentencing legislation in England and Wales and does not change the substantive law on sentencing. So for example, it does not alter the maximum penalties for any offence, nor does it reduce judicial discretion in sentencing or replace existing sentencing guidelines. But it does now provide a single reference point for sentencing legislation. The Code has re-written sentencing procedure with modern language and an overriding aim to bring a clear and logical structure to this area of practice.

Most defendants plead guilty to the offence with which they are charged (or sometimes to a lesser offence following negotiation with the prosecution or to a different version of facts – see **11.9.1** 'Basis of plea'). A smaller number of defendants will be convicted after a trial in either the magistrates' court or the Crown Court. The resulting sentence usually represents the final stage in the criminal process (subject to any appeal – see **Chapter 12**).

Section 57 of the Sentencing Act 2020 states that a court sentencing an offender aged 18 or over must have regard to the following five purposes of sentencing:

1. the punishment of offenders;
2. the reduction of crime (including its reduction by deterrence);
3. the reform and rehabilitation of offenders;
4. the protection of the public; and
5. the making of reparation by offenders to persons affected by their offence.

The court need not have such regard if the sentence is fixed by law (such as murder, which must attract a sentence of life imprisonment) or offences subject to a statutory minimum (see later), or if the defendant is classed as a dangerous offender.

Representing clients at a sentencing hearing is therefore a very important and regular feature of practising as a criminal defence solicitor.

11.2 Role of sentencing guidelines

Sentencing guidelines now play a key role in ensuring that when a court passes sentence it does so in a structured and consistent way.

11.2.1 The Sentencing Council of England and Wales

These guidelines are prepared and updated by the Sentencing Council (SC). The Sentencing Council (SC) is made up of eight judicial members and six non-judicial members.

The SC has the power to prepare sentencing guidelines in relation to any sentencing matter including guidelines for specific offences. In drawing up the guidelines, the SC must have regard to current sentencing practice, the need to promote consistency in sentencing, the impact of sentencing decisions on victims of crime, the need to promote public confidence in the criminal justice system, the cost of different sentences and their effectiveness in reducing re-offending and the SC's monitoring of the application of the guidelines.

Every court has a duty to follow any relevant guidelines unless it is satisfied that it would be contrary to the interests of justice to do so.

These guidelines can be found on the SC website at: https://sentencingcouncil.org.uk.

11.2.2 The principle of seriousness

One of the key concepts a sentencing court is required to consider when passing sentence is seriousness. Section 63 of the Sentencing Act 2020 requires that a court must consider:

(a) the offender's <u>culpability</u> in committing the offence, and

(b) any <u>harm</u> which the offence

    (i) caused,

    (ii) was intended to cause, or

    (iii) might foreseeably have caused.

11.2.2.1 Culpability

The sentencing guideline, 'Overarching Principles: Seriousness', identifies four levels of criminal culpability for sentencing purposes. In descending order of seriousness, the four levels are where the offender:

(a) has the intention to cause harm, with the highest culpability being when an offence is planned. The worse the harm intended, the greater the seriousness;

(b) is reckless as to whether harm is caused. This covers situations when the defendant appreciates that some harm would be caused but goes ahead, giving no thought to the consequences even though the extent of the risk would be obvious to most people;

(c) has knowledge of the specific risks entailed by their actions, even though the offender does not intend to cause the harm that results;

(d) is guilty of negligence.

11.2.2.2 Harm

Harm may be caused either to individuals, or to the community at large. The types of harm that may be caused include:

(a) physical injury

(b) sexual violation

(c) financial loss

(d) damage to health and

(e) psychological distress.

11.2.2.3 Prevalence

Although courts should pass the same sentence for the same type of offence, in exceptional circumstances, a court in a particular area may treat an offence more seriously than elsewhere. This may occur if the particular type of offence is prevalent in the area and the court has before it evidence that these offences are causing harm to the community at large.

11.3 Determining seriousness (aggravating and mitigating facts)

11.3.1 Statutory aggravating factors

There are four situations when the sentencing court is obliged to treat an offence as being more serious than it would otherwise have done:

(a) Previous convictions – the court must treat any previous convictions as an aggravating factor if, having regard to the nature of the previous conviction and the time that has elapsed since the conviction, the court considers it reasonable to do so. In practice, this means that previous convictions are likely to be regarded as aggravating factors if the offences have been committed recently and/or are for similar types of offence. For example, if a defendant convicted of a theft from a supermarket has several previous convictions for the same type of offence, these previous convictions will be seen by the sentencing court as an aggravating factor.

(b) Offences committed whilst on bail – if the offender was on bail in respect of another offence at the time of the current offence, the court must treat this as an aggravating factor.

(c) Racial or religious aggravation – any racial or religious motive for committing the offence must be treated as an aggravating factor.

(d) Hostility based on sexual orientation or disability – any hostility towards the victim of an offence based on that victim's sexual orientation or any physical or mental disability, must be treated as an aggravating factor.

11.3.2 Other aggravating and mitigating factors

The sentencing guideline on 'Seriousness' lists other factors which a sentencing court may consider to be aggravating or mitigating factors.

11.3.2.1 The list of aggravating factors

(a) offences that are planned or premeditated;

(b) offenders operating in groups or gangs;

(c) the deliberate targeting of vulnerable groups (such as the elderly or disabled victims);

(d) offences committed whilst under the influence of drink or drugs;

(e) the use of a weapon;

(f) deliberate and gratuitous violence or damage to property, beyond that required to carry out the offence;

(g) offences involving the abuse of a position of trust;

(h) offences committed against those working in the public sector or providing a service to the public;

(i) in property offences, the high value (including sentimental value) of property to the victim; and

(j) failure to respond to previous sentences.

11.3.2.2 The list of mitigating factors

(a) offences where the defendant has acted on impulse;

(b) when the defendant has experienced a greater degree of provocation than normally expected;

(c) defendants who are suffering from mental illness or physical disability;

(d) if the defendant is particularly young or old (particularly in the case of young offenders who are immature and have been led astray by others);

(e) the fact that the defendant played only a minor role in the offending;

(f) defendants who were motivated by genuine fear; and

(g) defendants who have made attempts to make reparation to their victim.

11.3.3 Reduction in sentence for a guilty plea

Section 73 of the Sentencing Act 2020 provides that when sentencing a defendant who has entered a guilty plea, the court must 'take into account' the stage in the proceedings at which the defendant gave their indication of a guilty plea and the circumstances in which the indication was given. The rationale behind a reduction in sentence for defendants who plead guilty is that a guilty plea avoids the need for a trial and, if made sufficiently early, saves victims and witnesses from stress and anxiety about having to attend court to give oral evidence.

The 'Reduction in Sentence for a Guilty Plea' Definitive Guideline applies to all defendants aged 18 or over and to all cases, regardless of the date of the offence(s). It applies in the magistrates' courts and the Crown Court. The guidelines make it clear that the level of the reduction is not dependent upon the strength or otherwise of the prosecution case. Nor should it be affected by whether or not the defendant feels any remorse for their offending behaviour. Whilst this may be an important feature at an earlier stage of the sentencing exercise (see below), it is not relevant to this statutory entitlement to a reduction for a guilty plea.

Under the Guideline, the full one-third discount on sentence will only be available where a guilty plea is indicated at the 'first stage of proceedings'. This will generally be:

*   on a guilty plea at the first hearing in the magistrates' court;

*   on a guilty plea at the first hearing in the magistrates' court where the case is then committed for sentence to the Crown Court;

*   on indication of a guilty plea in the magistrates' court to an offence triable only on indictment, followed by a guilty plea at the first hearing in the Crown Court.

There are some limited exceptions that may still entitle a defendant to this full reduction if it would have been unreasonable to expect the defendant to indicate a guilty plea at this first hearing.

However, where a guilty plea is usually indicated after this first stage of the proceedings, the 'maximum level of the reduction is one-quarter'. It follows that the one-quarter discount will be awarded where the guilty plea is only first indicated at the PTPH (and not earlier when the case was in the magistrates' court).

The reduction should then be decreased from one quarter to a maximum of one tenth where a guilty plea is entered on the first day the trial was meant to take place ('at the door of the court'). This may be reduced further, even to zero, where the guilty plea is entered during the course of the trial.

 R v Hodgin (Lee) [2020] EWCA Crim 1388 – the sole ground of appeal was whether H should have been afforded full credit of one third for indicating in the magistrates' court, when his case was sent to the Crown Court, that it was a 'likely guilty plea'. Was that an 'indication of a plea of guilty' entitling him to full credit of one third? In refusing the appeal it was held: 'where at the magistrates' court it is not procedurally possible for a defendant to enter a guilty plea, there must be an unequivocal indication of the defendant's intention to plead guilty. An indication only that he is likely to plead guilty is not enough'.

11.3.4 Totality principle

When an offender is being sentenced, the court will take into account both the offence they are being sentenced for and any associated offences. An associated offence is an offence for which the defendant has been convicted in the same proceedings or for which they are to be sentenced at the same time, or an offence which the defendant has asked the court to take into consideration when passing sentence.

 Example

Neil is convicted of three separate offences of theft in the same proceedings. When Neil is being sentenced, the court will not look at each offence separately, but will rather assess the total extent of Neil's offending in determining the sentence that Neil will be given. Only if the totality of Neil's offending passes the appropriate thresholds (see below) may a custodial or community sentence be imposed by the court.

11.3.5 Offences taken into consideration

Defendants who are being sentenced for a particular offence may ask the court to take other offences into consideration (TIC) when considering the sentence to be imposed. In addition to the offence for which they were charged and convicted a defendant may have committed several similar types of offence for which they have not yet been prosecuted, but for which they may subsequently face prosecution. It is likely to be in the defendant's interests that all matters outstanding (or potentially outstanding) against them should be dealt with at the same time.

The usual practice is for the police to present the defendant with a list of additional offences for which they are under investigation and may subsequently be charged. The defendant may ask the court to take some or all of these other offences into consideration when deciding the sentence they are to receive for the offence(s) for which they are currently before the court. The offences to be taken into consideration should be of a similar nature to, or less serious than, the offence(s) for which the defendant has been convicted.

The manner in which the court deals with offences taken into consideration depends on the context of such offences. Although in theory these additional offences should increase the severity of the sentence the defendant receives, in practice they might add nothing, or very little, to the sentence the court would otherwise have imposed.

The advantage to the defendant of having offences taken into consideration is that this 'wipes the slate clean', because they will not subsequently be prosecuted for such offences. The advantage to the police is that a large number of TICs improves their clear-up rates without the need to commence a fresh prosecution against the defendant.

11.4 How the Sentencing Guidelines work

Most offences now have their own definitive sentencing guidelines. These guidelines require a sentencing court to usually follow an eight-step approach to arrive at its sentence. The first two and fourth steps are usually the key steps that determine what sentence the court will impose.

STEP 1 – Determining the offence category

There are three categories identified to reflect differing levels in harm and culpability. So, an offence falling into Category 1 reflects both greater harm and enhanced culpability. An offence in Category 2 reflects either greater harm or enhanced culpability. Offences falling within Category 3 will be those involving lesser harm and a lower level of culpability. The relevant sentencing guidelines identify an exhaustive list of factors that will help determine which category will be the most appropriate for the offence in question. Having identified the relevant category, the court is then required to use the corresponding starting point sentence which will then be further shaped by the remaining steps. Note that under this format, the starting point sentence applies to all offenders regardless of how the offender pleaded or whether or not they have previous convictions.

STEP 2 – Shaping the provisional sentence: starting point and category range

Having identified the relevant category as a starting point sentence, the court will then start to fine-tune the sentence by reference to a list of aggravating and mitigating factors (see above). These factors are there to provide the context of the offence and the offender and they are considered together so that a holistic approach is taken. The sentencer is also required to consider the relevant statutory thresholds for custody (see later).

STEP 3 – Consider any factors which indicate a reduction in sentence, such as assisting the prosecution

This step allows the court to reduce the sentence where the offender has provided assistance to the police, usually in relation to other matters (not very common in practice).

STEP 4 – Reduction in sentence for a guilty plea

A reduction in sentence will be given for a guilty plea. The SC provides guidance on just how much of a reduction should be awarded depending on when the plea is entered (see **11.3.3**).

STEP 5 – Imposing an extended sentence

Section 61 of the Sentencing Act 2020 sets out the circumstances as to when a court will be required to consider imposing such a sentence, where for example the offender is classified as a dangerous offender (see **11.7.1.1**).

STEP 6 – Totality principle

The court must consider this where an offender is being sentenced for a number of offences to ensure that the overall sentence is proportionate (see **11.3.4**).

STEP 7 – Compensation and other ancillary orders

The court is reminded of their duty to consider whether or not to order the offender to pay compensation and also make any other appropriate ancillary orders such as confiscation, destruction and forfeiture orders.

STEP 8 – Giving reasons

Section 52 of the Sentencing Act 2020 obliges the court to give reasons for the sentence it is imposing. This includes explaining to the offender the effect of the sentence that has been passed; the effect of non-compliance with the sentence and to identify the definitive sentencing guidelines that have been followed at reaching the sentence passed, including any explanation as to why the court has imposed a lesser sentence than recommended in the guidelines if that is the case.

Not all these steps will apply to every case, but steps 1, 2, 4 and 8 are the most important in practice. The following example illustrates how the guidelines would apply in a case where the defence advocate should be able to persuade the magistrates to impose a sentence below the starting point sentence suggested in the guidelines.

 Example

> *Dean has pleaded guilty at his first appearance in the magistrates' court to an offence of assault occasioning actual bodily harm. Dean punched his victim once to the face during a five-a-side football game causing the victim a fractured nose that required surgery. The prosecution accept that it was not premeditated and was the result of some significant provocation by the victim. When interviewed by the police, Dean shows genuine remorse for what happened, and the police enquiries confirm this was an isolated incident. Dean is aged 24 and has no previous convictions.*

- *Step 1*

Harm – *likely to be regarded as greater harm as we are told the fracture required surgery.*

Culpability – *likely to be regarded as lower culpability as a greater degree of provocation and a lack of premeditation without any aggravating features is present.*

Category 2 *(greater harm and lower culpability)*

- *Step 2*

Starting point sentence *for Category 2 = 26 weeks custody (with a category range from low level community order to 51 weeks custody).*

- *No aggravating factors increasing seriousness*
- *Factors reducing seriousness include:*
  - *No previous convictions*
  - *A single blow*
  - *Remorse*
  - *An isolated incident*

These will suggest a lesser sentence from the above starting point sentence and Dean's advocate will use this to try and persuade the court to impose a community order for this offence rather than a custodial sentence.

- *Step 3*

Not applicable

- *Step 4*

Dean will be entitled to full credit for his timely guilty plea = a one-third reduction in his sentence.

- *Step 5*

Not applicable as Dean will not be classified as a dangerous offender.

- *Step 6*

Not applicable as Dean is only being sentenced for one offence.

- *Step 7*

The court is likely to award compensation to the victim (although the level of provocation by the victim may reduce the amount of any such award).

- *Step 8*

When passing sentence, the court will give its reasons in open court (these are likely to be reported in the local press).

Example

*In R v Arie Ali [2023] EWCA Crim 232, the appellant was a serving prisoner when he threw the boiling contents of his mug into a prison officer's face, causing a first-degree burn to the victim. Mr Ali did not have any previous convictions for violence. The Court of Appeal did not agree that a custodial sentence of six months' imprisonment was manifestly excessive (see **12.7.2** 'Appeal against sentence'), but it did agree that the sentencing judge erred in imposing a sentence of immediate custody for an offence of assaulting an emergency worker. The Court of Appeal reasoned that when the courts are considering sentencing an offence that crosses the threshold for a short custodial sentence, judges* *and magistrates can elect to suspend the sentence or impose a community order instead. The judgment in the case of Ali clarifies that, in such instances, and while there continues to be pressure on prison capacity, the courts can take into account the impact of the current prison population levels when making that decision as an exceptional factor to justify suspending a custodial sentence (see **11.8.2** 'Suspended sentences').*

11.5 Concurrent and consecutive sentences

These terms are relevant where a court is sentencing an offender to a custodial sentence for two or more offences. In such circumstances, separate sentences of imprisonment may be expressed by the sentencing court to be either concurrent or consecutive. A concurrent sentence means that the custodial terms are deemed to be served at the same time. A consecutive sentence means that one custodial sentence will start after the other one has finished.

✪ *Example*

Aisha is convicted in the Crown Court of unlawful wounding and theft. She is sentenced to three years' imprisonment for the unlawful wounding offence and one year's imprisonment for the theft. The judge tells Aisha that the sentences are to run concurrently. This means that Aisha has effectively received a total sentence of three years' imprisonment because the sentence for the theft will run at the same time as the first year of the sentence for the unlawful wounding.

Had the judge expressed the custodial terms to be consecutive, Aisha's total sentence would amount to four years. The one-year sentence for the theft would take effect after Aisha had served the three-year sentence for the unlawful wounding.

Consecutive sentences will not generally be imposed where matters of fact arise out of the same incident. So, in the above example, if the wounding and theft occurred at the same time in relation to the same victim, concurrent sentences would be more likely. A concurrent sentence may also be imposed even if they do not arise out of the same incident if the sentencing court applies the totality principle mentioned at Step 6 above.

11.6 Pre-sentence report before plea

Where an adult defendant will be pleading guilty and their case is likely to be sentenced in the magistrates' court, their legal representative can ask the Probation Service to prepare a pre-sentence report before the first hearing.

If the Probation Service decides to produce the report, the court will decide whether to use it to sentence the defendant.

The defendant's legal representative will only ask the Probation Service to prepare a pre-sentence report before plea if the defendant will:

- plead guilty to all offences charged on the full prosecution facts; and

- agree to co-operate with the Probation Service to prepare a report.

The legal representative must also be satisfied that:

- the defendant is likely to be sentenced in the magistrates' court;

- the offence(s) is serious enough for a community order and a pre-sentence report is likely to be necessary; and

- the defendant understands that:

  ○ a pre-sentence report before plea provides no indication of any sentence and that all sentencing options remain open to the court;

  ○ the court will decide whether to consider the pre-sentence report before plea, if the Probation Service produces one; and

  ○ the court may proceed to sentence without a pre-sentence report if the court considers a report unnecessary.

Moreover, s 30 of the Sentencing Act 2020 provides that the sentencing court must obtain and consider a pre-sentence report before forming an opinion on:

- whether the custody threshold has been passed and, if it has, how long the custodial sentence should be; and

- whether the threshold for imposing a community sentence has been passed and, if it has, the requirements that should be imposed on the defendant under a generic community order.

Note that a court is not required to obtain such a report if 'in the circumstances of the case, it considers that it is unnecessary'. For example, it may be unnecessary where a custodial sentence is inevitable because of the seriousness of the offence or where the court already has a recent pre-sentence report for that offender.

Whilst the requirement under s 30 sounds obligatory, the above qualification makes it clear that it is not. Section 30(4) also provides that if a court imposes either a custodial or community sentence before first obtaining or considering such a report, this will not invalidate any resulting sentence.

11.7 Mitigation

The penultimate stage in the sentencing process is for the defendant to have an opportunity to present mitigation before the sentencing court then considers and imposes its sentence. This entitlement is recognised in the Criminal Procedure Rules (r 25.16(6)) and in practice is one of the most frequent and important functions of defence advocates. The plea in mitigation usually just involves a speech by the defence advocate, but it can also include the calling of character witnesses on behalf of the defendant or introducing character letters to speak of the defendant's generally good character.

11.7.1 Objective and structure

The objective of the plea in mitigation is to persuade the sentencing court to impose upon the defendant the most lenient sentence which the court could reasonably be expected to give for that offence. Although there is no law or procedural rules on this, the structure of a plea in mitigation may be divided into four parts:

(a) The likely sentence – the defendant's solicitor may begin by identifying the likely sentence.

(b) The offence – the defendant's solicitor could then address the circumstances of the offence, minimising the impact of any aggravating factors and stressing the importance of any mitigating factors that are present.

(c) The offender – after dealing with the offence, the defendant's solicitor could then emphasise any personal mitigation which the defendant may have.

(d) The suggested sentence – the plea in mitigation should conclude with the defendant's solicitor suggesting to the court the type of sentence which he considers it would be most appropriate for the court to impose.

Each of these four parts will now be looked at in more detail.

11.7.1.1 The likely sentence

The defendant's advocate must research the likely range of sentences which will be in the mind of the court to identify what the 'starting point' sentence is likely to be (see above). The objective of the plea in mitigation is to persuade the magistrates to impose a sentence which is less severe than the 'starting point' sentence.

11.7.1.2 The offence

After identifying the likely sentence, the plea in mitigation could then focus on the offence itself. This requires the defendant's advocate to:

(a) minimise the impact of any aggravating factors surrounding the offence; and

(b) emphasise the importance of any mitigating factors.

The defendant's solicitor should identify any aggravating factors which would normally lead the court to impose a sentence in excess of the 'starting point' sentence, and attempt (if possible) to disassociate the defendant's case from those factors. Similarly, the defendant's solicitor should emphasise to the court the presence of any mitigating factors.

11.7.1.3 The offender

After dealing with the facts of the offence, the plea in mitigation should move on to consider any personal mitigation the defendant may have. Factors which may be relevant include:

- The age of the defendant

  This may be relevant where the defendant is young, especially where they are immature and impressionable. The courts are also generally more likely to give sympathetic treatment to a defendant of advanced years, particularly if this is their first offence, as the offending is out of character.

- The health of the defendant

  It is unwise to suggest to the court in mitigation that the defendant committed an offence only because he was under the influence of drink or drugs at the time. The court is likely to regard this as an aggravating feature of the offence. If, however, there is evidence that the defendant is a drug addict or an alcoholic, this may be used to suggest to the court that a sentence designed to help the defendant overcome this addiction (for example, a generic community order that incorporates a drug rehabilitation requirement or an alcohol treatment requirement – see **11.7.3.1**) may be more appropriate than a custodial sentence. Similarly, a defendant who is suffering from a long-term illness or injury is likely to receive some sympathy from the court, as is a defendant who may have been suffering from some form of mental illness (such as depression) at the time the offence was committed.

- Cooperation with the police/early guilty plea

  The court will give the defendant credit for entering an early guilty plea to the offence (since the sentencing guidelines are based on the appropriate sentence for a defendant who is convicted following a trial). We have already seen that the amount of credit the defendant will receive depends upon the stage in the proceedings at which the defendant entered their guilty plea. Such credit may amount to a maximum reduction of one third of the sentence (if the defendant has pleaded guilty at the first opportunity) down to one-tenth of the sentence (for a last minute change of plea at the door of the court). It would also be appropriate to tell the court if the defendant has positively assisted the police in their enquiries, for example by naming others involved in the crime or by revealing the whereabouts of stolen property. The fact that the defendant made a prompt confession when questioned by the police is also useful mitigation, showing that the defendant did not waste police time during the investigation process.

- Voluntary compensation

  A defendant who voluntarily makes good the damage which they caused, or who makes a voluntary payment of compensation to their victim, is likely to receive credit for this. This is particularly the case if the defendant is of limited means.

- Remorse

  Evidence of true remorse is effective mitigation. A mere apology made by the defendant's solicitor to the court on behalf of his client is unlikely to have much effect, but the court will take into account any positive steps which the defendant has made to tackle the problems which led them to commit the offence. For example, the court is likely to give credit to a defendant who has committed thefts to fund a drug habit, who has voluntarily sought treatment for their addiction.

- Character

  If the defendant has previous convictions, the court may view these as aggravating factors. The court is likely to view a defendant's previous convictions as being aggravating factors if the relevant offences either were committed recently or were the same type of offence as the offence for which the defendant is to be sentenced. If the defendant has any such convictions, the solicitor should attempt to distinguish such convictions from the facts of the current offence and 'explain' the circumstances of the defendant's previous offending. For example, a defendant convicted of theft may have several previous convictions for thefts which were committed in order to fund a drug habit. If the defendant is no longer taking drugs and the reason for the defendant having committed the current offence is different from his motive for committing the previous offences, their solicitor should explain this to the court.

  Just as having previous convictions may be seen as an aggravating factor, a defendant with no previous convictions (and so of previous good character) is entitled to have this taken into account. This is particularly important when there is a specific reason or explanation for a defendant of previous good character having committed an offence.

⭐ Example

Fien is 55 years of age and is of previous good character. She works on the check-out at her local supermarket and has been charged with stealing £500 in cash from her employers. The reason for Fien having committed the offence is that her husband has recently left her, taking all her savings and leaving her with insufficient funds to pay the rent on her house. Fien's solicitor can ask the court to take Fien's previous good character into account and suggest that there is a specific 'one-off' explanation for her committing a criminal offence.

*In R v Seed; R v Stark [2007] EWCA Crim 254, the Court of Appeal held that the absence of previous convictions was important mitigation that might make a custodial sentence inappropriate, even if the custody threshold had been crossed (see **11.7.1**).*

In such circumstances, the defendant's solicitor may call character witnesses to give evidence as to the defendant's previous good character.

- Family circumstances

If the court has requested a pre-sentence report from the Probation Service, this will look in depth at the defendant's personal background and family circumstances. The defendant's solicitor should also refer to the defendant's personal circumstances in the plea in mitigation, particularly if the defendant has a regular home and job, and has family who will be supportive in their attempts to stay out of trouble in the future. Equally, if the defendant has had a troubled family background, it would also be appropriate to refer to this in mitigation, particularly if the defendant is still young. For example, a defendant may have come from a broken home, or have been physically or sexually abused as a child. Similarly, young defendants will often have become addicted to drugs or involved in prostitution at an early age. This will be particularly effective mitigation if the defendant's solicitor is able to say that the client has made a genuine attempt to overcome such a background.

- Low risk of re-offending

The pre-sentence report from the Probation Service will address the risk of the defendant committing further offences. If this risk is assessed as being low, the defendant's solicitor should mention this in the plea in mitigation to support an argument that the defendant's offending was a one-off aberration for which the defendant has shown remorse and a willingness to change.

11.7.1.4 The suggested sentence

The plea in mitigation should conclude with the defendant's advocate suggesting to the court the sentence which they think the court should impose. This should be lower than the likely sentence and should reflect all the mitigating factors which the defendant's solicitor has placed before the court. The sentence which the defendant's solicitor suggests to the court must be realistic, and so should be at the lower end of the range of possible sentences which will be in the mind of the court. If the sentence which the defendant's solicitor suggests as being appropriate is the same sentence as is recommended in the pre-sentence report, the solicitor should emphasise this point (given that the pre-sentence report is requested by the court to assist it in determining sentence).

11.8 Types of sentence

Sentencing a defendant will not always result in a custodial sentence. Such sentences are not that common in the magistrates' court and youth court. Sentencing courts have a wide range of sentences at their disposal. This range of sentences is sometimes described as a 'sentencing pyramid'. Working from the top downwards, the range of sentences include:

- custody
- suspended sentence
- community sentence
- fine
- discharge (conditional or absolute).

We will just be considering the first three types of sentence.

11.8.1 Custodial sentences

Most offences which carry a custodial sentence allow the sentencing court a discretion as to whether a custodial sentence should be imposed, and the length of any such sentence. There are a limited number of exceptions where an offence carries either a mandatory sentence or a mandatory minimum term of imprisonment. For example, a defendant convicted of murder will receive a mandatory sentence of life imprisonment (Murder (Abolition of Death Penalty) Act 1965, s 1(1)).

Where the court has a discretion whether or not to pass a custodial sentence, it must apply the threshold test set out in s 230 of the Sentencing Act 2020:

> The court must not pass a custodial sentence unless it is of the opinion that the offence, or the combination of the offence and one or more offences associated with it, was so serious that neither a fine alone nor a community sentence can be justified for the offence.

This test is known as the custody threshold. Only if this threshold is passed may the court impose a custodial sentence. If the custody threshold has been passed, this does not necessarily mean that a custodial sentence should automatically be imposed. In *R v Seed; R v Stark* (2007), the Court of Appeal said that, where the custody threshold had only just been passed, a guilty plea or very strong personal mitigation might make it appropriate for a non-custodial sentence to be imposed.

Note that, according to s 230(4), the custody threshold test does not apply where an offender fails to express a willingness to take part in a community sentence.

 Example

Nathan is convicted of theft following a trial in the magistrates' court. According to the Magistrates' Court Sentencing Guidelines, Nathan should be eligible to receive a low-level community order. However, when the magistrates indicate their proposed sentence, Nathan makes it clear that he is not prepared to comply with the terms of the order. In these circumstances, even though the custody threshold has not been met, the magistrates will still be able to impose a custodial sentence on Nathan.

If the custody threshold is passed and the court decides to impose a custodial sentence, the court must then consider the length of the custodial sentence. To determine the length of the sentence, the court must apply s 231(2) of the Sentencing Act 2020. This provides that a custodial sentence

> must be for the shortest term (not exceeding the permitted maximum) that in the opinion of the court is commensurate with the seriousness of the offence, or the combination of the offence and one or more other offences associated with it.

The maximum custodial sentence which a magistrates' court may impose on a defendant is six months' imprisonment (note that s 13 of the Judicial Review and Courts Act 2022 amended s 224 of the Sentencing Act 2020 by increasing the magistrates courts' sentencing power for either-way offences from six months to 12 months' imprisonment – this was subsequently reduced back to six months' imprisonment on 30 March 2023 as a result of a further change to the law). Note though that a magistrates' court can impose up to a maximum period of 12 months' imprisonment for two or more either-way offences by imposing two consecutive periods of six months' imprisonment for each either-way offence.

 Example

Amir pleads guilty to offences of affray and assault occasioning actual bodily harm (two either-way offences) arising from the same public order incident. The magistrates sentence Amir to four months' imprisonment for the affray (having given him credit for his timely guilty plea) and four months' imprisonment for the common assault (again having given him credit for his timely guilty plea). In theory the magistrates could order these sentences to run consecutively since the overall term of eight months' imprisonment will be within the maximum of 12 months for two either-way offences, although it is likely the court will order them to run concurrently given that they both arise from the same incident.

Judges in the Crown Court have the power to sentence a defendant to a term of imprisonment up to the maximum permitted for that offence.

In practice though, very few defendants receive the maximum sentence which the offence carries. In determining the length of the sentence, the judge will have regard to guidelines issued by the SC and the guidelines considered by the Court of Appeal. The SC has put these cases together in a document entitled 'Guideline Judgments Case Compendium', which may be accessed from the SC website (see **11.2.1**).

Finally, note that where an adult offender is aged between 19–21 years, any custodial sentence they receive will not be served in prison, but in a young offender institution (YOI).

11.8.1.1 Dangerous offenders (Part 10, Chapter 6 of the Sentencing Act 2020)

In a limited number of situations, a defendant (both adult and juvenile) may be classified as a 'dangerous' offender. In such a situation, the sentencing court must impose one of the following forms of custodial sentence:

(a) automatic life imprisonment;

(b) discretionary life imprisonment; or

(c) an extended sentence of imprisonment.

The detail and requirements for the imposition of such sentences go beyond the SRA syllabus.

11.8.1.2 Early release

A defendant sentenced to custody will not usually serve all of their sentence behind bars. They will normally be released automatically halfway through their sentence.

Adult defendants who receive a custodial sentence of up to two years (for an offence committed after 1 February 2015) will be automatically released at the halfway point and then be on licence in the community to the end of the sentence. Upon release they must have a period of post-sentence supervision to ensure that they are supervised for a period of 12 months beginning on the day they leave custody.

Defendants who receive determinate sentences of over two years will also usually be released automatically after serving half their sentence and the remaining half is served on licence in the community, unless they are classified as an 'offender of particular concern'. For such an offender they will not be entitled to automatic release on licence after serving half the sentence. Instead they can apply for parole and may then be released at any time from this halfway point up until the end of their sentence. They will then be released on licence and subject to similar supervision. Such offenders include those convicted of much more serious offences such as terrorism and child sex offences.

11.8.2 Suspended sentences

Rather than imposing immediate custody, a sentencing court may sometimes order the sentence to be suspended.

11.8.2.1 When will a suspended sentence be imposed?

A custodial sentence of at least 14 days but no more than two years (or 12 months in the case of the magistrates' court) may be suspended for at least six months and not more than two years (Sentencing Act 2020, s 288(2)). The period during which the sentence is suspended is known as the 'operational period'.

The court will impose a suspended sentence only if it initially decides that the custody threshold (see above), but then considers that particular circumstances exist which justify the suspension of the sentence.

 Example

Berat is convicted of affray before the Crown Court. When sentencing Berat, the judge decides that the offence is so serious that the only appropriate sentence is custody. However, when giving the plea of mitigation on behalf of Berat, his advocate tells the judge that Berat is a single parent looking after a disabled child, and that a custodial sentence for Berat would mean the child needing to go into a care home. The trial judge considers that these particular circumstances justify the imposition of a suspended sentence. The judge therefore imposes a sentence of six months' imprisonment but suspends this for 12 months.

11.8.2.2 Requirements which the court may impose

When a court imposes a suspended sentence, it is likely to order the defendant to comply during a specified period (the *supervision period*) with one or more requirements falling within s 287 of the Sentencing Act 2020. The supervision period must end no later than the end of the operational period.

The requirements are the same type of requirements which the court may require a defendant to comply with when imposing a generic community order (see below for details of what each requirement entails).

11.8.2.3 Breach of a suspended sentence

The sentence of imprisonment will not take effect unless either the defendant fails to comply with any requirements which have been imposed or, during the operational period, the defendant commits a further offence and the court sentencing the defendant for the 'new' offence orders that the original sentence of imprisonment is to take effect.

If a defendant is found either to be in breach of a requirement or to have committed a further offence during the operational period, if the suspended sentence was imposed by the magistrates' court, they may be dealt with for the breach either by the magistrates' court or by the Crown Court. If the suspended sentence was imposed by the Crown Court, any breach may generally be dealt with only by the Crown Court.

A court dealing with a defendant who has breached a suspended sentence must do one of the following:

(a) order the custodial sentence originally suspended to take effect unaltered;

(b) order the custodial sentence to take effect, but for a shorter period of time, and/or substitute a lesser custodial period;

(c) amend the original order by imposing more onerous community requirements on the defendant; or

(d) amend the original order by extending the operational period, or by extending the supervision period.

The court must make an order under (a) or (b) above unless it considers that it would be unjust to do so in view of all the circumstances. So for example, the court may decide it would be unjust to make an order under (a) or (b) if the defendant is coming to the end of the supervision period (having complied with the requirements imposed) or if, in the case of a defendant convicted of a further offence, the new offence is a minor matter or is a completely different type of offence to the offence originally committed. The court will also take into account the time which has elapsed since the original offence was committed and any change in the defendant's circumstances.

If the court does make an order under (a) or (b), the term of imprisonment for the original offence will be consecutive to the sentence imposed for any new offence.

The court can also impose a fine of up to £2,500 for breach of a suspended sentence order where it decides not to give immediate effect to the custodial sentence.

Generally, the court will activate a suspended sentence and order it to run consecutively with any additional sentence imposed for the new offence.

 Example

Connor was sentenced five months ago in the Crown Court to a sentence of three months' imprisonment for an offence of theft. This sentence was suspended for a period of 12 months. Connor has now been convicted of a similar offence of theft and appears before the magistrates' court.

Connor is now likely to be committed to the Crown Court for sentence as he has re-offended during the operational period of a Crown Court suspended sentence. The Crown Court is likely to activate his suspended sentence for the full period of three months and sentence him to prison for the new offence and order this to run consecutively. So, if Conor was sentenced to four months' imprisonment for the new offence, he will serve a total of seven months' imprisonment (although he will be automatically released after serving half of this sentence).

11.8.3 Generic community orders

Section 204(2) of the Sentencing Act 2020 sets out the threshold which must be reached before a court can impose such an order:

(2) The court must not make a community order unless it is of the opinion that—

(a) the offence, or

(b) the combination of the offence and one or more offences associated with it,

was serious enough to warrant the making of such an order.

11.8.3.1 Contents of the generic community order

In making a generic community order, the court may choose from a 'menu' of options and select those which are most appropriate for the defendant.

The options from which the court may choose are as follows:

(a) Unpaid work requirement – this requires the defendant to perform unpaid work in the community for between 40 and 300 hours. This work must be completed within a 12-month period and in practice this is the most common requirement attached to a generic community order.

(b) Activity requirement – this requires the defendant to take part in specified activities which may be designed to help the defendant overcome a particular problem (such as finding work), or which may be activities to make reparation to the victim (such as repairing damage caused).

(c) Programme requirement – this requires the defendant to take part in one or more courses to address the defendant's offending behaviour, such as courses in anger management, sex offending or substance misuse.

(d) Prohibited activity requirement – this requires the defendant to refrain from taking part in specified activities.

(e) Curfew requirement – this requires the defendant to remain at a particular location (normally the defendant's place of residence) specified by the court between specified times. In order to check compliance with such a requirement, the defendant will be electronically monitored, which is known colloquially as 'tagging'.

(f) Exclusion requirement – this prohibits the defendant from entering a place or places (such as a city centre, or a particular type of establishment like a shop or a pub) for a period not exceeding two years. Again, the defendant will be electronically monitored.

(g) Residence requirement – this requires the defendant to live at a particular place as specified in the court order.

(h) Mental health treatment requirement – this requires the defendant to agree to treatment from a mental health practitioner for a specified period of time.

(i) Drug rehabilitation requirement – this requires the defendant to agree to treatment to reduce or eliminate their dependency on drugs, and to submit to providing samples to determine whether they have drugs in their body. This will be for a period of time specified by the court.

(j) Alcohol treatment requirement – this requires the defendant to agree, during a period of time specified by the court, to treatment to reduce or eliminate their dependency on alcohol.

(k) Supervision requirement – this requires the defendant to attend appointments with a member of the Probation Service. The purpose of such meetings is to promote the defendant's rehabilitation, and the meetings will involve confronting the defendant's offending behaviour, discussing how the defendant might 'manage' their life and generally monitoring the defendant's progress. A supervision requirement may be imposed for up to three years.

(l) Attendance centre requirement – this requires the defendant to attend an attendance centre for a total of between 12 and 36 hours. Such an order can only be imposed on defendants who are under 25 years of age.

(m) Foreign travel prohibition requirement – this enables a court to impose a prohibition on foreign travel as a requirement. The effect of this requirement is to prohibit travel to a country or countries outside the British Isles (the United Kingdom, the Channel Islands and the Isle of Man).

11.8.3.2 Guidance from the Sentencing Council

Given the extremely wide scope of the potential requirements a court may impose as part of a generic community order, the SC has provided guidelines as to how the court should approach the making of such an order.

The SC has identified three sentencing ranges (low, medium and high) within the community sentence band, and a court considering the imposition of such a sentence must also decide into which band the particular offence(s) with which it is dealing falls.

11.8.3.3 Breach of a community sentence

The first thing that will happen when a defendant, without reasonable excuse, breaches a community order, is that the defendant will receive a warning from the officer from the Probation Service who is supervising the defendant's compliance with his generic community order.

If, within the following 12 months, the defendant again fails without reasonable excuse to comply with the requirements of the order, the officer will report this matter to the court which imposed the order in the first place and the defendant will be required to appear before that court.

If the court is satisfied that the defendant has, without reasonable excuse, failed to comply with the requirements of the order, the court must:

(a) amend the order so as to impose requirements on the defendant which are more onerous (for example, by increasing the amount of unpaid work the defendant is required to complete); or

(b) revoke the order completely and re-sentence the defendant for the offence, but without taking into account the usual custody threshold; or

(c) where the defendant has wilfully and persistently failed to comply with the order, the court may revoke the order and impose a custodial sentence. This can be done even if the original offence was not punishable by way of a custodial sentence.

⭐ Example

Ahmet is convicted of assault occasioning actual bodily harm by the magistrates' court. He receives a generic community order which includes a requirement to complete 250 hours of unpaid work.

Ahmet fails to attend his first unpaid work session. The probation officer supervising Ahmet's sentence gives Ahmet a warning. Ahmet then fails to attend his second unpaid work session and is brought back before the magistrates' court. The magistrates must, if they are satisfied that Ahmet had no reasonable excuse for failing to attend the unpaid work sessions, either amend the generic community order to add more onerous requirements or revoke the order and re-sentence Ahmet. If the magistrates choose the latter course, the inevitable sentence will be custodial.

11.8.3.4 Further offences committed during a generic community order

It will often be the case that a defendant who has received a generic community order sentence is convicted of a further offence during the period when the generic community order is still in force. In such a situation, the magistrates may either allow the original generic community order to continue, or, if it is in the interests of justice having regard to the circumstances that have arisen since the original order was made, they may:

(a) revoke the order (this will be done if the magistrates are imposing a custodial sentence for the 'new' offence, since an offender in prison cannot comply with a community sentence); or

(b) revoke the order and re-sentence the defendant for the original offence as if they have just been convicted of it. If this is done, the court must have regard to the extent to which the defendant has complied with the original order.

11.9 Newton hearings

Sometimes a defendant may plead guilty to the charge they face but dispute the specific factual version of events put forward by the CPS. If the dispute concerning the correct version of events may have a bearing on the type of sentence the court imposes, the court must either accept the defendant's version of events, or allow both the CPS and the defendant to call evidence so that the court can determine the true factual circumstances of the offence on which the defendant's sentence will be based. This is referred to as a Newton hearing, following the case of *R v Newton* (1983) 77 Cr App R 13.

 Example

Simon pleads guilty to a charge of burglary of a dwelling. The CPS alleges that Simon broke into the dwelling by smashing a window, ransacked several rooms in the property, soiled the carpets and took several items of high value. Simon says that he got into the property through an open window (causing no damage to the window), denies ransacking the property or soiling the carpets, and says that he removed only a small transistor radio. The difference between the prosecution and the defence version of events is significant and is likely to affect the type of sentence the court will impose. The court must therefore either hold a Newton hearing, or alternatively accept Simon's account as being the correct version of events.

11.9.1 Basis of plea

One way the prosecution and defence may try to avoid having a Newton hearing is to agree a version of events upon which the defendant will be sentenced. This is known as a 'basis of plea' and it will usually be instigated by the defence. A basis of plea is a document that sets out the defendant's factual version of events to an offence which the defendant accepts they are guilty of.

The purpose of the basis of plea from the defence perspective is to remove various aggravating features of the case which would lead to a higher sentence and which the defendant does not accept are an accurate reflection of what actually happened.

If the basis of plea is accepted by the prosecution and the sentencing judge, the sentence will proceed on the version put forward by the defence.

If the basis of plea is rejected by the prosecution and the judge thinks that the version of events put forward by the prosecution is sufficiently more serious than the version put forward by the defence (so as to justify a higher sentence), then there will be a Newton hearing to determine the factual basis upon which the defendant will be sentenced.

It is also worth bearing in mind that the sentencing judge is entitled to reject a basis of plea which they consider to be absurd. If the judge takes the view that the basis put forward by the defence is patently absurd then sentencing will take place on the prosecution version of events without a Newton hearing taking place.

So the sentencing judge is the final arbiter on whether or not a basis of plea is accepted and is entitled to reject a basis even if accepted by the prosecution.

Summary

In this chapter you have considered a range of matters relating to sentencing. Notably:

- *The role of sentencing guidelines.* How these help a sentencing court to exercise their discretion when sentencing an offender to ensure a consistent and structured approach when sentencing an offender.

- *Aggravating and mitigating facts.* How the seriousness of an offence is determined with the use of both aggravating and mitigating factors which help a sentencing court to shape a starting point sentence.

- *The use of concurrent and consecutive sentences.* When and why sentences are ordered to run either concurrently or consecutively and what this means to an offender.

- *Mitigation and its impact on sentencing procedure.* How a defendant's advocate will structure and use a plea of mitigation to try and persuade the sentencing court to impose upon the offender the most lenient sentence which the court could reasonably be expected to give for that offence.

- *The types of sentence available to a sentencing court.* How and on what basis a custodial sentence may be imposed. When such a sentence may be suspended. The availability and range of community orders where the custodial threshold has either not been met, or where there is sufficient mitigation to persuade a court to impose a community sentence rather than a custodial sentence.

- *The role and function of a Newton hearing.* If an offender admits guilt but disputes the prosecution version of events, the defence may draft a basis of plea and invite the prosecution to agree to this as being the factual basis upon which the defendant will be sentenced. If no such agreement can be reached, or the sentencing judge is not prepared to accept the basis of plea, then the sentencing court will usually conduct a 'trial on the facts' (a Newton hearing) to determine the correct version of facts upon which the defendant will be sentenced.

Sample questions

Question 1

A man has been charged with an offence of robbery. When interviewed, he denied his involvement and later instructed his solicitor that he would plead not guilty. At his first appearance in the magistrates' court, the man's solicitor was given access to the prosecution evidence, which appeared to be compelling. Despite advice from his solicitor, the man was not prepared to indicate a guilty plea at this stage. The man's case was immediately sent to the Crown Court and a date for the plea and trial preparation hearing (PTPH) was set. At this hearing, the man changed his mind about the plea and entered a guilty plea at the PTPH. However, he made it clear he did not show any remorse for his offending behaviour.

What level of discount will the man be entitled to as a result of his guilty plea?

A   Somewhere between zero and one-tenth discount on his sentence since he has shown no remorse for his offending behaviour.

B   A one-tenth discount on his sentence since the evidence against him was overwhelming.

C   A one-quarter discount on his sentence since he only indicated his guilty plea after the first stage of the proceedings.

D   A one-third discount on his sentence since he indicated his guilty plea at his first appearance in the Crown Court.

E   The man will not be entitled to any discount on his sentence since he has shown no remorse for his offending behaviour and the evidence against him was overwhelming.

Answer

Option C is the correct answer. Under the 'Reduction in Sentence for a Guilty Plea' Definitive Guideline, where a guilty plea is indicated after this first stage of the proceedings, the maximum level of the reduction is only one quarter, and not the full reduction of one third. For this reason, option C is correct and option D is wrong because the first stage of the proceedings was when the man appeared in the magistrates' court and could reasonably have been expected to indicate a guilty plea at that stage.

Options A, B and E are all wrong because a reduction in discount to one-tenth or even to zero should only apply where a guilty plea is entered on the first day a trial is meant to take place (one-tenth discount) or it may be reduced further, even to zero, where the guilty plea is entered during the course of the trial. Not showing remorse or the strength of the prosecution case are not factors that will affect the level of discount.

Question 2

A man was sentenced six months ago in the magistrates' court for an offence of assault occasioning actual bodily harm. He received a suspended sentence order of three months' custody. The operational period of the suspended sentence is for 12 months. A requirement to complete 100 hours of unpaid work was attached to the suspended sentence order and the man has completed the unpaid work. The man has now pleaded guilty in the magistrates' court to an offence of affray.

Which of the following best describes the likely sentence the man will now receive?

A   The man will receive a custodial sentence for the present offence of affray and the suspended sentence of three months will be activated to run fully and concurrently with this sentence.

B   The man will receive a custodial sentence for the present offence of affray and the suspended sentence of three months will be activated but will be reduced to take into account the unpaid work the man has completed.

C   The man will receive a custodial sentence for the present offence of affray and the suspended sentence of three months will be activated to run fully and consecutively with this sentence.

D   The man will receive a custodial sentence for the present offence of affray and the suspended sentence of three months will be further suspended for another period of 12 months.

E   The man will receive a community order for the present offence of affray and the suspended sentence of three months will be further suspended for another period of 12 months.

Answer

All of these options are possible, but option C is the best answer. The general rule where a suspended sentence order is imposed and a further offence is committed during the operational period of the order is for a custodial sentence to be imposed for the present offence (assuming it is imprisonable, which affray is) and the suspended sentence will be activated to run fully and consecutively with this sentence. However, the sentencing court does have some discretion to impose other sentences. For example, if the present offence is not very serious and/or is very different in nature to the earlier offence, or the earlier sentence is very near the end of its operational period, the court may not activate the original sentence and further suspend it, or not activate it to run for the full period, or activate it to run concurrently with the present sentence as opposed to running consecutively with it.

Question 3

A woman is sentenced in the Crown Court for a number of dishonesty offences. For two unrelated offences of theft, she is sentenced to six months' imprisonment for each, which are ordered to run consecutively. For an offence of fraud, which is linked to the second offence of theft, she is sentenced to four months' imprisonment and this is ordered to run concurrently.

When should the woman be released from prison?

A   After serving four months in custody.

B   After serving six months in custody.

C   After serving 10 months in custody.

D   After serving 12 months in custody.

E   After serving 16 months in custody.

Answer

Option B is the correct answer. The woman has been sentenced to a total period of 12 months in custody as the two thefts are ordered to run consecutively (whereas the fraud offence will run concurrently and so does not count toward the overall total). However, a prisoner will generally be released after serving half their sentence, so here, after serving six months in custody. Because the woman's sentence runs to a total of 12 months, she will be released on licence and will be under the supervision of the Probation Service during the licence period. This will expire at the end of the 12-month period.

12 Appeals Procedure

SQE1 syllabus

This chapter will enable you to achieve the SQE1 Assessment Specification in relation to Functioning Legal Knowledge concerned with the following procedures and processes:

- appeal from the magistrates' court to the Crown Court;
- appeal from the magistrates' court to the High Court by way of case stated;
- judicial review of a magistrates' court decision;
- appeal from the Crown Court to the Court of Appeal.

Note that, for SQE1, candidates are not usually required to recall specific case names or cite statutory or regulatory authorities. These are provided for illustrative purposes only unless otherwise stated.

Learning outcomes

By the end of this chapter you will be able to apply relevant core legal principles and rules appropriately and effectively, at the level of a competent newly qualified solicitor in practice, to realistic client-based and ethical problems and situations in the following areas:

- How the defendant may appeal against conviction and sentence from the magistrates' court to the Crown Court and the Crown Court's powers when dealing with such appeals.
- Defence and prosecution appeals on a point of law from the magistrates' court to the High Court or challenging magistrates' court decisions by way of judicial review.
- Appeals against conviction and sentence by the defendant from the Crown Court to the Court of Appeal, including the relevant procedure, grounds of appeal and the Court of Appeal's powers.
- The limited extent to which the prosecution can appeal to the Court of Appeal.

12.1 Introduction

This chapter considers the options open to the defendant to appeal against conviction and/or sentence. It also examines the more limited rights of appeal that may be exercised by the CPS.

The rules which govern the procedure for the making of an appeal (either by the defendant, or by the CPS) are contained in Parts 34–43 of the CrimPR.

12.2 Appeals from the magistrates' court to the Crown Court

A defendant convicted in the magistrates' court (including the youth court) may appeal to the Crown Court in the following circumstances:

(a) if they pleaded guilty, they may appeal against the sentence they received;

(b) if they pleaded not guilty, they may appeal against any resulting conviction and/or the sentence they received.

The appeal will usually be heard by a recorder or a circuit judge who will sit with an even number of magistrates. This will normally be two magistrates, although up to four magistrates may sit on an appeal.

The prosecution does not have any rights of appeal to the Crown Court against the acquittal of a defendant, or the sentence imposed on a defendant by the magistrates' court. They can however appeal to the High Court on a point of law by way of case stated, as can the defence (see **12.5**).

12.2.1 Appeals against conviction

A defendant convicted following a trial in the magistrates' court may appeal against conviction to the Crown Court on the basis that the magistrates made errors of fact and/or law.

An appeal against conviction in the Crown Court is a full rehearing of the case (in effect another trial). The CPS and the defendant will need to call all those witnesses whose evidence they seek to rely on. New witnesses may be called, and new or different points of law may be relied upon.

12.2.2 Appeals against sentence

A defendant may appeal to the Crown Court against a sentence imposed by the magistrates' court on the basis that the sentence imposed by the magistrates is excessive. The Crown Court should carry out a full rehearing of the issues and take an independent view of what the correct sentence should be, rather than simply reviewing the sentence passed by the magistrates' court.

12.3 Procedure for appeal against conviction and/or sentence

A defendant wishing to appeal from the magistrates' court to the Crown Court must file a notice of appeal with both the magistrates' court and the CPS not more than 15 business days from the magistrates passing sentence (or the date sentence was deferred to – see CrimPR, r 34.2).

The clerk to the magistrates' court will send the notice of appeal to the relevant Crown Court, and the Crown Court will then arrange a date for the hearing of the appeal to take place.

If a defendant files their notice outside the 15 business days, a Crown Court judge does have the discretionary power to extend this time limit.

If the defendant's case before the magistrates' court was publicly funded by way of a representation order, a separate representation order will be required to cover the hearing of the appeal by the Crown Court. Any advice and assistance given to the defendant in preparing the notice of appeal will be covered by the original representation order.

If the defendant is appealing against a custodial sentence, the magistrates may grant bail to the defendant pending the appeal to the Crown Court. There is, however, no presumption in favour of bail, as s 4 of the Bail Act 1976 does not apply to defendants appealing against conviction or sentence (see **Chapter 7**). If the magistrates' court does not grant bail, the defendant may apply to the Crown Court for bail pending the hearing of the appeal.

 Example

Karim has been convicted of common assault following a trial in the magistrates' court. His case is then adjourned for the preparation of a pre-sentence report for three weeks. At his adjourned hearing Karim is made the subject of a community order. Karim decides to appeal against his conviction but does not want to appeal against his sentence.

Karim must file his notice of appeal against conviction not more than 15 business days from the date of sentence (not from the date of his conviction). If Karim files his notice outside the 15 business days, a Crown Court judge may, at their discretion, extend this time limit.

12.4 Powers of the Crown Court

The Crown Court may confirm, reverse or vary the decision. The Crown Court has the power to impose on the defendant any sentence, as long as it is a sentence which the magistrates' court had the power to impose. This means that a defendant appealing against a sentence imposed by the magistrates' court may have that sentence increased if the Crown Court takes a more serious view of the case.

Both the CPS and the defendant are then able to appeal to the High Court by way of case stated against any decision or order made by the Crown Court following an appeal from the magistrates' court. The appeal must be based either on a point of law, or on an argument that the Crown Court has exceeded its jurisdiction (see below).

12.5 Appeal to the High Court by way of case stated

Either the CPS or the defendant may appeal from a decision of the magistrates' court to the Queen's Bench Division of the High Court if:

(a) the decision which has been made by the magistrates is wrong in law; or

(b) the magistrates have acted outside their jurisdiction (Magistrates' Courts Act 1980, s 111).

Arguments often raised in an appeal by way of case stated are that:

(a) the magistrates misread, misunderstood or misapplied the law;

(b) the magistrates decided to hear a case when they did not have the jurisdiction to hear it;

(c) the magistrates made errors in deciding the admissibility or otherwise of evidence;

(d) the magistrates erred in their decision following a submission of no case to answer.

12.5.1 Procedure

A party wishing to appeal by way of case stated must apply to the magistrates' court within 21 days of the relevant decision being made by the magistrates' court (see CrimPR, r 35.2). This is normally done by writing to the clerk to the magistrates' court. The application must identify the question of law on which the aggrieved party seeks the view of the High Court. Following receipt of this letter, the magistrates must then 'state a case' for the opinion of the High Court.

To do this, the clerk to the magistrates (in conjunction with the magistrates or district judge who heard the case) will prepare a draft 'statement of case' that will:

(a) specify the decision in issue;

(b) specify the question(s) of law or jurisdiction on which the opinion of the High Court will be asked;

(c) include a succinct summary of:

   (i) the nature and history of the proceedings

   (ii) the court's relevant findings of fact and

   (iii) the relevant contentions of the parties

(d) if a question is whether there was sufficient evidence on which the court reasonably could reach a finding of fact:

   (i) specify that finding and

   (ii) include a summary of the evidence on which the court reached that finding.

Once an initial draft of the 'statement of case' has been prepared, the clerk will send this out to the CPS and the defendant's solicitor to enable them to suggest any necessary amendments. Once a final version of the statement of case has been agreed, the clerk will send this to the party making the appeal. That party must then lodge this with the High Court and give notice to the other party that this has been done.

12.5.2 The hearing

The appeal is then heard by the Divisional Court of the Queen's Bench Division and will normally be heard by three judges. No evidence is given by witnesses and the hearing will be confined to legal argument based on the agreed facts set out in the statement of case.

The Divisional Court has the power to reverse, vary or affirm the decision made by the magistrates' court. It may also remit the case back to the same magistrates' court with a direction to acquit or convict the defendant, or to remit the case to a different bench of magistrates (if the case needs to be reheard).

Both the CPS and the defendant are able to appeal to the Supreme Court in respect of any decision or order made by the High Court following an appeal to the High Court by way of case stated. Any such appeal must be on a point of law only, and the High Court must certify it to be a point of law of general public importance. Further, either the High Court or the Supreme Court must grant leave to appeal.

✪ Example

Elise has been acquitted of criminal damage following a trial in the magistrates' court. During the course of the trial the defence persuaded the magistrates to exclude a confession made by Elise to the police on the basis that it had been obtained in circumstances rendering it unreliable. The CPS appeal by way of case stated against the magistrates' exclusion of this confession, on a point of law.

If the High Court agrees with the CPS then they will either remit the case back to the magistrates' court with a direction to convict Elise, or remit the case to a different bench of magistrates to rehear the case, but on that occasion the confession will be admitted in evidence.

12.5.3 Advising a client

Although this would be the only avenue of appeal for the CPS, we have already seen that the defence can appeal straight to the Crown Court against both conviction and/or sentence. The following case highlights that appealing to the Crown Court would usually be the best approach to adopt.

 In Brett v DPP [2009] EWHC 440 (Admin) the use of appeal by way of case stated was discouraged by Lord Justice Leveson who was at pains to point out that a much speedier and more effective way to challenge a decision by the defendant that resulted in a conviction in the magistrates' court was to simply appeal against the conviction to the Crown Court. Leveson LJ observed that even if a case stated application succeeded it was still quite likely that the case would return to the magistrates' court for a retrial and a considerable amount of time will have elapsed, and he did not believe that such delay would ever be in the defendant's best interests.

✪ Example

Assume that in the above example of Elise, the magistrates refused to exclude the confession and convicted her of criminal damage. Elise could challenge, by way of case stated on a point of law, the magistrates' refusal to exclude her confession. However, even if this were to succeed, the case would be likely to be remitted back to the magistrates' court for a retrial and so it may well be much quicker and simpler for Elise just to appeal against her original conviction to the Crown Court.

12.6 Judicial review

An application for judicial review is not strictly a form of appeal. It does, however, represent an alternative (but not the usual) method of challenging a decision made by the magistrates' court. As with an appeal by way of case stated, an application for judicial review may be made either by the CPS or the defendant if:

(a) the magistrates' court has made an order that they had no power to make (and so have acted 'ultra vires', or beyond their powers); or

(b) the magistrates' court has breached the rules of natural justice (either by contravening a party's right to a fair hearing, or by appearing to be biased).

An applicant for judicial review will seek an order from the Divisional Court either quashing the decision made in the magistrates' court or compelling the magistrates' court to act (or not act) in a certain way.

As with an appeal by way of case stated, this would not be a usual route for the defence or even the CPS to take.

12.7 Appeals from the Crown Court by a defendant

A defendant who is convicted in the Crown Court has the following rights of appeal to the Criminal Division of the Court of Appeal:

(a) Appeal against conviction (Criminal Appeal Act (CAA) 1968, s 1(1)). The defendant may appeal against their conviction if either the Court of Appeal grants leave to appeal, or the trial judge grants a certificate that the case is fit for appeal;

(b) Appeal against sentence (CAA 1968, s 9). The defendant may appeal against the sentence they received if either the Court of Appeal grants leave to appeal, or the judge who passes sentence has granted a certificate that the case is fit for appeal against sentence.

12.7.1 Appeal against conviction

When will an appeal against conviction be allowed?

If the Court of Appeal considers a conviction to be '*unsafe*', it must allow the appeal (CAA 1968, s 2). In all other cases, the Court of Appeal must dismiss the appeal.

This means that a conviction may be upheld even if there was an error or mistake at the defendant's trial in the Crown Court, if the Court of Appeal considers that, had the mistake not been made, the correct and only reasonable verdict would have been one of guilty.

 So, for example, in R v Boyle and Ford *[2006] EWCA Crim 2101, two co-defendants were convicted of murder. There was significant DNA and other forensic evidence against them. The trial judge misdirected the jury as to the drawing of adverse inferences under s 34 of the Criminal Justice and Public Order Act 1994. The Court of Appeal held that the misdirection did not render the conviction unsafe because there was other compelling evidence against the defendants.*

In a very small number of cases, however, the Court of Appeal may allow an appeal and quash a conviction even if the court is satisfied that the defendant did commit the offence for which they were convicted. Such a situation is most likely to occur when there has been an abuse of process committed by the police or the prosecuting authorities, such as the 'bugging' of a privileged conversation between the defendant and his solicitor.

Examples of the most common factors raised by defendants to argue that their convictions are unsafe are:

(a) a failure by the trial judge to direct the jury correctly as to:

   (i) the burden and standard of proof;

   (ii) the substantive law concerning the offence(s);

   (iii) the fact that it is for the jury rather than the judge to determine what the facts of the case are (although the judge will remind the jury of the prominent features of the evidence when summing up, it is the jury's responsibility to judge the evidence and decide the relevant facts);

   (iv) the fact that the jury should try to return a unanimous verdict (and the judge will notify them when the time has arisen when the judge may be prepared to accept a majority verdict);

   (v) the jury's power to convict the defendant of any lesser offence which there was evidence to support;

(b) the trial judge wrongfully admitted or excluded evidence, for example:

   (i) the judge wrongfully admitted evidence of a disputed confession or the defendant's previous convictions;

   (ii) the judge wrongfully excluded hearsay evidence which would have assisted the defendant's case;

(c) the trial judge failed to administer the correct warnings to the jury, for example:

   (i) the judge failed to give a 'Turnbull' warning in a case of disputed identification, or a corroboration warning where the defendant alleges that a witness has a purpose of his own to serve in giving evidence against the defendant;

(ii) the judge failed to give a proper direction to the jury as to the drawing of adverse inferences from the defendant's silence;

(iii) the judge failed to give a proper direction to the jury as to the relevance of any previous convictions which may have been adduced in evidence;

(d) inappropriate interventions by the trial judge – if, for example, the judge had constantly interrupted defence counsel during the cross-examination of a prosecution witness;

(e) a failure by the trial judge when summing up the case to the jury to:

(i) deal with the essential points of the defence case;

(ii) identify any inconsistencies in the prosecution case;

(iii) summarise the evidence on which the jury may properly rely in order to convict the defendant;

(iv) tell the jury, when special measures have been used to enable a prosecution witness to give evidence, that they should not allow this to prejudice them against the defendant, nor assume that the use of special measures means the defendant has behaved improperly;

(f) fresh evidence – even if a trial has been conducted properly, the defendant may argue his conviction is unsafe if fresh evidence comes to light which casts doubt upon his guilt. For example, a new witness may come forward to substantiate an alibi which was disbelieved by the jury, or expert evidence relied on by the prosecution at trial may be shown to be flawed. Fresh evidence will not in itself render a conviction unsafe. The issue for the Court of Appeal is whether the fresh evidence is such that, had it been placed before the jury, the verdict might have been different.

At the end of the trial, defence counsel will normally prepare a written advice on the merits of an appeal against conviction which should be in accordance with the instructions contained in the brief.

12.7.1.1 Procedure for making an appeal against conviction

Only rarely will the defendant ask the trial judge to certify that the case is fit for appeal.

The usual method of commencing an appeal against conviction is for the defendant to seek permission to appeal from the Court of Appeal direct.

The procedure is as follows (CrimPR, r 39.2):

(a) Within 28 days of the conviction (not sentence), the defendant must serve their appeal notice, together with the draft grounds of appeal, on the Registrar of Criminal Appeals at the Court of Appeal. The grounds are a separate document prepared by defence counsel, setting out the detailed arguments as to why the conviction is unsafe.

(b) On receipt of these documents, the Registrar will obtain a transcript of the evidence that was given at trial and of the judge's summing up to the jury. The Registrar will then put the case papers before a single judge, who will determine whether permission to appeal ought to be granted. This is a filtering stage, designed to weed out appeals that have no chance of success. If permission is granted, the single judge will also grant the defendant public funding for the hearing of the appeal.

In appeals that are completely without merit, the single judge may, when dismissing the appeal, make a direction as to loss of time under s 29 of the CAA 1968. This means that any time spent by the defendant in custody awaiting the outcome of the appeal will not count towards the total time the defendant must serve for their sentence (as would normally be the case). This provision is designed to deter defendants from pursuing appeals that are without merit.

⭐ *Example*

Lucas has been convicted of an offence of robbery. Lucas was originally remanded in custody for three months before the date of his conviction. It then took a further month for the full Court of Appeal to refuse Lucas's appeal. Let us assume that when his case came before the single judge, it was assessed to be completely without merit and a direction as to loss of time under s 29 of the CAA 1968 was made by the single judge.

If Lucas decided to go ahead with his appeal and the Court of Appeal agrees with the single judge, Lucas will have deducted the time he has served in custody from the date of his conviction to the date the Court of Appeal refused his appeal. So here, Lucas will not have the later month he served in custody counting against his eventual sentence, although time spent in custody before his conviction will still count against his sentence.

If Lucas had accepted the views of the single judge and decided not to pursue his appeal, he would not lose any time that he has already served on remand.

(c) The hearing of the appeal will then take place before the full Court of Appeal, which will comprise a three-judge panel. The court will hear oral arguments from the parties, and may also hear fresh evidence if that evidence:

(i) appears to be credible;

(ii) would have been admissible at the defendant's trial; and

(iii) there is a reasonable explanation for the failure to adduce this evidence at the defendant's trial (CAA 1968, s 23).

12.7.1.2 Powers of the Court of Appeal at an appeal against conviction

Section 2 of the CAA 1968 permits the Court of Appeal to do any of the following:

(a) quash the conviction and acquit the defendant – if, for example, new evidence has come to light which the court considers would have led to the defendant's acquittal had such evidence been available at the defendant's trial;

(b) quash the conviction and order that a retrial take place – if, for example, the conviction is unsafe because the judge failed to direct the jury properly when summing up the case;

(c) allow part of the appeal and dismiss other parts of the appeal (if the defendant was appealing against conviction for more than one offence). In such a case the court will probably then re-sentence the defendant in respect of the offences for which his conviction was upheld;

(d) find the defendant guilty of an alternative offence (in which case the court will probably re-sentence the defendant); or

(e) dismiss the appeal.

The Court must dismiss the appeal unless it considers that the conviction is unsafe. If the conviction is unsafe, the Court must then decide whether to order a retrial. Section 7 of the CAA 1968 enables the Court of Appeal to order a retrial where the Court allows an appeal against conviction and where it appears to the Court that *'the interests of justice so require'*. If the Court is satisfied that the defendant would have been acquitted at trial (for example, had new evidence presented at the appeal been available at the original trial), the Court will not order a retrial. In other cases, the Court will normally order that a retrial take place unless a retrial would be unfair to the defendant or in some other way inappropriate.

12.7.2 Appeal against sentence

12.7.2.1 Procedure

A defendant may also appeal to the Court of Appeal against the sentence imposed by the Crown Court (CAA 1968, s 9). The procedure to be followed (CrimPR, r 39.2) when an appeal against sentence is made to the Court of Appeal is essentially the same as for an appeal against conviction, with the defendant either requiring a certificate from the sentencing judge that the case is fit for appeal, or the defendant seeking permission from the Court of Appeal to proceed. It is rare for the sentencing judge to grant a certificate, and most defendants will seek the permission of the Court of Appeal to proceed. If the defendant seeks permission from the Court of Appeal, a notice of application for permission to appeal together with draft grounds of appeal must be sent to the Registrar of Criminal Appeals at the Court of Appeal within 28 days of the sentence being passed. The draft grounds of appeal will state why it is considered that the sentence passed by the Crown Court is either wrong or excessive. Assuming leave to appeal is granted by the single judge, the appeal will then be considered by a two- or three-judge panel. The appeal will usually be confined to legal submissions on what the appropriate sentence (or sentencing range) is in the particular case.

12.7.2.2 When will an appeal be successful?

An appeal against sentence will be successful only if:

(a) the sentence passed by the trial judge is wrong in law (if, for example, the trial judge were to pass a sentence that they did not have the power to pass);

(b) the sentence passed by the trial judge is wrong in principle (if, for example, the trial judge passes a custodial sentence when the offence was not serious enough to merit such a sentence);

(c) the judge adopted the wrong approach when sentencing. Examples of a judge adopting the wrong approach when sentencing are:

    (i) if the judge increased the sentence because the defendant had pleaded not guilty (since the guidelines issued by the Sentencing Council start from the assumption that the defendant is convicted following a not guilty plea);

    (ii) if the judge failed to give the defendant an appropriate discount for entering a guilty plea;

    (iii) if the judge should have held a Newton hearing before determining the facts of the offence upon which the sentence was to be based;

    (iv) if the judge failed to take into account (or failed to give sufficient credit for) any relevant offence or offender mitigation put forward by the defendant;

(d) in the case of co-defendants, there is an unjustified disparity in the sentence each defendant receives, particularly where both defendants appear to have been equally culpable; or

(e) the sentence passed is manifestly excessive. This is the most common ground of appeal in practice. A Crown Court judge sentencing a defendant will impose a sentence within a range of possible sentences which may be appropriate for the offence. The Court of Appeal will interfere only if the sentencing judge has gone beyond the upper limit of this range. The Court of Appeal will not reduce a sentence simply because it would have imposed a lower sentence within the appropriate range.

After the defendant has been sentenced, defence counsel will normally provide a written advice on the prospects of a successful appeal against sentence in accordance with the instructions contained in the brief to counsel.

12.7.2.3 Powers of the Court of Appeal

The Court of Appeal may confirm a sentence passed by the Crown Court or quash the sentence and replace it with an alternative sentence or order as it thinks appropriate. The Court of Appeal cannot, however, increase the sentence imposed by the judge in the Crown Court (CAA 1968, s 11(3)).

A loss of time direction may also be made if the defendant makes an appeal against sentence that is deemed to be without merit (see above).

12.7.3 Prosecution appeals

12.7.3.1 Termination and evidential rulings (CrimPR, Part 38)

The CPS has no right of appeal in respect of a defendant who has been acquitted by a jury following a Crown Court trial (subject to the provisions of s 75 CJA 2003 below). Sections 58–63 of the CJA 2003 do, however, give the CPS a right of appeal to the Court of Appeal in respect of rulings made by a trial judge either before or during the trial which:

(a) either effectively terminate the trial ('termination rulings'); or

(b) significantly weaken the prosecution case ('evidential rulings').

These are not of much importance in practice though to a newly qualified solicitor.

12.7.3.2 Powers of the Attorney-General (CrimPR, Part 41)

The CPS has a right of appeal to the Court of Appeal if the Attorney-General considers that the Crown Court has passed a sentence which is 'unduly lenient'. Section 36 of the CJA 1988 allows the Attorney-General to refer such a case to the Court of Appeal, which in turn has the power to increase the sentence. The Attorney-General may refer a case to the Court of Appeal only if the offence is an offence triable only on indictment or is a specified either-way offence and the Court of Appeal has given permission.

If the referral is successful, the Court of Appeal will quash the sentence passed in the Crown Court and pass the sentence it considers appropriate. Any sentence imposed by the Court of Appeal must be a sentence that could have been passed in the Crown Court.

 Example

*Jakov has been sentenced by a judge in the Crown Court to four years' imprisonment for an offence of s 18 GBH which was assessed by the judge as being a Category 1 offence (see **Chapter 11**). The sentencing range for such an offence is between 9 to 16 years with a starting point sentence of 12 years. The offence is an offence that can only be tried on indictment and the CPS are therefore quite likely to make an Attorney-General's reference to challenge this sentence on the basis that it is unduly lenient. If the Court of Appeal agrees, it is likely to increase the sentence.*

12.7.3.3 Applications for a retrial by the CPS

The rule against double jeopardy

Prior to the enactment of the CJA 2003, a defendant could never be tried twice for the same offence (this was known as the rule against 'double jeopardy').

The CJA 2003 provisions

Section 75 of the CJA 2003 lists those offences for which a retrial is possible following the acquittal of a defendant. The list includes:

(a) murder and attempted murder;

(b) manslaughter;

(c) kidnapping;

(d) a number of sexual offences under the Sexual Offences Acts of 1956 and 2003, including rape, attempted rape and assault by penetration;

(e) various offences in relation to Class A drugs, such as unlawful importation and production; and

(f) arson endangering life or property.

The Court of Appeal will only quash an earlier conviction and order a retrial where the CPS can satisfy a two-fold test:

The evidential test

The evidential test is set out in s 78 of the CJA 2003. This requires that there be 'new and compelling' evidence of the defendant's guilt. 'New' evidence means evidence not adduced when the defendant was acquitted. To be 'compelling', this evidence must be reliable, substantial and highly probative of the case against the defendant.

An example of a case involving the powers of retrial is the case of Gary Dobson who, together with David Norris, was convicted of the murder of Stephen Lawrence in January 2012. Dobson had been acquitted in 1996 of the murder charge. In October 2010, the Director of Public Prosecutions made an application to the Court of Appeal for the acquittal to be set aside. This application was primarily based on new scientific evidence (at the trial it was established that this included tiny specks of blood on the defendant's clothes). In May 2011, the Court of Appeal set aside the acquittal, having found that the new evidence was compelling, and that a prosecution was in the public interest and the interests of justice.

The interests of justice test

This test is set out in s 79 of the CJA 2003, which provides that the Court of Appeal should have particular (but not exclusive) regard to the following factors:

(a) whether existing circumstances make a fair trial unlikely;

(b) the length of time since the offence was allegedly committed;

(c) whether it is likely that the new evidence would have been adduced in the earlier proceedings, but for the failure of the police or the prosecution to act with due diligence and expedition; and

(d) whether, since the earlier proceedings, the police or prosecutor have failed to act with due diligence or expedition.

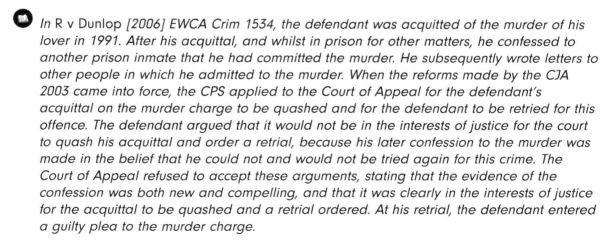 *In R v Dunlop [2006] EWCA Crim 1534, the defendant was acquitted of the murder of his lover in 1991. After his acquittal, and whilst in prison for other matters, he confessed to another prison inmate that he had committed the murder. He subsequently wrote letters to other people in which he admitted to the murder. When the reforms made by the CJA 2003 came into force, the CPS applied to the Court of Appeal for the defendant's acquittal on the murder charge to be quashed and for the defendant to be retried for this offence. The defendant argued that it would not be in the interests of justice for the court to quash his acquittal and order a retrial, because his later confession to the murder was made in the belief that he could not and would not be tried again for this crime. The Court of Appeal refused to accept these arguments, stating that the evidence of the confession was both new and compelling, and that it was clearly in the interests of justice for the acquittal to be quashed and a retrial ordered. At his retrial, the defendant entered a guilty plea to the murder charge.*

Summary

In this chapter you have considered a range of matters relating to appeals. Notably:

- *Appealing against conviction and sentence from the magistrates' court to the Crown Court.* How the defendant does this and the Crown Court's powers when dealing with such appeals.

- *Appeals on a point of law from the magistrates' court to the High Court.* How both the defence and prosecution can make such an appeal by way of case stated to the Divisional Court where either party will argue the magistrates' court has made an error of law.

- *Applying for judicial review of a magistrates' court decision.* How the defence and prosecution can challenge such decisions made in the magistrates' court on the basis the court acted ultra vires or breached the rules of natural justice when dealing with the case.

- *Appealing against conviction and/or sentence by the defendant from the Crown Court to the Court of Appeal.* How and on what basis the defendant makes such appeals to the Court of Appeal and the powers available to this appellate court when dealing with such appeals.

- *The limited extent to which the prosecution can appeal to the Court of Appeal.* How the prosecution can appeal termination and evidential rulings. The extent to which unduly lenient sentences can be appealed by the Attorney-General and the limited number of cases that can be retried where there is new and compelling evidence that has come to light since the original trial.

Sample questions

Question 1

A woman is convicted following a trial in the magistrates' court of an offence of low-value theft from a shop. The woman has extensive previous convictions for similar offending and is sentenced to four months' imprisonment. The woman is considering appealing to the Crown Court against this sentence.

Which of the following best describes the Crown Court's powers in relation to the woman's appeal against sentence?

A   The Crown Court may confirm or vary this sentence, including increasing the sentence up to a maximum of six months' imprisonment.

B   The Crown Court may confirm, reverse or vary this sentence, including increasing the sentence up to the statutory maximum for theft.

C   The Crown Court may confirm, reverse or vary this sentence, but they cannot increase the sentence that has already been imposed.

D   The Crown Court may confirm, reverse or vary this sentence, including increasing the sentence as this is an either-way offence.

E   The Crown Court may confirm, reverse or vary this sentence, including increasing the sentence up to a maximum of six months' imprisonment.

Answer

Option E is the best answer. The Crown Court has the power to impose any sentence, as long as it is a sentence which the magistrates' court had the power to impose. This means that a defendant appealing against a sentence imposed by the magistrates' court may have that sentence increased if the Crown Court takes a more serious view of the offence, but only up to the maximum available in the magistrates' court, which for this offence (a summary offence) would be six months' imprisonment (note the woman is not entitled to any discount of sentence for a guilty plea since we are told she was convicted following a trial, so the maximum sentence available would remain at six months).

Option A is not the best answer because the Crown Court can also reverse as well as confirm or vary the sentence, although in this case, reversing such a sentence would be unlikely. Option B is wrong because the sentence cannot be increased above the six months maximum the magistrates could impose for a summary offence. Option C is wrong because the Crown Court can also increase the sentence (unlike the Court of Appeal when hearing an appeal against sentence from the Crown Court). Option D is wrong because low-value shop theft is not an either-way offence and in any event, even if it were, this is not the reason why the Crown Court can increase the sentence.

Question 2

A man is convicted following trial in the Crown Court. During the trial, the judge failed to adequately direct the jury on the operation of the burden of proof. Following conviction, the man's case is adjourned for three weeks for the preparation of a pre-sentence report. At the adjourned hearing, the man is sentenced to a community order.

Can the man now appeal against his conviction?

A   Yes, because he has 28 days to appeal from the date of his sentence and his ground of appeal will be because of the trial judge's failure to direct the jury correctly.

B   Yes, because he has 28 days to appeal from the date of his conviction and he will argue his conviction is unsafe because of the trial judge's failure to direct the jury correctly.

C   No, because he has failed to appeal within the correct time period and his conviction will be upheld even if there was an error or mistake made by the trial judge when directing the jury.

D   No, because although he has 28 days to appeal from the date of his conviction, this will be upheld even if there was an error or mistake made by the trial judge when directing the jury.

E   Yes, because he has 28 days to appeal from the date of his sentence and his grounds of appeal will be that his conviction is unsafe because of the trial judge's failure to direct the jury correctly.

Answer

Option B is the best answer. The defendant has 28 days to appeal from the date of his conviction, rather than the date of his sentence. In this case the man still has seven days in which to serve his appeal notice, together with the draft grounds of appeal on the Registrar of Criminal Appeals at the Court of Appeal. Moreover, there is only one ground of appeal against conviction, namely that the conviction is unsafe (CAA 1968, s 2).

Option A is therefore wrong because the 28-day time period to appeal against conviction does not run from the date of sentence (unlike the magistrates' court where it does run from that date). Option C is wrong because the man has not failed to appeal within the correct time period. Moreover, although a conviction may be upheld even if there was an error or mistake made by the trial judge when directing the jury, this would only happen where the Court of Appeal considers that, had the mistake not been made, the correct and only reasonable verdict would still have been one of guilty. This explanation also applies to option D. Option E is wrong because it refers to the wrong grounds of appeal. As mentioned above, there is only one ground of appeal. The reference in option E is to the factors that could be used to support the one ground.

13 Youth Court Procedure

SQE1 syllabus

This chapter will enable you to achieve the SQE1 Assessment Specification in relation to Functioning Legal Knowledge concerned with the following procedures and processes in the youth court:

- youths charged with grave crimes;
- allocation;
- youths jointly charged with an adult;
- sentencing;
- appeals jurisdiction from the youth court.

Note that, for SQE1, candidates are not usually required to recall specific case names or cite statutory or regulatory authorities. These are provided for illustrative purposes only unless otherwise stated.

Learning outcomes

By the end of this chapter you will be able to apply relevant core legal principles and rules appropriately and effectively, at the level of a competent newly qualified solicitor in practice, to realistic client-based and ethical problems and situations in the following areas of youth court work:

- What the youth court is required to do when dealing with youths charged with a grave crime.
- The different approach taken in the youth court from an adult magistrates' court to the allocation procedure where a youth is charged with an either-way offence.
- Which court youths are dealt with where they are jointly charged with an adult.
- The powers given to the youth court when dealing with the question of bail.

- The range of sentences available in the youth court and the approach taken when sentencing youths, particularly:
  - the role of the Sentencing Children and Young People – definitive guidelines
  - referral orders
  - youth rehabilitation orders
  - detention and training orders.
- How the appeal jurisdiction operates when appealing a case from the youth court.

13.1 Introduction

In this chapter we will consider the procedures which take place in the youth court, and how these differ from proceedings in the adult magistrates' court. We will begin by describing the aims of the youth justice system and which categories of juvenile may be dealt with by the youth court. We will then consider the circumstances in which a juvenile who would ordinarily appear in the youth court may have their case heard before either the magistrates' court or the Crown Court. We will also consider the powers of the youth court in relation to the granting of bail, and the chapter concludes by describing the sentencing powers the youth court may exercise and how decisions from the youth court may be appealed.

13.2 The aims of the youth justice system

The principal aim of the youth justice system is to prevent offending by children and young persons (CDA 1998, s 37(1)). All those involved in the youth justice system (including solicitors representing juveniles) must have regard to this aim. The youth court must also have regard to the welfare of the juvenile, so the approach taken by the youth court is very different to that taken by an adult magistrates' court or the Crown Court.

13.2.1 Role of the Youth Offending Team (YOT)

YOTs are responsible for coordinating the provision of youth justice services in their particular local area. A member of the YOT will attend each sitting of the youth court. This is likely to be a member of the Probation Service who has received training in dealing with youth justice matters.

The YOT will assist the youth court with the following matters:

(a) investigating and confirming the personal circumstances and previous convictions of juveniles;

(b) providing support for juveniles who are granted bail;

(c) preparing pre-sentence reports; and

(d) administering any non-custodial sentence imposed by the youth court.

13.2.2 Role of parents/guardians

A juvenile appearing before the youth court who is aged under 16 must be accompanied by their parents or guardian during each stage of the proceedings, unless the court is satisfied that it would be unreasonable to require such attendance.

For juveniles aged 16 or 17, the court has a discretion as to whether to make an order requiring the attendance of the juvenile's parents or guardian.

Parents or guardians who attend the youth court play an active role in the proceedings. The court will want to hear their views (particularly in relation to sentencing) and may direct questions to them.

13.2.3 Reporting restrictions

The only people who are usually allowed to attend a hearing in the youth court are:

(a) the district judge/youth justices

(b) court staff (such as the court clerk and usher)

(c) the juvenile and his parents or guardian

(d) the CPS representative

(e) the juvenile's solicitor

(f) a representative from the YOT

(g) members of the press.

The press is restricted in what they are allowed to report about a hearing before the youth court. They cannot report the name, address or school, or any other details which are likely to lead to the identification of the juvenile or any other child or young person (such as a witness) involved in the case.

These reporting restrictions that apply specifically to children or young persons end automatically when they reach the age of 18.

Section 78 of the Criminal Justice and Courts Act 2015 allows for a lifelong reporting restriction in respect of a victim or witness who is under the age of 18 during the proceedings.

Section 49 of the Children and Young Persons Act 1933 allows the court to lift these restrictions either to avoid injustice, or, following conviction, if the court is satisfied that it is in the public interest to reveal the juvenile's identity. The courts should use this ability to 'name and shame' juveniles only when doing so will provide some real benefit to the community, such as making the public aware of the identity of a prolific offender. This power though should not be used as an 'extra' punishment imposed on the juvenile.

13.2.4 Legal representation

As well as observing the overriding aim of the youth justice system mentioned above (to help prevent offending by children), the solicitor representing a juvenile in the youth court plays the same role as they would were they representing an adult in the magistrates' court.

Representation orders are applied for in the same manner as in the adult court and will be determined by the Legal Aid Agency applying the same interests of justice test. The Legal Aid Agency must, however, take into account the age of the juvenile when deciding whether a representation order should be granted.

In respect of the means test, all juveniles under the age of 18 will be automatically eligible, regardless of their actual means.

13.3 The youth court's jurisdiction

The youth court is part of the magistrates' court system. A hearing in the youth court will therefore take place before either a district judge or a bench of youth justices. The youth court deals with cases involving defendants aged between 10 and 17 inclusive. Children aged 10 and over are subject to the criminal law in the same way as adults. There is a conclusive presumption that children under the age of 10 cannot be guilty of committing a criminal offence.

Juveniles in the youth court are sometimes referred to as either 'children' or 'young people'. 'Children' are juveniles aged between 10 and 13 inclusive. 'Young people' are juveniles aged between 14 and 17 inclusive. This distinction is relevant in terms of the sentencing powers of the court (see below).

Collectively, juveniles in the youth court are referred to as youths or 'juveniles'. There is a slight difference between the term 'juveniles' when applied to juveniles in the youth court and 'juveniles' at the police station. A 'juvenile' at the police station is a suspect who is, *or appears to be*, under 18 years of age. A 'juvenile' in the youth court is a juvenile who is under 18 years of age.

Some juveniles appearing before the youth court are classified by the court and the police as 'persistent young offenders' (PYOs). The Home Office categorises a PYO as a juvenile who has been sentenced on three separate occasions for one or more recordable offences (a recordable offence is any offence for which a juvenile may receive a custodial sentence). A juvenile who is a PYO will have their case expedited so the youth court may deal with them as quickly as possible.

13.4 Differences with the adult magistrates' court

Procedures in the youth court are modified to take account of the age of the juvenile. The layout of the court room is less formal than the magistrates' court, with all participants in the case sitting at the same level rather than there being a raised dock or bench. The juvenile will usually sit on a chair in front of the CPS representative and his own solicitor, and in full view of the magistrates. The use of straightforward language rather than legal terminology is encouraged, and solicitors remain seated when addressing the court. Juveniles (and any child witnesses) are usually spoken to and referred to by their first name. Witnesses 'promise' rather than 'swear' to tell the truth, and child witnesses under the age of 14 must give unsworn evidence (as, in fact, is the case in the adult magistrates' court). Emphasis is placed on there being as much communication as possible between the magistrates, the juvenile and his parent or guardian.

Magistrates receive special training in youth justice matters before being allowed to sit in the youth court.

Some of the terminology in the youth court also differs from that in the adult magistrates' court. For example, there will be a 'finding of guilt' rather than a conviction, and the court will make an 'order upon a finding of guilt' rather than give a sentence.

Most of the procedural and evidential issues that may arise in the context of a case before the youth court are the same as for the case of an adult juvenile before the magistrates' court. In particular, the magistrates will issue the same standard directions for the parties to comply with in advance of trial as would be issued were the case being tried before the adult magistrates' court. The only exception to this will be if the juvenile is a PYO (see above). If the juvenile is a PYO, the magistrates will issue revised directions to ensure that an expedited trial takes place. Whether or not standard directions have been issued, a trial in the youth court will follow the same procedure as a trial before the adult magistrates' court.

13.4.1 Age

If a juvenile is charged with an offence when aged 17, but turns 18 prior to their first appearance in the youth court, the court does not have jurisdiction to deal with them and the case must be dealt with in the adult magistrates' court.

If convicted, the juvenile will be subject to the full range of sentencing powers which the magistrates' court may exercise.

If a juvenile makes his first appearance in the youth court before their 18th birthday, but becomes 18 whilst the case is ongoing, the youth court may either remit the case to the adult magistrates' court or retain the case. If the youth court retains the case, it will have the full range of sentencing powers that the adult magistrates' court would have were it dealing with the juvenile.

13.4.2 Determining mode of trial of juveniles

As a starting point, most trials of juveniles should take place in the youth court. There are however five circumstances where a juvenile's case either must or may be sent to an adult court (a magistrates' court or Crown Court).

(a) *Homicide offences*

Where a juvenile is accused of a homicide offence (murder or manslaughter), the case *must* be dealt with in the Crown Court.

(b) *Firearms offences*

Where the juvenile has attained the age of 16 at the time of the alleged offence, the case *must* be sent to the Crown Court.

(c) *Grave crimes*

'Grave' crimes are offences for which an offender aged 21 years or over may receive a custodial sentence of 14 years or more (such as robbery, rape, assault by penetration, s 18 GBH), together with a number of specific sexual offences, including sexual assault.

The youth court *may* accept jurisdiction in a case involving a grave crime or send such a case to the Crown Court for trial.

The youth court should send for trial a case involving a grave crime only if it considers that its maximum sentencing powers (a 24-month detention and training order – see below) will be insufficient in the event that the juvenile is convicted, and that a sentence of long-term detention would be more appropriate.

⭐ *Example*

Zaina (aged 16) is charged with robbery and appears before the youth court. She has a previous conviction for the same offence. Zaina intends to plead not guilty to the charge. When they hear the facts of the case, the magistrates consider that, were Zaina to be convicted before them, their sentencing powers would be insufficient and that, were the case before the Crown Court, there is a real possibility that the judge would impose a sentence of long-term detention. The magistrates will send Zaina to the Crown Court for trial.

(d) *Specified offences*

Where a juvenile is charged with an offence of violence or a sexual offence their case *may* be sent to the Crown Court, but only where they can properly be regarded as a 'dangerous offender' (see **Chapter 11**). So if it appears to the court that the criteria would be met for the imposition of automatic life imprisonment, discretionary life imprisonment or an extended sentence, the juvenile is likely to have their case sent to the Crown Court.

(e) *Jointly charged with an adult*

(i) Adult's case dealt with in Crown Court

A juvenile *may* also be sent to the Crown Court, but only where this would be regarded as necessary in the interests of justice.

(ii) Adult's case dealt with in the magistrates' court

If the adult is to be tried in the magistrates' court, the adult and juvenile will be tried together in the adult magistrates' court. If the juvenile is convicted, the magistrates will normally remit their case to the youth court for sentence unless they propose to deal with the matter by way of a fine or a discharge, in which case they will usually sentence the juvenile themselves.

13.4.3 Plea before venue and allocation

This procedure applies to the cases listed above where the court *may* send the juvenile's case to the Crown Court. So, for grave crimes, specified offences and where a juvenile is charged with an adult whose case is to be dealt with in the Crown Court, the juvenile will be asked to indicate their plea.

If the juvenile indicates a guilty plea, the youth court will either sentence the juvenile or send them to the Crown Court for sentence where they believe their sentencing powers would be inadequate (ie the juvenile will receive a detention and training order in excess of 24 months).

If the juvenile indicates a not guilty plea, a similar allocation procedure will then be followed to that in the magistrates' court for an either-way offence (see **Chapter 6**). For such cases, the youth court will only decline jurisdiction and send the case to the Crown Court for trial where they believe their sentencing powers would be inadequate if the juvenile were convicted following trial (ie the juvenile will receive a detention and training order in excess of 24 months). However, unlike an adult magistrates' court, a juvenile does not have any right of election. If the youth court accepts jurisdiction, the trial must take place in the youth court.

13.5 Bail

Under the Bail Act 1976, the youth court has the power to remand a juvenile:

(a) on bail (with or without conditions)

(b) into local authority accommodation or

(c) in the case of 17-year-olds, into custody.

In deciding whether to grant bail, the youth court will normally have before it a report from the YOT providing details of the juvenile's antecedents and also their record in relation to previous grants of bail. In addition, the report will inform the court about the juvenile's home situation and their attendance record at school, college or work.

13.5.1 Consequences of refusal of bail

Where the court refuses bail, a juvenile may be remanded to local authority accommodation or to youth detention accommodation.

(a) Local authority accommodation

A remand to local authority accommodation is a remand to accommodation provided by or on behalf of a local authority. Note that this can sometimes include a return home but under the care of the local authority.

Ten- to 11-year-olds may only be remanded on bail or to local authority accommodation. They cannot be remanded to youth detention accommodation.

If a juvenile reaches the age of 12 during the course of a remand, it is possible that they may then be remanded to youth detention accommodation at the next court appearance should the relevant conditions be met (see below).

(b) Youth detention accommodation

There are four sets of conditions that must be met for a remand to youth detention accommodation to take place. These have recently been updated by s 158 of the Police, Crime, Sentencing and Courts Act 2022.

The starting point is that the youth court must first consider the best interests and welfare of the child, and s 158 introduces a presumption that children between the ages of 12–17 will be remanded into local authority accommodation rather than youth detention accommodation.

For a juvenile to be remanded into youth detention accommodation, the four sets of conditions are:

(i)   The juvenile must be aged 12 to 17 years.

(ii) The juvenile must usually have legal representation.

(iii) The offence will need to be either a violent or sexual offence or one for which an adult could be punished with a term of imprisonment of 14 years or more and that it is 'very likely the child will receive a custodial sentence' for the present offence. Alternatively, the juvenile will need to have a 'recent and significant history' of absconding whilst remanded to local authority accommodation or youth detention accommodation; or a 'recent and significant history' of committing imprisonable offences whilst on bail or remand to local authority accommodation or youth detention accommodation.

(iv) The court must believe a remand to youth detention accommodation is necessary either to protect the public from death or serious personal injury (physical or psychological) occasioned by further offences committed by the juvenile, or to prevent the commission by the juvenile of further imprisonable offences, and that the 'risk posed by the child cannot be managed satisfactorily in the community'.

⭐ *Example*

Jamie is aged 15. He has been charged with an offence of robbery, it being alleged that he stole a mobile phone from a fellow pupil at school whilst threatening the victim with a piece of wood. Jamie is not welcome home as he has fallen out with his parents following this latest incident. Jamie has a recent and significant history of committing acquisitive crime including several offences of theft and robbery, some of which were committed whilst on bail. Jamie has also recently failed to surrender to custody, and for his most recent offence he received a youth detention and training order for 24 months. The training part of the order has not yet been completed, and the youth court now takes the view that the risk posed by Jamie cannot be managed satisfactorily in the community. When Jamie appears in the youth court he is legally represented and indicates a not guilty plea. The youth court believes that its powers of punishment are inadequate to deal with Jamie and so his case is sent to the Crown Court for sentence. The CPS object to bail on the basis that there are substantial grounds to believe that if granted bail Jamie would fail to surrender to custody and commit further offences whilst on bail.

The youth court may now remand Jamie into youth detention accommodation as all four of the above conditions are satisfied.

13.6   Sentencing

Before a juvenile ever comes before a youth court, it is likely that they will have been through the formal system of youth cautions. When the youth court sentences a juvenile, it must balance the seriousness of the offence (and the juvenile's previous record) with the welfare requirements of the juvenile. The court must at all times have regard to the principal aim of preventing offending.

13.6.1   Sentencing procedure

Sentencing in the youth court follows a similar procedure to that in the adult magistrates' court. The CPS representative will give the facts of the case to the magistrates (assuming the juvenile has pleaded guilty rather than having been convicted following a trial), and the juvenile's solicitor will then give a plea in mitigation. The court is also likely to want to hear from the juvenile's parents or guardian before deciding the appropriate penalty.

A key document in the sentencing process is the pre-sentence report prepared by the YOT. The youth court must usually always obtain this report before sentencing the juvenile. The court is likely to indicate the type of sentence it has in mind when it orders a report, and the report will address the juvenile's suitability for that type of sentence. The court will place great emphasis on the contents of the report when deciding the sentence to impose. The youth court may either adjourn the sentencing hearing to enable the YOT to prepare the pre-sentence report, or may ask the member of the YOT who is present in court to prepare a 'stand down' report so that sentencing can take place without the need for the case to be adjourned.

13.6.2 Role of the Sentencing Children and Young People – definitive guidelines

As with adult offenders, a sentencing court is required to apply the relevant sentencing guidelines provided by the Sentencing Council. However, the approach taken is different to adults as can be seen from the extract below of the overarching principles of sentencing children and young people that apply to these guidelines.

Overarching principles – Section 1: General approach

1.1   When sentencing children or young people a court must have regard to:

- ◦ the principal aim of the youth justice system (to prevent offending by children and young people); and

- ◦ the welfare of the child or young person.

1.2   Whilst the seriousness of the offence will be the starting point, the approach to sentencing should be individualistic and focused on the child or young person, as opposed to offence focused. For a child or young person, the sentence should focus on rehabilitation where possible. A court should also consider the effect the sentence is likely to have on the child or young person (both positive and negative) as well as any underlying factors contributing to the offending behaviour.

1.3   Domestic and international laws dictate that a custodial sentence should always be a measure of last resort for children and young people and statute provides that a custodial sentence may only be imposed when the offence is so serious that no other sanction is appropriate.

1.4   It is important to avoid 'criminalising' children and young people unnecessarily; the primary purpose of the youth justice system is to encourage children and young people to take responsibility for their own actions and promote re-integration into society rather than to punish. Restorative justice disposals may be of particular value for children and young people as they can encourage them to take responsibility for their actions and understand the impact their offence may have had on others.

1.5   It is important to bear in mind any factors that may diminish the culpability of a child or young person. Children and young people are not fully developed, and they have not attained full maturity. As such, this can impact on their decision-making and risk-taking behaviour. It is important to consider the extent to which the child or young person has been acting impulsively and whether their conduct has been affected by inexperience, emotional volatility or negative influences. They may not fully appreciate the effect their actions can have on other people and may not be capable of fully understanding the distress and pain they cause to the victims of their crimes. Children and young people are also likely to be susceptible to peer pressure, and other external influences and changes taking place during adolescence can lead to experimentation, resulting in criminal behaviour. When considering a child or young person's age, their emotional and developmental age is of at least equal importance to their chronological age (if not greater).

1.6.   For these reasons, children and young people are likely to benefit from being given an opportunity to address their behaviour and may be receptive to changing their conduct. They should, if possible, be given the opportunity to learn from their mistakes without undue penalisation or stigma, especially as a court sanction might have a significant effect on the prospects and opportunities of the child or young person and hinder their re-integration into society.

These guidelines go on to adopt a similar structure and approach to those that apply to adult offenders but as can be seen from s 4 that sets out how a court should determine the sentence for a juvenile, they do so in a more sympathetic way:

Determining the sentence – Section 4

4.1. In determining the sentence, the key elements to consider are:

   ○ the principal aim of the youth justice system (to prevent re-offending by children and young people);

   ○ the welfare of the child or young person;

   ○ the age of the child or young person (chronological, developmental and emotional);

   ○ the seriousness of the offence;

   ○ the likelihood of further offences being committed; and

   ○ the extent of harm likely to result from those further offences.

4.2. The seriousness of the offence is the starting point for determining the appropriate sentence; the sentence imposed and any restriction on liberty must be commensurate with the seriousness of the offence.

4.3. The approach to sentencing children and young people should always be individualistic and the court should always have in mind the principal aims of the youth justice system.

4.4. In order to determine the seriousness of the offence the court should assess the culpability of the child or young person and the harm that was caused, intended to be caused or could foreseeably have been caused.

4.5. In assessing **culpability** the court will wish to consider the extent to which the offence was planned, the role of the child or young person (if the offence was committed as part of a group), the level of force that was used in the commission of the offence and the awareness that the child or young person had of their actions and its possible consequences. There is an expectation that in general a child or young person will be dealt with less severely than an adult offender. In part, this is because children and young people are unlikely to have the same experience and capacity as an adult to understand the effect of their actions on other people or to appreciate the pain and distress caused and because a child or young person may be less able to resist temptation, especially where peer pressure is exerted. Children and young people are inherently more vulnerable than adults due to their age and the court will need to consider any mental health problems and/or learning disabilities they may have, as well as their emotional and developmental age. Any external factors that may have affected the child or young person's behaviour should be taken into account.

4.6. In assessing **harm** the court should consider the level of physical and psychological harm caused to the victim, the degree of any loss caused to the victim and the extent of any damage caused to property. (This assessment should also include a consideration of any harm that was intended to be caused or could foreseeably have been caused in the committal of the offence.)

4.7. The court should also consider any aggravating or mitigating factors that may increase or reduce the overall seriousness of the offence. **If any of these factors are included in the definition of the committed offence they should not be taken into account when considering the relative seriousness of the offence before the court.**

For further detail see: https://sentencingcouncil.org.uk

We will now consider some of the sentences that can be passed on a juvenile offender.

13.6.3 Referral orders

A referral order must be made for a juvenile who pleads guilty to an offence (which carries a possible custodial sentence) and who has never previously been convicted or bound over by a court, unless the court is proposing either to impose a custodial sentence or to make an absolute discharge. Referral orders cannot be made unless the juvenile pleads guilty to the offence with which they have been charged, although if the juvenile has entered a mixed plea (ie guilty to one or more offences but not guilty to others), the court has the power to make a referral order but is not obliged to do so.

The court may also make a second referral order in exceptional circumstances.

If the court makes a referral order, the juvenile will be referred to a 'youth offender panel'. The youth offender panel comprises a member of the YOT and two community volunteers. At the meetings, the panel will speak to the juvenile and their family with a view to:

(a) stopping any further offending;

(b) helping the juvenile right the wrong they did to their victim; and

(c) helping the juvenile with any problems they may have.

The panel will agree with the juvenile a 'youth offender contract'. This is a programme of behaviour designed to prevent the juvenile re-offending and will last between three and 12 months. The terms of the contract are agreed between the juvenile and the panel members, rather than by the youth court.

13.6.4 Youth rehabilitation orders (YRO)

This is the equivalent of a generic community order for adult offenders. It allows the court to include one or more requirements to achieve punishment for the offence, protection of the public, reduction in re-offending and reparation (for a period of up to three years). The requirements are similar but not identical to the requirements that can be attached to an adult community order (see **Chapter 11**).

13.6.5 Detention and training orders

A detention and training order is the only type of custodial sentence that the youth court has the power to impose. The youth court should not impose a detention and training order unless it is of the opinion that the offence (or the combination of the offence and one or more offences associated with it) is *so serious* that neither a fine alone nor a community sentence can be justified for the offence, and the court must also consider whether a YRO with intensive supervision and surveillance is appropriate. The court would need to state the reasons why such a YRO was inappropriate.

Detention and training orders cannot be imposed on juveniles aged 10 or 11. If a juvenile is aged between 12 and 14 inclusive, an order may only be made if the court considers that the juvenile is a 'persistent young offender' (see above). For juveniles aged 15 or over, there is no restriction on the making of such an order.

Note that unlike an adult offender, the youth court has no power to suspend a detention and training order for a juvenile.

Initially it was the case that an order could only be imposed for fixed periods of four, six, eight, 10, 12, 18 or 24 months. That requirement has now been removed by s 236 of the Sentencing Act 2020 so that detention and training orders may now be ordered to run for at least four months but must not exceed a total of 24 months, so giving a youth court more flexibility when setting the length of such a sentence.

The length of the order must also be for the shortest period of time the court considers commensurate with the seriousness of the offence, or the offence and one or more offences associated with it. A detention and training order may be imposed only if the court has received from the YOT a pre-sentence report that specifically addresses custody as a possible sentencing option.

When the court makes such an order, the juvenile will be held in detention in a young offender institution for one half of the period of the order. They will then be released into the community under the supervision of the YOT for the second half of the order. The degree of supervision is decided upon by the YOT (not the court) but is likely to include electronic monitoring and intensive supervision.

A juvenile offender who breaches the supervision element of their sentence can be further punished for such a breach.

 Example

Kyle appears before the youth court and is convicted of the burglary of domestic premises. The youth justices impose a detention and training order for a period of 12 months. Kyle will spend the first six months in detention at a young offender institution. He will then spend the second six months in the community under the supervision of the YOT.

13.7 Appeal jurisdiction from the youth court

As the youth court is a type of magistrates' court, a juvenile convicted or sentenced by the youth court has the same rights of appeal as a defendant who is convicted or sentenced by the adult magistrates' court (see **Chapter 12**).

Summary

In this chapter you have considered a range of matters relating to the youth court. Notably:

- *Aims of the youth justice system.* How the principal aim of the youth justice system is to prevent offending by children and young persons.

- *The youth court's jurisdiction.* The relevance of a child or young person's age and how those aged between 10 and 17 (inclusive) will generally be dealt with in the youth court.

- *Differences between an adult court and the youth court.* Particularly how mode of trial operates differently in the youth court, including the five circumstances where a juvenile *must* or *may* have their case dealt with in an adult court. For those cases where the juvenile *may* be dealt with in an adult court, we also considered the approach taken at the plea before venue and allocation hearing and saw that a juvenile never has a right to elect trial in the Crown Court.

- *Bail.* How the same right to bail applies to juveniles and how very similar grounds and factors apply to refuse this right to bail. We also considered the consequences where a juvenile is refused bail and remanded either in local authority accommodation or in youth detention accommodation.

- *Sentencing.* The role of the Sentencing Children and Young People – definitive guidelines and the range of sentences that can be passed on a juvenile, particularly the use of referral orders, YROs and detention and training orders.

- *Appeals.* How an appeal from the youth court follows the same approach as an appeal from an adult magistrates' court.

Sample questions

Question 1

A boy, aged 16, has been jointly charged with a man, aged 18. They have been charged with an offence of theft of goods valued at £350 from a shop. The man consents to have his trial dealt with in the magistrates' court.

In which court will the boy's trial take place?

A   The trial may take place in the magistrates' court or the youth court. The boy does not have a right of election to have his trial dealt with in the Crown Court.

B   The trial may take place in the magistrates' court although the boy also has a right to elect trial in the Crown Court since he is charged with an either-way offence.

C   The trial must take place in the magistrates' court, although if convicted the boy may be sentenced in either the magistrates' court or have his case remitted for sentence to the youth court.

D   The trial must take place in the magistrates' court as the boy has no right of election since he is charged with a summary-only offence.

E   The trial may take place in the magistrates' court or the youth court depending on where the magistrates' court believe it will be in the interests of justice for the boy's case to be dealt with.

Answer

Option C is the correct answer. If the adult is to be tried in the magistrates' court, the adult and juvenile must be tried together in the adult magistrates' court. If the boy is convicted, the magistrates will normally remit the case to the youth court for sentence unless they propose to deal with the matter by way of a fine or a discharge, in which case, they will usually sentence the boy themselves.

Option A is wrong. Although it is correct to say the boy does not have a right of election to have his trial in the Crown Court, the case *must*, not *may*, be dealt with in the adult magistrates' court. Option B is also wrong for the same reason given for option A, but also because a juvenile will never have a right of election to have their trial in the Crown Court, even though the boy has been charged with an either-way offence. Option D is wrong because although it is correct to say the case must be tried in the magistrates' court, this is not a summary-only offence (the value of the goods stolen is not under £200). Option E is wrong because the magistrates do not have any discretion where the boy's case can be tried, although they do have a discretion where he can be sentenced if he is convicted.

Question 2

A girl, aged 13, has been charged with an offence of assault. It is alleged that she assaulted a teacher at school. When interviewed about the offence, the girl denied the assault and wrongly claimed the teacher had sexually assaulted her. The girl is to appear in the youth court and having received legal advice, now intends to plead guilty. The girl received a youth caution for an offence of assault on a fellow pupil two months ago and a conditional caution for an offence of criminal damage one month ago. The youth court will not take the view that the custody threshold has been met for this offence, nor will they deal with it by way of an absolute discharge.

Will the girl receive a referral order when she appears in the youth court?

A   Yes, because she will plead guilty to the offence and she has never previously been convicted or bound over by a court.

B   No, because the girl will now be classed as a persistent young offender and so will not be eligible to receive a referral order.

C   Yes, because the court has a discretion to impose such an order where the girl indicates a guilty plea.

D   No, because the offence will be regarded by the youth court as being too serious given the girl's wrongful allegation against the teacher.

E   No, because the girl did not make an early admission of guilt when first interviewed by the police.

Answer

Option A is the correct answer. A referral order *must* be made for a juvenile who pleads guilty to an offence (which carries a possible custodial sentence which assault does) and who has never previously been convicted or bound over by a court, unless the court is proposing either to impose a custodial sentence or to make an absolute discharge. Referral orders cannot be made unless the juvenile pleads guilty to the offence with which they have been charged. In this case, we are told the girl will plead guilty, she has no previous convictions and the court is not proposing either to impose a custodial sentence or to make an absolute discharge.

Option B is wrong because the girl will not be classed as a PYO as she does not yet have any previous convictions recorded against her (only two youth cautions). Option C is wrong because the youth court does not have a discretion – they must impose such an order (subject to the qualifications mentioned above which do not apply here.) Option D is wrong because we are told the offence does not meet the custody threshold, so a referral order must be made, even though the girl's wrongful allegation against the teacher is an aggravating factor in the case. Option E is wrong because the eligibility for a referral order is based on a guilty plea in court, not for an early admission of guilt when first interviewed by the police.

Question 3

A boy, aged 11, has been charged with an offence of sexual assault. It is alleged that he sexually assaulted another pupil at school. The boy will plead not guilty to the offence when he makes his first appearance in the youth court. The boy will be legally represented in court. The boy has a previous conviction for sexual assault for which he received a referral order nine months ago, along with a youth caution for an offence of common assault. The boy is estranged from his parents and is currently under the care of the local authority.

Which of the following best describes whether the prosecution is likely to seek a remand into youth detention accommodation when the boy's case is adjourned for trial?

A   The prosecution is likely to seek a remand into youth detention accommodation as the boy is legally represented and is charged with committing a sexual offence.

B   The prosecution will not seek a remand into youth detention accommodation as the boy is under the age of 12 years.

C   The prosecution is likely to seek a remand into youth detention accommodation as the boy is legally represented and has a recent and significant history of committing imprisonable offences.

D   The prosecution is unlikely to seek a remand into youth detention accommodation as the risk posed by the boy is likely to be able to be managed satisfactorily in the community.

E   The prosecution is likely to seek a remand into youth detention accommodation as the boy is legally represented and it is very likely the boy will receive a custodial sentence for the present offence if convicted.

Answer

Option B is the correct answer. A child under the age of 12 cannot be remanded into youth detention accommodation and so all the other options are wrong. Even if the boy were over the age of 12 years, there are three further conditions that must first be met, and although the other options refer to some of these conditions, they do not accurately deal with all of them (see **13.5.1** above).

Index